International Series in Operations Research & Management Science

Volume 132

T0134586

Series Editor
Frederick S. Hillier
Stanford University, CA, USA

Series Editorial Consultant
Camille Price
Stephen F. Austin State University, TX, USA

For further volumes:
http://www.springer.com/series/6161

Data Engineering

Mining, Information and Intelligence

Edited by

Yupo Chan
John R. Talburt
Terry M. Talley

 Springer

Editors

Yupo Chan
Department of Systems Engineering
University of Arkansas
Donaghey College of Info Sci.
2801 South University Avenue
Little Rock AR 72204-1099
USA
ychan@alum.mit.edu

John R. Talburt
Department of Information Science
University of Arkansas, Little Rock
2801 South University Ave.
Little Rock AR 72204-1099
USA
jrtalburt@ualr.edu

Terry M. Talley
Acxiom Corporation
P.O.Box 2000
Conway AR 72033-2000
USA
terry.talley@acxiom.com

ISBN 978-1-4614-2476-5   e-ISBN 978-1-4419-0176-7
DOI 10.1007/978-1-4419-0176-7
Springer New York Dordrecht Heidelberg London

Printed on acid-free paper

Springer is part of Springer Science+Business Media (www.springer.com)

Preface

Background

Many of us live in a world which is immersed in an overabundance of data. Not all this data, however, is either welcome or useful to the individual. The key is to bring the appropriate data together in a comprehensive and comprehensible way, then distill the data into information that is useful - information that will provide intelligence and insight for actionable strategies.

This volume describes applied research targeted at the task of collecting data and distilling useful information from that data. The work emanates primarily from applied research completed through collaborations between Acxiom Corporation and its academic research partners under the aegis of the Acxiom Laboratory for Applied Research (ALAR).

Acxiom Corporation is a global leader in customer and information-management solutions with international offices and operational units in the United States, Europe, Australia, and China. ALAR was created as a means to engage the intellectual resources of the academic community in applied research that addresses specific industry-defined problems and interests. The ALAR collaborations began in 2001 with several of the local universities near Acxiom's corporate headquarters in Little Rock, Arkansas, such as the University of Arkansas at Little Rock, the University of Central Arkansas, and the University of Arkansas, Fayetteville. Since then, the partnership has expanded to include other universities such as the Massachusetts Institute of Technology and Vanderbilt University.

ALAR holds an annual conference for its university partners, in which papers are solicited, refereed and compiled into Proceedings. The Laboratory also sponsors a focused annual conference for an invited audience where research results are presented. The top working papers from these conferences comprise the basis of this monograph. A working paper, once accepted, is required to go through another review for quality assurance.

Primary Audience

The issues discussed in these working papers include data integration, data management, data mining, and data visualization. These subjects are of interest to all those interested in data engineering, whether they are from academia, market-research firms, or business-intelligence companies. Notable research products are captured in this volume, consisting of reorganized chapters and extended results from those reported in the chosen working papers. The findings reported here represent not only the key issues facing Acxiom, but also other information-management concerns in the world. Because of the background from which these chapters are generated, the volume is ideally suited for researchers, practitioners, and postgraduate students alike. The contributions in this volume have their roots in problems arising from industry, rather than emanating from a basic research perspective. Each chapter includes Exercises at the end, making the book suitable for classroom use. Together with extensive references, and subject index, it can serve the academic, the research and industrial audiences.

Organization

The chapters in this book are roughly ordered to follow the logical sequence of the transformation of data from raw input data streams to refined information. The first half of the book addresses challenges associated with data integration and data management. These chapters particularly focus on two key problems within data integration: entity resolution and the challenges associated with very large scale data integration. The second half of the book is focused on the distillation of knowledge or information from data, with a particular focus on data mining, analytics and data visualization.

Specifically, we have organized our discussions using the following taxonomy:
- Data Integration and Information Quality
- Grid Computing
- Data Mining
- Visualization

In other words, we start out with how we organize the data and end up with how to view the information extracted out of the data. Following this taxonomy, we will further delineate (and in many cases reinforce) the future directions in data integration, grid computing, data mining and visualization.

Data integration and information quality are complementary areas that are maturing together. As is common in science, fields of study become increasingly inter-disciplinary as they mature. Information quality was essentially born from the 1980's movement to aggregate disparate operational data stored into a single repository (data warehouse), with the goal of extracting non-obvious business intelligence through data mining and other analytical techniques. From these efforts it became clear that independently held and maintained data stores were not easily integrated into a single, logically-consistent knowledgebase. It exposed problems with data accuracy, completeness, consistency, timeliness, and a myriad of other issues. In its earliest form, information quality was focused on methods and techniques to clean "dirty data" to the point that it could be properly integrated.

There has been a dramatic increase in the interest and visibility of grid computing during the preparation of this book. Once largely confined to the research community and a few targeted business domains, many of the concepts and techniques of grid computing have emerged as mainstream trends. Adoption of high throughput application paradigms such as Map-Reduce and high performance file systems such as the Google File System are becoming increasingly common across a variety of application domains. While some of the initial interest perhaps resulted from the publicity around the phenomenal demonstrated success of Google in exploiting massive processing power on very large amounts of data, the interest has been sustained and increased by the fact that these techniques have proven effectively and efficiently applicable to a wide range of problems. With the advent of processing chips containing many processing cores and with the development and refinement of both virtual machine hardware and software, parallel processing is increasingly considered the standard computing paradigm.

A focus of this book is to identify the correct person or object based on the data attributes associated with them. Future research into Entity Resolution could concentrate on integrating data provenance policies, i.e., when to insert, update, and delete based on sources. For law enforcement, for example, it could further refine the path-based prospecting approach, and positive or negative associations between entities. For instance, who bought guns from dealer X and also lived with known suspect Y?

The last part of our book examines how useful information can be shown visually to the user, including the authenticity of a document. In the "Image Watermarking" chapter, for example, a new, temper-proof method for image watermarking is developed using the phase spectrum of digital images. The watermarked image is obtained after multi-level "Inverse Difference Pyramid (IDP) decomposition with 2D Complex Hadamard Transform (CHT). The watermark data inserted in the consecutive decomposition layers do not interact, and the watermark could be detected without using the original image. The main advantages of the presented method, which result from the high stability of their phase spectrum, are the following. Perhaps the most important are the perceptual transparency of the inserted resistant watermark; its large information capacity; and the high resistance against noises in the communication channel and pirates' attacks for its removal.

The conclusion chapter lays out our vision of how each of these four areas—Data Integration and Information Quality, Grid Computing, Data Mining, and Visualization—are heading. Again, we combine both academic and industrial perspectives. In the editors' and authors' opinion, this volume complements other in the Int. Series In Operations Research & Management Science in the following ways. Most modeling procedures that are covered comprehensively in this series are built upon an available database. Yet few concern themselves with the compilation of the database. Still fewer people worry about the quality of the data once they arc compiled. Recent interests shown in *Analytics* suggest that businesses and other enterprises are increasingly concerned with the extraction of actionable decisions from data. We view the current volume as providing a much needed link in the long chain that connects data and decision-making.

Acknowledgements

The editors would like to thank the authors for their hard work and patience during the compilation of this volume. We are also grateful to Acxiom Corporation for their active engagement in and support of academic research through the Acxiom Laboratory for Applied Research (ALAR) without which this book would not have been possible. We would also like to thank Natalie Rego for her assistance in proof reading and editing suggestions.

Table of Contents

1 Introduction

Terry M. Talley[1], John R. Talburt[2], Yupo Chan[3]

[1] Acxiom Corporation
Conway, AR, USA

[2] Department of Information Science, University of Arkansas at Little Rock
Little Rock, AR, USA

[3] Department of Systems Engineering, University of Arkansas at Little Rock
Little Rock, AR, USA

1.1 Common Problem

Many companies and organizations face the common problem illustrated in Figure 1.1. The challenge is to take data from the real world and convert it into a model that can be used for decision making. For example, the model can be used as a tool to drive campaigns. The purpose of these campaigns is to affect the real world in a positive way from the perspective of the organization running the campaign. The general process is to collect data from a number of sources, then integrate that data into a consistent and logically related set of data. The integrated data is stored in a repository. This repository is often called a data warehouse and is often stored in a commercial relational database. Using the data, mathematical techniques, and algorithms, a model of the real world is constructed to support the decision making process. A variety of campaign management tools then use the model to drive campaigns executed in the real world.

As an example, a credit card issuer may collect credit and demographic data about the population of the United States. Using historical data on past customers, the credit card issuer builds a model of the attributes associated with "good" customers (e.g., customers that generate high profits for the credit card issuer) and seek to target new potential customers by identifying prospects with attributes similar to the good customers. The card issuer then runs a customer acquisition campaign to solicit these desirable prospects to acquire the credit card issuer's card. The product offered to the prospect may be constructed specifically to appeal to a subset of similar prospects. In this way, many distinct offers may be made to appeal to different segments of the overall prospect pool.

Y. Chan et al. (eds.), *Data Engineering*, International Series in Operations
Research & Management Science 132, DOI 10.1007/978-1-4419-0176-7_1,
© Springer Science+Business Media, LLC 2010

Only some percentage of the solicited prospects may respond to the campaign. To improve the performance of subsequent campaigns, the current campaign results are analyzed to potentially improve the data integration process, the model itself, or the resulting campaign process and products; and the cycle repeats.

The example of the credit card issuer is only one possible instance of the more general pattern. To take an example from a different realm, consider the task of an intelligence agency searching for potential terrorists. The details of the data sources available, the actual data collected, and the actual type of campaign executed may differ from the credit card example. Nevertheless, the basic system pattern is the same. In both cases, data are collected and integrated into some repository, a model of the real world is created or refined, and campaigns designed on the basis of the model are executed. The results of the campaigns are collected and analyzed to improve the process for the next campaign.

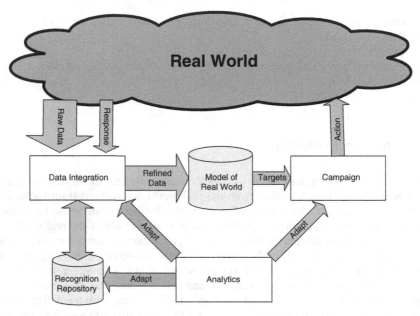

Fig. 1.1 A Common Problem

We can logically divide the supporting system into four subsystems: (1) data integration, (2) data management, (3) analytics, and (4) campaign execution. In Figure 1.1, the "Data Integration" box and the "Recognition Repository" represent the subsystem responsible for taking data sources from the outside world, performing the appropriate data quality processes on that data, identifying the entities of interest in that data, then passing that data on to the data management subsystem.

In Figure 1.1, the data repository labeled "Model of Real World" represents the data management subsystem. Most of data-management subsystem tasks consist of typical database update and administration functions. The data management subsystem is responsible for logically integrating data around core entities of interest, updating the core model with incoming data, and managing the persisted data state over time.

The "Analytics" subsystem in the figure is meant to represent model development, model validation, application of the model scoring routines to incoming data, data mining, and visualization. In other words, the analytics subsystem includes the tasks associated with developing and maintaining the model of the real world. This is the part of the system where information is derived from data.

In Figure 1.1, the "Campaign" box represents the applications or processes that take action based upon the model of the real world. In other words, this box represents the applications or systems associated with execution of actions. We distinguish this from the process of gathering insight on what to do in the Analytics subsystem. There is a wide spectrum of execution applications, depending on the specific type of campaign. As suggested by the book title, *Data Engineering: Mining, Information, and Intelligence* this book primarily focuses on the data integration, data management, and analytics subsystems. Since data access applications vary widely, less emphasis is placed here on campaign execution.

1.2 Data Integration and Data Management

1.2.1 Information Quality Overview

Building an accurate model of the world and then effecting the desired change are both fundamentally challenging problems. These fundamental challenges are further complicated by the pragmatic challenges associated with the data integration problem. The data collected from the real world is often of low quality. Obviously, the quality of the data supplied to the model and the subsequent campaign decision algorithms directly affect the efficacy of the campaigns. Much of the work required in the data integration process is targeted at reducing or eliminating data quality problems in the incoming data stream. Given the volume of data involved, the only practical way to address many data problems is to write and deploy computer programs to detect and correct data problems as part of the data-integration task.

For many people, the term *information quality* (used interchangeably with the term *data quality*) is usually equated with the degree of accuracy associated with the data. As a simple example, for a telephone number associated with a particular individual, this telephone number is considered to have high data quality if the number is correct to reach the individual. This is, however, a limited view of data quality. Researchers in the field of data quality now define many different dimensions of data quality. As suggested in Figure 1.2, adapted from Wang and Strong (1996), accuracy is only one of these many dimensions.

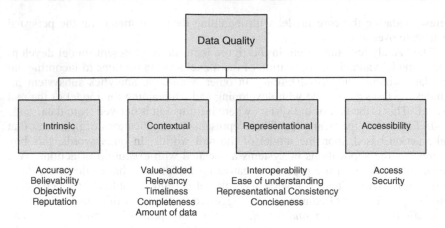

Fig. 1.2. Wang/Strong Data Quality Hierarchy

Interest in information quality is growing as organizations increasingly rely upon information for all aspects of their operations and decision making. The result is that the real costs of so called "dirty data" are increasing as well. Inaccurate, incomplete, inconsistent, and out-of-date information often lead to operational errors, poor decisions, and damaged customer relations that cost government and industry billions of dollars a year. For example, some experts have estimated that 40-60% of a service organization's expense may be consumed as a result of poor data (Redman 1998). Even worse, decisions based on poor quality data can have even more dire consequences including the loss of life (Fisher and Kingma 2001).

Information quality principles must be applied at almost every step of data integration and data management in order to be successful. Information quality processes are foundational to having accurate and consistent representations of the information.

1.2.2 Customer Data Integration

The collective set of techniques, tools, and processes for building and maintaining the core data with acceptable data quality, an acceptable level of logical integration at the entity level, and on an acceptable time schedule is sometimes known as Customer Data Integration (CDI). While some make distinctions between the term "data integration" and "customer data integration," we will use the terms interchangeably. Customer Data Integration covers almost any data transformation activity performed upon incoming data destined for a data repository (e.g., a data warehouse) and the subsequent process of integrating the new data into the existing data repository. Given the potential range of transformations that may have to be performed, categorizing CDI components into a limited set of descriptive terms may miss some data transformation cases, but we can give a general overview of the types of data transformations often seen in CDI processes.

1.2.2.1 Hygiene

The early stages of a CDI flow (i.e., the transformations that occur closest to the receipt of new data) can be described collectively as the *hygiene* phase. This part of the process is characterized by operations directly on the incoming data elements.

Encoding transformations deal with the translation of incoming data from one encoding format to another. For example, one common encoding transformation is converting data represented in EBCDIC into ASCII. Similarly, the translation of data from the Latin 1 character set into UTF-16 is an encoding transformation.

Conversion transformations convert incoming data from one data representation format to another. We usually refer to conversion as transformations fundamentally dependent on some computer format. For example, converting packed decimal into an ASCII representation is a conversion transformation as is the conversion of "big endian" integer to "little endian" and vice versa.

Standardization is similar to conversion, but the standardization transformations usually operate within some user defined representation scheme rather than a computer architecture format. For example, the "standard" encoding of gender in a particular database may be "M" for male and "F" for female. An incoming file may represent male as "0" and female as "1." A standardization transformation would translate the incoming "0" to "M" or "1" to "F" as part of the CDI process.

Standardization may also refer to transformations that reformat incoming data. For example, a standardization step may reformat the value "II" in a name suffix field to the value of "JR" or a standardization step might reformat a North American phone number like "(555) 555.0000" to "555-555-0000." There may be many standardization steps as part of a CDI process and many of these transformations may be field and data source specific.

Correction transformations fix problems in incoming data elements. This correction may be algorithmic, but is often based upon reference data available to the CDI process. For example, postal correction transformations can often correct United States zip codes on the basis of the city, state, and street address data. The distinction between *standardization* and *correction* is typically one of degree. We usually refer to a transformation as standardization if the result of applying the transformation to a data field is changing representational elements that do not affect the semantics of the field. We usually call it a correction if it fixes more substantive semantic problems in the data. In practice, both types of transformation are often done in a single code implementation.

Bucketing is similar to standardization but rather than a one-to-one translation of fields, one or more incoming fields are used to "bucket" or classify the data into some standard representation. For example, an incoming "income" field may be used to create a field called "income_group" with rules like "if income is between $25,000 and $50,000, then assign income_group the value 'A'."

Bursting is the process of breaking a single record from an incoming data file into multiple records for downstream processing. For example, a data record may contain information about a married couple with both names present in the record. If it is desirable to process the two individuals separately in the process, a bursting transformation produces a distinct record for each individual from the original record.

Validation transformations simply confirm the validity of a data field, but perhaps not its relationship to the remaining data in a record. For example, a validation transformation may confirm, through validation data available to the transformation code, that a given telephone number is a valid working number, but perhaps not that it is associated with the person's name contained in the same record.

As mentioned above, the range of possible hygiene transformations is quite large, so we will refer to those not covered by the categories above as *custom* transformations. These transformations may be highly specific to the data sources or problem space for the CDI process. Custom transformations are usually implemented in general purpose programming languages and may be arbitrarily complex.

1.2.2.2 Enhancement

After the hygiene transformations in a CDI flow, there are often a series of stages that augment the incoming data with additional data provided by a separate source (e.g., an external data provider). This part of the process is generically called *enhancement* and is characterized by using portions of the incoming data as a key to "look up" additional information or to compute additional information.

When performing "look up" enhancement, the data forming the key is usually some representation of an entity of interest (e.g., a person, place, or business). For example, one of the most common forms of enhancement for data about people is *demographic enhancement*. This type of enhancement takes a representation of an individual (e.g., a name and address combination) as the enhancement key and returns information about characteristics of that individual. Typical enhancement data may include information about age, ethnicity, income levels, marital status, number of children, etc. *Postal or address enhancement* may include information about an address (e.g., estimated property value) or may be combined with information about other entities, such as move information that associates both people and addresses. *Business enhancement* may provide information about business profits, corporate officers, credit ratings, etc.

Computed enhancements are often *analytic enhancements* that apply analytic models to compute a *score* (e.g., a credit worthiness score) or to classify entities into categories (e.g., "wealthy individuals" or "baby boomers"). *Association or grouping enhancements* are also often computed enhancements that associate a collection of entities on the basis of relationships between those entities (e.g., "known associates" or "household members"). This last category of enhancements is sometimes considered part of the entity resolution problem and leads to the discussion of data management.

1.2.2.3 Entity Resolution

Entity Resolution, sometimes also described as "customer recognition" or simply "recognition," is the process of resolving incoming data to an associated set of keys. These keys identify the entities associated with this new data. The purpose of this process is to get an accepted set of keys that can be used to logically join or merge the new data with existing data having the same keys. In other words, given a new data record as input, the intent of the recognition process is to return a set of data integration keys appropriate for that data.

Sometimes the incoming data has a set of associated *hard-keys* attached. These hard-keys are keys that, in the absence of errors within the key itself, uniquely identify an entity of interest in a particular domain. For example, an account number for existing customer present on an incoming data record may be used to associate the new data with existing data about that customer in the data repository. There is a wide variety of possible hard-keys. For example, in the United States, the Social Security Number (SSN) is used by many financial institutions as a hard-key for identifying individuals. The SSN is often treated as a unique, unambiguous identifier for a particular individual. Other hard keys, such as an account number for a bank account can identify a household entity, but not necessarily an individual. Often, incoming data records will have multiple hard-keys present on the data record, but this set of hard-keys may refer to different entity types (e.g., individual versus household) and may also give conflicting views of the associated entities.

Some data sources do not provide any hard-keys, but may provide *soft-keys* that may help identify the entities associated with the data. The distinction between hard-keys and soft-keys is that soft-keys are often ambiguous because of the representation of the key itself or by nature of the key itself. An example of a soft-key is a person's name. The representation of the name itself may change (e.g., "Jon M. Smith," "Jonathan Smith," "J.M. Smith", etc.) and names are not unique in the larger world (although perhaps in a given repository of data).

While the soft-keys provide hints to recognize the appropriate integration key, we may have to use multiple soft-keys (and indeed, hard-keys) to adequately identify the entities of interest. Building a recognition process is thus often dependent upon building an acceptable set of rules for examining collections of hard and soft keys to arrive at the appropriate data integration keys. We will refer to this set of rules and algorithms as a *entity resolution rule set*. While there are many accepted best practices for constructing this heuristic rule set, many consider the definition of the rules for a recognition process as much an art as a science.

1.2.2.4 Aggregation and Selection

Once incoming data records have passed through the hygiene, enhancement, and entity resolution process, the data management subsystem must decide what data to integrate. In some cases, multiple data records may be present, but only the "best" record should be used to update the persistent model. For example, suppose four distinct data records may provide the age of a particular person. If those sources conflict, there must be rules to define which data source is used to update the model repository. We refer to the task of choosing the best record as *selection*.

Similarly, some records may need to be combined before being used to update the model repository. In some cases, that may involve summing values across multiple records. For example, records representing sales transactions may need to be summed for a total sales amount before updating the model. We refer to this type of combination across records as *aggregation*. In other situations, the data from multiple records do not overlap or must be combined using more sophisticated decisions than simply summing the field contents. We refer to this type of combination as *blending*.

Finally, some data records should not be added to the repository. For example, in a credit card acquisition system, records for individuals that are bankrupt or in prison may be excluded from the model repository. Eliminating records from the repository based upon some criteria is referred to as *suppression*.

1.2.3 Data Management

Data management encompasses a very broad range of topics, often related to database operations such as query, update, deletion, insertion, backup, performance management, data security management, etc. However, for purposes of the discussion around the common problem in Figure 1.1, the ultimate objective of the system is to maintain an accurate model of some segment of the real-world. Several operations are required to keep the model current.

The real-world is dynamic, and keeping the model in synchronization is one of the greatest challenges in the entire process. In particular, there are four principal operations that keep the model in synchronizations. These are insert, update, consolidate, and split.

The insert operation is used to create a new model reference to a newly discovered entity such as a new customer. A new key along with the appropriate cluster of identity attributes must be added to the model to represent the entity. Interestingly the reciprocal operation of "delete" is rarely if ever used. Even though a customer may move away and technically no longer be an entity of interest, his or her entity reference in the model is usually retained, i.e., the model is cumulative. Deletion is sometimes used when an entity reference was erroneously created in the system, but even this is typically in conjunction with a consolidation operation.

The update operation is used to change the identity attributes of an existing entity reference. Attributes may change entirely such as when a customer moves to a new mailing address, or only partially, such as when zip codes are changed or a missing middle name is added.

The consolidation and split operations are used to correct errors in the model. It is often the case that real-world changes happen without prior notice to the model. For example, a new customer entity may be added to the model in response to purchase records related to customer named "Mary Smith" because no available information ties this customer with any entity already in the model. However, it may later be learned through other information sources that this customer is in fact the same as a previously defined entity named "Mary Jones", but who had recently married and changed her name. In order to maintain the integrity of the model, it becomes necessary to consolidate the two entity references into a single reference, update the identity attributes, and to delete one of the entity references.

A split occurs when the situation is reversed. For example, a single entity reference in the model may have been created for a customer named "John Smith". However, it may later be learned through other information sources that there are actually two customers, "John Smith, Sr." and "John Smith, Jr," residing at the same address. In this case it is necessary to create a new reference and split the information. Even though it is straight forward to create a new entity reference, it can be much harder, even impossible, to retroactively divide (re-label) the historical transactions that were accumulated under the single reference.

1.2.4 Practical Problems to Data Integration and Management

The volume of data required to build an accurate model and to measure the effects of a campaign can be staggeringly large. This leads to significant performance challenges associated with merely processing the required data. This challenge is exacerbated by the dynamic nature of data in the real world and the temporal value of that data. The data associated with particular entities changes frequently and the value of that data is often directly related to the age of the data, with recent data being much more valuable than dated data. This means that the data collection and data integration must be executed quickly enough to make the data available to the campaign while the data is still acceptably fresh. This temporal requirement, when coupled with the volume of data to be processed, makes the mechanics of integrating the data and positioning that data in the repository a difficult system performance challenge.

In addition, entity resolution is often a difficult and imprecise task. Entity resolution usually requires some heuristic matching of incoming data to existing data to determine the appropriate entity with which to associate the new data. The algorithms used for entity resolution can be CPU intensive for the match algorithms themselves and at the same time I/O intensive in fetching and sifting through the existing repository of known entities.

These practical problems of constructing and maintaining a useful repository of base data must all be addressed before the more fundamental problems of modeling the real world and executing campaigns can be done. The pragmatic technical challenges of performing the CDI processes for very large data volumes often stress the capabilities of traditional computer systems. This has led some to exploit the benefits of grid computing to address the CDI performance challenges. Later chapters in this book discuss a grid implementation specifically targeted at this problem.

1.3 Analytics

Decisions makers, investigators and scientists increasingly rely upon extracting relevant information from large repositories of data in order to make strategic decisions. The information is often used to test hypothesis or discover insights or intelligence. Businesses also rely upon such intelligence for their planning, including critical decisions about product lines, markets, and business reorganization. The support for these strategic decisions is usually based upon data collected from internal business operations, supplemented by relevant external information, and represented in the model of the real world.

In our simple description of the common problem in Figure 1.1, we logically associate all the tools, techniques, and processes associated with deriving insight from the core data as "Analytics." As shown by the arrows in Figure 1.1, the insights derived through the Analytics subsystem feed back into the entity resolution or recognition repository, the core data repository, and into the campaign strategy. We include many diverse techniques within the broad term analytics, including simple counts reporting, statistics, predictive models, data mining techniques, machine learning techniques, visualization systems, etc., that all may play a role in knowledge discovery from the core data.

1.3.1 Model Development

Let us take an example from a financial application to illustrate the role of analytics. Consider that one seeks to extract useful information about a financial client's customers or prospects using the associated demographic data, credit information, and purchase histories—as typically represented in a time-series description. An objective is to capture potential financial clients, including credit-card users and loan applicants—based on information of a potential client's background. Since the financial sector is greatly affected by the stock market and federal policies, these factors are assumed to be incorporated in the financial client's suite of models as well. Execution of this modeling process involves several steps.

    A. The "Customer Data Integration (CDI)" step prepares the historical data for use. This has been discussed amply in previous sections of this chapter.

    B. The "Model Development" (or "Modeling") step is usually performed by modelers within the client organization. Often the resulting models are delivered as "black box" algorithms. While some of these techniques are inherently parallel (e.g., neural networks), many of the more common techniques are difficult to execute in parallel or on a grid. Exploring improvements in the performance of the model-development process is one of the areas of investigation for this book.

    C. Model Application (or "Scoring") applies the models developed in the modeling step to the validation data. This part of the process, like data preparation, is "embarrassingly parallel" – many in the data-engineering business have been successful at exploiting grid processing for the scoring process. However, identifying changes in the historical data that force reassessment or re-scoring of a prospect, sometimes described as "incremental" or "evolutionary" scoring, is a potential area of investigation in analytics.

D.   As Figure 1.3 summarizes, the purpose of the Optimization step is to take the population of scored model subjects and select a subset of those subjects for the actual marketing campaign. The optimization step seeks to optimize some business criteria and may use techniques such as linear programming for overall ranking and selection. Exploring improvements in the performance of the optimization models is also one of the areas of investigation in analytics.

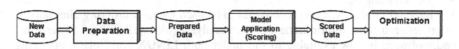

Fig. 1.3. Model Application Process

The objectives of this exercise are:
- Reduce the time required to develop and deploy financial models.
- Reduce the time required to optimize campaigns.
- Enable "evolutionary" or incremental modeling and optimization.

1.3.2 Current Modeling and Optimization Techniques

For the current discussion, our goal is to investigate methods of data parallelism (including data distribution and load balancing) and algorithm parallelism for regression, classification trees, genetic algorithms, optimization, and global ranking.

- *Classification trees*
Data mining has received much attention in extracting useful information from a massive database. Several primary data-mining methods have been defined the literature, including classification, neural networks, and regression.
- *Neural networks*
Existing neural network algorithms have exploited parallelism. We can take advantage of existing progress in this area.
- *Genetic algorithm*
Since the middle 1970s, genetic algorithms (GA) have been proposed to solve intractable computational problems through simulating evolution in simple populations

(Bockman & Wolf 2002). Genetic algorithms research in parallel GAs has led to several paradigms for how populations are evolved in parallel. One common method is known as the multideme or island-model approach, where isolated populations are evolved on separate nodes of a distributed memory cluster. Individuals from each node are evolved in a migration to other nodes every few generations. The island-model approach is useful for implementation on a broad array of parallel architectures, because the problem requires very little inter-process communication.

- *Optimization*

In linear-programming software, for example, a variety of parallel-processing versions of solvers continue to be available, some for multiprocessor shared-memory computers and some for distributed-processing networks, workstations, or PCs (Fourer 2001). Unfortunately, there is no obvious pattern or trend on how it would evolve in the future.

- *Global Ranking*

We interpret Global-Ranking techniques to be used for rank ordering alternatives, often referred to as multicriteria decision analysis (Maxwell 2002). Toward this end, software is now available to run under both LINUX and Solaris operating systems. A handful of packages are offered as web-based applications.

1.3.3 Specific Algorithms and Techniques for Improvement

Through the above cursory review, it appears that several algorithms are worthy of further investigation. It is important to examine parallelization from both the data and algorithm sides. Of particular interest is the interaction between them. The grid file, for example, has been designed to manage points in some k-dimensional data space, generalizing the idea of 1-dimensional hashing (Nievergelt et al. 1984). It partitions the data space into cells using an irregular grid. The split lines extend through the whole space, and their positions are kept in a separate scale for each dimension. The k scales define a k-dimensional array, the directory, containing a pointer to a page in each cell. All k-dimensional points contained in a cell are stored in the respective page. In order to achieve a sufficient storage utilization of secondary memory, several cells of the directory may be mapped into the same data page. Region queries can be answered by determining from the directory the set of grid cells intersecting the query region. This is accomplished by following the pointer to the corresponding data pages and then examining the points in these pages. The grid file is an adaptable, symmetric multi-key file structure that might play a role in the parallelizing model applications.

As far as *classification* algorithms, there are two common parallel formulations: synchronous tree construction and partitioned tree construction. In the former formulation, all processors construct a classification tree synchronously, and in the latter formulation, different processors work on different parts of the classification tree. Both formulations will have decreased efficiency as the number of processors increases to a certain degree. To attack this problem, we propose investigate a hybrid approach that contains elements of both parallel formulations; this is expected to be superior because its speedup keeps increasing with increasing number of processors. In addition, it adopts the advantages of the two basic parallel formulations for handling data parallelism.

For *regression* applications, Conway (2003) presented a small, general-purpose Unix script that allows SAS (and other) programs to be run in parallel when SAS Connect and other parallel processing ETL tools are not available or may be overkill for the task at hand. The script will primarily be of interest to those using Base SAS to process large amounts of data on Unix. Conway concluded that if one has excess processor capacity and the data is organized and/or can be processed in "convenient" groups (e.g., monthly files, area codes, states, account number ranges, etc.), dramatic reductions in run times can often be achieved by processing the data in parallel.

For *genetic algorithms*, it is advisable to investigate the parallelization technique – the island model (also called multiple-population coarse-grained model). In this model, an overall population is partitioned into a number of sub-populations, each of which evolves independently, trying to maximize the same function.

For *optimization*, it is important to examine the degree to which a model and data are pre-processed before being embedded in an application. The application developer may be able to use the modeling system to do some amount of model translation in advance, after which only a "compiled" version is embedded with the application. This alternative can greatly reduce the amount of modeling systems code that has to be included in the application. It also prevents users of the applications from seeing the original model, an important concern for security-conscious developers. Certain data values may be compiled with the model, but in general, an application depends on being able to optimize with different data values every time.

Although public optimization servers have received most of the attention recently, the same idea might be useful within large companies and other organizations. The callability of optimization modeling systems and servers might be put to work together, moreover, to produce specialized application packages. These packages will run locally, but they optimize remotely—to take advantage of the most attractive linear or integer programming resources, wherever they might happen to be.

As far as *global ranking* techniques, the continually increasing computational power of processors, advances in computer visualization techniques, and the Web are enabling support that was previously unimaginable. Quite a few packages now support decentralized group activities, which is often desirable in rank ordering alternatives.

The ability to exchange data with commercial applications, such as EXCEL and ACCESS, continues to emerge. A significant number of packages indicate that linear programming is now integrated into their tools.

1.3.4 Incremental or Evolutionary Updates

One can use Hoeffding bounds (Hoeffding 1963) to identify critical changes in data. Changes can be caused by noise or new information in data. We need to identify only the "significant" changes that are caused by new trends or information in the data.

Given a data model, Hoeffding bounds can give the lower bound on the number of data points that must fit the model to keep the model valid. We can detect when the given model no longer works for the data so that re-modeling and reassessment can be performed. For any percentage deviation ε, $0<\varepsilon<1$, we have the following Hoeffding Bounds

$$\Pr[X(t)/t > p+\varepsilon] \leq e^{-2t\varepsilon^2}$$

$$\Pr[X(t)/t < p-\varepsilon] \leq e^{-2t\varepsilon^2}$$

where t is the number of data points examined and $X(t)$ the number of data points that fit the current model, and p is the base percentage. In addition, we will investigate the techniques for updating the existing modeled population.

Once these bounds are exceeded, we need to re-examine the entire sequence in Figure 1.3. Particular attention is paid to the interface between the "scored data" and "optimization" steps. Optimal sampling procedures are required here in order to redesign a campaign. In recent years, heuristics have played an important role in optimization. Receiving most attention is the performance of a heuristics algorithm. Error bounds have been proposed as a way to compare heuristics. For a one-dimensional data-packing (bin-packing) problem, for example, the following bounds have been established.

Many bin-packing heuristics have been developed since the early 1970s. Some of the more popular ones are First-Fit (FF), Best-Fit (BF), First-Fit Decreasing (FFD), and Best-Fit Decreasing (BFD). FF and BF assign items to bins according to the order they appear in the list without using any knowledge of subsequent items in the list. FF can be described as follows: place the item in the next available bin that has the room. The BF heuristic is similar to FF except that it places the item in the fullest bin. In contrast to these heuristics, FFD first sorts the items in non-increasing order of their size and then performs FF. BFD first sorts the items in non-increasing order of their size and then performs BF.

Bramel and Simchi-Levi (1997) investigated the worst-case and average case bounds for the bin-packing problem. The best asymptotic performance bound for the FFD and BFD are reported as follows:

$$b^{FFD}(L) \leq 11/9 \, b^*(L) + 3$$

and

$$b^{BFD}(L) \leq 11/9 \, b^*(L) + 3$$

Here, $b^{FFD}(L)$ is the number of bins produced by the heuristic FFD on list L; and $b^*(L)$ is the minimum number of bins required to pack the items in list L; similarly for $b^{BFD}(L)$. The maximum deviation from optimality for all lists that are sufficiently "large" is no more than 22.2 percent (or $\lim_{L \to inf} b^{FFD}(L)/b^*(L) = b^{BFD}(L)/b^*(L)=11/9$) in the case of FFD and BFD.

The above is an asymptotic result for a long list of data items. It represents an example of asymptotic optimization that yields the best possible results based upon a given amount of computation. Most importantly, we know how far the answer is from optimum.

1.3.5 Visualization

Data visualization gives a direct view of complex data, which is especially helpful for analysis of large high dimensional datasets. However, existing methods often lose simplicity and clarity when rendering large amount of complex data. We will discuss some essential properties that a data visualization system should have. In addition, we present more than one interactive data visualization model that can effectively and efficiently visualize large, high-dimensional datasets.

Geospatial information is prevalent in our everyday lives. It is also an excellent example of visualization. Geospatial information is considered in such applications as our daily commute to work, mapping tools on the Internet, or through location-based services. However, a formalized standard is missing to extract useful intelligence from geospatial information. We propose several procedures and standards to unify the geospatial data sources. Specifically we include an ontology grammar for Vector and Raster imagery, data analysis based on Markov Random Field Theory, and visualization methods for the extracted information. Real-world examples are used to show how visualization can be an integral part of the Analytics subsystem.

1.4 Conclusion

Data integration and data management are fundamental to providing an integrated set of data with acceptable data quality for application use. Reflecting that importance, roughly half the chapters of this book are focused on specific challenges associated with data integration and data management. While there are many interesting problems associated with data integration and data management, chapters 2-10 largely focus on two primary challenges in this space: entity resolution and the practical problems of performing large-scale data integration.

Of course, the point of performing the data integration and data management is to enable the successful transformation of raw data into information. The second half of the book focuses on problems associated with analytics or knowledge discovery. Chapters 11-18 discuss several techniques extracting information from data. This collection of chapters has a particular focus on data visualization. Data visualization gives a direct view of complex data, which is especially helpful for analysis of large high dimensional datasets. However, existing methods often lose simplicity and clarity when rendering large amount of complex data. We discuss some essential properties that a data visualization system should have. In addition, we present more than one interactive data visualization model that can effectively and efficiently visualize large, high-dimensional datasets.

1.5 References

Bockman B, Wolf D (2002) "MPIGALib: A Library for Island Model Parallel Genetic Algorithms." Working Paper, CSCE Department, Pacific Lutheran University, May 28.

Bramel J, Simchi-Levi D (1997) The Logic of Logistics, Springer-Verlag, New York-Berlin.

Conway T (2003) "Parallel Processing on the Cheap: Using Unix Pipes to Run SAS® Programs in Parallel," Ted Conway Consulting, Inc., Chicago, IL, SUGI 28 Conference, SAS.

Fisher CW, Kingma BR (2001) Criticality of data quality as exemplified in two disasters. Information and Management, 39(2001), 109-116.

Fourer R (2001) "Linear Programming Solver or Modeling: Popular OR tool can take different approaches to reach common goal." OR/MS Today, August, pp. 58-68.

Hoeffding W (1963) "Probability Inequalities for Sums of Bounded Random Variables." *Journal of the American Statistical Association*, pp 13-30.

Maxwell DT (2002). Decision Analysis: Aiding Insight VI. OR/MS Today June, 44-51.s

Nievergelt J, Hinterberger, H; Sevcik, KC (1984). "The Grid file: An Adaptable, Symmetric Multikey File Structure." ACM Transactions on Database Systems, Vol. 9, No. 1, pp. 38-71.

Redman TC (1998) The Impact of Poor Data Quality on the Typical Enterprise. Communications of the ACM, 41(2), 79-82.

Wang RY, Strong DM (1996) Beyond Accuracy: What Data Quality Means to Data Consumers. Journal of Management Information Systems, 12(4), 5-34.

2 A Declarative Approach to Entity Resolution

Tanton H. Gibbs

Acxiom Corporation
Little Rock, AR, USA

2.1 Introduction

As companies gather and process more data from disparate sources, they are relying more heavily on entity resolution. Currently, creating an entity resolution system is a very procedural process. Blocking, transitive closure, and matching must all be pieced together whether by an Extract, Transform, and Load (ETL) tool or by a custom program (Galhardas et al. 2000). This is similar to the state of data querying before the advent of the Structured Query Language (SQL). In this chapter, a declarative approach to entity resolution is presented that gives the user the ability to specify what he or she would like resolved while allowing a code generator to determine the best way to resolve it. This chapter does not explore algorithms for blocking, transitive closure, clustering, or matching, but instead refers to papers on those subjects written by other authors (Baxter et al. 2003; Gu and Baxter 2004; Winkler 2000, 2003; Jaro 1989; Bhattacharya and Getoor 2006). Instead a background and defense of entity resolution and declarative languages is presented with a declarative solution and a possible representation. In section 2.2, a background of entity resolution is given. This covers both the rationale for and components of an entity resolution system. Section 2.3 begins the explanation of the declarative approach, focusing on the nouns of the taxonomy presented in this chapter. Section 2.4 continues the explanation, focusing on the adjectives followed by section 2.5 describing the verbs. The nouns, adjectives, and verbs are combined into an example representation in section 2.6 and then the chapter concludes in section 2.7.

Y. Chan et al. (eds.), *Data Engineering*, International Series in Operations
Research & Management Science 132, DOI 10.1007/978-1-4419-0176-7_2,
© Springer Science+Business Media, LLC 2010

2.2 Background

2.2.1 Entity Resolution Definition

Entity resolution is a fairly young field that stemmed from the commercial need for Customer Data Integration and record linkage. **Record linkage** is the task of identifying identical records across one or more record sources (Fellegi and Sunter 1969). It is also known as merge/purge (Hernandez and Stolfo 1995). Traditionally, record linkage was based around the Fellegi-Sunter statistical approach (Fellegi and Sunter 1969). This approach has been re-fined over the years to include modifications to approximate string matching (Winkler 1990) as well as the ability to better predict weights using an Expectation Maximization algorithm (Winkler 1988).

In recent years, the focus of record linkage has broadened to include training data (Cohen and Richman 2002), clustering techniques (McCallum et al. 2000), and even vector spaces (Jin et al. 2003) in order to bypass some of the deficiencies of the Fellegi-Sunter statistical approach.

Entity resolution can be viewed as an extension to record linkage that views the problem as a database problem (Benjelloun et al. 2006a) and expands the problem to include multiple entities and their associations (Bhattacharya and Getoor 2006).

2.2.2 Entity Resolution Defense

Data integration is quickly becoming one of the top needs of both public and private companies. From federal security to marketing campaigns, understanding the customer's interactions with your agency or company is vital. More-over, both real-time and offline entity resolution are required for today's businesses. Business call centers need to be able to access a customer's accounts across lines of business in order to understand the caller's relationship with the company. This interactive requirement necessitates a real-time component to the entity resolution framework. In addition, marketing campaigns may require the processing of millions or billions of prospect records. The computational requirements for this may necessitate different algorithms (Benjelloun et al. 2006b) and may need to be run offline so that interactive access can proceed with less latency. In other words, today's entity resolution system is the heart of the enterprise, equipping analysts and support representatives with the knowledge they need to do their jobs. To function effectively, it must be high throughput, low latency, flexible, scalable, and cost efficient.

2.2.3 Entity Resolution Terminology

The rest of this section explores existing entity resolution terminology. Creating a declarative language requires keen attention to the meaning of the terms used in that language. In this section, we will examine some of the operations regarding an entity resolution implementation since we will not describe those operations later. If the reader is interested in the implementation, he or she may follow the references in this section.

2.2.3.1 Prospecting

If performance is not a concern, or if the number of records is small, then it is satisfactory to match every record against every other record. In fact, many solutions propose to do that or minimize the cost of that (Benjelloun et al. 2006a, 2006b; Fellegi and Sunter 1969). Unfortunately, in today's world of massive datasets, it is often infeasible to perform that level of matching. Instead, entity resolution systems resort to prospecting. **Prospecting** is a function that quickly reduces the number of records that need to be sent to the matching engine. If we use the old analogy of finding a needle in a haystack, the goal of prospecting is to reach a hand in and pull out the needle with as little extra hay as possible.

2.2.3.2 Blocking

One common technique that is used for prospecting is known as blocking (Hernandez and Stolfo 1995; McCallum et al. 2000). **Blocking** segregates the input file into sections, or windows. Each record has its own window, or section of the file, that should contain the record of interest. Obviously, the wider the window is, the more sure you are that the record of interest is in the window. However, the wider the window is, the more records that you must match against and the longer it will take to get an answer.

2.2.3.3 Closure

Another common prospecting approach is closure. **Closure** treats the records as vertices in a graph with commonalities as the edges. It then uses the graph's connected components as the prospect set. So, if record A shares a phone number with record B, which shares an address with record's C and D, then all of those records would be connected and would be members of the prospect set. Another view of closure is shown by Bhattacharya and Getoor (2005). The authors view closure as a hyper-edge connecting entity references by associations.

As seen in Bhattacharya and Getoor (2006), closure can be computed on the fly to a specified depth. Limiting the depth helps prevent irrelevant or promiscuous data from expanding the prospect set. For instance, an apartment might have a large number of occupants across time, so its records derivatives should be quickly pruned from further analysis. It is worth noting that the results of the on-the-fly closure are stored so that future queries can be performed faster.

2.2.3.4 Matching

Matching is a function that determines whether two records represent the same real-world entity. Historically, approximate string matching (ASM) has been the center of the record linkage universe (Fellegi and Sunter 1969; Jaro 1989; Winkler 1990; Navarro 2001). With entity resolution, ASM is still important, but the system must also consider associations that ASM cannot handle such as changes of address, married name changes, aliases, and address standardization changes. In (Benjelloun et al. 2006a), matching is treated as a generic function that could encapsulate all of those associations. Furthermore, clustering approaches to entity resolution include matching, but also focus on the structural similarities between entity graphs (Bhattacharya and Getoor 2006).

2.2.4 Declarative Languages

A declarative language focuses on what the user wants accomplished rather than how the user wants it accomplished. A language such as the SQL represents many complicated procedural statements in just a few high level sentences. "SELECT * FROM TABLE WHERE X = Y" has behind it numerous optimizers, cache detection algorithms, file reading algorithms, etc..., but all of that is hidden from the SQL user.

A declarative language is, by nature, domain specific. The language uses business terminology to encapsulate the procedural statements into a form that is widely recognized and understood by the business analysts. For example, in Galhardas et al. (2000), the author uses a SQL-like language to provide a declarative language for the data cleansing domain, replacing a traditionally ETL-driven process with a concise, descriptive language.

2.3 The Declarative Taxonomy: The Nouns

The primary contribution of this chapter is the declarative taxonomy that begins in this section and continues through section 2.5. This taxonomy gives precisely defined terms that can be flexibly implemented to create a tailor made entity resolution system. This section focuses on the taxonomy's nouns. Some of the nouns currently exist in entity resolution literature. Others were created and defined in conjunction with the taxonomy. This section will distinguish between the two where appropriate.

The taxonomy's nouns promote the needs of businesses that offer many services around the same set of data. For instance, customers might be linked together based on individual attributes in order to determine credit worthiness. However, those same customers might be linked together into a household to ensure only one flyer gets sent to each family. The taxonomy clearly separates incoming records (what we will call references) and the entities that they belong to, thereby allowing a more flexible system. In the following subsections, we will explore the nouns of the declarative taxonomy: *attributes, references, paths and match functions, entities, super groups, and matching graphs.*

2.3.1 Attributes

Attributes are the building blocks of the other nouns. They are atomic values that represent such constructs as *first-name, last-name, street, SSN,* or *date-of-birth.* An attribute may also identify a specific collection of attributes due to database normalization (e.g., a key representing all the attributes of an address [street, city, state, zip] that are located in a separate address table). An attribute may also be algorithmically generated. For example, search keys are often generated to facilitate fast lookup of records with similar name or address attributes. On its own, an attribute is without *context*, or additional information that provides meaning, and therefore, to be useful, attributes must be collected together. In other papers, attributes are known as fields (Singla and Domingos 2006), features (Benjelloun et al. 2006a), or attributes (Benjelloun et al. 2006a).

2.3.2 References

The taxonomy defines a **reference** as a heterogeneous, fixed length collection of attributes. A reference typically represents a real world person, place, or thing. More specifically, a reference represents someone's representation of a real world person, place, or thing. For instance, a reference given by a web site might have only a username and email address. However, a reference to the same person given by a bank will likely have much more information, such as account number, social security number, and street address. Therefore, references are scraps of information, or clues, that must be analyzed to piece together the entity resolution puzzle. The taxonomy defines the term **input reference** to mean information that is input into the entity resolution system, whereas a **managed reference** is information that has been processed and persisted by the entity resolution system and will be managed over time. Each managed reference can be identified by a unique reference link. In other papers, the term record is used because the data is often a record in a database or file and because of the historical tie between entity resolution and record linkage (Benjelloun et al. 2006a; Winkler 1988). However, the taxonomy uses the term reference because the data is a reference to one or more entities, whether or not it exists as a unique record (Benjelloun et al. 2006a). A UML view of references and attributes can be seen in Figure 2.1.

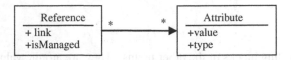

Fig. 2.1. The relationship between references and attributes is many to many.

2.3.3 Paths and Match Functions

To find a managed reference when presented with an input reference, the entity resolution system follows one or more paths and uses a match function. A **path** is a collection of prospectors coupled with a well defined traversal sequence. In addition, a path has one or more **required attributes** that must exist on the input reference before the entity resolution system will follow the path. If the required attributes exist on the input reference, then that path is said to be *valid*, and the entity resolution system will use the path's prospectors to search for similar records. Intra-path prospecting is short-circuited when prospects are found. Each prospector is tried until a prospector returns a set of managed references. The resulting (possibly empty) managed reference set is the output set of the path. If more than one path is valid, then each path's output sets are unioned to form the final set of candidate references. The input reference and the candidate references are then fed into the **match function** (Benjelloun et al. 2006a, 2006b) to determine the most closely matching managed reference. The intra-path logic for two prospectors is shown by the UML sequence diagram in Figure 2.2. Inter-path logic is shown by the UML sequence diagram in Figure 2.3. It is worth noting that while there are multiple prospectors per path and multiple paths per reference type, there is only one match function per reference type. This is shown visually in the UML diagram in Figure 2.4.

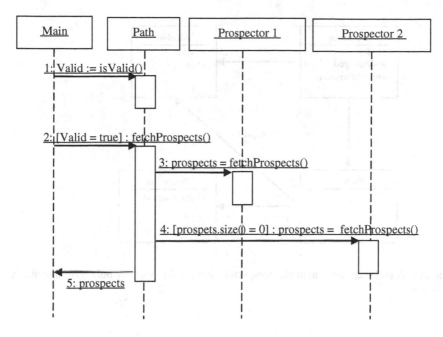

Fig. 2.2. A UML sequence diagram representing the logic of a single path

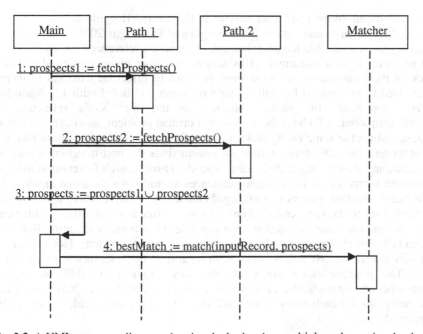

Fig. 2.3. A UML sequence diagram showing the logic when multiple paths are involved.

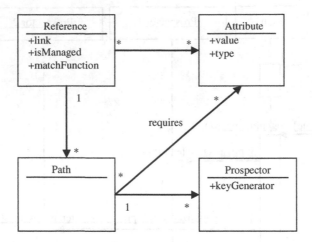

Fig. 2.4. A path may have multiple prospectors, but a reference may only have one match function.

2.3.4 Entities

The core of an entity resolution system is the entity (Benjelloun et al. 2006a, 2006b; Bhattacharya and Getoor 2005; Singla and Domingos 2006). An **entity** is a homogeneous, variable length collection of managed references. A good example of an entity is a consumer. Business-to-consumer companies need to keep track of their customers, or consumers, in order to effectively market to them. They need to understand the call center's reference to "Bob Smith 123 Main St. 21543" represents the same consumer as the web site's reference to "bsmith@isp.com." To help them solve that critical problem, an entity resolution system assigns the same **entity link** to both references. To find an entity link for an input reference, the entity resolution system finds the best matching managed reference and uses its associated entity link. An **entity match function** is used to determine if two different managed references should have the same entity link. This match function accepts two managed entities and analyzes them to determine if they belong to the same entity. The entity match function will often be different from the reference match function. For example, for a household entity, Bob and Melinda Smith at the same address may represent a valid match. However, it is unlikely that these two would match with regards to the reference's match function. This example shows how a reference may belong to two different entities (Consumer and Household). Nevertheless, a reference will never have more than one entity link for each entity. Our UML diagram with entities added is shown in Figure 2.5.

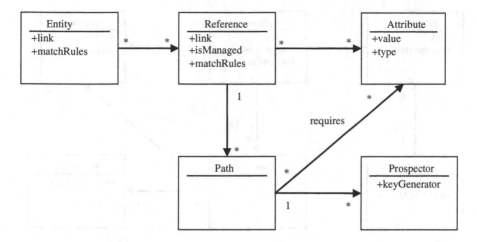

Fig. 2.5. Entities are homogeneous collections of references.

2.3.5 Super Groups

In order to efficiently determine related entities, entities are divided into super groups. A **super group** is formed when references from two different entities share the same closure attribute (discussed later). In other words, super groups are the connected components in the closure graph described in section 2.3.3. Each entity instance (represented by an entity link) will belong to exactly one super group. Furthermore, a super group only contains entities of the same type (e.g., Consumer or Household). Extending our UML diagram with super groups leads to the Figure 2.6. While other authors have discussed the role of transitive closure in entity resolution (Singla and Domingos 2006), this is the first instance of a term to denote the structure formed after closure occurs. An interesting use of super groups is shown in Bhattacharya and Getoor (2005) where the authors mine latent similarity structures in the closure graph of a super group in order to find unspecified associations.

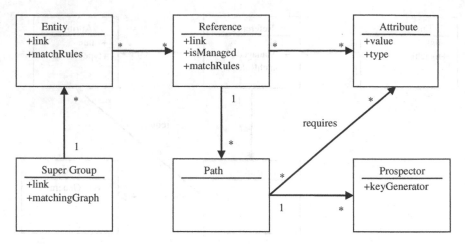

Fig. 2.6. Super Groups are collections of entities.

2.3.6 Matching Graphs

To maintain information on the connections between managed references, entities use a matching graph. A **matching graph** is a graph that contains a vertex for each managed reference associated with the entity and an edge for each positive association between managed references. For instance, "Bob Smith 123 Main St. 21543," "Robert Smith 123 Main St. 21543," and "Bob Smith 18 East Dr. 93253" are three different managed references that belong to the same entity. The first two are connected by an edge that represents a fuzzy match. The last might be connected to the first by external information. For instance, the edge might represent the fact that Bob Smith has moved and has filled out a change of address form. The resultant matching graph for the entity is visually represented in Figure 2.7.

There is a one-to-one correspondence between matching graphs and super groups; therefore, there are typically many entities participating in one matching graph. The difference between the matching graph just described and the closure graph described in section 2.3.3 needs to be stressed. The *closure graph* is used to find which entities participate in the matching graph. The edges on the closure graph directly correspond to identical closure attributes. The vertices on the closure graph correspond to managed references. The *matching graph* is used to determine how managed references are organized into entities. The vertices again refer to managed references, but the edges refer to fuzzy or logical associations between references. So, the vertices between a closure graph and a matching graph will be identical, but the edges will be very different.

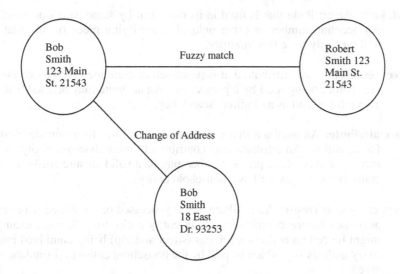

Fig. 2.7. Bob Smith and Robert Smith represent the same consumer entity. Two references have been joined by a fuzzy matching algorithm. The other two references have been joined by a change of address processed from post office data.

The nouns presented in this section form the foundation of the taxonomy. In the next section we will augment these nouns with adjectives and in section 2.5 we will give them actions via verbs.

2.4 A Declarative Taxonomy: The Adjectives

Some nouns from the previous section can take different forms and therefore may have adjectives attached to them. Specifically, attributes and references can be augmented in the system by descriptive terms.

2.4.1 Attribute Adjectives

An attribute is a very flexible and vague piece of information; therefore, it stands to reason that it may have the most adjectives defined to clarify its purpose. Some attributes with little relative importance, such as a street pre-directional (N, S, E, W), may have no adjectives assigned to them. Others with more importance, such as a name, may have multiple adjectives. All of the attribute adjectives are orthogonal to one another and may be used simultaneously to describe an attribute. The attribute adjectives defined by our taxonomy include the following

Search key: An attribute that is used in its raw form by some path's prospector. An account number or other uniquely identifying piece of information will typically have this modifier.

Indirect search key: An attribute that is processed or combined with other attributes before being used by a prospector. An attribute may be used both as a search key and as an indirect search key.

Closure attribute: An attribute that is used in its raw form to formulate closure for an entity. An attribute may contribute to more than one entity's closure. For example, a phone number may be a valid closure attribute for a consumer entity as well as a household entity.

Indirect closure attribute: An attribute that is processed or combined with other attributes before contributing to an entity's closure. A good example might be certain address attributes (street and zip) being combined into a fuzzy address key which is used by the household entity to formulate closure.

Identity attribute: Two references are identical if all of their identity attributes are equal. Identity attributes help to prevent duplicate references being persisted. Typically, more distinguishable attributes such as *first-name*, *last-name* and *street* are identity attributes. Attributes that are typically not identity attributes include title and gender.

Implied attribute: An entity uses implied attributes to prevent invalid reference combinations. For instance, we might wish to prevent a reference with a name suffix of SR from being in the same entity as a reference with a name suffix of JR. In that case, we would say that name suffix is an implied attribute. Once an attribute is designated implied then all references that belong to an entity must have the same attribute value (or no value at all for that attribute).

Constrained attribute: An attribute that has certain business rules around its format. For example, the entity resolution system might wish to store name suffix values as the integers 1 to 9. If this were the case, then the name suffix field is said to be constrained. Other constraints might include all digits for an account number, a certain format for a phone or social security number, or a birth date field matching a given regular expression.

Nullable attribute: A given reference type may decide that certain attributes are so important that they cannot go missing. These attributes are non-nullable. A nullable attribute may be either present or absent without any ill effects. If an input reference is missing a non-nullable attribute, it may still receive a link from a managed reference, but it will never be persisted.

2.4.2 Reference Adjectives

Adjectives that augment references do so to describe how references relate to entities. Does a reference type exist to be grouped into various entities, or is the reference type only there to help conceptualize the domain model? The adjectives that answer those questions are

Linkable: A **linkable** reference is a managed reference that has been assigned a unique id, known as a link. The entity resolution system will assign that link to any input reference that matches the managed reference. These links may be used to later update or delete references that are in need of maintenance.

Non-linkable: A **non-linkable reference** is purely logical and has no linkage. For instance, we can think of a Person reference as consisting of a *first-name, middle-name, last-name, name-suffix, primary-number, street, secondary-number,* and *zip*. Or, we can think of a Person reference consisting of a Name reference and an Address reference. These references are not members of other entities; therefore, we don't need to manage them individually and we don't assign them links. They are present only to help conceptualize the system.

2.5 The Declarative Taxonomy: The Verbs

An entity resolution system must also exhibit actions. These actions can be configurable in many different ways, thus the taxonomy defines verbs that are often implemented as pluggable strategies rather than as hard-coded modules. Verbs can be applied at the attribute level, reference level, or entity level.

2.5.1 Attribute Verbs

Since the attributes are the atomic data elements, attribute verbs describe various manipulations that may be performed on the data. The verbs are

Standardize: This action mutates an attribute to ensure consistency and adherence to database rules. For instance, all input fields might be trimmed and certain illegal characters (', -) might be removed. Standardization for US name suffixes might entail translating I and SR to 1, II and JR to 2, and so on. Standardization might also be used to ensure only certain values are allowed. For instance, if a *first-name* attribute consisted of only numbers, then it might be considered invalid and changed to blanks. Because of possibility of mutation, standardization must occur before anything else that uses the input references (e.g., path selection, prospecting, or matching). Furthermore, it is important to distinguish between standardization, which merely ensures database constraints, and hygiene, which is more encompassing in nature. For instance, address hygiene is an important part of data cleansing, but would be too involved for standardization. Though the line is a fine one, the important decision factor is whether or not the rule enforces a database constraint. If so, it belongs in standardization. If not, it belongs outside the entity resolution system.

Validation: A subset of standardization in which an attribute is either accepted or rejected. If the attribute is rejected, the attribute may be removed (replaced with blanks), or the entire reference may be removed from the input source or the reference have its insertion prohibited. Validation ensures that attributes exist, only contain certain characters or values, or only occur in conjunction with other attributes. For instance, a *primary number* might only exist when the *street* is not a PO Box.

2.5.2 Reference Verbs

Actions involving references revolve around reference management and linkage. References are independent of entities, so the reference actions do not involve their associations with entities. The reference verbs are

Match: The most basic question that can be asked is whether or not two references are equivalent. To ask this question programmatically, the reference match function is used. At a minimum, the match function should return back whether the references are close enough to be considered the same reference. A more useful function will return additional information such as the strength of match. In general, match functions can be divided into two types. **Attribute-aware** match functions have knowledge about the attributes that compose the reference. Their usefulness comes from their ability to use the attribute type to make a better match. For instance, if the match function knows that a reference has a *first name* it can use a *first name* nickname algorithm to provide a more accurate match. **Attribute-neutral** match functions do not have special knowledge of a reference's attributes. Their usefulness comes from their ability to work regardless of locale or reference genre. Often, an attribute-neutral match function will work equally well across languages or even on something as diverse as barcodes.

Create: To manage an input reference, we must create a managed reference in our database. The creation function will need to generate a unique reference link for the new reference.

Remove: For various reasons, references will need to be removed. Occasionally, the provider of the managed reference will request that their information be removed from a database. Another removal reason would be an incorrect entity resolution run. Removal of a reference may also affect the structuring of entities, so analyzing the matching graph after removal is a necessity.

Update: Often, a reference will need to be updated due to inaccurate or incomplete information. For instance, a customer may call in to say that his phone number or email address is incorrect, or a government might change the postal code or street address for a particular person. Like the remove operation, update may affect the entity structure and requires the matching graphs to be reanalyzed.

Reconcile: Reference reconciliation is a strategy for deciding when to create or update a reference. It reconciles new information with the information that is already known. A reconciliation strategy should use the proximity of match between the input and managed references as well as the data provenance to determine what action needs to be taken. A common strategy might include doing nothing if the input reference is a subset of the managed reference. However, if the managed reference is a proper subset of the input reference, then the managed reference might be updated. Furthermore, the reconciliation strategy may take into account information about the source of the input or managed reference. For example, if the input reference was taken from a marketing file, it may not be allowed to update a managed reference that came from an internal account file. Moreover, some sources should never be added to the database for legal reasons, so the reconciliation strategy should refuse to insert records from those sources. Therefore, reconciliation is a way to ensure the entity resolution system treats sources as first class citizens with regards to its persistence policies.

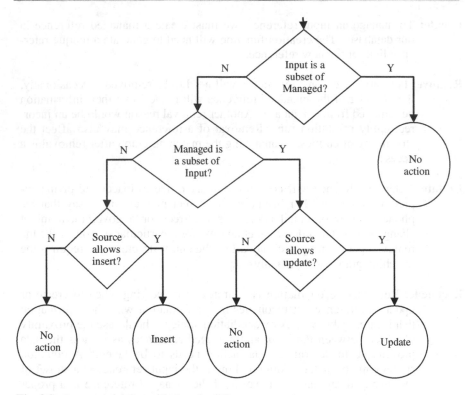

Fig. 2.8. An example reconciliation algorithm

2.5.3 Entity Verbs

Entities are more volatile than references, because they may be organized and re-organized often. Therefore, the taxonomy defines entity verbs that concern them-selves with the merging and unmerging of entities as well as with determining membership for references. The verbs defined for entities are

Includes-reference: This verb decides if an entity should contain a given refer-ence. This takes into account the entity match rules as well as the im-plied attributes of the references. Typically, to determine membership, the candidate reference is compared to each reference in the entity. If the entity match rules ever return a positive match, then the candidate refer-ence should be included (assuming no implied field conflicts); otherwise, it should not.

Split: A split occurs when one reference needs to change entities. An input refer-ence is added to its first entity by splitting it from the null entity. When a managed reference is deleted, it is split from its current entity to the null entity. Splits do not affect closure and should not affect the matching graph, since it should have already been updated, thus causing the split.

Reconcile: If the entity needs to include a new reference or split out an old reference, then it should invoke the reconciliation action. This action is designed to preserve the integrity of the database when presented with the myriad of changes that a split or new reference can entail. First, the database needs to be locked against any changes to the closure (since we'll be updating the matching graph). The lock needs to extend to any references that will be split. Second, the references being split need to have their group links updated to the new group link. Third, the matching graph needs to be updated and finally, the records need to be unlocked.

Entity reconciliation is also responsible for reconciling super groups. If a reference is added whose closure attributes correspond to more than one closure key, then those super groups must be consolidated. This occurs in two steps. First, the matching graphs for the various super groups are joined together by use of the entity match rules. Second, the lowest closure key is chosen as the new closure key. Third, all references with the other closure keys will have their closure key changed to match the lowest. Fourth, the consolidated closure keys' matching graphs will be removed from the base and the new matching graph will be added and associated with the lowest closure key. A possible entity reconciliation algorithm is shown in Figure 2.9.

Lock appropriate matching graphs and included occupancies
Update managed references with new group links
If (input reference spans super groups)
   lowestClosureKey := min(input reference closure keys)
   update managed references, set closure key to lowestClosureKey
   delete matching graphs with closure key != lowestClosureKey
End if
Update matching graph
Unlock all locks

Fig. 2.9. A possible entity reconciliation algorithm.

2.6 A Declarative Representation

A key factor in making a system declarative is the representation of the system. It must be focused on describing the data and relationships and not in describing the algorithms. For that reason, the XML is used as the representation language. The

XML is known for its flexibility and suitability for describing data, which is needed for the entity resolution system.

2.6.1 The XML Schema

Since attributes are the most atomic unit of the taxonomy, it makes sense to start by representing them. An attribute needs an identifier. This identifier should be unique across the system. An attribute may also have a maximum length, a standardization or validation routine, a nullable property, and whether or not it is an identity attribute for the enclosing reference. Other attribute adjectives are applied when describing other nouns. An XML snippet would look like Figure 2.10.

```
<attribute id="first-name"
        max-length="25"
        nullable="false"
        identity="true"
        validation="[A-Za-z ]+"/>
```

Fig. 2.10. The XML representation of an attribute. The validation routine is an inline regular expression ensuring the attribute only consists of alphabetic characters.

References are the next component of the system and are composed of attributes. Therefore, it seems natural to represent references as a composite element. In addition, references have paths, which are themselves composed of prospectors. The prospectors are constructed via a dependency injection framework such as Spring (Spring 2008); therefore, they may have configuration parameters in the declarative XML representation. A reference XML snippet is shown in Figure 2.11.

```
<reference id="PersonAtAddress" matchrules="paa.matchrules">
  <attribute id="first-name" maxlength="25"
             nullable="false" identity="true"/>
  <attribute id="middle-name" maxlength="25"
             nullable="false" identity="true"/>
  <attribute id="last-name" maxlength="25"
             nullable="false" identity="true"/>
  <attribute id="name-suffix" maxlength="25"
             nullable="true" identity="true"/>
  <attribute id="street" maxlength="25"
             nullable="false" identity="true"/>
  <attribute id="zip" maxlength="9"
             nullable="false" identity="true"/>
  <attribute id="phone" maxlength="25"
             nullable="true" identity="false"/>
  <path id="nameAddressPath">
    <required-attributes>
      <required-attribute ref="first-name"/>
      <required-attribute ref="last-name"/>
      <required-attribute ref="street"/>
      <required-attribute ref="zip"/>
    </required-attributes>
    <prospectors>
      <prospector id="exactMatchProspector"
                  class="com.recognition.ExactMatchProspector"/>
      <prospector id="streetProspector"
                  class="com.recognition.FieldProspector">
        <variable id="prospectField" value="street"/>
      </prospector>
    </prospectors>
  </path>
  <path id="phonePath">
    <required-attributes>
      <required-attribute ref="phone"/>
    </required-attributes>
    <prospectors>
      <prospector id="phoneProspector"
                  class="com.recognition.FieldProspector">
        <variable id="prospectField"
                  value="phone"/>
      </prospector>
    </prospectors>
  </path>
</reference>
```

Fig. 2.11. A reference with two prospecting paths, name/address and phone.

Finally, the entity representation is shown in Figure 2.12. Entities need to be associated with a reference type, entity match rules, and closure attributes. The closure attributes need not be part of the reference type, they can be generated attributes as well. Furthermore, the implied attributes can be specified in the match rules, in the XML schema itself, or in both.

```
<entity id="Consumer"
        reference="PersonAtAddress"
        matchrules="consumer.matchrules'>
  <closure-attributes>
    <closure-attribute ref="Phone"/>
    <closure-attribute
      generator="com.recognition.AddressKeyGenerator"/>
  </closure-attributes>
</entity>
```

Fig. 2.12. The XML for the *Consumer* entity.

2.6.2 A Representation for the Operations

The operations would typically be configured in a more dynamic way than XML due to their implementation as strategies. For instance, one could envisage managing a data source's retention and update policies through a web interface. However, the declarative schema can be used for more static decisions such as whether or not to allow or disallow operations such as splits, deletions, or reference creation. For more control, operations such as update could be specified at the attribute level. Figure 2.13 shows such a representation.

```
<reference id="PersonAtAddress" ...>
  ...
  <operation id="delete" status="disabled"/>
  <operation id="update">
    <legal-attributes>
      <legal-attribute ref="Phone"/>
      <legal-attribute ref="Zip"/>
      <legal-attribute ref="Street"/>
    </legal-attributes>
  </operation>
</reference>
```

Fig. 2.13. Static decisions such as whether or not to allow deletes and which attributes may be updated should be placed in the declarative XML.

2.7 Conclusion

In this chapter, the entity resolution problem is described and defended. In addition, we have proposed a declarative taxonomy for defining an entity resolution system and laid the foundation of a declarative language based on the XML. The contributions include a consistent taxonomy for entity resolution including nouns, adjectives and verbs. Moreover, the taxonomy is structured in such a way that it promotes pluggable strategies, enabling the re-use of other author's research. Finally, the XML is used to apply our taxonomy to an actual implementation. The declarative approach in conjunction with the XML definition will facilitate easier entity resolution system deployment and may make the data integration problem more agile. The author's team at Acxiom Corporation is currently investigating this approach to specifying an entity resolution system. Java and J2EE are being used to allow for pluggable strategies in the form of JavaBeans. So far, the results have been very positive with the ability to define entity resolution systems in a matter of hours instead of days or weeks with the current ETL based approach. Future research into this area could concentrate on integrating data provenance policies (when to insert, update, and delete based on sources), further refining the path-based prospecting approach, and positive or negative associations between entities for law enforcement (who bought guns from dealer X and also lived with known suspect Y).

2.8 Exercises

1. Describe how your school or workplace might use entity resolution.
2. Name the attribute adjectives. For each adjective, tell whether its meaning has the most effect on the attribute itself, the reference, or the entity.
3. Would a postal (or zip) code make an effective closure attribute? Why or why not? How could you modify the zip code to make it more attractive as a closure attribute?
4. Maintaining associations between entities are critical for law enforcement agencies. How would you extend this language to handle those associations? In addition, negative associations are also important. These associations ensure that two references never belong to the same entity. How do positive and negative associations affect the verbs of our taxonomy? How do they affect the XML representation?

2.9 References

Baxter R, Christen P, and Churches T (2003) A Comparison of Fast Blocking Methods for Record Linkage. Proceedings of the ACM SIGKDD'03 Workshop on Data Cleaning, Record Linakge, and Object Consolidation.

Benjelloun O, et al. (2006a) Swoosh: A Generic Approach to Entity Resolution. Stanford University Technical Report.

Benjelloun O, et al. (2006b) DSwoosh: A Family of Algorithms for Generic, Distributed Entity Resolution. Stanford University Technical Report.

Bhattacharya I, Getoor L (2005) Entity Resolution in Graphs. University of Maryland Technical Report CS-TR-4758.

Bhattacharya I, Getoor L (2006) Collective Entity Resolution in Relational Data. IEEE Data Engineering Bulletin, Special Issue on Data Quality, June 2006.

Cohen W, Richman J (2002) Learning to Match and Cluster Large High-Dimensional Data Sets for Data Integration. Proceedings of the eighth ACM SIGKDD International Conference on Knowledge Discovery and Data Mining.

Fellegi I, Sunter A (1969) A Theory for Record Linkage. Journal of the American Statistical Association.

Galhardas H et al. (2000) An Extensible Framework for Data Cleansing. International Conference on Data Engineering.

Gu L, Baxter R (2004) Adaptive Filtering for Efficient Record Linkage. Proceedings of the Fourth SIAM International Conference on Data Mining.

Hernandez M, Stolfo S (1995) The merge/purge problem for large databases. Proceedings of the 1995 ACM SIGMOD International Conference on Data Engineering.

Jaro M (1989) Advances in Record-Linkage Methodology as Applied to Matching the 1985 Census of Tampa, Florida. Journal of the American Statistical Association.

Jin L, Li C, Mehrotra S (2003) Efficient Record Linkage in Large Data Sets. Proceedings of the 8th International Conference on Database Systems for Advanced Applications.

McCallum A, Nigum K, Unger L (2000) Efficient Clustering of High-Dimensional Data Sets with Application to Reference Matching. Knowledge Discovery and Data Mining.

Navarro G (2001) A Guided Tour to Approximate String Matching. ACM Computing Surveys.

Singla P, Domingos P (2006) Entity Resolution with Markov Logic. Proceedings of the Sixth International Conference on Data Mining.

Spring (2008) retrieved 2008 from http://www.springframework.org.

Winkler W (1988) Using the EM Algorithm for Weight Computation in the Fellegi-Sunter Model of Record Linkage. Proceedings of the Section on Survey Research Methods, American Statistical Association.

Winkler W (1990) String Comparator Metrics and Enhanced Decision Rules in the Fellegi-Sunter Model of Record Linkage. Proceedings of the Section on Survey Research Methods, American Statistical Association.

Winkler W (2000) Machine Learning, Information Retrieval, and Record Linkage. Proceedings of the Section on Survey Research Methods, American Statistical Association.

Winkler W (2003) Data Cleaning Methods. Proceedings of the ACM Workshop on Data Cleaning, Record Linkage, and Object Identification.

3 Transitive Closure of Data Records: Application and Computation

Wing Ning Li[1], Roopa Bheemavaram[2], and Xiaojun Zhang[3]

[1] CSCE Department, University of Arkansas
Fayetteville, AR, USA

[2] Acxiom Corporation
Fayetteville, AR, USA

[3] WCOB Department, University of Arkansas
Fayetteville, AR, USA

3.1 Introduction

This chapter considers a record-grouping problem, which is called the transitive closure problem. The problem arises from the area of efficient information processing aiming at improving data quality and information quality. To provide a context in which the problem could be better understood, we consider the importance of data quality and information quality and discuss samples of related work in this introduction. Motivating discussion and examples are given first and reviews of related work come next.

The remainder of the chapter is organized as follows. The transitive closure problem is formally defined in section 3.2. Two sequential algorithms are developed in section 3.3. In addition to the specification of the algorithms, an example is given to illustrate how one of the algorithms works and experimental results are provided for the implementations of the two algorithms. Parallel and distributed algorithms are presented in section 3.4. The last section of the chapter contains a chapter summary and a discussion of the future work.

Y. Chan et al. (eds.), *Data Engineering*, International Series in Operations
Research & Management Science 132, DOI 10.1007/978-1-4419-0176-7_3,
© Springer Science+Business Media, LLC 2010

3.1.1 Motivation

The impact of information quality upon an organization has been indicated via use and user satisfaction (Delone and Mclean 1992). There is a wide array of data quality problems that can be classified into four categorizations (Redman 1998):

1. Data views: how the real world is captured in the data, such as relevancy, granularity and level of detail.
2. Data values: data accuracy, redundancy, consistency, currency and completeness.
3. Data presentation: appropriateness of the data format, ease of interpretation.
4. Other data issues: data privacy, security and ownership.

Poor information quality has direct impact on organizational performance. According to the study by Data Warehousing Institute, it is estimated that an annual loss of $600 billion is due to poor data (Agostino 2004). Another study indicates the estimated cost associated with poor data quality to be 8-12% of the revenue of a typical organization, and informally speculated to be 40-60% of a service organization's expense (Redman 1998). The impact of poor data quality is summarized as: "customer dissatisfaction, increased operational cost, less effective decision-making, and a reduced ability to make and execute strategy, ...hurts employee morale, breeds organizational mistrust, and makes it more difficult to align the enterprise" (Redman 1996). The reader is referred to Ballou (1999); Ballou et al. (1998); Depompa (1996) for further discussion of the impact of poor data and issues concerning of data quality management.

Most companies have realized the importance of data quality. According to a survey in 2000 by InformationWeek Research of 300 IT executives, over 80% agreed improving customer data quality was their top priority (Faden 2000). The market for database-cleansing service has been growing, up to 20% annual growth rate through 2008 (Agostino 2004). However, the cost of cleansing data is also very high, in addition to the complexity of implementing such task. The reported cost ranges from "$100,000 and $500,000, depending on company size and the amount of data you need to clean" (Agostino 2004).

Another sometimes less obvious area, where data quality is highly critical, is in data mining. Many of the data mining algorithms, which depend on the quality of data, would be rendered useless unless a satisfactory solution to the data quality problem exists (Goiser and Christen 2006).

Among the four categories of data quality, this chapter addresses the second category, which measures data quality in terms of data accuracy, redundancy, consistency, currency and completeness. To illustrate some of the issues, let us consider the four records shown in Table 3.1.

Table 3.1. A sample record set of similar records

Record Number	Name	Address	Phone Number	SSN
1	Peg M Smith	123 Main St. Apt. 3	870-123-4567	220-43-1234
2	Peggy Smith	123 Main St.	870-123-4567	220-34-1234
3	Peg R Smith	213 Main St. Apt. 3	870-321-4567	220-43-1233
4	Robert P Smith	213 Main Street	870-321-4566	220-43-1233

The reader should have no difficulty in observing the similarities among the records in Table 3.1. Further analysis of this record set might reveal that all four records belong to the same household. This realization might lead to another process in which the discrepancy in the address field is resolved. Hence, data accuracy and consistency are improved. The same idea might be used to correct the typos or errors in the telephone field in the example. Now, let us imagine that the addresses are all quite different in this example, reflecting the old and new addresses resulted from moves or change of addresses. By realizing that all four records belong to the same household, we might initiate another process that identifies the current address of the household. Hence, data currency is maintained.

Another analysis of the same record set might also reveal that record 1 and record 2 refer to the same individual. As a result, we might have duplicate records if both records are from the same database. Such information is useful to address the data redundancy issue. Now, let us imagine that record 1 and record 2 are from different databases. In addition to the four fields shown, record 1 has an email address field and record 2 has a cell phone number field. Knowing record 1 and record 2 refer to the same individual, we might fill in the cell phone information for record 1 if this field is blank or enhance the database of record 1 by adding a cell phone column. Likewise, record 2 might be made more complete by having an email address. We might even build and develop a new database, which "combines" the two databases with enhancement, such as the example illustrates. Notices that relational operator "joint" cannot be performed due to the lack of common key from different data sources.

The preceding discussion demonstrates the importance of the analysis tools for achieving data quality in terms of data accuracy, redundancy, consistency, currency and completeness. Usually such analysis tools are nontrivial and demand a lot of computing time. The run time of these tools is at least quadratically related to the number of records given and has large coefficients for the polynomial. Such tools might spend days and weeks if not months or years when they are given a data source having billions of records.

To use these analysis tools more effectively and efficiently for dealing input records which are in the range of hundred millions to billions, a fast preprocessing step is needed. Depending on which analysis tools are to be used, the preprocessing step partitions the input records into many smaller groups, where seemingly similar records are grouped together. The idea of grouping is that only those records within a group might lead to further improvement of data quality when the analysis tools process them. We may think of the records of Table 3.1 as one of the groups produced in a preprocessing step. The preprocessing step makes all "related" records into a single group. Typically, the relation of "relatedness" is an equivalence relation[1], and the relation partitions the input records into equivalent classes. Another view of these groups is that all the records in a group are roughly "related" to one another in some fashion. As a result of grouping more relations might be added. For example, suppose we are given two relations (R_1, R_2) and (R_2, R_3). Due to transitivity, we conclude that (R_1, R_3). Therefore the grouping process may be viewed as a process of computing the transitive closure[2]. This chapter uses the term "transitive closure" to refer to the grouping problem that has to be addressed in a preprocessing step.

3.1.2 Literature Review

The grouping process this chapter addresses is often referred to as "blocking methods" in the literature by Baxter et al. (2003), which have been found beneficial in solving problems such as record linkage, data cleaning, data purging/merging, and data enhancement. The notion of "grouping" or "blocking" is to divide the whole data set into relatively smaller subsets for which pairwise record analysis is performed. One of the requirements of the subsets is that the sum of the number of pairwise analysis within each subset over all subsets is minimized. Notice that if each subset contains a single element, then this sum is zero since no pairwise analysis is ever performed within each subset. On the other hand, another contrary requirement of the subsets is that the pairwise comparisons within each subset are sufficient to discover records, usually from different data sources and without a unique identifier or primary key, identifying the same real world entity (e.g., a customer, a patient, a business, or an organization) for the whole data set. Notice that if the only subset is the input data source itself, then it is ensured that the pairwise comparisons within each subset are sufficient since all possible pairs are compared. In addition to the two requirements, the third requirement has to be met as well. This requirement states that the subsets, meeting the two requirements above, must be computed much more efficiently relative to performing pairwise analysis over all pairs. The transitive closure formulation of the grouping problem is a new "blocking" method suggested by our project sponsor that satisfactory meeting the first two requirements in practice. The algorithmic study reported in this chapter demonstrates the third requirement can be also met by using clever algorithm design, implementation, and parallel and distributed grid processing.

The "blocking methods" could be categorized as *Standard Blocking* (Jaro 1989), *Sorted Neighborhood* (Hernandez and Stolfo 1998), *Bigram Indexing* (Baxter et al. 2003), and Canopy Clustering with TFIDF (McCallum et al. 2000). In Standard Blocking, records are grouped together because they share the identical *blocking key* value. A blocking key could be a single attribute or composed of

---

[1] A relation that is reflexive, symmetric, and transitive is said to be an equivalence relation (Hopcraft and Ullman 2001).

[2] R is a relation. The transitive closure of R, denoted R^+, is defined by 1) if (a, b) is in R, then (a, b) is in R^+, 2) if (a, b) is in R^+ and (b, c) is in R, then (a, c) is in R^+, and 3) Nothing is in R^+ unless it so follows from 1) and 2) [10].

several attributes and is application dependent. For example, in the instance of Table 3.1, the Name attribute could be the blocking key or the first four characters of the Name attribute could be the blocking key. In Sorted Neighborhood, records are sorted based on a *sorting key*. Similar to the concept of blocking key, a sorting key could be a single attribute or composed of several attributes. Once the records are sorted, a window of a certain size, which is also application dependent just as the sorting key, is moved along the records. The records fall into a window form a group implicitly and are paired with each other in the detailed analysis step.

In Bigram Indexing, the blocking key as introduced in the standard blocking is first transformed into a set of bigrams (all sub-strings of length two). For example, a key value "baxter" will result in a bigram set (ba, ax, xt, te, er). The resulting bigram set is then used to derive its all possible subsets of a certain size. The size of subset is determined by some application dependent size factor. For example, if size factor is 0.8, the size of the subset, in the above example, is 5 x 0.8=4 (notice that the number of bigrams in (ba, ax, xt, te, er) is 5). The new subsets are (ax, xt, te, er), (ba, xt, te, er), (ba, ax, te, er), (ba, ax, xt, er), (ba, ax, xt, te). Two records are compared if the corresponding lists of subsets of the two records contain a common element. The subsets become the conceptual blocking keys to increase the number of record pair analyses compared to standard blocking.

In Canopy Clustering with TFIDF (Term Frequency/Inverse Document Frequency), records are group together if they are in the same canopy cluster. Picking a record at random from a candidate set of records, which is initialized to all records, and then including all records within a certain "loose-threshold" distance to it forms a canopy cluster. The record chosen at random and any records within a certain "tight-threshold" distance to it are removed from the candidate set. Then the above process is repeated with the current candidate set, and continues until the current candidate set is empty. Notice that blocking process is in essence a clustering process. Empirical studies of the various blocking methods are reported in Baxter et al. (2003).

The blocking technique considered here is similar to the standard blocking in that records with the same blocking key are grouped. Unlike the standard blocking, the transitive closure blocking method allows the consideration of multiple keys at the same time and relates different keys through transitivity. The final groupings are obtained by a transitive closure computation. The precise formulation is given next.

3.2 Problem Definition

In general, a record may have many attributes varying from a half of a dozen to a few hundreds. Not all attributes will be considered as keys in the blocking process. In fact, for most applications, only a small number of the attributes is selected as keys. Without loss of generality, in our formulation of the transitive problem those attributes that are not chosen as keys are ignored and a record contains the key attributes only. We should also point out that depending on what applications the grouping is aiming at, such as consumer resolution, household resolution, or business resolution, a different set of attributes may be selected as keys to compute the transitive closures. The keys in the formulation that follows are those selected keys for one particular closure computation.

Definition 1: *A record is a n-tuple (or a relation), $(V_1, V_2 ... V_n)$, V_i denotes the value of ith key.*

In the example of Table 3.1, the first record may be viewed as (V_1, V_2, V_3, V_4) where V_1, V_2, V_3, and V_4 are respectively Peg M Smith, 123 Main St. Apt. 3, 870-123-4567, and 222-43-1234.

Definition 2: *Two relations $(V_1... V_n)$ and $(U_1... U_n)$ are "related" if there exists i, $1 \leq i \leq n$, such that $V_i = U_r$ In other words, two records are "related" if for some key the two records share the same value.*

Note from the above definition, all keys are treated the same. As long as one key is identical, two records are "related". This may be desirable in the preprocessing step that intends to capture all the possibly related information. An alternative approach is to assign different weights to different keys. For example, in most cases, SSN can be used as the unique identifier of the real world entity (not always the case though, sometimes the son may use his father's SSN). If the application is to identify individual consumer records, we may place more weight on SSN key than other keys. However, in this chapter, we assume equal weight in the definition of relatedness.

Definition 3: *Two records $V= (V_1... V_n)$ and $U= (U_1... U_n)$ are "**transitively related**" if either the two records are related or there exists records $R_1, R_2...R_k$ for $K \geq 1$ such that V and R_1, R_k and U are related, and R_i and R_{i+1} are related, $1 \leq i < k$.*

In the example of Table 3.1, records 3 and 4 are related because the value of their 4th key is 220-43-1233. Suppose we only use first name and last name to test the value of the name field. Then records 1 and 3 are related. From transitively related definition, records1 and 4 are transitively related.

Definition 4: *Let S be a set. $P_1, P_2... P_k$ is a **partition (cluster)** of S iff $S = P_1 \cup P_2 ... \cup P_k$ and $Pi \cap Pj = \Phi$, $i \neq j$, $1 \leq i, j \leq k$. Pi is an element of the partition, which has k elements.*

Let S be {1,2,3,4,5,6,7,8}. A partition of S could be {1,3,5}, {2,8}, and {4,6,7}; or it could be {1,2,3} and {4,5,6,7} among other possibilities.

Transitive Closure Problem:

Input: a set of records.

Output: the partition of input record set such that all records transitively related are in one element of the partition.

In the example of Table 3.2, the record set has twelve records and each record has four keys. Records 1 and 2 are related due to the first key. Records 2 and 6 are related due to the third key. Records 5 and 6 are related due to the first key. Hence, records 1 and 6 are transitively related. We leave to the reader the verification that the partition of the twelve records is {1,2,3,5,6,9,10,11,12} and {4,7,8}.

3.3 Sequential Algorithms

Two sequential algorithms are proposed and studied in this section. Through the study of these algorithms, we could understand the nature of transitive closure problem better and deeper. The study also prepares us to see the rationales leading to the development of the parallel and distributed algorithms to be presented in the section that follows, and allows us to comprehend the parallel and distributed algorithms, which are more complicated to develop than the sequential ones.

Any algorithm that solves the transitive closure problem must address two fundamental problems. One is to determine if two records are related or not for any two records. This task amounts to computing the complete relation using definition 2. The other task is to partition the records based on the relation and transitivity definition (definition 3).

The first algorithm, called a breadth first search based algorithm, essentially carries out pairwise evaluation of relatedness between two records and relies on the breadth first search algorithm to assign records to the elements of the partition. More details of the algorithm will be provided later. The second algorithm is based on the ideas of sorting and disjoint set data structures. Instead of using all the key values of two records to determine if the records are related, the algorithm considers one key at time and repeats the process for all keys to capture the transitively relatedness information completely. The partition or transitive closure sub problem is effectively solved by disjoint set find and union operations.

3.3.1 A Breadth First Search Based Algorithm

The description of the algorithm assumes that input records from an input file have already been stored in an array data structures r[j], where j represents a record number. Records are numbered from 1 to n. A record has k keys, numbered from 1 to k. The notation r[j].key[2] refers to the second key of record j. In addition to the key fields, a record has one extra field called partition. The partition field of record j is denoted by r[j].partition. The partition field keeps track of the records in each element of the partition. All those records having the same partition field value belong to the same partition element. The algorithm also assumes the availability of a queue data structure, denoted by q, which supports operations for adding an item, removing an item, and testing of queue emptiness. Indentation indicates block structure in the specification of the algorithm.

The pseudo code of the first sequential algorithm is given in Fig. 3.1. Notice that one-of-the-keys-equal() function returns true if there exists a key for which both argument records have the same value, and false otherwise. The function tells us if the given two records are *related* or not. For record r[i], if its partition has not been identified (indicated by its partition field being 0), then after the execution of lines 4 to 11 all the records having the same partition as r[i] have been correctly identified. We leave the correctness proof of the algorithm to the reader.

```
Algorithm 1: computing the transitive closure or partitions
Assuming records are numbered from 1 to n; q is empty initially
Assuming partition field of each record is 0 initially.
1      nextPartition = 1;
2      for ( i = 1; i ≤ n; i ++)
3          if ( r[i].partition == 0)
4              r[i].partition = currentPartition;
5              adding r[i] to q;
6              while (q is not empty)
7                  removing record r from q;
8                  for (j = i + 1; j ≤ n; j++)
9                      if (r[j].partition == 0 and one-of-the-keys-equal (r, r[j]))
10                         r[j].partition = nextPartition;
11                         Add r[j] to q;
12             nextPartition++
```

Fig. 3.1. Algorithm 1 for Transitive Closure Computation

The algorithm in fact handles two related but independent tasks. One is to determine if two records are related or not for virtually all pairs of records. The other is to identify the transitive closures (or equivalent classes) based on the related information. These two tasks may be separated provided the relation R is given. We will address and stress this point again in later sections. Observing that the two tasks could be separated, we could develop an alternative algorithm based on the same idea, where the algorithm first computes R using the two loops at line 2 and line 8 and then performs either the breadth first search as in Algorithm 1 or the depth first search based on R. The details of the alternative algorithms are left as exercises for the reader.

Conceptually, the related information may be represented as a graph, where a vertex represents a record and an edge between vertices U and V represents that records U and V are related, that is, one-of-the-keys-equal (U, V) is true. Consequently, the transitive closure problem becomes graph connected components problem, a well-known graph theoretic problem (Cormen et al. 2001). Based on the depth first search or the breadth first search graph traversal approach, connected components problem can be solved in linear time in the number of vertices and edges of the graph. However, in general we may need to spend quadratic time to find the related information between all pairs of records for an arbitrary given relatedness function.

However, we may take advantage of the particular property of definition 2 of relatedness to reduce the quadratic time (see the sorting and disjoint set based algorithm in Fig. 3.2). The time complexity of algorithm 1 is $O(n^2)$.

3.3.2 A Sorting and Disjoint Set Based Algorithm

The pseudo code of the second sequential algorithm is given in Figure 3.2. Sorting and disjoint set find and union are the two key ideas used. Both topics are covered thoroughly in Cormen et al. (2001). The disjoint set data structures maintain a group of sets that are pair-wise disjoint. Given an element findSet returns the set in which the element belongs. Given two elements from two disjoint sets, union combines the two sets into a single one.

```
Algorithm 2: computing the transitive closure or partitions
Assuming there are n records and k keys, numbered from 1 to n, and 1 to k respectively.
Each record also has a record number field, recNum, for identification purpose.
djs is the data structures for disjoint set find and union.
It is assumed that djs is initialized with each record forming a set of its own
1    for ( i = 1; i ≤ k; i ++)
2        sort all records based on the ith key;
3        preKey = r[1].key[i];
4        recNum = r[1].recNum;
5        for ( j = 2; j ≤ n; j ++)
6            If (preKey == r[j].key[i] && (djs. findSet (recNum) != djs.findSet (r[j].recNum)))
7                djs.union (recNum, r[j].recNum);
8            preKey = r[j].key[i] ;
9            recNum = r[j].recNum;
10   for ( j = 1; j ≤ n; j ++)
11       r[j].partition = djs.find (r[j].recNum);
```

Fig. 3.2. Algorithm 2 for Transitive Closure

The same record structure used in Algorithm 1 is used in algorithm 2. Algorithm 2 passes through the record set K times, where K is the number of keys. In each pass, algorithm 2 considers a new key and uses that key to further refine the transitive closure computed thus far. The transitive closure computed thus far has been determined by the keys already processed, meaning key 1 through key j-1, if the new key is key j. The refinement is carried out very efficiently using disjoint set find and union data structures. Due to definition 2, sorting of a given key can be used to derive all needed record relations associated with that key. If a perfect hashing is available, the same information may be derived using hashing, which is even more efficient than sorting. However, for non-perfect hashing, collisions may happen, which introduces fictitious relatedness between records. These fictitious relations might lead to bigger transitive closures. Nonetheless, the idea of using hashing is very interesting and should be investigated further for possible gain in efficiency in time and space. The time complexity of algorithm 2 is O(nlogn), where K is treated as a constant here and n is the number of records in a input file.

To give the reader a clearer picture of how Algorithm 2 works, let us consider the records in Table 3.2 (all rows and columns 1 to 5). These records will be the input to the algorithm. The last column of the table shows the initial values of the disjoint set.

Table 3.2. An Example of Transitive Closure

RecordNo.	Key 1	Key 2	Key 3	Key 4	Set Number
R1	C1K1V4	C1K2V10	C1K3U30	C1K4U31	1
R2	C1K1V4	C1K2U2	C1K3U3	C1K4V2	2
R3	C1K1V4	C1K2V5	C1K3U8	C1K4V5	3
R4	C2K1U18	C2K2V3	C2K3V3	C2K4V3	4
R5	C1K1V5	C1K2V7	C1K3U21	C1K4V7	5
R6	C1K1V5	C1K2V4	C1K3U3	C1K4V4	6
R7	C2K1V9	C2K2V3	C2K3U5	C2K4V4	7
R8	C2K1V16	C2K2V3	C2K3U6	C2K4V5	8
R9	C1K1V7	C1K2U13	C1K3U14	C1K4U15	9
R10	C1K1V7	C1K2V42	C1K3U14	C1K4V34	10
R11	C1K1V23	C1K2V6	C1K3U14	C1K4V6	11
R12	C1K1V23	C1K2V1	C1K3U14	C1K4V5	12

Figure 3.3 shows two transitive closures for these 12 records. The first one includes R1, R2, R3, R5, R6, R9, R10, R11, and R12. The second one includes R4, R7 and R8. Figure 3.3 also shows which key or keys make a pair of records related to one another. For example, R4 and R7 are related to one another by Key 2, which means their second key values are identical. Similarly, R9 and R10 are related to one another by Key 1 and Key 3, indicating not only their first keys are identical, but the third keys as well.

As commented in the pseudo code, the disjoint set is initialized as shown in Table 3.2 last column. Each record forms a set of its own. In this example, we have four keys. The loop at line 1 of Algorithm 2 will iterate four times. Tables 2.3 to 2.6 show the outcomes in the corresponding iterations.

Tables 3.3 to 3.6 share the same structure. Each table consists of two sub tables (Table 3(a) and Table 3.3(b)). The three rows of Table 3.3(a) represent first key value, record number, and set number respectively. The twelve columns represent the twelve records. The results at the end of the sorting step are shown in Table 3.3(a). Notice that the key values in the first row are sorted in lexicographical order. Colors are used to highlight the consecutive records having the same key values. Conceptually, the sorting step rearranges the records as shown in the table. The results after disjoint set find and union step are shown in shown in Table 3.3 (b). The only difference between Table 3.3(a) and (b) is in their respectively last rows, since the disjoint set find and union operation modifies the set to which a record belongs. Arrows and bold fonts are used to indicate changes in set membership.

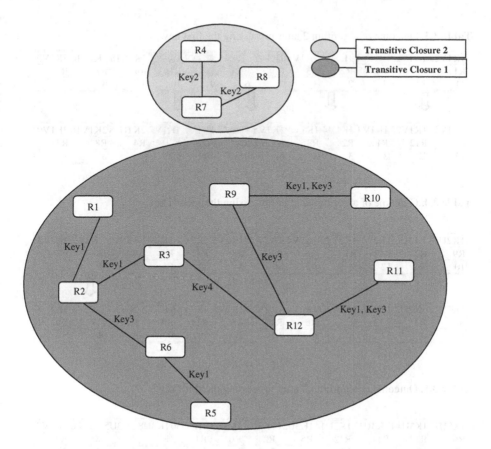

Fig. 3.3. Transitive closure problem for Algorithm 2

Table 3.3. Outcome of algorithm 2 after processing the first key

1K1V23	1K1V23	1K1V4	1K1V4	1K1V4	1K1V5	1K1V5	1K1V7	1K1V7	2K1U18	2K1V16	2K1V9
R11	R12	R1	R2	R3	R5	R6	R9	R10	R4	R8	R7
11	12	1	2	3	5	6	9	10	4	8	7

(a)

1K1V23	1K1V23	1K1V4	1K1V4	1K1V4	1K1V5	1K1V5	1K1V7	1K1V7	2K1U18	2K1V16	2K1V9
R11	R12	R1	R2	R3	R5	R6	R9	R10	R4	R8	R7
12	12	3	3	3	6	6	10	10	4	8	7

(b)

Table 3.4. Outcome of algorithm 2 after processing the second key

1K2U13	1K2U2	1K2V1	1K2V10	1K2V4	1K2V42	1K2V5	1K2V6	1K2V7	2K2V3	2K2V3	2K2V3
R9	R2	R12	R1	R6	R10	R3	R11	R5	R4	R7	R8
10	3	12	3	6	10	3	12	6	4	7	8

(a)

1K2U13	1K2U2	1K2V1	1K2V10	1K2V4	1K2V42	1K2V5	1K2V6	1K2V7	2K2V3	2K2V3	2K2V3
R9	R2	R12	R1	R6	R10	R3	R11	R5	R4	R7	R8
10	3	12	3	6	10	3	12	6	8	8	8

(b)

Table 3.5. Outcome of algorithm 2 after processing the third key

1K3U14	1K3U14	1K3U14	1K3U14	1K3U21	1K3U3	1K3U3	1K3U30	1K3U8	2K3U5	2K3U6	2K3V3
R9	R10	R11	R12	R5	R2	R6	R1	R3	R7	R8	R4
10	10	12	12	6	3	6	3	3	8	8	8

(a)

1K3U14	1K3U14	1K3U14	1K3U14	1K3U21	1K3U3	1K3U3	1K3U30	1K3U8	2K3U5	2K3U6	2K3V3
R9	R10	R11	R12	R5	R2	R6	R1	R3	R7	R8	R4
12	12	12	12	6	6	6	6	6	8	8	8

(b)

Table 3.6. Outcome of algorithm 2 after processing the forth key

1K4U15	1K4U31	1K4V2	1K4V34	1K4V4	1K4V5	1K4V5	1K4V6	1K4V7	2K4V3	2K4V4	2K4V5
R9	R1	R2	R10	R6	R3	R12	R11	R5	R4	R7	R8
12	6	6	12	6	6	12	12	6	8	8	8

(a)

1K4U15	1K4U31	1K4V2	1K4V34	1K4V4	1K4V5	1K4V5	1K4V6	1K4V7	2K4V3	2K4V4	2K4V5
R9	R1	R2	R10	R6	R3	R12	R11	R5	R4	R7	R8
12	12	12	12	12	12	12	12	12	8	8	8

(b)

The results after sorting the second key are shown in Table 3.4(a), and the results after disjoint set find and union step are shown in Table 3.4(b). Similar results after processing the third key and the forth key are shown in Tables 3.5 and 3.6 respectively. As can be seen, at the end two transitive closures (8, 12) are obtained. This example confirms the correctness of Algorithm 2.

Conceptually, we may view Algorithm 2 having two phases. Phase one generates related records (or edges of the graph with possible repeated edges); and phase two computes record transitive closures (or connected components of the underlining graph).

3.3.3 Experiment

The two algorithms in the previous section are implemented in C^{++}. Empirical study is conducted. The record files used in the experiment are generated by a synthetic data generator, called "Ruby Data Generator" (Li 2008). The example used to illustrate how Algorithm 2 works is generated by the same data generator.

Table 3.7. Experimental results

Distribution	Nbr of Records	Sorted Alg 1	Sorted Alg 2	Sorted Alg 2*	Ran Alg 1	Ran Alg 2	Ran Alg 2*
100,000 clusters. Each cluster has one record	100000	1288	89	3	1293	90	3
10,000 clusters. Each cluster has 10 records	100000	1296	529	3	1954	525	3
1,000 clusters. Each cluster has 100 records	100000	1301	605	3	1966	604	3
100 clusters. Each cluster has 1000 records	100000	1317	612	3	1993	611	3
10 clusters. Each cluster has 10,000 records	100000	1463	610	3	2258	611	3
1 cluster, which has 100,000 records	100000	2803	611	3	2835	612	3
5 clusters. Each cluster has 20,000 records	100000	1617	614	3	2395	613	3
50 clusters. Each cluster has 2,000 records	100000	1339	611	3	2040	613	3
500 clusters. Each cluster has 200 records	100000	1309	608	3	1986	607	3
5,000 clusters. Each cluster has 20 records	100000	1306	570	3	1978	568	3
500 clusters of which 25% has size 80, 160, 240, 320 (totally 108,400 records)	108400	1536	715	3	2328	715	3
100,000 clusters, of which 80% has 1 record, 10% has 2 records, 5% has 3 records, 2.5% has 4 records and 2.5% has 5 records (totally 137,364 records)	137364	2429	390	3	2825	390	3

The experimental results are shown in Table 3.7. Twelve files are used in the experiment. Each file has roughly one hundred thousand records. Column 1 of the table lists the parameters given to the Ruby data generator to generate the files. Column 2 lists the number of records in each file. In the files generated by Ruby data generator, all records belonging to the same transitive closure are located consecutively in the file. In other words, records in a file are "sorted" according to their transitive closures. The "sorted" property might affect the efficiency evaluation of the algorithms and produce bias results.

A tool, developed in house, is used to randomize the data files produced by the data generator. Both the original, "sorted" files and the corresponding randomized files are used in the experiment. Columns 3 to 5 list the run times (in seconds) for the "sorted" files, and column 6 to 8 for the "unsorted" files. The results were obtained from C++ programs ran on a single 1.3 GHz Dell computer with 512 MB main memory under Windows XP.

Columns 3 and 6 list the run times of Algorithm 1. Columns 4 and 7 list the run times of Algorithm 2 where C^{++} template class design has been used to implement disjoint set to allow set element to be of any object (including string object). Columns 5 and 8 list the run times of Algorithm 2 where the implementation requires that set elements be restricted to integers from 1 to n, where n is the largest integer used. Both the design and the implementation of the disjoint set find and union data structures are optimized by using union by rank and path compression algorithms (Cormen et al. 2001). The experiment shows that for Algorithm 2, the implementation using an integer set runs 30 to 200 times faster than the implementation using an object set. Algorithm 2 runs 400 to 900 times faster than Algorithm 1. For certain transitive closure distributions, "sorted" files impact the performance of Algorithm 1. (See rows 3, 4, 5, 6, 8, 9, 10, 11, and 12 of Table 3.7). Regardless the files are "sorted" or not, Algorithm 2 delivers the same performance.

In all three implementations of the proposed algorithms, that the processing can be done internally is assumed, meaning all the records can be stored in main memory or virtual memory. However, the assumption is not valid for files with billions of records and each record may take hundreds of bytes. For example, for many 32-bit systems, the maximum virtual memory an application can have is 2GB or 4GB. To overcome the problems caused by large file size, two alternatives exist: one is single machine solution and the other is multi-machine solution. A single machine solution may have to use external processing and external files. External processing in general is very slow relative to internal processing. The evidence is very clear when file sizes are really large. Therefore, we will not investigate this alternative any further. A multi-machine solution, combining memory of each machine into a large memory, may have to use distributed processing and requires algorithmic development in a parallel and distributed setting. This alternative will be further investigated due to many successful stories in parallel and distributed processing and grid computing. Nonetheless, the proposed sequential algorithms may be applied to improve the performance of both single and multi-machine solutions because both solutions have an internal processing component.

The proposed algorithms assume that they must compute both the relation between records (see definition 2) and the transitive closure that the relation set defines. As mentioned earlier, computing the relation set and computing the transitive closure are two independent but related activities. A slightly different way of formulating the transitive closure problem is that the relations are given and the corresponding transitive closure must be computed. One way of specifying the relations is by providing a set of record pairs or key pairs. An algorithm has also been developed for this version of the transitive closure problem. It uses the disjoint set find and union concept and efficient data structures. As an example, it takes the prototype algorithm less than 21 minutes to finish the transitive closure computation for an input file consisting of 442,658,820 integer key pairs, where key values are integers. The number of distinct key values is 122,915,040. The file size is about 8GB. The program ran on a single 2.8 GHz Dell computer running Windows XP with 1 GB main memory. The reader is referred to Zhang et al. (2006) and Li et al. (2006) for additional discussions and empirical studies of these algorithms.

3.4 Parallel and Distributed Algorithms

As pointed out in the preceding, one main challenge of processing a huge data set in transitive closure computation is insufficient internal memory of a single machine. Using parallel and distributed processing, we have developed algorithms that allow data to be partitioned and distributed among grid nodes, and memory of each grid node to be combined to hold the data structures, such as a disjoint set or a map. The algorithmic design goal is to be able to handle efficiently (both space and time) the computation of transitive closure of huge data files with hundreds of millions to billions of records.

The proposed parallel and distributed algorithms assume the input to the transitive closure process is a set of record pairs or key pairs, where a record identifier or a key is represented by an alphanumeric string. Our project sponsor has a massively parallel process using grid computers to produce key pairs from a record file, whose structure is similar to those defined and considered in the previous sections. The distributed process of producing the key pairs from a record file will be briefly discussed.

3.4.1 An Overview of a Parallel and Distributed Scheme

Finding transitive closures of records require 3 steps to be executed in sequence with each step performed in parallel on distributed processors. These steps are:

1. transform an input file to record pairs (or key pairs)
2. convert alphanumeric string pairs to integer pairs
3. compute closure on integer pairs

Efficiency of the first two steps

We know that every distributed or parallel algorithm requires data to be communicated among the processing elements by passing messages except for shared memory architectures. But communicating large volumes of data degrades the performance. Thus, to avoid large volumes of data communicated among the processors, in step 1 records are processed and a new file containing all record pairs is generated (or all record pairs could be sent directly to the processors of step 2). In step 2 the string pairs of step one are converted to equivalent integer pairs, where each record is uniquely represented by an integer. Step 1 helps in communicating the related record identifiers instead of the records as whole, thus reducing the data volumes being communicated. *Step 2 is required only in case if record identifiers in record pairs are none integers.* This step further reduces the size of communicating messages because in real time implementations, size of integer (in machine representation) is far less than the size of any formatted string (character representation) and time taken to send a set of strings will be far more than sending the corresponding mapped integers. This is demonstrated by the run-times of a simple communication given in Table 3.8.

Table 3.8. Run-times of string Vs integer communications

Data sent from one processor to other	Time taken
300,000 - 32-byte strings	0.85 seconds
300,000 integers	0.15 seconds

Table 3.9. Scan-times and sizes of the Text Vs Binary file formats

Number of Matching Pairs	Text/Binary	Size of the file	Number of processors	Time (seconds)
120 million pairs	Text	7.8 GB	4	1361
120 million pairs	Binary	1 GB	4	55
120 million pairs	Text	7.8 GB	8	1134
120 million pairs	Binary	1 GB	8	45

Table 3.9 gives the run-times for each processor to just go through the whole file once. The input file in text format represents character-based string record pairs before conversion process, while the input file in binary format represent the mapped integer pairs in machine representation after the conversion process.

Thus the first two steps help in improving the performance both in terms of memory and time. The first two steps also lead to a more efficient parallel and distributed closure algorithm to be described later. In our current application, if all records may be viewed as vertices of an undirected graph then vertices are connected by edges if and only if they are *related* [see section 3.2] records. The problem of finding transitive closures is equivalent to finding the connected components in an undirected graph. The pairs of related records are stored as record pairs in a data file, which acts as an input file to the step 2.

3.4.2 Generate Matching Pairs

This step is similar to finding pairs of directly related records that match by at least one key and can be performed in several ways. For instance, this step is performed by some sets of processors working in parallel in different stages where those residing in the last stage will generate matching pairs.

Let us suppose we have data records with four key fields. Then there exist 4 processors (one for each key) in the first stage reading the input file in parallel using some parallel file system such as PVFS and taking the required information from it. That is, each processor will be associated with one key field and collects the record identifier and key value pairs, where key values are hashed and directed to the appropriate processor working in the second stage. This is to make sure that all key values that are equal with respect to one key field go to the same processor, although some of the unequal ones with the same hash value will go to that processor as well.

Each processor in the first stage is associated with 'n' parallel processors in the second stage. Thus, in the current case, a total of 4n processors work in the second stage. Thus the 4n processors in the second stage collect all record number and key value pairs, do some internal sorting, and generate the matching pairs (i.e., pairs of record numbers) for which key values match. Since keys are processed independently, the distributed process may generate duplicated record pairs. A variation of the above process is to use key pairs instead of record pairs, which is currently implemented by our project sponsor. The clustering algorithm described in the next Section can handle such data with ease. The detail of the distributed process of producing the key pairs from a record file is beyond the scope of this chapter and will not be addressed further.

3.4.3 Conversion Process

We shall use grid node or node to refer to processor in our parallel and distributed systems. Nodes are identified by their ranks from 0 to p-1, for a system having p nodes. Records (or record identifiers to be more precise) are "distributed" or "assigned" to nodes using some hashing scheme so that records are evenly distributed. A record assigned to a node is referred to as a *local record* to that node; otherwise the record is referred to as *non-local*. A record pair is a *local pair* with respect to a node if both records in the pair are local to the node. A pair of records is a *global pair* with respect to a node if the pair contains a local record and a non-local record.

In this step, each node processes all pairs containing its local records, and produces the corresponding integer pairs associated with its local pairs and only specific form of global pairs, which contain pairs of records (a, b) such that *a* is its local record and *b* is a non local one. In this conversion algorithm, a node ignores all global pairs in the format (a, b) such that *a* is its non local record and *b* is its local record. Note that the conversion of such pairs is taking care of by the node of which *a* is a local record. In the clustering algorithm that is developed in next section, each node processes all its local and global pairs.

Here is how to decide what records belong to which nodes. Records are distributed equally among the processors by finding modulo *p* on the hash value of the record number (which is in a string). That is, a record belongs to the processor with rank *r* if and only if the resulting hash modulo value is *r*.

This phase has 2 steps to be performed in sequence:

- *Constructing the Map:* A map is a data structure that holds the record numbers (alphanumeric strings) and their associated integral values assigned uniquely to all record numbers distributed among parallel processors. In this phase, each node first constructs a local map that contains all local records mapped to a sequence of integral numbers starting from 1. Then unique mapping values for all records, distributed across the participating processors, are found by a sequence of processor communication that is as follows. The first processor with rank 0 initiates the process by sending the maximum integer value assigned to one of its local record (i.e., maximum mapped value) to the next processor in the sequence (i.e., processor with rank 1), which in turn increments all its map values by the offset received from its previous processor and sends the maximum mapped value to the next processor. This process continues until the last processor in the sequence (processor with rank *p*-1), which increments its map values and stops the communication sequence.

- *Finding integer pairs:* In this phase, each processor first converts all its local pairs to the equivalent integer pairs by using the local map constructed in the previous phase. Then all global record numbers are sent out to the appropriate participating processors to acquire their equivalent integer values. Then all global pairs are also converted to the equivalent integer pairs that are finally written to the output file in binary format. This phase is performed iteratively by reading the input file in blocks such that the above steps are repeated for each block. The size of the block can vary depending on the hardware and software used. That is it depends on the capacity of internal memory and the maximum amount of data that can be communicated. This helps in converting the input files scalable to any extent.

3.4.4 Closure Process

The main logic involved in finding the transitive closures is described as follows:

In many applications, we find certain records that are *directly* or *transitively related* to the other records [see Problem Definition Section]. The task of finding the transitive closures involves three basic processes to be executed repeatedly for

$\log_2$ n steps, where n is the number of processors on which the current closure process is being executed, after an initial preprocessing step.

The initial step performs local clustering, where all records that are directly or transitively related are grouped to form local clusters. Each node performs this step independently on its local pairs. Then, each node using its global pairs (the globally related records), generates new pairs (either local or global pairs) belonging to all other processors. That is, if (a, b) and (c, d) are global pairs of the current processor P and either $a=c$ or a & c belong to the same local cluster group, then (b, d) forms either a new local pair for some other processor Q, if b and d are local to the participating processor Q or a new global pair for both processors Q and R if $b \in$ Q and $d \in$ R, and Q and R are different processors. Note that in our convention, for a global pair its first element refers to the local record and its second element refers to non-local record.

Let us illustrate the algorithm of finding transitive closures using the records given in Fig. 3.4 and Fig. 3.6. The diagrams assume that all records are represented as vertices in a graph, with bigger circle enclosing them represent the parallel processors. Also the edges connecting the nodes in the graph represent the relation 'directly related to.' The term edge and pair will be used interchangeably in the following discussion.

Processor : 0

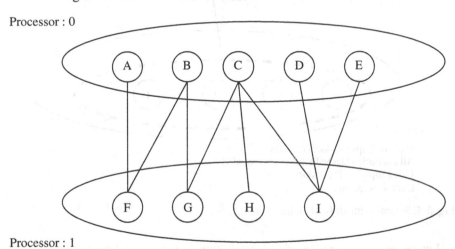

Processor : 1

Fig. 3.4. A sample of records and edges representing directly related records

In the preprocessing step, all local clusters are formed. In the above figure all records individually form the local clusters because there is no local pair (or local edge) in either processors. Thus in the next phase, each processor separately generates new edges belonging to the other participating processor. As a part of this step, processor 0 generates (F, G), (G, H), (H, I) edges that are local to processor 1 and processor 1 generates (A, B), (B, C), (C, D), (D, E) edges that are local to the processor 0, though we ignores the possibility of generating edges (A, B), (B, C)...etc by processor 0 where both A and B point to the same record in the other processor because this mechanism may only generate the new local edges if and only if both the local records relate to the same non-local record, instead of the same non local cluster at the other processor, which is more general and is the main hub for the algorithm.

Now, both the processors exchange the newly generated edges concurrently and process the new edges independently to form new local clusters (transitive closures). Since the number of nodes involved is 2, the entire process of forming global clusters stops after just one iteration. By the end of this process, all local clusters, located at different processors, belonging to the single global cluster are connected in the form of a complete graph with local clusters as vertices and final global pairs as edges. This can be viewed as a graph given below in Fig. 3.5, where all records form a single global cluster.

Processor : 0

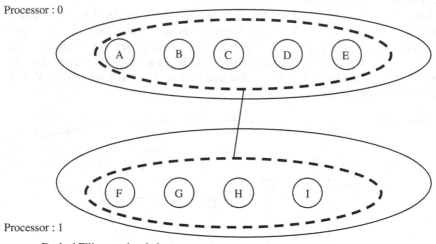

Processor : 1

Dashed Ellipse –> local clusters
All connected Dashed ellipses –> global clusters
Line Ellipse –> Processors
Circles -> records

Fig. 3.5. Sample with all final global clusters

Let us see an illustration with 3 processors in Fig. 3.6, where the process of generating edges, communicating and processing edges is repeated twice.

The new edges generated in each node after local clustering is shown below. Observe that each record in the above figure forms a local cluster.

- Processor 0: (F, I), (E, H), (D, G)
- Processor 1: (B, G), (A, H)
- Processor 2: (C, E), (B, F)

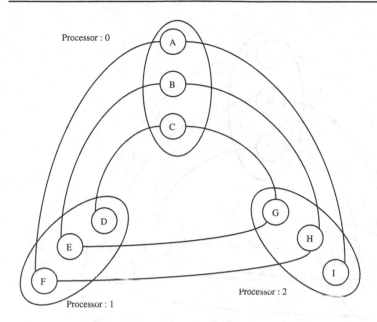

Processor : 0

Processor : 1

Processor : 2

Fig. 3.6. A given sample of records

Hence each node receives following pairs:
- Node 0: (B, G), (A, H), (C, E), (B, F)
- Node 1: (F, I), (E, H), (D, G), (C, E), (B, F)
- Node 2: (F, I), (E, H), (D, G), (B, G), (A, H)

Now the resultant graph is shown in Fig. 3.7 below after processing the received edges.

The new edges generated in the second iteration are:
- Processor 0: (H, I), (G, H)– to Processor 2, (E, F), (D, E)– to Processor 1
- Processor 1: (C, G), (B, C), (A, B)- to Processor 0, (C, G), (G, H), (H, I)- to Processor 2
- Processor 2: (B, C), (A, B)- to Processor 0, (D, E), (E, F), (A, F)- to Processor 1

Many new edges that can be generated are being filtered by considering them as duplicate edges. Hence we can save the amount messages that are being communicated. Let us observe one case where the duplicate edges are filtered:

In iteration 1, (H, E) is generated since processor 0 has two global edges (B, H) & (B, E).

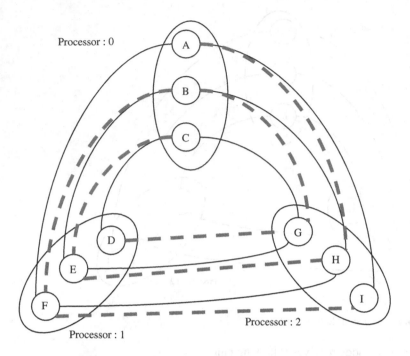

Fig. 3.7. All related records after first iteration

In iteration 2, local edges (G, H) and (E, F) are generated because it has (B, G), (B, H) & (B, E), (B, F) edges. Now the possible global edges that can be generated are (G, E), (G, F), (H, E), (H, F). In the future step, after processing the newly generated local edges in the other two processors G & H forms one group and E & F forms one group, in which case only one global edge need to be maintained between the two groups. Hence edge (H, E) sent over in first iteration serves the purpose and hence all newly generated global edges can be ignored. Thus, we can reduce the number of pairs communicated among the processors to a greater extent.

After processing new edges received, the local and global clusters will be shown in Fig. 3.8 below and the whole process of global clustering process stops.

We now provide more details about the parallel and distributed closure algorithm. We could divide the process into two basic steps executed in sequence. These steps are:

    1)   Local Clustering
    2)   Global Clustering

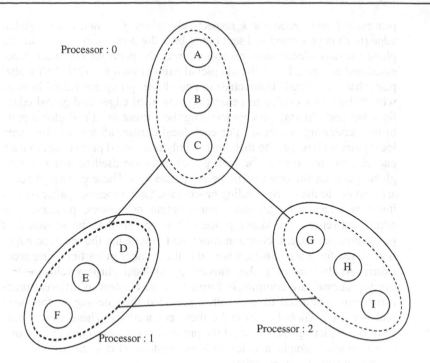

Fig. 3.8. Single global cluster, in the form of complete graph of local clusters, formed after two iterations

- *Local Clustering:* This is an initial phase in which each processor reads its own local pairs and global pairs from an input file and performs local clustering by processing all local pairs. It takes advantage of the Disjoint Set Union and Find data structure to group all related local records. The Disjoint Set allows online processing of local pairs. Hence, each local pair is processed immediately after it is read and there is no need to store it anywhere. Disjoint Set Find and Union data structure is basically a fast accessible array data structure that is accessible through some operations such as UNION, MAKE_SET and FIND_SET that implements Union by rank and Path Compression techniques as mentioned in the earlier section. As for global pairs, encountered during the input file scanning, they are stored in an intermediate storage in order to generate new edges (pairs) that are to be sent out to other participating processors. As illustrated earlier, the generation of additional pairs to be sent to other processors is based on the current local clusters and global pairs of the generating processor.

- *Global Clustering:* This phase is mainly responsible for finding transitive closures of all related records. That is, if node i contains two global pairs (a, b) and (c, d) where either $a=c$ or a and c belongs to single cluster group then if b and d are local to some processor j then node i generates a new local edge (b, d) and sent to processor j. But, if b and d belongs to processor j and processor k respectively where $j{\neq}k$ then a new global edge (b, d) is generated and sent out to both the processors j and k. In this phase the new global pairs received during the previous phase are processed and organized with the old global pairs in such a way that all global pairs that are related (connected) to one cluster group are stored in node wise fashion. This helps in generating new local edges and global edges for other participating processors using the current local and global pairs of the generating processor. For each local cluster, after generating new local pairs with respect to that cluster, only one global pair is kept to each participating processor. The kept global pairs are used to generate new global pairs for the other participating processors. These generated edges are sent out to the corresponding processors. Each processor, after receiving new edges from all other participating processors, processes the edges and repeats the above process. It is proven that the sequence of generating new edges, communication and processing the received edges is repeated for $\log(p)$ times, where p is the number of participating processors. At the end of global clustering, all local clusters (closures) in every processor are completely formed. Local clusters in different processors are connected to each other provided they belong to the same global cluster. Global pairs make these connections. These connections form a complete graph. Now all the processors can communicate through those complete graphs and form global clusters. This is demonstrated in the two examples given earlier.

3.4.5 A MPI Based Parallel and Distributed Algorithm

The conversion and closure algorithms are implemented on cluster computers. The operating system used is Red Hat LINUX that is supported on x86, x86_64 and IA_64 processors and requires 512 MB minimum memory capacity. The networks connecting these cluster nodes are Ethernet and Myrinet.

Since at the time of this study, MPI did not support process management and multi-threading, we have decided to use SPMD model to implement the proposed algorithms. In SPMD model, all processors will execute the same program at the same time. Even though all processors execute the same program, the processors could behave differently (e.g., sending and receiving) by executing different sections of the program. This is possible because the control logic of the program refers to the processor executing the program (a variable initialized with a processor ID, myrank is such a variable in the sample code shown later).

The hardware and software mentioned above support the medium-grained parallel clusters that support SPMD (Single Program Multiple Data) mechanism and Message Passing Architecture with static network. The parallel algorithms described in the previous section are implemented in C++ using MPI (Message Passing Interface). Blocking `MPI_Send` and `MPI_Recv` are used for synchronous communication between nodes.

We have decided not to give an introduction to MPI in this chapter. The reader is referred to Snir et al. (1995) for a complete discussion and description of MPI. Nonetheless, two code fragments of MPI from our implementation will be used to illustrate the SPMD model and how processes communicate under such a model in MPI.

The following code fragment is used to compute the largest integer used in the map of node k and to communicate that integer to node $k+1$, where k varies from 0 to p-2 and p is the number of processors. The variable serial gives the next integer value to be used when a string is inserted into the map. The code used to build the map and to update variable serial is omitted here. Variable incr is the buffer for receiving serial value sent. Variable myrank is the rank of the node executing the code. Notice that even though every node will execute the following code (a loop), at any moment only two nodes are active. The active nodes are those nodes having ranks i and $i+1$, for sending and receiving respectively. This example shows how SPMD paradigm and blocking send and receive work in general.

```
1 MPI_Status status;
2 int incr=0;
3 serial--;
4 for(i=0;i<p-1;i++){
5     if(myrank==i)
6         MPI_Send(&serial,1,MPI_INT,i+1,100,MPI_COMM_WORLD);
7     if(myrank==i+1){
8         MPI_Recv(&incr,1,MPI_INT,i,100,MPI_COMM_WORLD,&status);
9         mapIncrement(incr); //add in all mapped integer
10        serial = serial+incr;
11    }
12}
```

Fig. 3.9. MPI sample code for map offset computation

The next code segment implements the map value look up from other nodes' maps. This code segment assumes the node executing the code is ready to send. Due to synchronous communication, all the nodes must be ready to send to complete the execution of the code. Furthermore, the sending begins with rank 0 node. Any node with rank greater than 0 that executes this code gets blocked at line 7 when it tries to receive from rank 0 node. After sending the values for look-up to each node, rank 0 node could be blocked at line 18 waiting the messages from rank 1 node, rank 2 node, and so on in that order.

Additional discussions and descriptions of the algorithms and their implementation can be found in Bheemavaram (2006); Li et al. (2007); Li and Schweiger (2007).

```
 1 for(x=0;x<p;x++){// each node needs to perform look-up from
                    // other nodes. The loop makes it possible.
 2  if(myrank==x){  // sending to each node strings to look up
 3    for(y=0;y<p;y++){
 4      if(x!=y)
 5        MPI_Send((sendbuf+MAXSENDATA*y),*(ind+y),sendtype,y,
                 100,MPI_COMM_WORLD);
      }
 6  }else{ // receiving strings
 7    MPI_Recv(recvbuf,MAXSENDATA,sendtype,x,100,MPI_COMM_WORLD,
             &status);
 8    MPI_Get_count(&status, sendtype, &nc);
 9    recvind = recvbuf;
10    for(i=0;i<nc;i++){//look up the integer values in the map
11      mapIter = mapKeys.find(atoi(recvind->key));
12      *(key2+i) =mapIter->second;
13      recvind++;
      }
      // sending the corresponding integer values back
14    MPI_Send(key2,nc,MPI_INT,x,100+myrank,MPI_COMM_WORLD);
    }
15  if(myrank==x){ // receiving the integer values
16    for(y=0;y<p;y++){
17      if(x!=y){
18        MPI_Recv(key2,MAXSENDATA,MPI_INT,y,100+y,
                 MPI_COMM_WORLD,&status);
19        MPI_Get_count(&status, MPI_INT, &nc);
20        idy=copylist(idy, nc, y);
      }
    }
  }
}
```

Fig. 3.10. MPI sample code for string-to-integer look-up

3.4.6 Experiment

Empirical study has been conducted to study the performance of the proposed parallel and distributed algorithms implemented in MPI. The runtime of the algorithms are collected under various circumstances and are shown in Tables 3.10 through 3.14. It should be noted that the run-times recorded may not be very accurate with respect to our algorithm's behavior since the run-time environment might be affected by various factors such as workload, number of I/Os, maximum memory supported and the number of other users running different programs at the same time as our program runs. The gird computer hardware is shared among many users. As the number of users increases, the workload on different processors increases and hence the number of I/Os and memory consumed might increase, which directly affects the execution time.

The run-times of the conversion algorithm (the mapping of alphanumeric string pairs to integer pairs in machine representation) are recorded with respect to varying number of processors under the same input size (i.e. the same input file) and are shown below. The purpose is to observe speed up effects and the actual run time in a production environment.

Number of processors	Time taken (seconds)
2	3500
3	3498
4	3172
5	2676
6	2728
7	2740
8	2653
9	2804
10	2578
11	2317
12	2358

Table 3.10. Parallel Run-time for the Conversion Algorithm.

Table 3.10 and Figure 3.11 show the run-times of the conversion algorithm when executed on different numbers of processors using the same input file containing about 220 million string pairs. From Figure 3.11, it can be observed that the run-time decreases as the number of processors increases. This is due to the distribution of workload among all processors processing the data in parallel. But this curve is not ideal (the ideal case is that if T is the time taken by a single processor to complete the task, then T/P would be the time for all P processors to complete the task in parallel) because of the overhead caused by communication. As discussed earlier, processors have limited memory and can handle only limited amounts of data. That is the reason why the conversion algorithm could not hold all the intermediate data when implemented on a single processor for the current input file of size 220 million pairs. Hence, a case in point, parallel and distributed processing and algorithms are needed.

The run-times of the clustering algorithm are shown in Table 3.11 and Figure 3.12. It can be observed from the graph in Figure 3.12 that there is an increase in run-time from one processor to 2 processors, which is because of the additional overhead due to spreading a single data structure (disjoint set) among many nodes and distributed processing. The reason for breaking up a data structure and partitioning it among a group of processors is that a single processor does not have enough main memory. For comparison sake, we make sure the size of the test file is such that it is sufficiently large and still can be handled by a single processor.

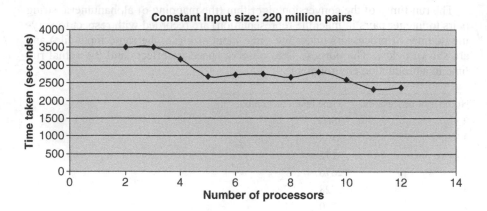

Fig. 3.11. Parallel Run-time for the Conversion Algorithm

Table 3.11. Parallel run-time for clustering program

Number of Processors	Time (seconds)
1	183.72
2	255
3	256.2
4	266.1
5	254.7
6	279.7
7	327.9
8	354
9	384
10	395
11	447.6
12	368
13	403.7
14	436.7
15	443.4
16	498

The curve is more or less constant from 2 to 4 processors and shows the minimum time recorded for that particular file in distributed processing, which indicates the algorithm is effective in this particular case. From 6 processors on, the overhead due to distributed processing dominates and makes the execution less efficient. Small fluctuations in the run-times could be either due to discrepancies in the run-time environment or an unpleasant data distribution among different processors. An ideal condition for the clustering algorithm arises when the data pairs are distributed in such a way that no global pairs exists, in which case the algorithm behaves like the sequential algorithm of section 3. Thus, the run-time of the algorithm also depends on the distribution of the data. An initial partition of the input pairs that results in fewer global pairs (or edges) generally takes less time to execute.

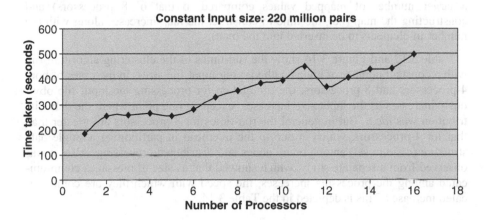

Fig. 3.12. Parallel run-times for clustering program

Table 3.12. Parallel run-time for Conversion algorithm - on constant number of processors with varying input size

Input size	4 – processors	8 – Processors
7,377,658	54.1	45.1
36,888,285	339.9	305.2
73,776,580	704.3	651.6
110,664,870	1092	1002.4
147,553,160	1579.4	1519.5
184,441,450	2214	2150
221,329,740	3172	2653

Next, the run-time of the parallel algorithms with respect to varying input sizes on a constant number of nodes (or processors) is observed.

Table 3.12 and Figure 3.13 show the run-times of the conversion algorithm when executed on two constant numbers of processors, 4 and 8 respectively, with respect to various input file sizes. It can be observed that the run-times are less when executed on 8 processors compared to that of 4 processors. This is due to more internal processing in the case of 4 processors than that of 8 processors. Internal processing includes look-up of the map values (i.e., look up time increases as the map size increases, which is the case for 4 processors where each one holds a larger number of mapped values compared to that of 8 processors) and constructing the map (i.e., the time to construct the map increases along with the number of elements to be inserted into the map).

Table 3.13 and Figure 3.14 show the run-times of the clustering algorithm run with a constant number of nodes with varying input file sizes. In the cases of both 4-processors and 8-processors, the time taken for processing the input file obviously increases as the input size increases, except at one point where the data distribution was *ideal*. But in general the run-times for 8-processors are greater than that for 4-processors, which is due to the overhead in partitioning a single data structure (disjoint set) among many nodes and distributed processing. Also, it was observed from a separate study, which showed that as size of messages communicated among the processors increases, the speed with which they are communicated increases. This is depicted in the Table 3.14.

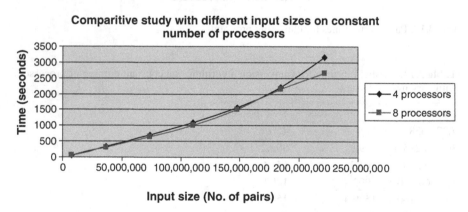

Fig. 3.13. Parallel run-time for Conversion algorithm - on a constant number of processors with varying input size

It was observed that the sizes of messages communicated among the 4 processors are always greater than that of messages communicated among 8 processors for these particular input files. Though the speed of the communication is faster in the case of 4-processors, the time taken for each single communication is longer. Note that the number of iterations is two for 4-processors and three for 8-processors. An iteration consists of generating and communicating new pairs along with processing the received ones. As the number of iterations decreases, the inter-processor communication time reduces considerably. This is due to reduction in overhead of making and closing the connections and extra internal processing.

Table 3.13. Parallel run-time for Clustering program – on constant number of processors with varying input size

Input Size	4 – processors	8 – processors
7,377,658	19.47	14.3
36,888,285	62.9	55.4
73,776,580	91.1	127.57
110,664,870	204.5	271.3
147,553,160	167.38	234.04
184,441,450	227.6	299.5
221,329,740	266.1	354

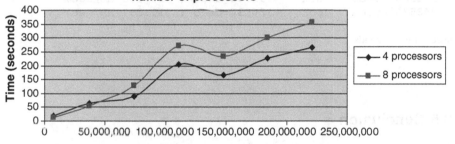

Fig. 3.14. Parallel run-time for Clustering program – on constant number of processors with varying input size

Table 3.14. Run-times for the communicating the messages of different sizes between two processors

```
       8 bytes    took       210 usec (    0.076 MB/sec)
      16 bytes    took       209 usec (    0.153 MB/sec)
      32 bytes    took       210 usec (    0.305 MB/sec)
      64 bytes    took       218 usec (    0.587 MB/sec)
     128 bytes    took       242 usec (    1.058 MB/sec)
     256 bytes    took       335 usec (    1.528 MB/sec)
     512 bytes    took       380 usec (    2.695 MB/sec)
    1024 bytes    took       593 usec (    3.454 MB/sec)
    2048 bytes    took       819 usec (    5.001 MB/sec)
    4096 bytes    took      1180 usec (    6.942 MB/sec)
    8192 bytes    took      1894 usec (    8.650 MB/sec)
   16384 bytes    took      3306 usec (    9.912 MB/sec)
   32768 bytes    took      6170 usec (   10.622 MB/sec)
   65536 bytes    took     11913 usec (   11.002 MB/sec)
  131072 bytes    took     23993 usec (   10.926 MB/sec)
  262144 bytes    took     47288 usec (   11.087 MB/sec)
  524288 bytes    took     93740 usec (   11.186 MB/sec)
 1048576 bytes    took    186637 usec (   11.237 MB/sec)
```

usec – 1.e-6 seconds

3.5 Conclusion

In this chapter, the importance of data quality is discussed. Why analysis tools might improve data quality in terms of data accuracy, redundancy, consistency, currency and completeness is articulated and illustrated through an example. To improve the performance of the analysis tools, transitive closure problem is introduced and formulated. Transitive closure processing reduces the number of records fed to the analysis tools by grouping related records into groups. The size of each group is much smaller than the size of the data source. The analysis tools are applied to records within each group instead of the whole data source. Therefore, the number of pairwise comparisons is reduced drastically. Two sequential algorithms are proposed to solve the transitive closure problem, one based on the idea of breadth first search and the other the ideas of sorting and disjoint set find and union. The two algorithms with implementation variations are programmed and studied empirically. The experimental results strongly favor algorithm 2, in particular the disjoint set of integer implementation. Hence, using integers as record identifiers should improve the performance of transitive closure computation. This idea as well as disjoint set idea are incorporated into the development of parallel and distributed algorithms aiming at handling large file sizes for which the sequential algorithms cannot handle. Parallel and distributed algorithms are proposed and implemented in C++ MPI. The preliminary empirical study demonstrates that the algorithm is able to handle huge data set efficiently in closure computation.

The related work is briefly considered here. For the analysis tools mentioned in the introduction, two fundamental questions that need to be answered are: 1) Do the two records refer to the same real-world entity of interest or not? 2) Are two fields similar, same, or approximately same or not? To see how two records compare, we could select the same set of fields from both records and base the results of the field comparison to determine the outcome of the record comparison (Hernandez and Stolfo 1995; Navarro et al. 2001). Approximate string match techniques and its variations are typically applied to address the field comparison question (Jokinen et al. 1996; Hall and Dowling 1980). Several commercial products (for example, Acxiom, Trillium, Vality) have proprietary algorithms, which might leverage characteristics peculiar to a particular domain, such as address, for matching addresses and individual or business records.

The distributed disjoint set allows us to maintain the transitive closures in memory. This property will be investigated and explored further to implement a closure service and a transactional closure computation where closure information is updated as new edge pairs are introduced.

We are currently studying how to further speed-up the proposed parallel and distributed algorithms. Other competing definitions of relatedness and other parameters that might affect the effectiveness of transitive closure computation need to be investigated, for example, applying different weights to different keys. Last, but not the least, we need to improve the analysis tools, which process the records in a transitive closure, so that ultimate data quality can be achieved. One technique might be to use clustering to regroup the over-grouped records in a transitive closure.

3.6 Exercises

1. Consider the sample record set shown in Table 13.1. Determine the transitive closures under the following conditions.

   A The last name of the Name field is used as the key.
   B The last four digits of a telephone number in the Phone Number field and the last four digits of a social security number in the SSN field are used as keys.
   C The last seven digits of a telephone number in the Phone Number field and complete social security number in the SSN field are used as keys
   D The first name of the Name field and complete phone number in the Phone Number fields are used as key

2. Modify algorithm 1 in such a way that the algorithm first computes relation R, R(i,j) is 1 iff record i and record j are related, and 0 otherwise, and then uses breadth first sesearch to find the transitive closures.

3. Modify algorithm 1 in such a way that the algorithm first computes relation R, R(i,j) is 1 iff record i and record j are related, and 0 otherwise, and then uses depth first sesearch to find the transitive closures.

4. Implement the two algorithms of exercises 2 and 3. Perform empirical study of the two algorithms.

5. Consider the record set shown in Table A.

   A   Draw the diagram similar to Fig. 3.3 for the record set.
   B   How many clusters are there?
   C   Compute the tables similar to Tables 3.3 to 3.6 for the record set.

6. Using any simple hash function and the scheme described in 4.2 to generate the matching pairs based on Record ID field for the record set of Table A. Let us assume that we have 12 nodes or processors, where 4 nodes for the four keys in stage one and 2 nodes for each stage one node.

Table A. A sample data set for exercises 5 through 8

RecordID.	Key 1	Key 2	Key 3	Key 4	Record ID
R1	C1K1U3	C1K2V1	C1K3U4	C1K4V1	K2P1K3P4
R2	C4K1U19	C4K2V4	C4K3U20	C4K4V4	K2P8K3P5
R3	C2K1U11	C2K2U12	C2K3V2	C2K4V2	K2P10K3P3
R4	C4K1U23	C4K2V4	C4K3U24	C4K4V4	K2P3K3P6
R5	C2K1U5	C2K2U6	C2K3U10	C2K4V1	K2P10K3P7
R6	C1K1V1	C1K2V1	C1K3U1	C1K4U2	K2P13K3P10
R7	C3K1V3	C3K2U15	C3K3U16	C3K4V3	K2P17K3P3
R8	C2K1U11	C2K2V2	C2K3U14	C2K4V3	K2P2K3P4
R9	C4K1V4	C4K2U21	C4K3U22	C4K4V4	K2P14K3P1
R10	C5K1V5	C5K2V5	C5K3U25	C5K4U26	K2P19K3P1
R11	C3K1U17	C3K2V3	C3K3U18	C3K4V3	K2P9K3P5
R12	C2K1U8	C2K2U9	C2K3U10	C2K4V2	K2P6K3P9

7. Using any simple hash function and the algorithm described in 4.3 on 3 nodes, that is p is 3, to convert the alphanumeric string pairs produced from problem 6 to the corresponding integer pairs.

8. Using the same hash function used in problem 7 to draw the diagram similar to Fig. 3.6 on 3 nodes for the integer pairs of problem 7. Using the algorithmic idea of 4.4 and the diagraming convention of Fig. 3.7 and Fig. 3.8 to diagram the parallel and distributed computation of transitive closures.

9. Repeat problems 5 to 8 for the record set shown in Table B.

10. In the development of the proposed parallel and distributed algorithms, which aims at handling huge data sets, three separated but related processes have been introduced. These are a) transforming an input file to record pairs (or key pairs); b) converting alphanumeric string pairs to integer pairs; and (c) computing closure on integer pairs. Discuss whether we should combine the three processes into a single process and propose a framework in which the three processes may be combined effortlessly.

Table B. A sample record set for exercise 9

RecordID.	Key 1	Key 2	Key 3	Key 4	Record ID
R1	C1K1V1	C1K2U7	C1K3U8	C1K4V1	K2P9K3P8
R2	C4K1V4	C4K2U26	C4K3V4	C4K4V4	K2P10K3P4
R3	C6K1V6	C6K2V6	C6K3U32	C6K4V6	K2P11K3P5
R4	C2K1V2	C2K2U20	C2K3U21	C2K4V2	K2P7K3P6
R5	C2K1V2	C2K2U14	C2K3U15	C2K4V2	K2P14K3P6
R6	C7K1U33	C7K2V7	C7K3U38	C7K4U39	K2P6K3P8
R7	C3K1U23	C3K2V3	C3K3U24	C3K4V3	K2P3K3P4
R8	C2K1V2	C2K2U22	C2K3V2	C2K4V2	K2P16K3P3
R9	C1K1U3	C1K2V1	C1K3U5	C1K4U6	K2P8K3P7
R10	C5K1U30	C5K2V5	C5K3U31	C5K4V5	K2P18K3P7
R11	C2K1V2	C2K2U11	C2K3U12	C2K4U13	K2P16K3P2
R12	C7K1U40	C7K2U41	C7K3U42	C7K4V7	K2P6K3P2
R13	C1K1U9	C1K2V1	C1K3U10	C1K4V1	K2P17K3P1
R14	C4K1U27	C4K2U28	C4K3U29	C4K4V4	K2P16K3P4
R15	C2K1U16	C2K2U17	C2K3V2	C2K4U19	K2P7K3P9
R16	C3K1V3	C3K2V3	C3K3U25	C3K4V3	K2P6K3P9
R17	C7K1U33	C7K2U34	C7K3U35	C7K4V7	K2P6K3P3
R18	C1K1U1	C1K2V1	C1K3U2	C1K4V1	K2P9K3P7

3.7 Acknowledgments

This research was supported in part by Acxiom Corporation through the Acxiom Laboratory for Applied Research.

3.8 References

Agostino D (2004) Getting Clean. CIOINSIGHT.

Ballou D (1999) Enhancing data quality in Data Warehousing Environment. Comm. ACM (42:1), pp. 73-78.

Ballou D, Wang H, Pazer G (1998) Modeling Information Manufacturing Systems to Determining Information Product Quality. Management Science (44:4), pp. 462-484.

Baxter R, Christen P, Churches T (2003) A Comparison of Fast Blocking Methods for Record Linkage. ACM SIGKDD '03 Workshop on Data Cleaning, Record Linkage, and Object Consolidation, Washington, DC, pp 25-27.

Bheemavaram R (2006) Parallel and Distributed Grouping Algorithms for Finding Related Records of Huge Data Sets on Cluster Grid. MS thesis, University of Arkansas.

Cormen T, Leiserson C, Rivest R, Stein C (2001) Introduction to Algorithms Second Edition. McGraw-Hill Higher Education.

Delone W, Mclean E (1992) Information Systems Success: The Quest for the Independent Variable. Information Systems Research (3:1), pp. 60-95.

Depompa B (1996) Scrub Data Clean. InformationWeek (610), pp. 88-92.

Faden M (2000) Data Cleansing Helps E-Business Run More Efficiently. InformationWeek (781).

Goiser K, Christen P (2006) Towards Automated Record Linkage. Proceedings of the 5th Australasian Data Mining Conference, pp. 23-31.

Hall P, Dowling G (1980) Approximate String Matching. ACM Computing Surveys, 13(4), pp. 381-402.

Hernandez M, Stolfo, S (1995) The merge/purge problem for large databases. In Proceedings of the 1995 ACM SIGMOD International Conference on Management of data, pp. 127-138.

Hernandez M, Stolfo S (1998) Real-world Data is Dirty: Data Cleansing and the Merge/Purge Problem. Journal of Data Mining and Knowledge Discovery, 1(2).

Hopcroft J, Ullman, J (2001) Introduction to Automata Theory, Languages, and Computation. Addsion-Wesley Publishing Company.

Jaro M, (1989) Advances in Record Linkage Methodology as Applied to Matching the 1985 Census of Tempa, Florida. Journal of the American Statistical Society, 84(406), pp. 414-420.

Jokinen P, Tarhio .J, Ukkonen E (1996) A comparison of approximate string matching algorithms. Software Practice and Experience, 26(12): pp. 1439-1458.

Li W (2007) A Parallel and Distributed Approach For Finding Transitive Closure of Data Records: A proposal. Submitted manuscript.

Li W (2008) Private Communication With Project Sponsor.

Li W, Schweiger T (2007) Distributed Data Structures and Algorithms for Disjoint Sets in Computing Connected Components of Huge Network. Proceedings of the International Conference on Parallel and Distributed Processing Techniques and Applications, Volume II, 905-909.

Li W, Hayes D, Zhang J, Bheemavaram R, Portor C, Schweiger T (2007) Parallel and Distributed Grouping Algorithms for Finding Related Records of Huge Data Sets on Cluster Grids. Proceedings of the Acxiom Laboratory for Applied Research (ALAR) 2007 conference on Applied Research in Information Technology.

Li W, Zhang J, Bheemavaram R (2006) Efficient Algorithms for Grouping Data to Improve Data Quality. Proceedings of the 2006 International Conference on Information and Knowledge Engineering, pp. 149-154.

McCallum A, Nigam K, Ungar L (2000) Efficient clustering of High-Dimensional data Sets with Application to Reference Matching. Proceedings of the 6th ACM SIGKDD int. Conf. on KDD, pp. 169-178.

Navarro G, Baeza-Yates R, Sutinen E, Tarhio J (2001) Indexing mechods for approximate string matching. IEEE Data Engineering Bulletin 24(4): pp. 19-27.

Redman T (1996) Data Quality for the Information Age. Artech House, Norwood, MA.

Redman T (1998) The Impact of poor data quality on the typical enterprise. Comm. ACM (41:2), pp. 79-82.

Snir M, Otto S, Huss S, Walker D, Dongarra J (1995) MPI: The Complete Reference. MIT Press.

Zhang J, Bheemavaram R, Li W (2006) Transitive Closure of Data Records: Application and Computation. Proceedings of the Acxiom Laboratory for Applied Research (ALAR) 2006 conference on Applied Research in Information Technology, pp. 71-81.

4 Semantic Data Matching: Principles and Performance

Russell Deaton[1], Thao Doan[1], and Tom Schweiger[2]

[1]Computer Science and Computer Engineering, University of Arkansas, Fayetteville, AR, USA

[2]Acxiom Corporation, Fayetteville, AR, USA

4.1 Introduction

Automated and real-time management of customer relationships requires robust and intelligent data matching across widespread and diverse data sources. Simple string matching algorithms, such as dynamic programming, can handle typographical errors in the data, but are less able to match records that require contextual and experiential knowledge. Latent Semantic Indexing (LSI) (Berry et al. 1995; Deerwester et al. 1990) is a machine intelligence technique that can match data based upon higher order structure, and is able to handle difficult problems, such as words that have different meanings but the same spelling, are synonymous, or have multiple meanings. Essentially, the technique matches records based upon context, or mathematically quantifying when terms occur in the same record.

A study of LSI indicated that it could handle abbreviations, short record sizes, and typographical errors in business name data, as well as match synonyms and reveal higher order structure in the data, such as matching financial institutions though no words are shared. It was found that shared terms among documents affected LSI performance negatively. Thus, preprocessing to remove shared terms, which tend to be common or generic words, numerals, or abbreviations, improves LSI performance for semantic data matching. Some of these shared terms, however, contain information that can be used for record classification, which is revealed by representing these terms as a network. Thus, though LSI can match records based on contextual semantic information, for short records, like business

Y. Chan et al. (eds.), *Data Engineering*, International Series in Operations
Research & Management Science 132, DOI 10.1007/978-1-4419-0176-7_4,
© Springer Science+Business Media, LLC 2010

names, care must be taken when pruning shared terms in an effort to improve performance. Otherwise, information about the type of business may be lost.

4.2 Problem Statement: Data Matching for Customer Data Integration

In order to be successful, companies need to build relationships with customers, and to understand their wants and needs. Technology can support customer relationship matching by creating a real-time, single view of the customer from transaction information that is distributed across diverse and dispersed data sources. The problem of customer data integration is difficult because of errors, both machine and human, incomplete and misleading information, and the size and diversity of the data sources. Systems can enable and ease the task of customer data integration by processing customer records from widespread data sources, merging customer information in a data warehouse, and providing links to the customer information in an appropriate format.

A difficulty in this process is the accurate matching of customer information in different records. This information can include, among other things, business names, addresses, consumer names, and purchases. The problem is the imprecise nature of the customer information across different records. As an example, let's take business names. Business names can include typographical errors, phonetic spelling, homonyms (words that are spelled the same, but have different meanings), synonyms (different words, but different spellings), polysemy (words with multiple meanings), and different combinations of word breaks (Fellbaum 1998). Business names can be abbreviated or aliased. Frequently, human intelligence is able to deal with these difficulties by using context and experience, or in other words, the meaning or semantics of the information. The challenge in automated data integration is to reproduce the human capability in machine intelligence (Manning and Schutze 1999).

4.3 Semantic Data Matching

In this work, a technique called latent semantic indexing will be applied to data matching for customer data integration.

4.3.1 Background on Latent Semantic Analysis

In approaches such as dynamic programming (Manning and Schutze 1999), information is matched by literally comparing and scoring pairwise string symbols in the data records. Higher scoring pairs of strings are matches, while low scoring pairs are mismatches. While perhaps adequate for overcoming typographical errors in data records, string matching is inadequate for the problems of homonyms, synonyms, and polysemy.

Latent Semantic Indexing (Manning and Schutze 1999) attempts to classify records based upon higher order structure (meaning) in the data space that is present, but not obvious, in the patterns of word usage and groups. For a given query, the quality of its classifications is determined by the other words in a record and the size and completeness of the data space, corresponding to context and experience, respectively. It has been applied to a variety of data matching applications, such as intelligent tutoring systems, web-based search and information retrieval, and cross-language matching, and is capable of dealing with the complex problems associated with data matching for customer data integration.

The technique is based on linear algebra, and singular value decomposition, in particular. The data is represented in a term by document matrix, A, where for example, individual terms are the rows, the documents, or records, are the columns, and the entries

$$A = [a_{ij}], \tag{4.1}$$

are the frequency of occurrence of term i in document j. This is typically a sparse matrix, as every term does not appear in every document. Local or global weights can be applied to increase or decrease the importance of terms among documents. The matrix, A, is factored using singular value decomposition as

$$A = U\Sigma V^{T}, \tag{4.2}$$

where U (term) and V (document) contain the left and right singular vectors of A, and Σ is a diagonal matrix containing the singular values. These matrices represent, in a sense, the decomposition of the original information into a linearly independent set of vectors, or factor values. Typically, only the k largest factor values are saved, and thus, the original, and possibly noisy, term-document matrix is approximated by the reduced matrices. These reduced factors are a set of indices with which to represent each term and document as a vector in a k-dimensional space. This truncation of the original dimensionality enables higher order structure to be resolved, while dampening the effects of noise and variability in the data. This means that terms, which might never appear in the same document, can be near each other in the k-dimensional space. Nearness is typically calculated with cosines, Euclidean distance, or dot products. Once derived, the SVD matrices can be used to classify new queries composed of terms or documents. In addition, the entire SVD can be updated with new information by the process of folding-in new terms and documents without redoing the entire SVD.

The quality of the of the LSI results depends upon several factors (Wild et al. 2005; Baeza-Yates and Ribeiro-Neto 1999), including filtering of "stop" words, weighting methods, document preprocessing, dimensionality, and similarity measures. The effect that will be studied in what follows is related to "stop" words.

4.3.2 Analysis

Business name data usually consists of short documents with few terms. LSI is usually applied to much larger documents. In order to verify that LSI was appropriate for business name data and using an evaluation copy of a commercial program from Telecordia (2007), the LSI technique was tested on a sample set of data. The measure of nearness was the dot product, with a score nearer to 1 indicating greater similarity. As a sanity check, documents were used as queries in order to verify that a document would perfectly match itself, which was the case. Then, various key word searches were done to explore the capabilities of the technique. Though not a systematic study, overall, the results were promising. In most cases, terms in a query were matched with appropriate documents. In addition, synonyms for query terms were detected, and higher order relationships emerged. Running times were reasonable. It was discovered that when certain common terms, such as office, center, etc..., were removed from the analysis, results improved.

The results for an example query of "richardson" on a set of 132 documents are shown in Table 4.1. The results for the same query, but with the word "center" removed are shown in Table 4.2. As is evident, the results for the correct matches were improved, but another common word, "services," introduced relationships between records, thus revealing a higher order structure, i.e. all business that are services, in the database.

Table 4.1. LSI results for query "richardson."

Term	Score
richardson center	0.934
richardson center incorpora	0.933
richardson center adult services	0.935
lumbermart building center	0.910
soderquist center	0.911
soder quist center	0.911
meeks building center	0.910
interface computer center	0.908

Table 4.2. LSI results for query "Richardson" with common term "center" removed

Team	Score
richardson center	1.0
richardson center adult services	0.996
allclean	0.996
allclean services	0.995
ibm global services	0.994
vice pres student services	0.994

In another example, the term, "bank," was used to query a database of over a 100,000 documents. Some of the results are summarized in Table 4.3. Lines 1 and 2 obviously have a semantic relationship, and identify the same entity. In addition, the abbreviation for bank in line 3 was correctly identified. Lines 4 and 5 show entities that are related to 'banks' in their function, revealing the synonym "financial" for bank.

Table 4.3. LSI results for query "bank."

Number	Term	Score
1	arvest	0.957
2	arvest bank opps	0.997
3	mcilroy bk & tr	0.919
4	federal taxct dls rtl wn	0.976
5	national financial servics	0.935

Thus, the study shows that the LSI technique has promise for addressing some of the problems for data matching. This indicated that LSI might be useful in identifying groups of records that represent the same business entity, and in retrieving business entity records in response to incomplete or erroneous user queries.

Several variables that affect LSI performance could be evaluated to improve performance. When the document-term matrix is parsed from the raw data, preprocessing can improve LSI performance, specifically, deletion of common terms, keyword identification by frequency of occurrence, and word order. In the singular value decomposition, global and local weighting of commonly occurring terms ('company'), abbreviations ('Inc.'), symbols ('&'), and numbers are an issue since they frequently occur in business name and address data. Other variables that could receive emphasis include the dimensionality of the LSI space, record sizes, noise in the data, and the effect of different fields on the results.

4.4 Effect of Shared Terms

4.4.1 Fundamental Limitations on Data Matching

In textual data, data are matched by identifying similarities among long strings. For string matching, this involves alignment of characters that compose the strings so that either the distance between them is minimized, or a similarity score is maximized. Metrics can include Hamming distance, edit distance, or various alignment scoring systems that weight matches, mismatches, insertions, deletions, and spaces in various ways. Alignment and scoring of biological sequences are important applications, and fundamentally, do not different from applications to other textual data. For LSI, the task is to find those strings (or terms) that occur in similar contexts. In both techniques, noise or randomness in the data induces deviation from the globally best match.

An example would be computing the best alignment for two strings using dynamic programming (DP). If the two strings are identical, then, a complete match results, and the alignment is given by the diagonal entries in the DP comparison matrix. As one of the strings diverges from the original by character changes, insertions, and deletions, then, alignment diverges from the diagonal. Hwa and Lassig (1996) showed that as the similarity between the two strings decreases, the ability to compute the optimal alignment undergoes a fundamental change. In fact, below some critical value of similarity, the match is essentially random, and conclusions about relationships between the strings are meaningless. Thus, a fundamental limitation exists on the performance of this type of matching algorithms.

In customer integration applications, queries are matched to documents in the database on a term-by-term basis. Thus, in a dynamic programming or other approach, each query term is compared to document terms, and similarity is based upon the number of matches. Certainly, as the number of matches falls below a critical threshold, the ability to determine a good match becomes more difficult. This is where the role of common, shared terms among documents becomes significant. In effect, these common terms inflate the similarity between documents, and therefore, reduce the ability of data matching algorithms to correctly match queries to them. A simple example would be comparison of "Tom Davis American Accounting Agency Associates Incorporated," and "Tom Smith American Insurance Agency Associates Incorporated." By both LSI and term matching, these documents would be measured as similar.

Thus, the challenge is three-fold. First, the effects of the common terms on the ability to match data has to be understood, quantified, and modeled, so that second, algorithms can be designed and implemented to reduce their effects and improve data matching performance. A third consideration is to only prune those common terms that do not represent significant information about the record.

4.4.2 Experiments

In order to study the effect of shared terms, an artificial data set was created that allowed the number of shared terms to be controlled. The test data included a set of short terms resembling business name data. The individual terms were letters from the alphabet, and a document or query, a string of letters. These terms were divided into five categories, four of which were specific term categories, and one, which was a shared term category. The latter represents shared terms that are common in many documents of a database and that affect the outcome of LSI. With four terms in each category, we constructed 60 queries and 16 documents (4 documents for each specific category). During the experiments, shared terms were added systematically into these queries and documents so that the results reflect the influence of shared terms in queries and documents on the LSI performance. In all cases, the LSI score was the cosine of the angle between the query and document vectors in the reduced LSI space. In this study, as the previous one, an evaluation copy of a commercial program from Telecordia (2007) was used to perform the LSI technique on the test database.

In the first experiment (LSA 1) (Fig. 4.1), no shared terms were allowed in either documents or queries. The result reflects LSI performance in a noise-free environment, and thus, served as both a baseline and control for subsequent tests. From the second experiment, the proportion of shared terms in queries, as well as documents, were raised gradually as follows:

1. LSA 2: 25% shared terms in documents and queries (Fig. 4.2)
2. LSA 3: 50% shared terms in documents and queries (Fig. 4.3)

In-category queries refer to those constructed from the terms in a given document. Out-category queries refer to those constructed from terms not in a given document. One type of data matching of interest is matching a query with its proper category. For instance, the query might represent a bank that should be matched with entries in the financial institution category. The metrics for this type of match were in-category average and out-category average LSI scores, which indicate how the performance changed within the group of queries of one document category and the group of queries out of that category. A second type of result is to match a query with best scoring document in the database. For example, we would like to match Computer Science with the CSCE department at The University of Arkansas, since both sets of terms represent the same entity. Therefore, how shared terms affect the best-matched documents of each query was also analyzed.

4.5 Results

Fig. 4.1 represents the LSI query results with no shared terms. The in-category queries were numbered 46 and above. These were the queries selected from the terms m, n, p, q. As can be seen, the LSI scores for in-category and out-category queries were appropriate. Fig. 4.2 shows the results when q occurred as a shared term among the document database. The quality of the LSI matching was degraded. Finally, in Fig. 4.3, both documents and queries contained 50% shared terms. While the in-category queries scored slightly better, the results are essentially random, and LSI has lost both the ability to correctly match documents to queries and to identify categories.

In Fig. 4.4, the average in-category scores for all documents over all queries are shown, and in Fig. 4.5, the average out-category scores are shown. It is evident that 50% shared term composition is a threshold to accurate LSI matching of queries to documents.

For each query, there was a document scoring the highest. However, this best-matched document varied with the adjustment of shared terms in the database. The following data indicates the magnitude of this change in the results of the experiments.

Thus, with the addition of 25% shared terms, 70% of the best matches changed, and with 50% shared terms, 73% changed. There was even variation between the best matches for 25% and 50% shared terms.

1. LSA 2 VS. LSA 1: Number of best-matched documents changed (/60): 42

    2. LSA 3 VS. LSA 1: Number of best-matched documents changed (/60): 44

    3. LSA 3 VS. LSA 2: Number of best-matched documents changed (/60): 33

The results showed that shared terms in documents and queries have a significant impact on the outcome of the LSI technique. Moreover, the higher the proportion of overlap in data, the smaller the gap between in-category query and misclassified query matching probabilities. For example, the difference in average performance between the two groups in LSA 1 (0% shared terms) is 0.6247, whereas it is only 0.3570 in LSA 3(50% shared terms). This reduction apparently makes it more difficult to differentiate one group from the other. Another interesting observation from the results is that shared terms had more influence on misclassified query performance than on the correct category classification.

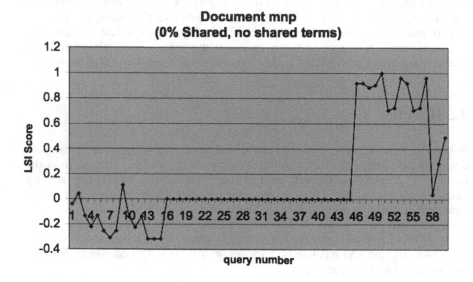

Fig. 4.1. Test case LSA 1: LSI Score versus query number for document "mnp." Queries numbered 46 and above were in-category. Higher score is better, indicating a closer match.

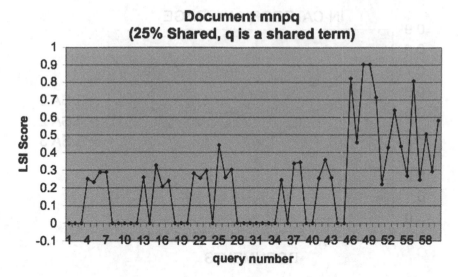

Fig. 4. 2. Test case LSA 2: LSI Score versus query number for document "mnpq." q was chosen as a shared term in both documents and queries. Queries numbered 46 and above were in-category. Higher score is better, indicating a closer match.

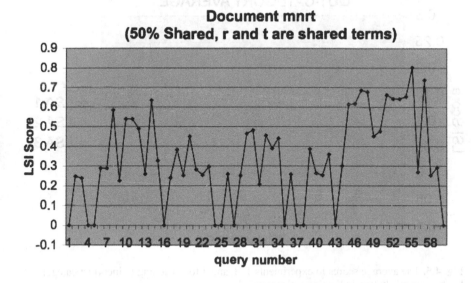

Fig. 4.3. Test case LSA 3: LSI Score versus query number for document "mnrt." r and t were chosen as shared terms in both documents and queries. Queries numbered 46 and above were in-category. Higher score is better, indicating a closer match.

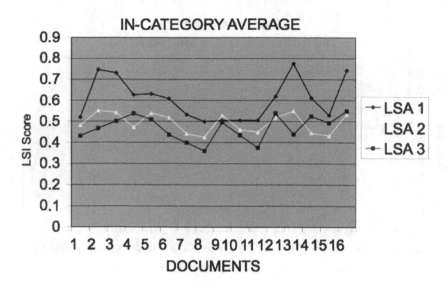

Fig. 4.4. The average scores in experiments 1, 3, and 4 for matching to correct category.

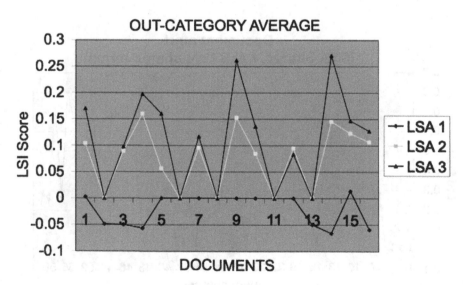

Fig. 4.5. The average scores in experiments 1, 3, and 4 for matching to incorrect category. Higher score is better, indicating a closer match.

4.6 Conclusion

Thus, an obvious conclusion would be to get rid of shared terms in order to improve LSI performance. Because the shared terms may contain significant information about the classification of the record, however, this has to be done with caution.

For example, consider the records in Table 4.4. If the terms are vertices in a graph, and vertices are connected if the corresponding terms occur in the same record, then, the graph if Fig. 4.6 results. The shared terms here are Arkansas, College, and University. In particular, the latter two terms are identifying of the category of the record, i.e. is the institution a college or university.

Table 4.4. A sample of Arkansas colleges and universities.

Arkansas State University
Harding University
Henderson State University
John Brown University
Mississippi County Community College
Northwest Arkansas Community College
WestArk College

It appears as if a database of business names is a "small world." The small world phenomenon (Watts and Strogatz 1998) is that any two people in the world are linked together by short chains of people that they know. Recently, it has been discovered that such diverse systems as communication networks, hyperlink structure on the Web, and communities of scientists exhibit the small world effect.

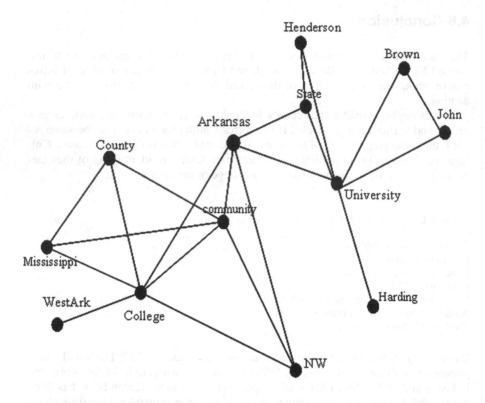

Fig. 4.6. Graph of data in Table 4.6.

For the database of names, the small world takes the form of documents that are linked together by the terms that they share. Thus, a graph is formed in which each term is a vertex, and an edge is placed between vertices if those terms occur in the same document. In this way, a graph representing the database of documents is constructed. Categories of documents would form clusters of connected vertices in the graph. For example, financial institutions share sets of terms like "bank, financial, savings, loan, etc...." It is the common terms, however, that link category clusters together, and thus, provide a short path in the graph between any given pair of vertices to produce the small world effect. Examples of common terms are "company, services, inc.," but this depends on the context. This effect is characterized in several ways that could be applied to database data. In small world graphs, the characteristic path length, or the average number of edges in the shortest path between any two vertices, and the clustering coefficient, or the average number of adjacent vertices of a given vertex that are also adjacent to each other, have characteristic behavior that might be used to identify the common terms. In addition, various network and graph algorithms (Gibbons 1985) might be applied to identify the common terms. A good possibility might be based on efficient algorithms to

find minimum cut-sets, sets of edges that when removed, make the graph disconnected.

Latent Semantic Analysis is a promising technique for data integration. Nevertheless, the results of this study show that increasing the proportion of shared
terms in the data causes degradation in the performance of LSI. For the most part,
this degradation is the result of more misclassification with increasing percentages
of shared terms. In addition, the best match to a query is highly variable with
changing percentages of shared terms. Thus, identification and elimination of
shared terms is key to increasing LSI performance. Nevertheless, shared terms often contain information that is useful for classification of records. Therefore, un-
important shared terms have to be distinguished from meaningful ones.

4.7 Exercises

1. Research three other applications of Latent Semantic Indexing.
2. What is another machine intelligence technique that attempts to capture
   semantic information?
3. Research other applications of "small world" networks in data matching
   applications.

4.8 Acknowledgments

This work was supported by a grant from the Acxiom Corporation. We also thank
Ms. Ameera Jaradat for contributions to the small world model.

4.9 References

Baeza-Yates R, Ribeiro-Neto B (1999) Modern Information Retrieval. ACM Press, New
    York.
Berry MW, Dumais ST, O'Brien GW (1995) Using Linear Algebra for Intelligent Informa-
    tion Retrieval. Siam Review 37 pp 573–595.
Deerwester S, Dumai ST, Landauer TK, Furnas GW, Harshman RA (1990) Indexing by
    Latent Semantic Analysis. Journal of the Society for Information Science 41 pp 391–
    407.
Fellbaum C (1998) WordNet. MIT Press, Cambridge, MA.
Gibbons A (1985) Algorithmic Graph Theory. Cambridge University Press, Cambridge,
    England.
Hwa T, Lassig M (1996) Similarity Detection and Localization. Phys. Rev. Lett. 76 pp
    2591–2594.

Manning CD, Schutze H (1999) Foundations of Statistical Natural Language Processing. MIT Press, Cambridge, MA.

Telecordia   (2007)   Latent   Semantic   Indexing.   Retrieved   from http://lsi.research.telcordia.com.

Watts DJ, Strogatz SH (1998) Collective Dynamics of Small World Networks. Nature 393 p 440.

Wild F, Stahl C, Stermsek G, Neumann G (2005) Parameters Driving Effectiveness of Automated Essay Scoring with LSA. In Danson, M., ed.: Proceedings of the 9th CAA, Loughborough, Professional Development pp 485–494.

5 Application of the Near Miss Strategy and Edit Distance to Handle Dirty Data

Cihan Varol[1], Coskun Bayrak[1], Rick Wagner[2], and Dana Goff[2]

[1]Computer Science Department, University of Arkansas at Little Rock
Little Rock, AR, USA

[2]Acxiom Corporation,
Conway, AR, USA

5.1 Introduction

In today's information age, processing customer information in a standardized and accurate manner is known to be a difficult task. Data collection methods vary from source to source by format, volume, and media type. Therefore, it is advantageous to deploy customized data hygiene techniques to standardize the data for meaningfulness and usefulness based on the organization. A standardized and accurate data set can have the following advantages (Varol et al. 2006):

- Lowering cost by limiting erroneous data used in marketing.
- Increasing performance since post-processing can assume that the input field is formatted the same every time.
- Allowing multiple data sets to be run through one standardized process.

It is also important to understand which techniques can be used to improve data accuracy. Because of human errors, data collection methods can often produce incorrect and meaningless data. Extracting the most relevant information is a complex process because data can be freely formatted and voluminous. Moreover, understanding the impact on customer satisfaction caused by ill-defined/dirty data (misspelled or mistyped data) is more challenging. Most of the time, the use of data administrators or a tool that has limited capabilities to correct the mistyped information can cause many problems. Therefore, the more accurate the selected word is, the more useful the information that is retrieved. This is why one goal of the data processing industry is to make source data more meaningful. This can be accomplished by utilizing more effective tools and sequences or statistical approaches

Y. Chan et al. (eds.), *Data Engineering*, International Series in Operations
Research & Management Science 132, DOI 10.1007/978-1-4419-0176-7_5,
© Springer Science+Business Media, LLC 2010

to provide a suggestion table. For these reasons, the *Personal Name Recognizing Strategy* (PNRS) was developed to provide the closest match for a misspelled name. In Section 5.2, some relevant definitions and background of the system are introduced. The strategies and methodology that are used in PNRS to overcome the problem are discussed in Section 5.3. In the final section, the paper is concluded by summarizing the test result.

5.2 Background

Before discussing the techniques that are being used, it is necessary to point out the different types of errors targeted in this research to judge the effectiveness of the solutions. The study presented here deals primarily with four types of errors. The primary type of errors is an *isolated-word error* (Kukich 1992). This is a single misspelled or mistyped word that can be captured with simple techniques. As the name suggests, isolated-word errors are invalid strings, properly identified and isolated as incorrect representations of a valid word (Becchetti and Ricotti 1999). There are many isolated-word error correction applications (for an exhaustive list, see (Kukich 1992)) and different issues and techniques may pertain to specific applications. The primary isolated errors are as follows:

- Typographic errors
- Cognitive errors
- Phonetic errors
- OCR errors

Typographic errors (also known as fat-fingering) occur when one letter is accidentally typed in place of another. For example, in the case of *"teh"* while trying to type *"the."* These errors are based on the assumption that the writer or typist knows how to spell the word, but may have typed the word in a rush (Kukich 1992). *Cognitive errors* refer to situations where the writer or typist chooses an incorrect spelling due to lack of knowledge of the correct one. For example, the incorrect spelling of *"piece"* as *"piexe"* (Kukich 1992). *Phonetic errors* can be seen to be a subset of cognitive errors. These errors are made when the writer substitutes letters into a word where the sound of it is mistakenly believed to be correct, which in fact leads to a misspelling. For example, spelling *"naïve"* as *nyeve* (ASPELL 2007). *Optical Character Recognition (OCR) errors* arise from OCR misinterpretations of the original document (Taghva and Stofsky 2001). These errors include the merging and splitting of words and characters, or incorrect framing of characters that usually results in one-to-many mappings, insertions of characters, deletions of characters, and rejections of characters due to low confidence levels in recognition. OCR based errors are as follows: _Threshold error:_ Since each OCR device has a minimal recognition threshold that determines the confidence level in recognizing a particular character or symbol, some characters may not be understood. This is called Threshold error in OCR. _Substitution error:_ This error appears when one character or symbol in a document is translated as another, i.e., different from the intended character or symbol. For example, an *i* can become a *1*, or an *o* becoming a *0* (zero). *Insertion or Deletion error:* This error happens when the OCR device picks up an additional character or deletes a character from the original document. The frequent insertion of white space characters, due to inconsistent font spacing, is good example of insertion or deletion type errors. *Framing error:* This is the case when the mapping between a character and its output is not one to one. For example, an *m* might become *iii* or the *cl* character set becoming a *d* (Beitzel et al. 2002).

The distinctions among these categories of spelling errors are quite subtle and, in fact, the categories overlap, making it impossible to categorize all errors precisely. Fortunately, spelling correction techniques generally do not require that errors be placed precisely into one of the above categories.

5.2.1 Techniques used for General Spelling Error Correction

Once a potential problem associated with a word has been detected, then the correction of that word is another issue in the spelling correction process. As stated, there are many isolated-word error correction applications and these techniques decompose the problem into a sequence of three sub-problems (Kukich 1992): detecting the error, generating the candidate corrections, and ranking the candidate solutions. Five main categories can be defined for the techniques used for isolated-word error correction, as follows:

5.2.1.1 Minimum edit distance techniques

The edit distance is defined as the smallest number of insertions, deletions, and substitutions required for changing one string into another (Levenshtein 1965). The edit distance from one string to another is calculated by the number of operations (replacements, insertions or deletions) that need to be carried out to transform one string to another (Levenshtein 1965). Minimum edit distance techniques have been applied to virtually all spelling correction tasks, including text editing and natural language interfaces. The spelling correction accuracy varies with applications and algorithms. Shortly after the definition of the edit distance, Damerau (Damerau 1990) reports a 95 percent correction rate for single-error misspellings for a test set of 964 misspellings of medium and long words (length 5 or more characters) while using a lexicon of 1,593 words. However, his overall correction rate was 84 percent when multi-error misspellings were counted. On the other hand, Durhaiw et al. (1983) reports an overall 27 percent correction rate for a very simple, fast, and plain single-error correction algorithm accessing a keyword lexicon of about 100 entries. Although the rates seem low, the authors report a high degree of user satisfaction for this command language interface application due to their algorithm's unobtrusiveness.

In recent work, Brill and Moore (2002) report experiments with modeling more powerful edit operations, allowing generic string-to-string edits. Moreover, additional heuristics are also used to complement techniques based on edit distance.

For instance, in the case of typographic errors, the keyboard layout is very important. It is much more common to accidentally substitute a key by another if they are placed near each other on the keyboard.

AGREP (Wu and Manber 1992a, 1992b), which is a tool based on an extension of the Edit Distance algorithm to find the best match, uses several different algorithms for optimal performance with different search criteria. For simple patterns with errors, AGREP uses the Boyer-Moore algorithm with a partition scheme (see Wu and Manber (1992b) for details of partitioning). AGREP essentially uses arrays of binary vectors and pattern matching, comparing each character of the query word in order to determine the best matching lexicon word.

Moreover, similar measures are used to compute a distance between DNA sequences (strings over {A, C, G, T}), or proteins. The measures are used to find genes or proteins that may have shared functions or properties and to infer family relationships and evolutionary trees over different organisms (Needleman and Wunsch 1970).

5.2.1.2 Soundex and Phonetic Strategy

The SOUNDEX (Philips 1990), which is used to correct phonetic spellings, maps a string into a key consisting of its first letter followed by a sequence of digits. It takes an English word and produces a four-digit representation, which is a primitive way to preserve the salient features of the phonetic pronunciation of the word. On the other hand, the metaphone algorithm is also a system for transforming words into codes based on phonetic properties (Philips 1990, 2000). Unlike Soundex, which operates on a letter-by letter scheme, metaphone analyzes both single consonants and groups of letters called diphthongs according to a set of rules for grouping consonants and then maps groups to metaphone codes (Kukich 1992). The disadvantage of the metaphone algorithm is that it is specific to the English language.

A significant and meaningful study by Veronis (1998) devised a modified dynamic-programming algorithm that differentially weights edit distances based on phonemic similarity. This modification is necessary because phonetic misspellings frequently result in greater deviation from the correct orthographic spelling (Kukich 1992).

5.2.1.3 Rule-based techniques

Rule-based techniques attempt to use the knowledge gained from spelling error patterns and write heuristics that take advantage of this knowledge. For example, if it is known that many errors occur from the letters *"ie"* being typed *"ei"*, then we may write a rule that represents this (Yannakoudakis and Fawthrop 1983).

5.2.1.4 N-gram-based techniques

The character n-gram-based technique coincides with the character n-gram analysis in non-word detection. However, instead of observing certain bi-grams and trigrams of letters that never or rarely occur, this technique can calculate the likelihood of one character following another and use this information to find possible correct word candidates (Ullman 1977).

5.2.1.5 Probabilistic techniques and Neural Nets

Naturally, n-grams can be used to calculate probabilities and this has led to the probabilistic techniques demonstrated by Lee (1999). In particular, transition probabilities can be trained using n-grams from a large corpus and these n-grams can then represent the likelihood of one character following another. Confusion probabilities state the likelihood of one character being mistaken for another (Golding and Schabes 1996). Neural net techniques have emerged as likely candidates for spelling correctors due to their ability to do associative recall based on incomplete and noisy data. This means that they are trained on the spelling errors themselves and carry the ability to adapt to the specific spelling error patterns that they are trained upon (Trenkle and Vogt 1994).

5.2.2 Domain-Specific Correction

An approach to spelling error correction that has received relatively less attention is the domain-specific approach. Corpus-specific approaches may fall in the same category, although the text found in the same corpus does not necessary imply that they fall in the same domain. For example, the British National Corpus2 (BNC) is a 100 million word collection of samples of written and spoken language from a wide range of sources, and these samples do not pertain to any particular domain. In contrast to this, the ACL Anthology is a corpus in the domain of Computational Linguistics. Tillenius (1996) reports on a method for generating and ranking spelling errors. This approach investigated an efficient way to combine the edit distance metric between two strings using a word frequency dictionary and word bi-grams to achieve better results for spelling error corrections. After having analyzed both a corpus of unedited news articles and a corpus of student essays, when using both edit distance and word frequencies, Tillenius (1996) finds that word frequencies should be more important than edit distance according to the work. Tillenius (1996) concludes that both modified edit distance and word frequencies gave a good ranking of valid candidate words for the spelling errors, with a combined correction percentage of 76%. More recently Mihov et al. (2003) report on using the web as a dynamic secondary dictionary, based on the assumption that the content of web pages belonging to a specific thematic area will provide a better basis for a relevant dictionary. They experiment with building the dictionary from words gathered from the body of web pages that were retrieved by sending a relevant query to the AllTheWeb3 search engine. The resulting top 100 web pages returned would then be used to build the dynamic dictionary. Using this method, they report a slightly increased accuracy rate in error corrections when using the dynamically built domain-specific dictionary combined with a conventional one.

5.3 Individual Name Spelling Correction Algorithm: the Personal Name Recognition Strategy (PNRS)

The PNRS, introduced in this study combines not only strategies discussed above but also includes new ones to find the closest match (Figure 5.1). Before applying any techniques to suggest a valid word for a particular field, the information in the proper place needs to be free of non-ASCII characters. The PNRS approach for removing the non-ASCII characters requires (1) keeping the original blank spaces in the data and later using them as delimiters, (2) removing the non-ASCII characters from the records, and (3) consolidating the partitioned word pieces. After removing the non-ASCII characters from the input data, PNRS invokes certain algorithms to produce the alternative suggestions.

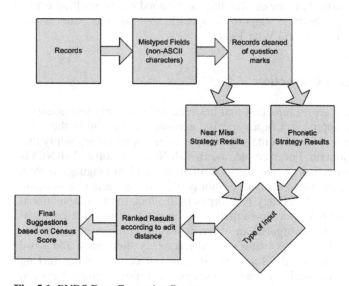

Fig. 5.1. PNRS Data Correction Process

The *near miss strategy* is a fairly simple way to generate suggestions. Two words are considered near, if they can be made identical by inserting a blank space, interchanging two adjacent letters, changing one letter, deleting one letter or adding one letter (NetSpell 2007). If a valid word is generated using these techniques, then it is added to the temporary suggestion list. However, the near miss strategy does not provide the best list of suggestions when a word is truly misspelled. That is where the phonetic strategy takes place. As discussed above, a phonetic code is a rough approximation of how the word sounds (Kukich 1992). The English written language is a truly phonetic code, which means each sound in a word is represented by a symbol or sound picture. The applied phonetic strategy compares the phonetic code of the misspelled word to all the words in the word list. If the phonetic codes match, then the word is added to the temporary suggestion list.

If the input data contain names, possibly of international scope, it is difficult to standardize the phonetic equivalents of certain letters. Therefore, an intelligent decision mechanism is placed before the ranking algorithm is applied. The input data is compared with a domain-specific English names dictionary.

- If the input data contains an English name, the algorithm that is used moves the results of the near miss strategy and phonetic strategies into the permanent suggestion pool at the same time and makes them of equal weight.
- If the input data contains an international name, then the phonetic results are omitted and the permanent suggestion pool consists only of the results from the near miss strategy.

Once the PNRS has a list of suggestions (based on the data type) an edit-distance algorithm is used to rank the results in the pool. In order to provide meaningful suggestions, the threshold value is defined as 2. In case the first and last characters of a word do not match, we modified our approach to include an extra edit distance. The main idea behind this is that people generally can get the first character and last character correct when trying to spell a word.

At the final stage it is possible to see several possible candidate names which have an edit distance of one or two from the original mistyped word. Relying on edit distance doesn't often provide the desired result. Therefore, we designed our decision mechanism based on the content of the input information and added the U.S. Census Bureau decision mechanism to it. The decision mechanism data is a compiled list of popular first and last names which are scored based on the frequency of those names within the United States (Census 2007). This allows the tool to choose a "best fit" suggestion to eliminate the need for user interaction. The strategies are applied to a custom dictionary which is designed particularly for the workflow automation. A sample of the popular names file is shown in Table 5.1. For the sake of this investigation, the rank associated with a name will be called the census score. Names with lower census scores occur more frequently in the Census data.

Table 5.1. Sample from U.S. Census popular names file

Name	Census Score
James	1
Miller	7
Margaret	9
Eric	33
Morgan	57
Annie	97
Robinette	2428
Kulaga	40211

The census score portion of the algorithm is implemented using the following steps:

1. *Step:* Compare the current suggested names to the census file. If there is a match, store the census score associated with the suggestion.
2. *Step:* Choose the name with the lowest census score as the "best fit" suggestion.
3. *Step:* If all suggestions are unmatched on the census file, choose the suggestion with the lowest edit distance.
4. *Step:* If there are several suggestions that share the lowest edit score, choose the first suggestion on the list.

5.3.1 Experiment Results

Experimental data is a real-life sample which involves personal and associated company names, addresses including zip code, city, state, and phone numbers of 1,850 individuals. Dirty data is present in total of 129 records, including misspelled names and some non-ASCII characters. In order to evaluate the effectiveness of the tool, experiments are conducted not only on current correction algorithm (NameCheck[1]) and PNRS but also on the well known ASPELL (ASPELL 2007), JSpell HTML (JSPELL 2007), and Ajax Spell Checkers (AJAX 2007). As illustrated in Figure 5.2 and Table 5.2, PNRS achieved a 68 percent correction rate while the runner-up algorithm was only able to fix 47 percent of the records. Although JSPELL proposed the most number of corrections, its exact match rate is under 48 percent. While PNRS failed to provide any other suggestions for 28 individual names out of 129, only 5 of them were omitted and 23 of them qualified as valid names.

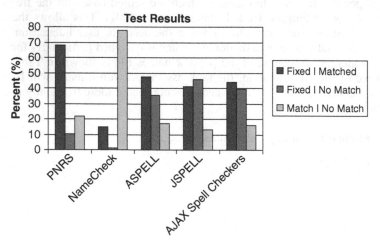

Fig. 5.2. Comparison of the Tools

---

[1] NameCheck is an algorithm currently being used by Axciom.

Table 5.2. Statistical Results

	Corrections		
Algorithms-Attributes	[1]Fixed I Matched	[2]Fixed I No Match	[3]Match I No Match
NameCheck	19	0	110
PNRS	88	13	28
ASPELL	61	46	22
JSPELL	53	59	17
Ajax Spell Checkers	57	51	21

[1]Exact correction of the misspelled name
[2]Corrections that provide no match with the original name
[3]Either the input is accepted as a valid name or the system failed to provide any suggestions

5.4 Conclusion

In today's environment of information explosion, it is very difficult to retrieve relevant data. As data sources become larger, current techniques of information retrieval fail in terms of their efficiency. Also, extracting the most relevant information in a system is a complex process: data is free-formatted, voluminous, and consists of multiple media types. Although quite a number of spelling algorithms exist for general purpose use, it is hard to distinguish and correct individual names with them. In this study a custom name spelling checking algorithm is presented in order to overcome the lack of spelling correction tools for personal names. The results are compared with other known tools to reflect the success of the study. Not only did PNRS provide the most Fixed I Matched corrections, but it also achieved 21 percent more exact corrections than the runner-up algorithm. Although the success rate of PNRS was about 68 percent, another 10 percent were fixed but provided different results (Figure 5.1). In future work, a combination of Kullback-Leibler divergence (Pedro et al. 2004) and Information theoretic distortion measures (Cardinal 2002) will be applied to predict how close the obtained results are to the expected ones.

5.5 Exercises

1. List the main sources of isolated word errors and explain them briefly?
2. What are the main techniques used to correct the spelling corrections?
3. How important is the Phonetic Strategy in spelling correction? Discuss it in terms of English language and individual names?
4. Discuss the pros and cons of including an extra edit distance if the first and last characters of a word do not match?
5. Why matching of personal names are more challenging compared to matching of general text?
6. What improvements can be made to strengthen PNRS algorithm?

5.6 References

AJAX (2007) AJAX Spell Checker. Retrieved from http://www.broken-notebook.com/spell_checker/.

ASPELL (2007) ASPELL. Retrieved from http://aspell.net/metaphone/.

Becchetti C, Ricotti LP (1999) Speech Recognition: Theory and C++ Implementation. John Wiley & Sons.

Beitzel SM, Jensen EC, and Grossman, DA (2002) Retrieving OCR text: A survey of current approaches. White Paper.

Brill E, Moore RC (2002) An improved error model for noisy channel spelling correction. In: Proceedings of ACL-2000, the 38th Annual Meeting of the Association for Computational Linguistics, pp 286-293.

Cardinal J (2002) Quantization with an information-theoretic distortion measure. Technical Report 491, ULB.

Census (2007) Census Bureau Home Page, www.census.gov.

Damerau FJ (1990) Evaluating computer generated domain-oriented vocabularies. Information Process. Management. 26: 791 – 801.

Durhaiw I, Lamb DA, and Sax JB (1983) Spelling correction in user interfaces. CACM 26: 764–773.

Golding A, Schabes Y (1996) Combining trigram based and feature-based methods for context-sensitive spelling correction. In: Joshi A, and Palmer M, (eds.). Proceedings of the 34th Annual Meeting of the ACL. San Francisco.

JSPELL (2007) JSPELL HTML. Retrieved from http://www.thesolutioncafe.com/html-spell-checker.html.

Lee L (1999) Measures of distributional similarity. In: Proceedings of the 37th Annual Meeting of the ACL.

Levenshtein VI (1965) Binary codes capable of correcting deletions, insertions and reversals. Doklady Akademii Nauk SSSR 163: 845-848, also {1966) Soviet Physics Doklady 10: 707-710.

Kukich K (1992) Techniques for Automatically Correcting Words in Text. ACM Computing Surveys, Vol. 24, No. 4.

Mihov S, Ringlstetter C, Schulz KU, and Strohmaier C (2003) Lexical post-correction of OCR-results: The web as a dynamic secondary dictionary? In: Document Analysis and Recognition Proceedings Volume 2, pp 03–06.

NetSpell (2007) Near Miss Strategy. Retrieved from http://www.codeproject.com/csharp/NetSpell.asp.

Needleman SB, Wunsch CD (1970) A general method applicable to the search for similarities in the amino acid sequence of two proteins. Journal of Molecular Biology 48: 443-453.

Pedro JM, Purdy PH, Vasconcelos N (2004) A Kullback-Leibler divergence based kernel for SVM classification in multimedia application. In: Thrun S, Saul L, Scholkopf B (eds) Advances in Neural Information Processing Systems 16, MIT Press, Cambridge, MA.

Philips L (1990) Hanging on the metaphone. Computer Language, 7(12): 39-43.

Philips L (2000) The double-metaphone search algorithm. C/C++ User's Journal, 18(6).

Taghva K, Stofsky E (2001) OCRSpell: an interactive spelling correction system for OCR errors in text. IJDAR, 3: 125-137.

Tillenius M (1996) Efficient generation and ranking of spelling error corrections Master's thesis, Royal Institute of Technology, Stockholm, Sweden.

Trenkle JM and Vogt RC (1994) Disambiguation and spelling correction for a neural network based character recognition system. In: Proceedings of SPIE. Volume 2181, pp 322-333.

Ullman JR (1977) A Binary n-Gram Technique for Automatic Correction of Substitution, Deletion, Insertion, and Reversal Errors in Words. Computer J., 20 (2): 141-147.

Varol C, Robinette C, Kulaga J, Bayrak C, Wagner R, Goff D (2006) Application of Near Miss Strategy and Edit Distance to Handle Dirty Data. In: ALAR Conference on Applied Research in Information Technology, March 3, Conway, Arkansas, USA.

Veronis, J (1998) Morphosyntactic correction in natural language interfaces. In: Proceedings of the 12th International Conference on Computational Linguistics. Budapest, Hungary, pp 708-713.

Wu S, Manber U (1992a) AGREP - A Fast Approximate Pattern Matching Tool. In: Proc. Usenix Winter 1992 Technical Conf., pp 153-162.

Wu S, Manber U (1992b) Fast Text Searching With Errors. Comm. ACM, Vol. 35.

Yannakoudakis EJ, Fawthrop D (1983) The rules of spelling errors. Information Processing Management 19 (2): 87–99.

6 A Parallel General-Purpose Synthetic Data Generator[1]

Joseph E. Hoag and Craig W. Thompson

Computer Science and Computer Engineering Department,
University of Arkansas,
Fayetteville, AR, USA

6.1 Introduction

The IT industry needs synthetic data generation tools for a number of applications including (but not limited to):

- *Regression testing.* Repeatedly generate the same large data set for testing enterprise applications. Allow the data set to be removed between regression tests.
- *Secure application development.* Allow developers access to data that looks very much like the real data, but does not contain any sensitive information.
- *Testing of data mining applications.* Generate data sets with known characteristics to gauge whether data mining tools can discover those characteristics.

Several synthetic data generation tools already exist in the commercial world (TurboData n.d.; GS Data Generator n.d.; DTM Data Generator n.d.; RowGen n.d.). These tools can generate modest amounts of easily described data. However, they do not scale for generating "industrial-sized" (i.e., terabyte) data sets.

Data generation tools have recently been developed in the academic world as well (Bruno and Chaudhuri 2005; Houkjaer et al. 2006; Samadi et al. 2006). These present new concepts in the form of graph- and language-oriented synthetic data description, providing greater flexibility in the description and generation of synthetic data.

In this chapter, we present the Parallel Synthetic Data Generator (PSDG). PSDG is designed to generate data across multiple processors. This allows PSDG

---

[1] This chapter is adapted from an article of the same name published by the authors in the March 2007 issue of the ACM *SIGMOD Record*.

Y. Chan et al. (eds.), *Data Engineering*, International Series in Operations
Research & Management Science 132, DOI 10.1007/978-1-4419-0176-7_6,
© Springer Science+Business Media, LLC 2010

to harness the power of cluster/grid computing to generate huge data sets with linear speedup. Parallel execution involves more than launching several generators simultaneously. PSDG will generate consistent output (for a given input file) regardless of the degree of parallelism. This repeatable determinism is a requirement for regression testing applications.

PSDG is written in Java so it is portable across platforms. Although PSDG supports direct-to-database data generation, it is generally quicker to generate the data to file(s) and then use a fast load utility to upload data into a database.

This chapter also describes Synthetic Data Description Language (SDDL). SDDL files serve as input to PSDG. SDDL is an XML-based language that codifies the manner in which generated data can be described and constrained. Rich description mechanisms available in SDDL enable generation of a variety of kinds of synthetic data.

In the following section, we document features of SDDL. Next, we discuss the concept of pools. Then we describe mechanisms that produce deterministic data sets over an arbitrary number of processors. We conclude with performance data, applications and future directions.

6.2 SDDL

SDDL is an XML-based language that provides the user flexibility in describing and constraining synthetically generated data. While SDDL was developed along with PSDG, it is intended to be expressive and could be used as input by other synthetic data generators. SDDL is similar in concept to DGL (Bruno and Chaudhuri 2005), but SDDL is XML-based while DGL is C-like, and they have some functional differences as well.

SDDL describes at its outer level a "database" element, which is composed of zero or more pool elements and one or more table elements. Pools will be described later. The following is a valid (if trivial) SDDL file:

```xml
<?xml version="1.0" encoding="UTF-8"?>
<database>
 <seed>1240958412</seed>
 <pool name="colors">
  <choice name="red"/>
  <choice name="green"/>
  <choice name="blue"/>
 </pool>
 <table name="PAIRS" length="5">
  <field name="F1" type="int">
   <min>1</min>
   <max>50</max>
  </field>
  <field name="F2" type="CHAR(5)">
```

```
<formula>colors</formula>
  </field>
 </table>
</database>
```

The file above, when input to PSDG, would result in the synthesis of a relation named *PAIRS*, which would look like this[2]:

Table 6.1. Output from PSDG

F1	F2
28	blue
24	green
50	red
3	blue
3	red

A table element contains all information needed to synthesize a table, including a name attribute, a length attribute, and one or more embedded field elements. The attributes associated with the generated table are defined by the field elements within the table element.

Each field element has "name" and "type" attributes. Field types can be one of *int*, *real*, *string*, *bool*, *date*, *time* or *timestamp*. Field types can also be defined as standard SQL data types, i.e., *CHAR(n)*, *VARCHAR(n)*, *NUMERIC(m,n)*.

Each field also contains a generation constraint. SDDL currently supports five types of generation constraints: min/max, distribution, formula, iteration, and queryPool. Each are described below.

6.2.1 Min/Max Constraints

The user can specifies a minimum and maximum value for a field, e.g.,

```
<field name="age" type="int">
  <min>20</min>
  <max>65</max>
</field>
```

In this example, generated values for the *age* attribute are randomly distributed between 20 and 65, inclusive.

---

[2] The actual values could change with a different random seed.

6.2.2 Distribution Constraints

A distribution constraint is a set of min/max constraints (called "tiers"), each of which has a specified statistical probability of being selected:

```
<field name="age" type="int">
  <dist>
    <tier prob="0.50" min="20" max="30"/>
    <tier prob="0.30" min="31" max="50"/>
    <tier prob="0.20" min="51" max="65"/>
  </dist>
</field>
```

In this example, the generated *age* column values would have a 50% chance of being between 20 and 30, a 30% chance of being between 31 and 50, and a 20% chance of being between 51 and 65.

6.2.3 Formula Constraints

Using a formula constraint, a field can be defined in terms of a mathematical formula consisting of operators, constants, built-in functions, and other field values, for example:

```
<field name="ship_date" type="date">
  <formula>order_date+IRND(4)</formula>
</field>
```

In this example, the *ship_date* field will be equal to the *order_date* field plus anywhere from 0 to 3 days.

Formula constraints can also contain pool references as discussed in the Pools section below.

6.2.4 Iterations

Iterations constrain the generator to iterate through a set of values for a specified column. If a table contains one or more iteration-constrained fields, then the length of the table will be governed by the iteration results. SDDL supports three kinds of iterations: query, pool, and count iterations.

Query iterations allow a column to iterate through the results of a query. For example:

```
<field name="store_nbr" type="int">
  <iteration query="select store_nbr from stores"/>
</field>
```

In this example, the generated *store_nbr* column values would iterate through the *store_nbr* column values in the *stores* table.

Similarly, iterations can iterate through pool choices:

```
<iteration pool="states"/>
```

or numeric values:

```
<iteration base="1" count="100"/>
```

By default, an iteration results in one row of output for each element of its set. However, the user can specify repetition of iteration elements:

```
<field name="F1" type="int">
  <iteration base="1" count="5">
    <repeatMin>3</repeatMin>
    <repeatMax>6</repeatMax>
  </iteration>
</field>
```

In the example above, the *F1* attribute would contain the values 1 through 5, each repeated anywhere from 3 to 6 times. Iteration repeat constraints can also be specified with a statistical distribution:

```
<field name="F1" type="int">
  <iteration base="1" count="5">
    <repeatDist>
      <tier prob="0.70" min="3" max="5"/>
      <tier prob="0.30" min="6" max="6"/>
    </repeatDist>
  </iteration>
</field>
```

If there are multiple iteration-constrained fields in a table, they are considered to be nested, with the nesting order the same as the order of appearance in the table description. Consider the following table definition:

```
<table name="nesting_example">
  <field name="A" type="int">
    <iteration base="5" count="3"/>
  </field>
  <field name="B" type="int">
    <iteration base="100" count="2"/>
  </field>
</table>
```

The output from the *nesting_example* is shown in Table 6.2.

Table 6.2. Table generated by *nesting_example*

A	B
5	100
5	101
6	100
6	101
7	100
7	101

6.2.5 Query Pools

Query pools are used to enforce referential integrity constraints. Using query pools, the value of a field is chosen from the result of a query. In the following example, values generated in the *StudentID* field would be valid IDs from the *students* table:

```
<field name="StudentID" type="int">
  <queryPool>select ID from students</queryPool>
</field>
```

6.3 Pools

Pools are hierarchically structured SDDL elements that can serve as user-defined domains, sources of reference information, and modeling tools.

In SDDL, a pool element must have a *name* attribute and is composed of one or more choice elements. Each choice element must have a *name* attribute and can optionally be composed of sub-pools and auxiliary data items. Pools are modular. Reusable pools can be stored in separate files and imported into SDDL files.

The following pool provides a domain for *states*:

```
<pool name="states">
  <choice name="AK"/>
  <choice name="AL"/>
  <choice name="AR"/>
  ...
  <choice name="WV"/>
  <choice name="WY"/>
</pool>
```

The pool can be accessed from a formula constraint as follows:

```
<field name="state" type="CHAR(2)">
 <formula>states</formula>
</field>
```

Using the formula, each entry in the "states" pool has a 1-in-50 chance of being output for each row of the "state" field. However, we could make the "states" pool more interesting:

```
<pool name="StateZip">
 <choice name="AK">
  <pool name="zips">
   <choice name="99501">
     <city>ANCHORAGE</city>
     <county>ANCHORAGE</county>
     <weight>16211</weight>
   </choice>
   <choice name="99502">
     <city>ANCHORAGE</city>
     <county>ANCHORAGE</county>
     <weight>18626</weight>
   </choice>
    ...
  </pool> <!--end of "zips" sub-pool-->
  <weight>624992</weight>
 </choice> <!--end of "AK" choice-->
  ...
 <choice name="WY">
  <pool name="zips">
   <choice name="82001">
     <city>CHEYENNE</city>
     <county>LARAMIE</county>
     <weight>34767</weight>
   </choice>
   <choice name="82007">
     <city>CHEYENNE</city>
     <county>LARAMIE</county>
     <weight>15840</weight>
   </choice>
    ...
  </pool> <!--end of "zips" sub-pool-->
  <weight>493502</weight>
 </choice> <!--end of "WY" choice-->
</pool> <!--end of "StateZip" pool-->
```

The *StateZip* pool above is a population model of the U.S. taken from publicly available *2000 Census* data (www.census.gov). At the top level, there are still 50 states in the pool. Each state contains a pool of zip codes; each choice in the *zips* sub-pool contains the city and county associated with the zip code. Both the top-level *states* pool and the nested *zips* pools are weighted by population.

Consider the following SDDL table definition that uses the *StateZip* pool:

```
<table name="offices">
  <field name="OfficeID" type="int">
    <iteration base="1000" count="1000"/>
  </field>
  <field name="state" type="CHAR(2)">
    <formula>StateZip</formula>
  </field>
  <field name="zip" type="CHAR(5)">
    <formula>StateZip[state].zips</formula>
  </field>
  <field name="city" type="CHAR(25)">
    <formula>StateZip[state].zips[zip].city</formula>
  </field>
</table>
```

The *offices* table generated from the definition above will have information for 1000 offices. Offices will be distributed within the U.S. according to inter-state and intra-state population statistics. The *state*, *city*, and *zip* fields generated for each row will be consistent with each other.

Given this structural and semantic flexibility, pools can be used to describe a variety of complex data types. Using pools, we have so far modeled such diverse concepts as graphs, maps, state machines, and context-free grammars.

6.4 Parallel Data Generation

Multi-processor systems (clusters, grids) are increasingly affordable. The size of data sets is growing – terabyte-sized tables are not uncommon. Why not take advantage of the former to synthetically generate the latter?

We designed PSDG with parallel generation capability as a requirement. We wanted to minimize communication between generation processes and maintain deterministic output (for a given input) regardless of the degree of parallelism.

Previous synthetic data generation frameworks have supported parallelism to some degree. (Gray et al. 1994) described methods for writing special-purpose data generators in parallel. The MUDD generator (Stephens and Poess 2004) provided a general purpose (though simple) input language, and decoupled the data description from the parallelization details. The KRDataGenerator (KRDataGeneration n.d.), which is a commercialization of (Houkjaer et al. 2006), is graph-based and has a distributed generation capability, but can not describe data with the detail of SDDL.

PSDG distinguishes itself by providing a very descriptive input language (SDDL) while supporting easy parallelism. Like MUDD, PSDG decouples data generation details from data description; users need not take parallelism details into account when constructing an SDDL file.

Each PSDG generation process is launched with the knowledge of how many processes are participating, as well as its own process index. With this information, a generation process can determine the extent of the data that it is responsible for generating without the need for inter-process communication. Because there is no need for inter-process communication, it is possible to launch PSDG processes on heterogeneous, loosely coupled processors (i.e., a grid environment), as well as on homogenous, tightly coupled processors (i.e., an SMP/cluster environment).

PSDG slices the generated data horizontally between generation processes. Generation processes handle slices in a "striped" fashion: process 0 of N will generate slices $\{0, N, 2N,...\}$, process 1 of N will generate slices $\{1, N+1, 2N+1,...\}$, and so on. We can use two separate methods of data slicing: Algorithm 1 is used when there are no iterations in the SDDL description (for a table), and Algorithm 2 is used when iterations are present.

6.4.1 Generation Algorithm 1

With no iterations present, a table's row structure is predictable, and its rows are divided into "swaths", each of size *SWATHSIZE*. The generation processes generate swaths in an alternating round-robin fashion. Before generating a swath, the generation process will call the re-seed function *RF(seed, row)* (where *seed* is the user-specified seed, and *row* is the start row of the swath), which uses *seed* and *row* to re-seed the random number generator.

If there is only one generation process, generation proceeds as shown in Fig. 6.1. (assuming *SWATHSIZE = 100*):

Process 0:
*RF(seed,*0)
Generate rows 0-99
*RF(seed,*100)
Generate rows 100-199
*RF(seed,*200)
Generate rows 200-299
...

Fig. 6.1. One generation process

If there are two generation processes, the generation proceeds in parallel as shown in Fig. 6.2.

Process 0:	Process 1:
$RF(seed,0)$	$RF(seed,100)$
Generate rows 0-99	Generate rows 100-199
$RF(seed,200)$	$RF(seed,300)$
Generate rows 200-299	Generate rows 300-399
...	...

Fig. 6.2. Two generation processes

The random number generator is always re-seeded to a deterministic value (based on the user-specified seed and the row number) before generating a swath. Thus any particular swath will be generated identically regardless of the number of processes participating in the generation.

Note that the load balancing for Algorithm 1 is even; each generation process generates at most *SWATHSIZE* more rows than any other generation process.

6.4.2 Generation Algorithm 2

When iterations are present, it becomes more difficult to deal out constant-sized swaths to each generation process. Consider the following SDDL snippet:

```
<table name="iteration_example">
 <field name="deptID" type="int">
  <iteration query="select ID from departments"/>
 </field>
 <field name="courseID" type="int">
  <iteration query="select ID from courses where deptID = [deptID]"/>
 </field>
</table>
```

How many *courseID* rows will be generated for each *deptID* value? We can't really tell before running the actual queries. As a consequence, we don't know *a priori* how to divide the output into equal-sized slices.

However, we do know the number of elements in any outer iteration element. For query iterations, it is the number of elements returned by the given query. For pool iterations, it is the number of choices in the specified pool. For numeric iterations, it is the value of the *count* attribute. Therefore, the table is sliced up into outer iteration elements (OIEs).

When a single generation process performs generation algorithm 2, the result is shown in Fig. 6.3.

```
Process 0:
RF(seed,0)
Generate OIE 0
RF(seed,1)
Generate OIE 1
RF(seed,2)
Generate OIE 2
...
```

Fig. 6.3. Single generation process on algorithm 2

With 2 processes, the generation proceeds as shown in Fig. 6.4.

```
Process 0:           Process 1:
RF(seed,0)           RF(seed,1)
Generate OIE 0       Generate OIE 1
RF(seed,2)           RF(seed,3)
Generate OIE 2       Generate OIE 3
...                  ...
```

Fig. 6.4. Two generation processes on algorithm 2

Again, the random number generator is always re-seeded to a deterministic value before generating the rows associated with an outer iteration element. Thus the rows associated with any OIE will be generated identically regardless of the number of processes participating in the generation.

Note that Algorithm 2 is balanced with respect to the number of OIEs assigned to the generation processes; each generation process will handle the generation of at most one more OIE than its peers. However, the number of rows associated with an OIE is not guaranteed to be constant. Therefore, it is possible for the generation to be unbalanced in terms of the number of rows generated per generation process.

6.5 Performance and Applications

This section details some of the problem spaces toward which PSDG has been applied.

<u>Benchmarks:</u> As a reference point for generation speed, we generated the SetQuery (O'Neil n.d.) and TPC-C (TPC-C n.d.) benchmark data sets with the results shown in Table 6.3.

Table 6.3. Performance on benchmark data sets

Data Set	Generated MB/Second	
	1 processor	2 processors
Set-Query	5.41	10.69
TPC-C (W=1)	3.58	6.73

The results above were obtained using Pentium 4 processors running at 3 GHz. The slightly sub-linear speedup is due to serial functionality embedded in our current iteration logic (which we are removing).

Ten years of store/item/sales data: We collaborated with a major retailer on a project involving the generation of 10 years worth of realistic store-item-sales data, resulting in 70 billion rows, or nearly 5 Terabytes of data. This data had fairly complex inter- and intra-row dependencies. Running PSDG across 16 1.6-GHz Itanium processors, we were able to reach data generation speeds of over 500,000 rows/second.

Synthetic music industry database: We collaborated with the University of Arkansas Walton College of Business to produce a realistic music industry database called "Hallux." The database had 25 industry-related tables such as "Band," "Album," "Song," "Agent," "Venue," "Performance," "Order_Detail," and "Order_Header." There were a number of inter- and intra-table dependencies to preserve, as well as a number of business rules to thread into the generated data. The Hallux database is used for educational purposes in the business school, and will eventually be made available to multiple universities.

Legal strings for context-free grammars: In our first non-tabular application, we were able to create an SDDL pool format capable of representing arbitrary context-free grammars (CFGs). We were then able to write SDDL code that took such a pool as input and produced legal strings from the CFG represented by the pool.

Mailing lists: PSDG was used to generate realistic mailing lists in both fixed-column-width format and comma-delimited format. These synthetically generated mailing lists were used to test algorithms for processing mailing lists. In a slight variation of this application, PSDG was also used to generate "parallel" mailing lists: the first list was a "canonical", error-free, fixed format mailing list; the second list contained the same information as the first, but with errors injected and multiple formats exhibited. These "parallel" lists were used to test whether the mailing list processing algorithms could properly derive the "canonical" list from the flawed, multiply-formatted second list.

6.6 Conclusion and Future Directions

SDDL provides the functionality and expressiveness needed in a synthetic data description language. Formulas and pools allow for intra-row dependencies. Min/max and distribution constraints support loose inter-row dependencies, and iteration variables (not discussed here) support tight inter-row dependencies. Query pools and query iterations allow for inter-table dependencies. SDDL pools allow for modeling a rich array of concepts, from simple domains and reference tables to graphs, maps, state machines and context-free grammars.

While SDDL does not explicitly support the complex statistical distributions found in (Bruno and Chaudhuri 2005) and (Gray et al. 1994), it does support the use of user-defined plug-in functions in formulas. Complex data distributions (such as Gaussian and Zipfian distributions) can be enforced using this plug-in mechanism.

The data generator itself (PSDG) provides partitioning algorithms that allow for the parallel generation of data sets without the need for communication between generation processes. This parallel capability makes it possible to generate large "industrial size" data sets quickly. Our partitioning algorithms balance processor loads and make sure that the data generated from a given input will be the same regardless of the number of processors across which it is generated. Such deterministic behavior makes PSDG useful for generating regression test data sets.

In our design of both SDDL and PSDG, we aimed to satisfy two goals: (1) provide a rich, flexible, extensible synthetic data description language, and (2) support efficient, deterministic parallel generation of data sets. When these two goals have conflicted, we have so far given priority to the latter. For example, allowing for "side-by-side" iterations, in addition to nested iterations, would enhance the descriptive power of SDDL. However, side-by-side iterations would be difficult to partition and parallelize, so we have chosen not to implement them.

We have identified a number of research areas and potential improvements to PSDG/SDDL:

- While PSDG does have a functional graphical user interface (GUI), it could use some enhancement, primarily in the area of generating obfuscated versions of existing tables. Currently, the GUI can assist in extracting attribute and domain data from existing tables. It would be nice if it could also deduce intra- and inter-column statistical data about existing tables.

- Allow for the specification of a discrete obfuscation level for an attribute when producing obfuscated versions of existing tables. This would relieve the user of the necessity of implementing his/her own obfuscation algorithms.

- Provide streaming, real-time capabilities in the PSDG generation engine. This would allow PSDG to be more useful in a simulation environment.

- Research the idea of compositional constraints for SDDL table fields. Currently, only one constraint is allowed per field. Would it make sense to allow multiple constraints? Would they be AND-ed together, or OR-ed together?

- Write a translator that could convert an E-R diagram into an SDDL file. This would allow data creators a more comfortable data description mechanism.

- Support logical assertions ("Jazz musicians do not play the harmonica") and fuzzy logic constraints ("Many of the employees are tall") in SDDL table and field descriptions. It is currently possible to describe such constraints, but the SDDL required can be monstrously complicated. It would be nice if the user were allowed to specify such simple assertions.

- We would like to explore additional application areas for synthetic data generation. Could SDDL be used to capture some music theory rules, which could be used to generate random (but theoretically sound) music? Could geography and cartography rules be captured in SDDL and used to synthetically generate landscapes? What kind of new functionality would need to be added to SDDL to accommodate these applications?

6.7 Exercises

1. Create an SDDL description for a 100-row table with the following fields:
    - ID: An integer whose values run sequentially from 100 thru 199
    - DOB: A date between January 1, 1960, and December 31, 1979
    - Salary: An integer between 50,000 and 100,000

2. Create an SDDL description for a pool whose choices represent 10 different colors. Each choice should also contain auxiliary data items "redvalue," "greenvalue," and "bluevalue" to represent the RGB components of the color being represented.

3. Consider the following SDDL table description containing nested iterations. Does the order of the iterations affect the degree of parallelism than can be employed to generate the data set? Explain.

    ```
    <table name="sample">
     <field name="A" type="int">
      <iteration base="1" count="10"/>
     </field>
     <field name="B" type="int">
      <iteration base="1" count="100000"/>
     </field>
     <field name="C" type="int">
      <iteration base="1" count="20"/>
     </field>
    </table>
    ```

4. Discuss some specific applications of synthetic data generation not described in this chapter.

5. Many real data sets contain personally identifying information (PII). Many corporations do not want to release PII data to their partners to assure privacy to their customers but they may still need to run large-scale tests at vendor or customer sites. How does SDDL help?

6. Discuss some possible enhancements for the PSDG/SDDL framework. Are there additional constraint types that would be useful? Would it be possible to import ER diagrams into SDDL diagrams? Can you think of some useful functionality in a PSDG/SDDL graphical user interface?

6.8 References

Bruno N, Chaudhuri S (2005) Flexible Database Generators. Proceedings on Very Large Data Bases, pp.1097-1107.

DTM Data Generator (n.d.), DTM Data Generator home page. Retrieved March 2007 from http://www.sqledit.com.

Gray J, Sundaresan P, Englert S, Baclawski K, Weinberger P (1994) Quickly Generating Billion-Record Synthetic Databases. Proceedings of the ACM International Conference on Management of Data (SIGMOD).

GS Data Generator (n.d.), GS DataGenerator home page. Retrieved March 2007 from http://www.GSApps.com/products/datagenerator.

Houkjaer K, Torp K, Wind R (2006) Simple and Realistic Data Generation. Proceedings on Very Large Data Bases, pp. 1243-1246.

KRDataGeneration (n.d.). KRDataGeneration home page. Retrieved January 2007 from http://www.data-generation.com.

O'Neil P (n.d.) The Set-Query Benchmark. Retrieved March 2007 from www.cs.umb.edu/~poneil/SetQBM.pdf.

RowGen (n.d.), RowGen home page. Retrieved March 2007 from http://www.iri.com/products/rowgen.

Samadi, B., Cipolone, A., Jeske, D., Cox, S., Rendón, C., Holt, D. and Xiao, R. (2006). "Development of a Synthetic Data Set Generator for Building and Testing Information Discovery Systems," *Proceedings of the Third International Conference on Information Technology: New Generations*, IEEE Computer Society, Las Vegas, USA, April 10-12, 2006, pp. 707-712.

Stephens, J. and Poess, M. (2004). "MUDD: a Multi-Dimensional Data Generator", *International Workshop on Software and Performance*, Redwood City, California, January 2004, pp. 104-109.

TPC-C (n.d.). TPC-C Home page. *Transaction Processing Performance Council.*, Retrieved March 2007 from http://www.tpc.org/tpcc.

TurboData (n.d.). TurboData home page. Retrieved March 2007 from http://www.turbodata.ca.

7 A Grid Operating Environment for CDI

Terry M. Talley

Acxiom Corporation
Conway, AR, USA

7.1 Introduction

The purpose of this chapter is to discuss how a grid operating environment is well suited to the tasks associated with Customer Data Integration (CDI) and describe a logical organization of a grid that is targeted at addressing this application. More specifically, recall from the introductory chapter of this book that many organizations face a common problem of collecting data from the outside world and integrating that data into a model of the real world that can be used to direct effective campaigns. This chapter discusses how a grid can be organized into a computer that directly supports the task of building and maintaining the model. We will describe a logical organization of that computer and some desirable features for the components or subsystems within that computer given the target CDI problem.

We will use the grid developed at the Acxiom Corporation as a case study of a grid constructed specifically to support CDI work. The intent here is not necessarily to evangelize the way that Acxiom approached the problem, but instead to give concrete examples of the challenges and possible implementations associated with exploiting a grid for CDI processing.

In particular, we will use the evolution of the grid at Acxiom as a path to introduce the components of a complete grid environment for CDI processing. Many implementations of grids (albeit in different problem spaces) followed a similar path of discovery and we include the Acxiom experience only as an example. Nevertheless, the Acxiom grid is widely recognized as one of the first grids constructed specifically to address the challenges associated with CDI, so the case study provides not only insight into the final organization of a CDI grid computer, but also on the motivations and process that guided the Acxiom grid through its evolution. A complete description of a grid processing environment is beyond the scope of this book. This chapter attempts to give the reader a conceptual understanding of CDI processing on a grid and to provide context for the remaining chapters in this section of the book that discuss specific areas within the context of a CDI grid.

Y. Chan et al. (eds.), *Data Engineering*, International Series in Operations
Research & Management Science 132, DOI 10.1007/978-1-4419-0176-7_7,
© Springer Science+Business Media, LLC 2010

7.2 Grid-Based Service Deployment

7.2.1 Evolution of the Acxiom Grid (A Case Study)

Acxiom did not set out to create a grid. The Acxiom grid evolved from efforts to solve a specific pair of related problems. In the late 1990s, Acxiom created a product called AbiliTec®. The purpose of the AbiliTec product is to resolve different representations of specific entities (i.e., individual names, business names, and addresses) to consistent, persistent entity keys (also called "links") that represent the particular entity instance. The input to AbiliTec is one or more names and addresses of an individual or business. The output is one or more entity keys (i.e., an AbiliTec consumer link, business link, and/or address link) that can be used to abstractly represent the specific entities.

Using the terminology from our description of Customer Data Integration in the introductory chapter of this book, AbiliTec is a recognition or entity resolution service. In particular, it is a recognition service where the caller knows little about the individuals or businesses to be recognized other than a name and address. This is a common situation, particularly when businesses are attempting to acquire new customers. Traditionally, this type of "prospect" recognition was done using approximate string algorithms to match similar representations of names and addresses together. AbiliTec not only uses approximate string algorithms to match, but also uses a very large knowledge base, compiled separately by Acxiom using Acxiom data sources, that contains significant information about the linkage between people, businesses, and addresses. This approach is similar to expert systems that apply both algorithmic rules and domain-specific knowledge to solve specific problems. The result of this combination approach is that AbiliTec can not only match similar names and addresses to the same entity key (using approximate string match), but can also correctly identify entities with dissimilar representations (using the accumulated proprietary data in the knowledge base). This was a breakthrough in the CDI industry. AbiliTec was rapidly and widely accepted and Acxiom experienced a dramatic growth in both the number of customers and the volume of records being processed.

While this situation was good from an Acxiom business perspective, it presented significant financial and technical challenges as well. The AbiliTec service consumes both significant CPU resources, due to the approximate string scoring algorithms, and also significant I/O resources, due to the references to the large knowledge base, which is too large to be stored in RAM on traditional machines.

As a result, Acxiom faced a pair of related challenges. First, to make a single given job run fast, the growing knowledge base was forcing Acxiom to buy increasingly larger and more expensive machines. The original AbiliTec implementation ran on large Unix machines. These machines had many CPUs (e.g., 16 CPUs) and a large amount of RAM (e.g., 96 GB). At the time, machines of this class were very expensive. Second, the success of the product caused a dramatic increase in the volume of data to be processed. The resulting capacity problem was expensive to solve given the number of machines required to meet the peak demand.

In 2000, Acxiom addressed these challenges by implementing a new version of AbiliTec that spread the single logical service across many commodity servers. All the commodity servers in the implementation were logically homogeneous (at the time, 2 CPU Intel architecture servers with 4 GB of RAM and 1 or 2 disk drives running Linux), although the actual manufacturer and models of the machines were not necessarily identical. To the service client, these machines looked like a single service, but the processing was in fact spread across many actual machines and service instances. A given service instance could only process work associated with a subset of the full knowledge base, but in aggregate the set of service instances implemented the full logical service.

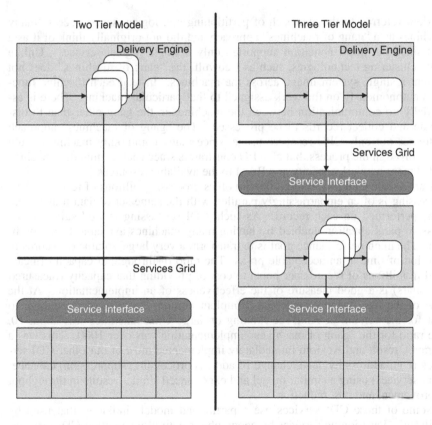

Fig. 7.1. "Gang of Machines" AbiliTec Implementation Models

This distributed version of AbiliTec was deployed in two models (Figure 7.1). In the Two Tier Model, the match base is spread across many physical servers. Each server supports one or more services associated with a particular geography (e.g., a particular zip code). The calling client (e.g., a batch delivery engine or a transactional delivery engine) is aware of which geographies reside on different nodes and routes requests appropriately. Each geography is replicated on two or more nodes. If one node should fail, the client switches to one of the other nodes providing the same geography.

The Three Tier Model is similar, but inserts a "Director" layer service that presents a geographically independent interface and the client is not aware of the geographically specific services at the lowest tier. The advantage of the Three Tier model is that the client is insulated from changes to the geographic split. The disadvantage is that there is an extra call across the network over the Two Tier model.

7.2.2 Services Grid

Acxiom referred to the approach of partitioning one logical service across many machines as a "gang of machines" approach and did not originally think of it as a grid since the implementation supported only a single logical service. Unlike some clustering technologies, such as Beowulf, the "gang of machines" does not present a single system image across the machines. Instead each machine functions autonomously on the work assigned to that particular machine. There is essentially no communication between the machines in the gang other than to distribute and collect records to be processed. The "gang of machines" approach addresses not only CPU resource usage, since many commodity machines could be involved in the process, but also I/O constraints since each commodity machine added more network capacity and RAM to the available resources.

Large-scale CDI processing often involves processing billions of records. This processing is often embarrassingly parallel, with the same set of data transformations performed on each record. As such, CDI processing is well suited to the massive parallelization enabled by having many machines available to the problem. The main performance goal is to transform a very large volume of records in a period of time at an acceptable price. The ratio of throughput capacity (measured in millions of records per hour) to cost of providing that capacity (measured in dollars) is a good measure of the effectiveness of an implementation. At the time of the first "gang of machines" implementation, the ratio of throughput to cost for the version of AbiliTec running on large Unix machines was about 10. The ratio for the "gang of machines" implementation was over 1000. This was a dramatic result and Acxiom immediately implemented most of our other CDI services (e.g., address hygiene, change of address processing, suppression, enhancement services) using a similar model and experienced similar results in throughput improvement and cost reduction.

Some of these CDI services use a partitioned model similar to that used by AbiliTec. Partitioning services by geography is natural many other CDI services, particularly those oriented around addresses. Other services were partitioned using other criteria for splitting the service. For example, many of Acxiom's demographic enhancement services are partitioned by the actual value of the AbiliTec consumer link since this link is the basic input value for calling the enhancement services. Acxiom also deploys services using more traditional horizontal scaling. For example, the complete implementation of Acxiom's United States postal hygiene product can run on a single server, but is deployed as a replicated set of services on a set of servers for performance and redundancy.

Eventually, all Acxiom CDI products were implemented using this "gang of machines" approach, exploiting both a Common Object Request Broker Architecture (CORBA) and Web Services infrastructure. Acxiom began to refer to the collection of commodity servers supporting these services and the collection of services themselves as the Services Grid.

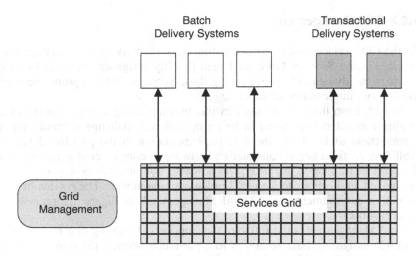

Fig. 7.2. Batch and Transactional Delivery Systems Connected to Services Grid

Acxiom has many delivery channels for CDI services, including batch delivery systems (e.g., via ETL engines), transactional delivery systems (e.g., call center applications), infrastructure technologies (e.g., CDI "Hubs," stored procedures), and web applications. The Service Oriented Architecture (SOA) provided by the Services Grid proved a good implementation for serving all these channels. For example, for transactional delivery, implementing priority queues within the services allowed the same set of servers to support both transactional and batch, meeting both low latency and high throughput requirements. As another example, since the CDI services running in the Services Grid were highly redundant, transactional delivery systems could dynamically adapt to server failures by choosing another service instance on failure, providing very high availability to the end users. From the batch perspective, carefully implemented CDI services can meet any of the throughput capabilities of the batch delivery engines themselves. For example, horizontally scaling services (i.e., adding redundant servers for additional capacity) and batching multiple records on a single request to the service enables batch delivery engines to achieve very high throughput calling the services. As another example, the low unit cost of additional servers allows the Services Grid to be incrementally scaled to meet a growing batch load either through a long term capacity planning process or by dynamically adding servers "on demand" during unexpected peak periods.

Figure 7.2 shows a conceptual view of the Services Grid with multiple delivery engines connecting with the grid implementation of a variety of CDI services. At first, only the CDI services themselves ran in the Services Grid, but it quickly became obvious that the transactional delivery systems, which are fundamentally services, could also run in this environment and, in particular, exploit the horizontal scaling opportunities in the grid.

7.2.3 Grid Management

As the CDI services and many of the transactional delivery systems migrated into services in the Services Grid, we began flexibly assigning machines to different services and dynamically provisioning those services. At this point, we began to think of our implementation as a true grid.

In fact, from the start, it was obvious that managing a large number of commodity computers was going to be an operational challenge without supporting management tools. From the first implementation of the grid-based version of AbiliTec, Acxiom began constructing software to control, configure, and manage the services running in the grid. This software continued to evolve and expand as we moved applications to the new implementation model. The portion of the grid operating environment called "Grid Management" in Figure 7.2 represents this control software.

Grid Management is the software that supports (1) adding new resources to the grid, (2) assigning those resources to a particular service, (3) provisioning those resources to support the assigned service, (4) providing an interface to configure and control services, and (5) monitoring currently running services.

Grid resources include compute elements, storage elements, and network elements. Compute elements are the base level computational hardware available to the grid. For the Acxiom grid, like many other grids, a compute element is a rack-mounted commodity server running some number of Intel-architecture processors. Storage elements are, from a hardware perspective, more varied than compute elements, but we can logically think of the storage elements as physical units providing data storage. Network elements are primarily network switches.

One of the main functions of Grid Management is to allow new resources to be defined to the grid and then provide the initial provisioning of those resources. In general, the provisioning and management of storage elements and network elements is relatively static compared with compute elements, so we will focus on the provisioning, control, and monitoring of services running on compute elements here.

The first task to provisioning a new compute element is to install a base operating system on the computer. In the Acxiom grid, the compute elements have a local disk drive and the primary purpose of this drive is simply to hold the base operating system and allow the machine to boot. Assuming that the compute elements do not come preinstalled from the computer vendor, the machines are configured to network-boot when powered on and then connect to an image service running within the grid. The image service provides the base image compatible with the compute element hardware. The maturing of CPU virtualization technologies has opened more options for software provisioning. It is now possible for the base provisioning of a hypervisor rather than a full operating system. Many of the more dynamic provisioning concepts are the same for either implementation of the bootstrap environment.

Once the compute element is bootable, it can be assigned as a platform for services. Software and data provisioning a particular service can either position the software and data directly on the compute element's local disks or mount the data and software from a file server. There are advantages to each method, but with CDI services it often advantageous to mount data and software rather than directly install. CDI services often have significant data backing the services. It is expensive and time consuming to propagate that data to individual nodes. This becomes particularly important if service instances are dynamically deployed to meet service demand since the data transfer time may dramatically affect the time to start a new instance.

Installing service software directly to the node may have similar, though less pronounced, effects. For example, software provisioning must be fast when compute elements are dynamically assigned to relatively short-lived (when compared with CDI services) jobs as discussed later in this chapter. However, the challenges with software provisioning are more often a challenge of selecting the granularity of the software distribution and managing the "stacking" of software to create a deployable service. Three common strategies for "stacking" software to deploy a service are (1) a native service deployment strategy, (2) a container deployment strategy, and (3) a virtual machine deployment strategy.

A native service strategy deploys software on top of the base operating system on the compute element. Regardless of whether the service software is physically installed on the compute element or mounted prior to service implementation, the service software is "stacked" or layered on top of the base operating system software resident on the compute element. The advantage of this method is that it may minimize the need for discrete deployment packages because a given service may, for example, be able to be deployed on a number of distinct base operating systems (e.g., different operating system update levels or different hardware-specific configurations). The disadvantage is that the software stack must be consistent and the software provisioning process may have to enforce this consistency. Also, this model may mean that the application services are aware they are running under a grid operating environment and introduce some dependency upon that environment for the startup, shutdown, and configuration of that service.

A container service strategy packages an application deployment container (e.g., a J2EE environment) as a grid service that is instantiated and managed via the Grid Management interfaces. Application services (e.g., CDI services) are then provisioned into the container, using either Grid Management services or, more likely, using tools directly provided by the container itself. This eliminates some consistency issues and also insulates the application service from the specifics of the grid operating environment. The disadvantage is that operational management of the environment must deal with the conceptual and implementation details of running services within a cascading set of containers (e.g., a base operating system running a guest virtual machine which is in turn running an application container hosting an application service).

We can collapse the cascaded container strategy by deploying a complete virtual machine. In a complete virtual machine deployment, the stacking problem is largely eliminated since the virtual machine contains the complete deployment of the entire software stack (indeed, the underlying data supporting the service may also be included in the virtual machine image). However, the tradeoff for this simplicity is the complexity of management of a potentially large number of virtual machine images.

For CDI services, provisioning issues are primarily an issue for service startup. Since CDI services are typically relatively long lived, any of the provisioning schemes above are probably viable. However, later in this chapter, we will see that dynamic provisioning schemes become much more important when CDI jobs run on the same grid infrastructure as the services.

Once a service is provisioned, the Grid Management software must provide some way to configure the execution-time parameters for an application service. The parameters to be configured are service specific, but an example of this type of configuration is setting the service name to distinguish between development, test, and production versions of the service, all of which are potentially running in the same grid.

Once configured, the Grid Management provides some mechanisms for control of the application services. The degree of the control depends primarily on the sophistication of the application service and the degree to which that service is aware that it is running on a grid. At minimum, Grid Management must be able to invoke the start script for the application service and probably an associated script to stop the service.

Once running, the Grid Management software monitors active services. At minimum, this monitoring is able to determine if the specific service is up or down, but more sophisticated monitoring may be provided. For example, the Grid Management software may monitor the CPU, memory, and network usage on the physical servers supporting the service. The Grid Management software may then dynamically create new service instances on other nodes if the load on the original machines exceeds a defined threshold.

It is important to note that the Grid Management software provides management of a collection of related services as a single entity. As described above, CDI services may require many physical servers and component services to implement a single logical service. For example, the logical AbiliTec service is implemented as a set of director nodes, providing clients a geographically-independent service interface, and a set of geography-specific nodes. The Grid Management software supports monitoring all these services as a single logical AbiliTec service. Similarly, a grid administrator can start and stop the entire logical AbiliTec service as a single logical service. The capability to interact at lower levels services also exists. For example, it is possible to start a particular geography-specific service to address a spike of activity in that geography and have that new service instance join a running instance of the overall logical service.

7.3 Grid-Based Batch Processing

7.3.1 Workflow Grid

With the deployment of the Services Grid, virtually all of Acxiom's CDI services and transactional delivery systems were running in a grid environment and being managed by the Grid Management infrastructure software. However, other critical parts of the CDI process, such as data storage and the batch processing platforms (i.e., the client programs reading and writing records and calling the CDI services), continued to run on traditional single machines. Prior to their implementation on the grid, the throughput of the CDI services was the bottleneck for batch processing, but the "gang of machines" implementation of the CDI services greatly improved the throughput on the services to the point that the CPUs on the batch delivery engines were now the bottlenecks. This new bottleneck had to be removed in order to continue to improve the throughput of individual jobs. The approach to addressing this bottleneck was to use the same strategy that had worked for services, namely to exploit the relatively low price commodity hardware and process work in an embarrassingly parallel fashion on both the batch delivery system and the CDI services.

Like many CDI batch implementations, the Acxiom batch delivery systems are implemented on either home-grown or commercial Extract-Transformation-Load (ETL) systems. There are many commercial ETL engines, but conceptually they all approach batch CDI processing the same way. A batch job is defined and executed as an ETL flow, which is a series of data transformations that are coordinated by the ETL engine. The terminology differs by ETL engine, but we will refer to a step in the flow as an "operator." The ETL engine provides a set of standard operators for common functions. For example, the standard operators handle most of the routine data sources and sinks associated with ETL processing, such as operators for reading and writing to flat files, extracting and loading data into many commercial databases, etc. The standard operators also provide common data transformation functions such as sorts, joins, and simple data manipulation logic. In addition, ETL engines also allow users to create custom operators. These custom operators allow programmers to create operators that are too application-specific or complex to be implemented from the standard operators. In particular, these custom operators can be the clients to specialized CDI services running in the Services Grid.

Most ETL engines allow a given CDI flow to be parallelized across multiple CPUs within a single physical server and potentially across multiple physical servers. Usually, the set of servers available for this parallel processing is statically defined in the ETL engine configuration. The ETL engine will manage work in this environment, but the servers in the ETL pool typically must be dedicated to a single governing ETL engine instance.   Operators within a flow execute as separate processes or threads.

Figure 7.3 shows an example of this environment.   The ETL flow runs in a Delivery Engine on a single machine.   The specific operators ("Reader," "A," "B," "C," and "Writer") implement the CDI flow.   The Reader operator reads the source data and the Writer writes the output file resulting from the application of transformations A, B, and C to the data passing through the flow.   Multiple instances of the data transformation operators are executed in parallel in the flow and the Reader has the responsibility of distributing data records to each of the four streams of execution.   In this figure, data storage is represented as being within the Delivery Engine which implies disks that are physically connected to the Delivery Engine server, but the data source and sink storage could also be a network file system such as NFS.

The data transformation operators may execute completely within the Delivery Engine or may call external services running in the Services Grid.   Figure 7.4 shows an example of CDI services ("B", "C", "D", and "X") running on servers within the Services Grid.   The Grid Management interfaces were used to map the servers to the specific services.   Within the Delivery Engine, operator A runs completely within the Delivery Engine, but operators B and C make services calls to the corresponding CDI service running in the Services Grid.   Note that for clarity of illustration, Figure 7.4 only shows connecting lines for some one pair of clients and services.

There may be many instances of the CDI services running in the Services Grid and the associated operator chooses which instance to invoke either implicitly (e.g., through transparent network level load balancers) or explicitly (e.g., selection via a Naming Service).   If one of the CDI service instances fails, the clients may implicitly or explicitly be transferred to another CDI service instance.   Many CDI services are stateless and transfer on failure is relatively straightforward.   The problem is a bit more challenging with stateful servers.   Of course, there are potentially many services also running in the Services Grid (e.g., D and X) that are not used by the particular ETL flow.

While servers could be dedicated to a particular ETL instance, in a large data center with multiple users and perhaps multiple tenants, it is often more efficient to pool a large number of machines and make them dynamically available to many ETL instances at run-time for a particular CDI batch job.   Using a pool of resources, when a CDI job is submitted, the scheduling system can analyze the contents of the flow, the input data consumed by that flow, and the throughput requirements for that flow, then map the appropriate number of compute elements from the pool of compute elements to the flow in order to meet the throughput requirements of the specific job.   This not only allows dynamic matching of resources to the needs of a particular job, but also allows data center policies to be enforced at the scheduler for all jobs.

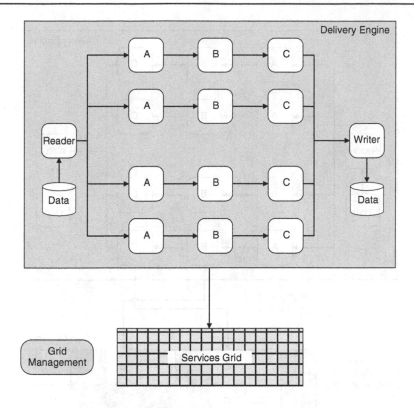

Fig. 7.3. External Batch Delivery Engine with Services Grid

Fortunately, some ETL engines provide customization points in the flow submission process to tailor the flow invocation process. Requests to start jobs within a given ETL instance can be intercepted at this customization point and a script can then allocate compute resources to the job just prior to starting the job.

Acxiom created a special resource manager grid service to support dynamic acquisition of compute elements. This service runs on a set of compute elements that form the dynamic compute pool. We refer to this service as the Workflow Grid Resource Reservation Service or, more simply, as the Workflow Grid. Technically, the Workflow Grid is simply another service running in the Services Grid, but because of the dynamic allocation of compute elements to a specific job at run-time, we conceptually separate the Workflow Grid from the Services Grid.

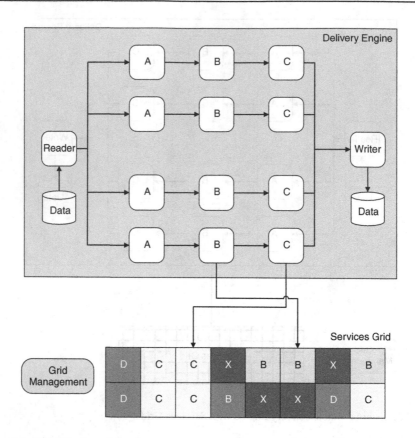

Fig. 7.4. CDI Clients and Services

The process of defining and executing a job using both the Workflow Grid and the Services Grid is illustrated in Figure 7.5. A user first defines a CDI flow using a user interface. This interface is typically provided by the ETL vendor and supports a flow-chart metaphor for defining the CDI flow. When the user submits the flow, we exploit the customization points of the ETL engine to intercept the request and send the request to a data center wide scheduler. The scheduler analyzes the job definition then requests the appropriate set of nodes from the Workflow Grid on behalf of the submitting user. The Workflow Grid resource manager identifies which compute elements are to be assigned for the job and sets up the security environment on these compute elements so that only the original requesting user may execute work on those compute elements. The resource manager also mounts any file systems listed in the allocation request. These mounts serve two purposes. The most obvious use is to make any input data required by the CDI flow available to the allocated compute elements. The second use is to dynamically provision software to the allocated compute elements. This provides a low overhead way to provide job-specific software to compute elements at runtime.

After setting up the security environment and mounting any required file systems, the allocation service then returns the selected set of compute elements to the scheduler. The scheduler picks one of the returned compute nodes and runs a configuration agent on that compute element. The configuration agent constructs the specific run-time environment for the ETL engine, then invokes the actual ETL engine with this job-specific configuration. Using this configuration and the defined flow, the ETL engine executes the job, which typically results in the ETL engine exploiting the other allocated compute elements to execute the flow. Specifically, the ETL engine is responsible for launching flow instances on the allocated nodes and flowing data through the distributed flow. Note that the ETL engine is unaware of the dynamic allocation of nodes in this environment. The ETL engine simply sees a set of resources available to it at run-time and is not aware of whether those resources were statically or dynamically provisioned.

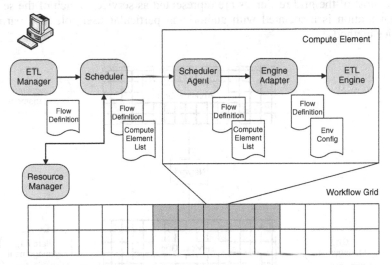

Fig. 7.5. CDI Flow Invocation

When the job completes, the scheduler's agent notifies the scheduler, which then releases the reserved node back the Workflow Grid resource manager. The resource manager removes any vestige of the previous user, removes the security authorization for that user from the compute elements, then returns the compute elements back to the pool for reallocation.

Using this implementation, we can run a complete CDI job within the grid environment. Data access and simple transformations are performed as operators running on the compute elements allocated from the Workflow Grid. In addition, operators in the CDI flow can also invoke CDI services in the Services Grid.

Providing this dynamically allocated execution environment for the ETL flows implies some additions to the grid operating environment over that required simply to support CDI services (see Figure 7.6). The Workflow Grid joins the Services Grid to provide the dynamically allocated compute resources. The entire environment is managed using the same Grid Management capabilities discussed in connection with Services Grid. A new part of the grid operating environment, Execution Management, provides all the capabilities to schedule, monitor, and control jobs. The dominant element in Execution Management is the set of schedulers used to manage work in the data center. By introducing one or more data center schedulers, we can also map resources to the needs of a particular job and enforce data center policies for all submitted work.

Running user-defined ETL flows that directly access user data also requires an expanded set of security services for the authentication and authorization of users and their delegates. This allows for jobs to run securely under the security context of the submitting user. Security Management includes services providing a repository for user authentication and authorization (e.g., an LDAP cluster) and also mechanisms to allow security administrators to manage users and permissions. Since most of the grid resources are represented as services, much of the security administration is associated with authorizing particular user roles for particular service methods.

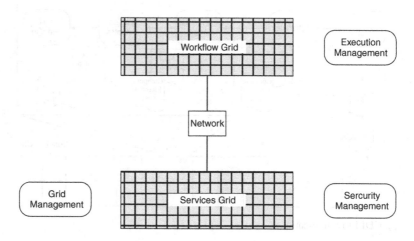

Fig. 7.6. Grid-based CDI Computation Environment

Naturally, this is actually only a subset of the Security Management functions. A full discussion of security functions associated with managing a grid is beyond the scope of this chapter, but some examples of functions provided by Security Management include mechanisms to harden compute elements, management of network containment (e.g., firewall configurations around and within the grid), intrusion detection, software validation, access and action logging, data access authorization, data transfer authorization, and mechanisms to control the input and output destinations for data transfer. Unlike the more general grid community, particularly the academic grid community, a CDI Grid is typically completely contained within a company, so there is often less emphasis on inter-organization security and more on internal security, particularly on the threat of inappropriate data access or use by a trusted insider. Inter-organization communication is usually limited to invocation of a specific set of CDI services (e.g., demographic enhancement) from a trusted business partner through a well defined published interface and is thus more easily contained and certified.

It is important to note that while we logically distinguish between the Services Grid, Workflow Grid, and the management services, all services actually execute upon the same grid fabric formed by the compute, storage, and network elements. The logical distinctions are conceptual and the actual mapping of all these services to resources is done through Grid Management.

7.3.2 I/O Constraints

With the construction of the Workflow Grid and the integration of this resource pool with the scheduler services in Execution Management, we are now able to allocate a number of compute elements to the client side of CDI flow processing. Coupled with the Services Grid implementation of CDI services, most computation bottlenecks in a given CDI flow can now be addressed by allocating a sufficient number of compute resources to the job. Once the computation bottleneck is removed, I/O becomes the governing bottleneck.

In particular, after the implementation of the common CDI services in the Services Grid and the ETL transformation flows in the Workflow Grid, reading and writing the data associated with CDI flow became the limiting factor on job throughput. Most CDI work is record based and is inherently parallel since each transformation in the CDI flow executes on a given record without regard to others. Similarly, group-based CDI (e.g., processing all the records about individuals within a household) can also be viewed as inherently parallel if the unit of work is defined as the collection of records comprising a group. However, ETL engines often distribute data to transformation streams by having all data pass through a single distributing reader (see Figure 7.4). Furthermore, a single collecting writer produces the resulting output files. Together, the Workflow Grid and Services Grid fully parallelize all of the execution parts of the flow. Data flows through multiple compute elements in the Workflow Grid due to parallelization by the ETL engine and each operator in the flow may have independent connections to compute elements in the Services Grid. However, reading and writing remain serialized (Figure 7.7).

A potentially better scheme is for each stream of execution in the ETL flow to have its own reader and writer (Figure 7.8). This can be done on a single computer with direct attached storage by creating a new form of Reader and Writer that reads a specified subset of the file (e.g., given n transformation streams, each stream computes the starting point of its nth and reads or writes just that section). However, this scheme does not work with local disks on a given server when some of the CDI streams are executing on other servers. In particular, the server providing the data storage may become an I/O bottleneck since it must forward data to all servers involved in the flow.

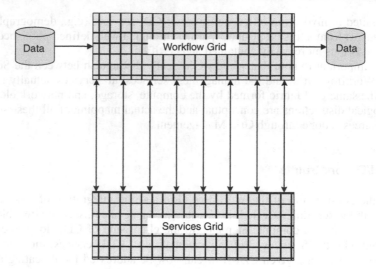

Fig. 7.7. Parallel Transformation Flows and Service Calls

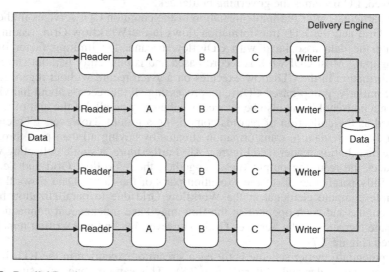

Fig. 7.8. Parallel Readers and Writers

We can allow each independent stream to directly read the data if the data storage is provided by a distributed file system. The distributed file system servers provide data storage and data access for all servers involved in the CDI flow. Unfortunately, traditional distributed file systems, such as NFS, may only move the bottleneck to the file system server.

To address the performance challenges associated with traditional distributed file systems, a number of parallel distributed file systems have been created. The main idea behind all these parallel file systems is to spread data across a number of hardware resources, both storage and compute. Many client machines can access the data simultaneously, but the parallel nature of the file system implementation means that clients are often accessing files or portions of files that are served by distinct hardware resources.

Unfortunately, while parallel file systems are very good at providing access to large files, particularly when accessed sequentially, they are often not as well suited to other uses, where traditional file systems excel. To get the best of both worlds, it is useful to think of storage resources as a grid of services. We refer to such a collection of storage resources as a Data Grid.

7.3.3 Data Grid

A Data Grid is a logical file system used to potentially store unstructured and structured data. The Data Grid does not hold relational databases, but stores most everything else. Of particular importance to the CDI process, the Data Grid is typically used to hold all data not directly associated with the world model and associated analytic data. As such, the Data Grid holds data files being received from the outside world, any intermediate files produced as part of the CDI process, historical files, etc. We usually refer to the files in the Data Grid as "flat files" meaning that to the repository these files are viewed and stored as a sequence of bytes, although they may have some additional structure inside the file contents (e.g., XML tags) that provide additional logical structure when processing the files.

The Data Grid is viewed as a single file system, but is actually constructed of a set of one or more independent file systems. There may be multiple file system types represented in the set. For example, a Data Grid may have both Network File System (NFS) and Parallel Virtual File System (PVFS) file systems as component file systems (see Figure 7.9). All the component file systems are logically integrated at the file system client by mounting the component file systems under a single directory on the client machines (e.g., by the Workflow Grid resource manager at job invocation). From the perspective of the applications running on the client machines, the Data Grid looks like a single directory tree.

One of the reasons for using multiple independent file systems rather than a single monolithic file system is for the CDI processing system to survive loss of any single file system. Independent file systems can fail without affecting other branches of the logical Data Grid file system.

Depending upon the particular file system technology employed, the component file systems may be fault tolerant in their own right, but this is not necessarily the case. Also, even fault tolerant systems may be subject to failure in some disaster scenarios. Naturally, if a component file system does go down, data on that file system is unavailable from that file system until the file system returns to service. For this reason, important data stored on the Data Grid may be replicated across multiple component file systems within the Data Grid and perhaps also stored in some off-line media (e.g., tape). Also, since the component file systems are independent, different component file systems may be deployed at different physical sites and replication may occur between sites to limit the impact of losing a given site. For example, in the configuration shown in Figure 7.9, the independent file systems comprising the Data Grid are geographically spread across two sites and data may be replicated across file systems to provide redundancy for disaster recovery.

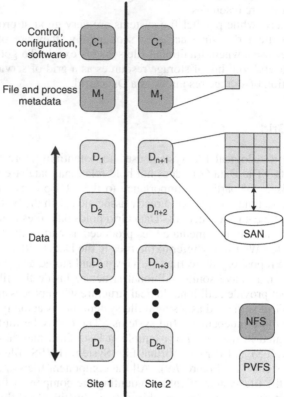

Fig. 7.9. Data Grid Implementation

A second reason for using multiple independent component file systems is to allow the Data Grid to provide different qualities of service for different data. Put another way, allowing multiple component file systems and only restricting the implementation of the file system to the fact that it must be mountable across a network allows the Data Grid to deploy specialized file systems for particular tasks. This is particularly important if we want to exploit the power of a grid on CDI processing.

In a CDI system, some files in the Data Grid have usage characteristics consistent with the majority of files on traditional computer systems (e.g., files are small, are infrequently accessed, etc.). For example, CDI job definitions and transformation configuration files often have these qualities. On the other hand, many of the data files processed in a CDI environment have characteristics more like data files collected in HPC applications (files are very large, are typically processed from start to finish, etc.).

In the example Data Grid (Figure 7.9), both NFS and PVFS are used to provide file system support. An NFS file system is used to hold control files, configuration files, and software. A separate NFS system holds file and process metadata. NFS is well suited to providing occasional access to these types of small files. The NFS file systems are implemented as a single compute element with on-board storage since the performance requirements associated with the types of data placed in this example on these systems does not require high throughput.

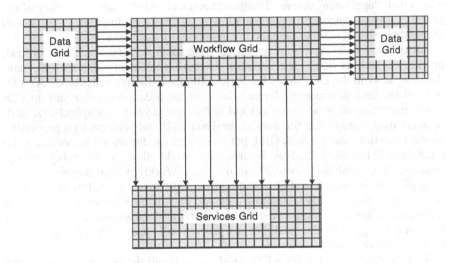

Fig. 7.10. Parallel Data Access

PVFS systems are used to hold the data files arriving from the outside world and intermediate or output files resulting from CDI processing. The PVFS file systems are implemented as a set of compute elements attached to a SAN. This allows PVFS to partition data across many physical disk drives (in the SAN) and support concurrent file system access by many client compute elements through multiple I/O servers (i.e., the 16 node PVFS cluster shown in the figure). This provides for much higher data throughput for I/O bound CDI flows. Consider our earlier Figure 7.7, where a single compute element supported a file server. With a parallel file system, the logical data paths now look like Figure 7.10.

7.3.4 Database Grid

The Data Grid houses most of the non-relational data within the CDI Grid. The Data Grid is well suited to managing and processing the very large volumes of source data input into a large CDI system. However, the reason for performing the CDI processing is to effectively build a repository of information that represents our model of the real world. The intent is to use this information in decision support, analytical, or campaign management systems to effect positive change in the real world. Commercial software suites are usually used for this task and most of those commercial systems expect to access the information from a relational database.

Today, the relational databases holding this information are deployed on a wide range of server platforms. Many are deployed on general purpose computers under a commercial database management system. Others are deployed on "database appliances," which are special purpose hardware and software systems that provide RDBMS capabilities, but are advertised as simpler to install and maintain due to their "appliance" nature. Database vendors have also taken a variety of approaches to the database implementation (e.g., clustered implementations with shared disk, shared nothing architectures, in-memory databases, etc.).

All of these database implementations have multiple access methods to load, update, and extract data. The common database implementations all have standard operators in the ETL suites for performing these routine functions. As a result, all of these database implementations can be a data source or sink to CDI flows running in the Workflow Grid and/or the Services Grid. A hybrid CDI environment may manage flat file data in the Data Grid and perform CDI processing on the Workflow and Services Grid, but load or update the model information into a database. The ideal database environment would allow the flexibility and dynamic scaling capabilities available in the Data, Workflow, and Services Grid to be applied to the database. For example, it would be useful to allow compute resources to be dynamically added to a database implementation when needed, then reallocated when not. Some of the "shared nothing" database implementations are beginning to approach this goal, but the process still lacks the flexibility of other parts of the CDI system.

To complete our vision for a CDI Grid, we will call the portion of system that provides relational storage the Database Grid. Like the independent file systems in the Data Grid, the Database Grid may be composed of many independent, but logically affiliated database implementations. Similarly, like the parallel file systems in the Data Grid, some database implementations in the Database Grid may exploit multiple compute and storage elements to improve performance and redundancy. Current database implementations may not yet provide this flexibility in exploiting the grid infrastructure, but we expect database implementations to continue to evolve toward this model.

7.3.5 Data Management

Distinct component file systems in the Data Grid may provide different storage quality of service. Similarly, databases in the Database Grid may be tuned for a particular usage (e.g., data analytics, transaction processing). The general issue of matching storage quality of service to the particular data is a challenging problem that requires not only the appropriate file system and database technology to provide the needed quality of service, but also some mechanism to assist human administrators in controlling the placement and movement of files within the Data Grid and the Database Grid.

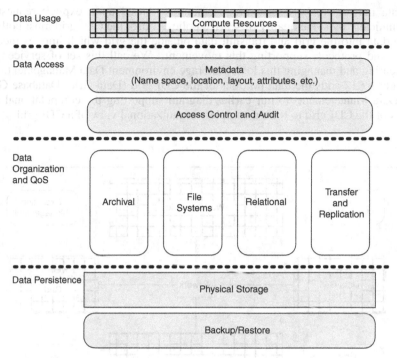

Fig. 7.11. View of Storage Virtualization

Figure 7.11 shows a logical view of the storage virtualization and storage quality of service problem. The ideal situation is that from the perspectives of compute resources, all storage is viewed as an undifferentiated pool of storage and all data resides in that storage. Access to that data is managed and achieved consistently. There may be multiple ways to access the data (e.g., fopen, SQL, etc.), but metadata associated with the data (location, layout, etc.) are accessed and managed consistently. In addition, all access control and audit logging is managed consistently. This provides a view of a "virtual" storage system with logical, apparent characteristics created from the physical storage resources underlying the virtual illusion.

Underneath these logically consistent metadata layers, the storage containers providing the various data organization and quality of service characteristics are implemented. We refer to this as the organization layer because part of the quality of service characteristics is how the data is logically organized (e.g., relational, read-write flat files, read-only archival flat files, etc.). This organization layer is largely a software layer (e.g., the file system protocol implementation) running on some of the compute elements in the grid. The physical data is stored on some storage elements in the grid. Both the compute elements and the storage elements also provide elements of the overall quality of service provided by the virtualized storage system.

Data may move between storage containers based upon explicit request or automatically by some quality of service policy. Also, the CDI grid must both receive data into the grid and transmit data outside the grid which implies mechanisms and protocols supporting this movement. We call this set of services implementing and managing this logical storage environment Data Management.

Figure 7.12 adds the data portions of the CDI grid (Data Grid, Database Grid, and Data Management) to our earlier diagram supporting the computational elements of the CDI grid to form a complete organizational view of a CDI grid.

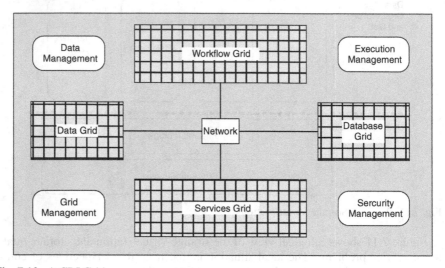

Fig. 7.12. A CDI Grid

7.4 Conclusion

This chapter has discussed the logical organization of a grid built to support the tasks surrounding Customer Data Integration (CDI) and particularly around the data transformation tasks for the very large data volumes common for large scale CDI systems. We have referred to such a grid as a CDI Grid. We have used the evolution of the CDI Grid at Acxiom Corporation to motivate many of the important parts of a CDI Grid. The Acxiom CDI Grid maps to the logical architecture in Fig. 7.12 and has been in production since 2001. As of 2008, this grid routinely transforms more than 1.5 trillion records per month through a variety of CDI process flows.

Several of the other chapters of this book focus in more detail on some aspects of a CDI Grid. Our discussion of the Data Grid in this chapter introduced the importance of file systems in achieving high throughput. Chapter 8 "Parallel File

Systems" by Ross, Carns, and Metheny gives a more detailed description of the challenges associated with creating a parallel file system and some of the design approaches taken to address these challenges. Our discussion of the execution environment for a CDI flow in this chapter hints at the complexity of running work in a distributed environment. Managing the service level agreements, capacity, and performance of such a complex data center is very challenging. Chapter 9 "Performance Modeling of Enterprise Grids" by Hoffman, et al. describes their work on creating an analytical model of a CDI Grid and characterizing the associated workload in order to provide data center managers a tool to efficiently predict and manage all parts of a CDI Grid. Finally, most of the elements of Figure 7.12 have been discussed at least briefly in the chapter, but it is important to point out that exploiting the full power of this distributed environment is dependent upon the network infrastructure connecting all the compute and storage elements. Network performance is critical to the operation of a CDI Grid. Duan's Chapter 10 on switch performance goes into more depth on this fundamental issue.

7.5 Exercises

1. Discuss the distinctions, if any, between "grid computing" and "distributed computing."
2. Discuss the relative advantages and disadvantages of performing CDI work on a grid rather than on a single symmetric multiprocessor.
3. Some CDI processes are record oriented. For example, standardizing postal addresses in a file can be done independently for each record in the file. Other CDI processes are group oriented. For example, entity resolution must often compare collections of records to determine which records represent the same entity. Discuss how whether a given CDI process is record or group oriented might influence how that process was implemented on a CDI grid.
4. Computer and data security is sometimes described as a set of perimeters of defense. Consider Figure 7.12 and discuss the appropriate points and mechanisms for security control in a CDI grid.
5. The misuse of data by a person authorized to access that data is sometimes described as the "insider threat." Discuss the challenges with managing the insider threat in a CDI grid and ways to mitigate the risk associated with this threat.
6. This chapter describes logical CDI services that are implemented as many complementary actual services spread across multiple compute elements. Discuss the relative advantages and disadvantages of this implementation pattern.
7. Describe how CDI services and data may be deployed on a CDI grid to improve the fault tolerance and disaster recovery attributes of the overall system.

8. ETL processes often operate on very large amounts of data. Describe how use of a CDI grid can improve the execution time of such processes.
9. Discuss how ETL environments can detect compute element failures during a job. Describe how ETL environments can adapt to and/or mitigate the impact of compute element failures during a job.
10. Describe the resources that job schedulers should consider when scheduling work into a CDI grid. Describe how resource reservation and consumption might be managed in a job scheduler.
11. Operational management of a CDI grid is complex because of the large number of component resources (e.g., compute elements, storage elements, network elements, file systems, services, etc.). Discuss the types or categories of management tools needed in such an environment.
12. Discuss how the virtualization of compute, storage, and network elements might influence the configuration and management of a CDI grid.
13. Discuss the relative advantages and disadvantages of flat file storage to relational storage for CDI processing.
14. Describe some of the challenges associated with implementing a relational database management system that can exploit the resources of a CDI grid, particularly in dynamically allocating and releasing resources such as compute elements.

8 Parallel File Systems

Robert Ross[1], Philip Carns[1], and David Metheny[2]

[1] *Mathematics and Computer Science Division, Argonne National Laboratory*
Argonne, IL, USA

[2] *Acxiom Corporation*
Conway, AR, USA

8.1 Introduction

The success of a CDI Grid is dependent upon the design of its storage infrastructure. As seen in Chapter 7, processing in this environment revolves around the simultaneous movement and transformation of data on many compute elements. Effective storage solutions combine hardware and software to meet these needs. The storage hardware selected must provide enough raw throughput for the expected workloads. Typical storage hardware architectures also often provide some redundancy to help in creating a fault tolerant system. Storage software, specifically file systems, must organize this storage hardware into a single logical space, provide efficient mechanisms for accessing that space, and hide common hardware failures from compute elements.

Parallel file systems (PFSes) are a particular class of file systems that are well suited to this role. This chapter will describe a variety of PFS architectures, but the key feature that classifies all of them as parallel file systems is their ability to support true parallel I/O. Parallel I/O in this context means that many compute elements can read from or write to the same files concurrently without significant performance degradation and without data corruption. This is the critical element that differentiates PFSes from more traditional network file systems, and it is this characteristic that makes PFSes an integral part of an effective CDI Grid.

While databases play a significant role in data engineering for the grid, they are not appropriate for all types of data. PFSes are particularly well-suited to storing large amounts of structured data that can reside within flat files. This type of data can be dynamically distributed and processed across almost any number of compute elements by simply assigning each compute element a unique portion of the file. Compute elements can then be added incrementally to increase the processing rate. This corresponds well with CDI processes that will be discussed in greater

Y. Chan et al. (eds.), *Data Engineering*, International Series in Operations
Research & Management Science 132, DOI 10.1007/978-1-4419-0176-7_8,
© Springer Science+Business Media, LLC 2010

detail in the next section. In these cases, the raw bandwidth of the storage system is more important than the latency of individual transactions. Databases, on the other hand, perform much more efficiently for transactional operations and are therefore better suited for accessing or analyzing information distilled from the data after it has been processed using a CDI Grid.

The remainder of this chapter is organized as follows. Section 8.2 presents background on the characteristics and access patterns of data found on CDI Grids. Section 8.3 provides an overview of the basic concepts of PFSes. Section 8.4 presents specific design challenges that must be met in order for a file system to be successful in a CDI Grid environment. Section 8.5 presents four file system case studies to illustrate the diversity of existing file system architectures.

8.2 Commercial Data and Access Patterns

Chapter 7 introduced the concept of a data grid as storage for almost all CDI grid data. This includes historical files, temporary files used during CDI processing, data ingested from external sources, and metadata. A data grid may contain more than one file system. Multiple file systems may be used for organizational reasons, to meet capacity requirements, or to take advantage of different file system characteristics for different types of data.

The largest files stored in the data grid range from gigabytes to terabytes in size. Examples include national credit records, retail transaction records from a large company, and cellular telephone call records. In each of these cases, the files are organized using a highly structured pattern of records and fields. The records are stored in a fixed size throughout the file in order to simplify the format and make it easier to process in parallel.

CDI applications typically process an entire file and perform an independent transform on each record or group of records. The file can therefore be divided among multiple compute elements for parallel processing as shown in Fig. 8.1. In order to make the most efficient use of a PFS, multiple compute elements should simultaneously read and/or write the data rather than funneling I/O through a single compute element bottleneck. The most straightforward way to accomplish this is to have each process directly read and/or write the records that it is responsible for. The number of compute elements should be adaptable at run time in order to meet business needs or fit available resources. Often applications simply assign M/N records to each compute element, where M is the total number of records and N is the number of compute elements. Load balancing, expected output format, file system characteristics, and other factors could motivate alternative algorithms.

A data grid will also contain small files. One example would be nightly updates of transaction records from a retailer. While the complete historical record for a major retail chain could be quite large, daily updates from a particular franchise will be much smaller. Updates such as these will likely be staged into individual files for organizational purposes until they are integrated as part of a CDI transform. A second example of a small file type would be a *layout* file. A layout describes the organization of records within a data file. It may provide labels that describe fields within each record or indicate the size of each record. Layouts are stored separately from the actual data file in order to avoid disrupting the natural pattern of the file. The layout files could be stored in an independent database, but storing them on the same file system simplifies organization by keeping the layout logically close to the data that it describes. A final example of small files within a CDI data grid would be configuration or control files that are used by the CDI process or other applications.

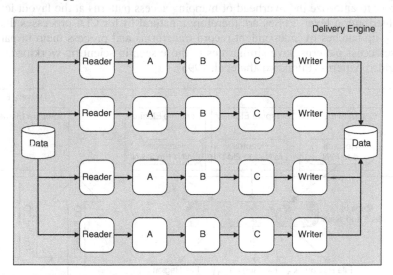

Fig. 8.1. Parallel I/O and transformation

The smaller files in a data grid are not normally read in parallel. This might be because there is no throughput advantage in dividing such a small file, or because this type of data is only needed by one process at a time. It is therefore desirable for a PFS to be able to perform efficiently for brief serialized accesses to small files in addition to sustained parallel streaming of large files. A data grid may elect to use a more traditional network file system such as NFS to serve this small file role, rather than using a parallel file system for all file types.

8.2.1 Large File Access Patterns

Although the data grid will contain both large and small files, the large files that are accessed in parallel account for the majority of the I/O traffic. These files offer the best opportunity to take advantage of a PFS. Figure 8.2 illustrates how a typical CDI application access pattern (such as generated by the readers and writers in Figure 8.1) is broken down to storage device accesses within a PFS. As outlined earlier, each compute element is assigned to read M/N records within the data. The file layout is used to determine the size of the records and map them into file regions with specific offsets and sizes. These file regions then are read from the file system in parallel. The file system uses its own internal mapping, known as a *distribution*, to then determine exactly which underlying storage devices will provide the data. Reading from multiple compute elements in parallel allows the file system to leverage the aggregate throughput of several network links and underlying storage devices. Furthermore, reading in large sequential chunks from each compute element allows the file system to stream enough data with each operation in order to amortize the overhead of mapping access patterns at the layout level or the distribution level. PFSes are therefore a natural fit for CDI processes that can divide up batches of independent record transforms and process them in parallel. These access patterns have similarities to those seen in scientific workloads, such as strided patterns (Purakayastha et al. 1995).

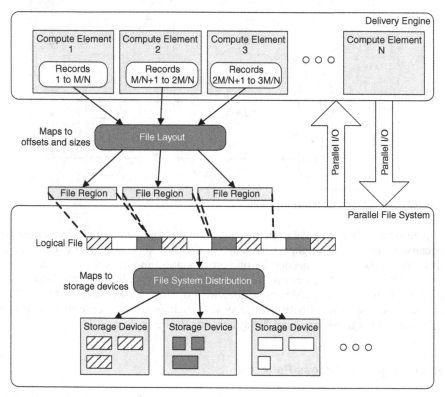

Fig. 8.2. Mapping access patterns to storage devices for parallel I/O

8.2.2 File System Interfaces

The interface used for reading and writing data may vary considerably depending on the application, and this can have a significant impact on how the access patterns are viewed by the file system. Some applications may elect to use a POSIX file system interface in order to allow for the most portability across different file system types. Others may be optimized to use interfaces such as MPI-IO that are designed specifically for parallel I/O. MPI-IO is an I/O interface designed as an extension to the Message Passing Interface (MPI), the de facto standard programming model for writing message-passing parallel programs. MPI is commonly used in scientific computing for writing parallel simulation codes that need to efficiently communicate and perform I/O at very large scales. MPI has seen limited use in commercial settings outside computational science so far, but it may play a more important role as grids grow in number of compute elements. For MPI applications, the MPI-IO interface provides the ability to organize I/O by groups of processes through *collective I/O* calls and allows applications to describe *noncontiguous I/O* operations, such as the strided pattern mentioned previously, as a single I/O operation, improving efficiency in many cases.

Another example file system interface is MapReduce, which has become popular in the last few years due to its use by Google (Dean and Ghemawat 2004). MapReduce provides a model for performing processing on large datasets in an independent manner (the *map* operation), followed by a combining phase (the *reduce*). MapReduce is a significant departure from standard file system APIs and requires that applications be written to use this API and to manage some unusual scenarios that may occur in concurrent I/O situations. However, it appears to be very effective for large-scale data processing.

8.3 Basics of Parallel File Systems

As discussed in the introduction to this chapter, one of the main tasks of a PFS is organizing storage hardware into a single logical space. Typically the PFS presents a single "name space" to users, a tree organization in which directories and files are stored. This is the same organization that users are accustomed to seeing on local file systems, such as their workstations or laptops. The data that makes up this name space is then distributed over storage elements. Small files are often simply assigned to a single storage element. Large files are typically split up into regions of contiguous data, and these regions are spread across storage elements so that many disks and network links may be used concurrently to access different regions of the file. The algorithm used to perform the distribution of these regions varies widely from one PFS to another. Information about the files and the name space, called *metadata*, must also be stored. Examples of this type of information include the owner, permissions, and time stamp of a file. PFSes may also store internal metadata that is necessary to organize and coordinate access to data. Some PFSes store this information separately on dedicated "metadata servers," while others simply distribute this data on the same storage elements on which file data is stored.

Figure 8.3 depicts an example file system and name space distribution. Users of the file system, the file system *clients*, run on compute elements and access storage elements over a network of some type. In this example, individual directories and file metadata are placed on different storage elements to help balance the metadata load. Likewise, large files, such as national credit screening files, are also distributed to help balance I/O load. Small files, such as incremental input of new customer accounts, are stored on single storage elements.

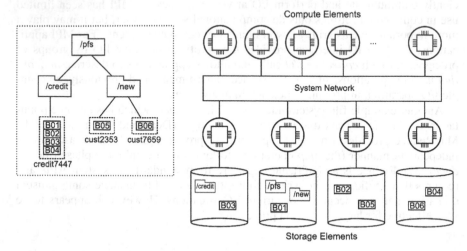

Fig. 8.3. In a PFS, name space components are spread across storage elements

8.3.1 Common Storage System Hardware

Storage element hardware varies widely, with some systems using commodity components and other systems requiring specialized hardware. Covering the specifics of this range of storage hardware is beyond the scope of this text; however, there are some broad categories of storage hardware that are commonly deployed as part of a storage system solution.

Commodity disks are standard consumer grade IDE, SATA, or SCSI hard drives. Commodity disks are inexpensive and can provide high throughput when used in parallel across many servers, but are typically considered less reliable than *enterprise disks*, which are usually of the fibre channel (FC) variety. Recent work has questioned the conventional wisdom of disk reliability assumptions, however (Schroeder and Gibson 2007). *Storage arrays* are hardware systems that combine many disks into a logical unit (LUN) that can be accessed as if it were a single disk. Storage arrays often provide RAID (Patterson et al. 1988) capabilities in order to tolerate failure of one or more disks in the array. Storage arrays are available that use both commodity and enterprise disks. Storage arrays can be attached to single computers and used for storing local file systems, but often they are used as a building block for PFSes.

An *object storage device*, or OSD, is a type of storage device that distinguishes itself by presenting a higher level of abstraction than the typical block device interface. Rather than representing storage as a linear array of data blocks, an object storage device instead structures storage into objects that contain raw data as well as metadata attributes. The intention of this approach is to simplify file systems by offloading the work of common data allocation and metadata operations to the storage device itself. The OSD interface was formalized by the Storage Networking Industry Association (SNIA) OSD working group. OSDs can be accessed using extended SCSI commands.

A *storage area network*, or SAN, refers to a dedicated network connecting one or more computers with one or more storage arrays. The three most common transports used to connect a SAN are fibre channel (FC), InfiniBand (IB), and iSCSI. Fibre channel refers to both a cabling type and an interface protocol. It requires a FC switch to connect components and FC host bus adapters (HBAs) to be installed on the compute elements. Likewise, IB SANs require both IB HBAs and storage that can be attached to IB. iSCSI is a protocol standard that allows SCSI traffic to be carried over a TCP/IP network. iSCSI can utilize general purpose Ethernet switches and host Ethernet adapters, allowing traffic to be moved over existing communication networks rather than a dedicated SAN, if desired.

Network attached storage, or NAS, is a type of storage hardware that can be attached to a standard computer network in order to provide file system services. It uses disks, storage arrays, or even OSDs as its underlying storage, but it presents this storage through a standard file system protocol such as NFS. NAS devices are popular for commercial use because they combine a complete storage implementation into a single consolidated product. NAS devices do not normally provide parallel I/O capabilities, but we will discover in later case studies how vendors are extending this model.

PFSes are often built on top of storage arrays and SANs, taking advantage of the RAID capabilities of storage arrays and connectivity of SANs to tolerate component failures. This will be discussed in greater detail later in the chapter. First, however, we will discuss some of the challenges in designing PFSes and how different approaches to these challenges can lead to dramatically different implementations.

8.4 Design Challenges

PFS architectures are shaped by a variety of unique technical challenges that require compromise between competing goals. Understanding these challenges is helpful in comprehending how PFSes fit into the grid environment as a whole, and they also help to motivate some of the fundamental architectural decisions that distinguish one file system implementation from another.

8.4.1 Performance

Performance is the most significant factor that impacts PFS design. Given adequate underlying hardware, the designers will design a system that performs well for a large number of clients, as well as for a single client. The typical workload for a CDI Grid will involve many clients simultaneously accessing a large collection of data. In order to satisfy this workload, the underlying hardware must provide multiple independent paths through which data may flow: efficiency will be compromised if all data must flow through a single server, a single disk, a single network link, or a single SAN link. Further, the file system must also avoid introducing additional software bottlenecks.

A common feature of all PFSes is that they allow multiple paths to storage to be utilized concurrently. This is accomplished by spreading data across multiple disks. These disks are then accessed by clients either indirectly through a collection of servers, or by allowing clients to directly access the disks via multiple network links. In addition to distributing data, the manner in which metadata is accessed and maintained can have an impact on performance. If metadata in one location must be updated any time a file grows, appending to a file will not proceed concurrently because of this bottleneck. This is one example of how a PFS implementation might introduce a software bottleneck where no hardware bottleneck is present.

A more subtle factor in performance is how well the interface to the file system allows application programmers to describe their accesses. If this interface matches poorly with the application programmer's needs, then it is likely that inefficient access will occur. We will discuss two specific examples of interfaces tuned to application needs later in the chapter.

8.4.2 Consistency Semantics

The file system semantics define the rules followed by the file system when accessed through an application interface. *Consistency semantics* are the subset of these rules related to multiple compute elements interacting with the file system, and they define such things as when changes from one compute element become visible to others and what the results of concurrent changes to the same file region will be. These semantics must be clearly defined so that application programmers know what should be expected from the file system and how to impose a consistent view of data when it is needed. For example, one compute element's process flow may depend upon correctly reading a file region that was just written by a different compute element. Knowing what steps, if any, are necessary to guarantee that the writer's changes are visible to the reader is critical to correct application behavior.

This does not necessarily mean that a PFS must behave exactly like a local workstation file system, which is typically POSIX compliant. Maintaining or imposing a consistent view in a PFS requires communication because data is distributed, and communication takes time and uses system resources. Imposing certain traditional file system semantics may have a negative impact on performance, even if typical grid applications have no need for them. For this reason, none of the case study file systems in this chapter are strictly POSIX compliant, choosing to relax their consistency semantics in different ways to attain higher performance for specific types of access. One example is consistency of file system writes. Sequential consistency, the consistency model imposed by POSIX, dictates that overlapping writes to the file system appear to occur atomically and in the same order for all processes (Culler et al. 1999). In a CDI Grid environment, however, the ETL engine coordinates the application processes so that overlapping writes never occur. The overhead of implementing this semantic requirement may therefore not be worthwhile in this problem domain.

Locking is a commonly used technique for enforcing consistency semantics in a PFS, so it is worth mentioning specifically. When locks are used in a file system, clients must obtain a lock on resources before reading or writing to it. Locks are only granted when the consistency semantics are met. Locks may be handed out by a single server or may be managed in a distributed manner. Locks in PFSes always allow a file to be broken up into separate regions that may be accessed concurrently, but the granularity of those locks may limit locking to particular sizes, such as a file system stripe. In addition to file region locking, a PFS may also elect to use internal locking to protect metadata resources such as directories. This approach could have subtle performance ramifications. An example would be the simultaneous creation of new files within a single parent directory. If clients must acquire a write lock on the parent directory each time a new entry is added, then lock contention will degrade performance if enough clients attempt to create files simultaneously. When a PFS uses locks, it can be important for applications to adjust their access patterns to interact efficiently with the locking system.

8.4.3 Fault Tolerance

Fault tolerance, or the ability of a system to continue operating in the event of component failures, is a characteristic that is desired in any storage system. However, fault tolerance takes on additional significance in PFSes due to the number and complexity of the underlying components. As mentioned under the topic of performance and scalability, a PFS leverages multiple storage devices and I/O paths. Failure at any one of these devices or paths has the potential to disrupt the file system as a whole. Hiding, or at least mitigating, the impact of failures is an important consideration in designing a PFS, although tools outside the file system may also be useful in providing this capability. In Fig. 8.4 we show how redundant links to storage arrays can allow one PFS server to take over service for another, if the PFS supports this capability.

One consideration is that components of the file system should avoid propagating failures. In server based file systems, for example, the failure of one server should not prevent other servers from responding to unrelated requests. Clients should also be able to continue operation in the event that some other client fails.

This implies careful consideration of how state is shared across file system components.

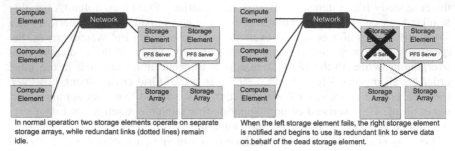

In normal operation two storage elements operate on separate storage arrays, while redundant links (dotted lines) remain idle.

When the left storage element fails, the right storage element is notified and begins to use its redundant link to serve data on behalf of the dead storage element.

Fig. 8.4. When a storage element fails (*left*), redundant links maintain operation (*right*)

8.4.4 Interoperability

Interoperability should take into account both how applications interact with the file system as well as how the file system interacts with underlying storage components. Some file systems provide proprietary interfaces for application use, but these can cause portability challenges. These challenges should be avoided through the use of standardized interfaces unless there is a compelling reason to tightly bind applications to the file system or a priorietary interface. The most common file system interfaces are the standard POSIX/Unix file interface (IEEE 1996), and the MPI-IO parallel interface (MPI 1997).

Interoperability with respect to storage components can become important as a grid deployment evolves. One of the key advantages of the grid approach is scalability. If the number of compute elements and application size are increased, then it follows that the storage capacity or performance will need to increase as well. An ideal PFS will be portable across a variety of storage hardware technologies and at a variety of scales, allowing larger and more powerful hardware to be deployed as part of the grid life cycle.

Finally, many grid environments employ an assortment of hardware platforms and operating systems. Ideally a PFS will support a broad collection of different operating systems as clients, allowing convenient access to the storage system from all the relevant systems. Unfortunately, because of the specialized nature of PFSes, this is often not the case. For example, a PFS that was originally designed for high performance scientific computing may only support the operating system of a particular HPC vendor. Likewise, a commercial file system may only certify a subset of available operating system versions in order to streamline technical support.

8.4.5 Management Tools

System management can be a challenge within a PFS consisting of many underlying components, distributed data, unique architectures, and a dynamic number of clients. It is therefore helpful if the file system provides integrated tools to aid in common management tasks. Examples of common storage management tasks in a CDI Grid environment include diagnosing failures, understanding application and environment I/O behavior, and tuning the PFS for different workloads.

Failure diagnosis is closely associated with the fault tolerance design challenge outlined earlier. We have already established that fault tolerance is a desirable characteristic, but it is even more powerful if the file system enables an administrator to react to the fault in an efficient manner. The first goal is to identify the fault. It may not be immediately obvious what component has failed due to the number of I/O devices and data paths available. Effective fault identification can be enhanced through simple design considerations such as clear and detailed error logging. More sophisticated approaches may include integration with alarm mechanisms or utilities to interactively probe the status of underlying hardware. These tools should make an effort to not only identify failed components but indicate how they failed. Once a failure has been diagnosed, the next logical administrative step is to repair it. File systems can aid in this task by allowing replacement of hardware components. It may also be necessary to provide tools to repair the file system itself in the event that its integrity has been compromised.

Understanding application and environment I/O behavior can impact an administrator's ability to manage the PFS. In CDI Grid environments, it is likely that many different applications will be accessing the PFS concurrently. This makes it difficult for an application developer to anticipate the behavior of a PFS. It is therefore important to be able to understand how an existing application interacts with the file system, both as a single application running by itself and as a subset of applications running concurrently in a CDI Grid environment. This task can be aided by relatively simple features such as the ability to monitor resource load while applications are running in order to identify bottlenecks. More sophisticated techniques may include tracing both of the application system calls and the underlying file system operations in order to correlate fine grained behavior.

Finally, once an application's access pattern is well understood, this information can be applied to tuning of the file system. Examples of common PFS tuning parameters include cache policies, cache limits, block sizes, and network buffer sizes. In addition, some PFSes allow control over how data is distributed across storage resources. This allows administrators to match application access patterns to the appropriate level of storage device concurrency and granularity. As mentioned in Section 8.2 of this chapter, it is most helpful if tuning can be applied to specific files or directories so that different parameters may be used for particular applications. Depending on the workload, however, it may still be a significant benefit to simply tune the entire file system for its most common application.

8.4.6 Traditional Design Challenges

The design challenges that have been outlined thus far in this section focus on issues that are either unique to PFSes or take on a special significance in that domain. However, it may also be helpful to understand that there are also traditional design challenges that may *not* be as significant for a CDI Grid. One that was already mentioned briefly is POSIX compliance. Another feature which may not be as important in this environment is desktop interoperability. Most CDI Grid environments do not utilize desktop workstations for processing or data management. This type of access can be a significant security concern and can also increase management complexity for a grid environment. Likewise, CDI Grids do not necessarily require file systems to be wide-area network aware. Performance requirements typically rule out the use of remote data for commercial production environments. If a WAN is considered for geographical failover purposes, data synchronization and similar tasks may be best handled by tools or middleware that reside above the file system level.

8.5 Case Studies

In this section we look at four examples of PFSes. We will start by looking at an example of what might be considered the "enterprise approach" to PFS architecture: the Multi-Path File System. Following that we will examine the Parallel Virtual File System, a PFS tailored to scientific computing but also very useful in CDI Grid environments. We will then discuss the Google File System, a custom file system tailored specifically to the needs of Google's data-intensive applications. This section will conclude with a discussion of pNFS, which is a standard for integrating parallel I/O into the ubiquitous NFS file system.

8.5.1 Multi-Path File System (MPFS)

The Multi-Path File System is a commercial PFS developed by EMC Corporation. It works in conjunction with EMC hardware products including the Celerra NAS platform and the Clariion storage platform. MPFS was first released in 2000 under the HighRoad product name.

MPFS is a relevant case study in PFS architecture because it illustrates two architectural concepts. The first is that its fundamental design classifies it as a "shared disk" or "SAN" file system. This means that all entities in the file system, including both servers and clients, have direct access to the same shared storage devices. In the MPFS case, storage connectivity is provided via either fibre channel or iSCSI.

The second key architectural concept of MPFS is that it extends the standard NFS file system. MPFS leverages existing NFS semantics and protocols for handling metadata. However, it uses a bypass mechanism so that clients can read and write to disks in parallel without the direct intervention of an NFS server. MPFS was motivated by observations across EMC's NAS and SAN product lines. A large SAN is capable of providing a high throughput volume to concurrent compute elements. However, this capability is negated if all data must flow through a single NAS device. MPFS is intended to offer the abstraction layer and simplified management of a NAS device in conjunction with the raw throughput and parallel data paths available in a SAN connection. We will find in the final case study that this relates closely to the proposed Parallel NFS (pNFS), protocol, which is an official IETF standard being developed by several industry groups including EMC (Welch et al. 2005).

8.5.1.1 Architecture

Figure 8.5 illustrates the basic architecture of MPFS. The Celerra is a NAS device that provides standard NFS and CIFS file access while simultaneously acting as the metadata server for MPFS. Compute elements connect to the Celerra via Ethernet. The Celerra is typically attached to the storage array via fibre channel, while compute elements are attached to the storage array via either iSCSI over Ethernet or fibre channel. The topology can be interconnected using a stand alone SAN switch or integrated ports within the storage hardware.

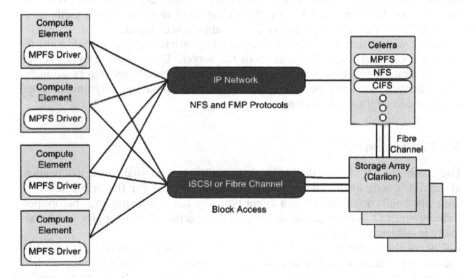

Fig. 8.5. MPFS architecture

The disks in the Clariion storage array are bound into RAID groups and exposed to clients and servers as SCSI LUNs. The MPFS file system itself is then striped across these LUNs. This distribution method causes large I/O operations from compute elements to fan out across disks and achieve higher overall throughput than is possible with an individual RAID set (EMC 2006).

8.5.1.2 File Mapping Protocol

The Celerra coordinates three primary activities within the MPFS file system: metadata management, block allocation, and distributed locking. Basic metadata operations (such as name space and attribute operations) are handled using the NFSv4 protocol. Block allocation is handled using a custom protocol known as FMP, or the File Mapping Protocol (Fridella et al. 2003).

The first responsibility of the File Mapping Protocol is to describe the layout of files to compute elements. When a file is opened, the client receives a set of file maps, or extents, that describe the volume ids, offsets, and block counts for the data within the file. At this point, a client has enough information to understand how to access file data directly on the SAN. However, it must also obtain a delegation for a region in order to have permission to perform I/O. This is handled with block level granularity. Each block can either be unlocked, locked for reading from multiple readers, or locked for writing from a single writer. The process of acquiring file maps and delegations is normally grouped into a single FMP request in order to improve efficiency. Delegation locks are lease based. This allows clients to access blocks efficiently if there is no block level contention. The process becomes more complicated if multiple clients require conflicting access to the same blocks, however. In this case the Celerra will use notification methods to contact clients if a lock is revoked or a file mapping is changed.

Before writing data for a new file or extending an existing file, a client must reserve a preallocated set of blocks from the server. The Celerra uses a delayed commit strategy for these blocks, so that no data is actually set into position for other clients to see until the writer issues a commit operation. Any uncommitted blocks are freed if the file is closed.

8.5.1.3 Caching

The Clariion SAN storage device implements its own internal cache independent of the file system. MPFS clients perform caching as well. The file map extents are prefetched and cached such that a client typically has a complete map before performing any I/O. As mentioned in the previous section, file mappings can be actively invalidated if needed.

Clients also cache file data. File data is automatically prefetched during reads, and on writes data is cached and committed using a write behind policy. Coherency and consistency are maintained using the FMP protocol. In addition to notification messages, the Celerra and clients exchange heartbeat messages to verify that FMP connections are still operable. If a connection is lost, then the client will stop all I/O and invalidate its data and file mapping caches.

8.5.1.4 Fault Tolerance

Both the Celerra and Clariion products from EMC include fault tolerance in their hardware design. The Clariion LUNs utilize standard RAID techniques to protect against disk failures, while the data caches utilize mirroring to protect cached information. The storage array can also be configured with several hot spare disks to take the place of failed disks without service interruption. The Celerra server supports redundant management and service components with failover capability.

8.5.1.5 Similar File Systems

Examples of other shared disk file systems include Clustered XFS (CXFS) from SGI, the Global File System (GFS) from RedHat Inc., and the General Parallel File System (GPFS) from IBM. The PanFS file system from Panasas Inc. is another example of a file system that is based on a NAS device concurrently providing NFS and CIFS service along with a bypass mechanism for parallel I/O, although PanFS differs in that it uses an object storage abstraction rather than the block abstraction used in MPFS.

8.5.2 Parallel Virtual File System (PVFS)

The Parallel Virtual File System is an open-source PFS developed by an international team of researchers and software developers from national laboratories, industry, and academia. The project grew out of early PFS work at Clemson University, and core project members are now located at Argonne National Laboratory, Clemson University, and Ohio Supercomputer Center. These members oversee the source code repository and steer the project, while many others contribute to the overall success and quality of the project.

The overall goal of the PVFS project is to provide the community with a production-quality PFS that is tailored to the needs of the high-performance computing community and that is also useful as a basis for further research in parallel I/O. The architecture that the PVFS team has chosen reflects this emphasis and makes PVFS an interesting case study. In particular PVFS is designed to deal with a very large number of clients in the most efficient, cost effective, and reliable manner possible.

8.5.2.1 Architecture

The architecture of a typical PVFS deployment is shown in Figure 8.6. Multiple PVFS servers provide metadata and data storage to file system clients. File data can be striped for greater overall bandwidth or kept on a single server to minimize overhead for metadata operations. Servers store their data using locally accessible data storage, either on local disks or on storage attached via iSCSI, InfiniBand, or Fibre Channel. In this model, servers manage their own storage, eliminating the need for expensive storage area networks and making PVFS deployable on commodity hardware in a scratch file system role, which is perfect for research work. However, when SAN infrastructure is deployed behind the PVFS servers, access to storage by multiple servers allows server failures to be tolerated, enabling high availability configurations necessary in most production environments.

Clients run a small amount of PVFS client software that allows them to communicate with PVFS servers over the cluster network, which could consist of any combination of TCP/IP, InfiniBand, Myrinet MX, or Portals protocols.

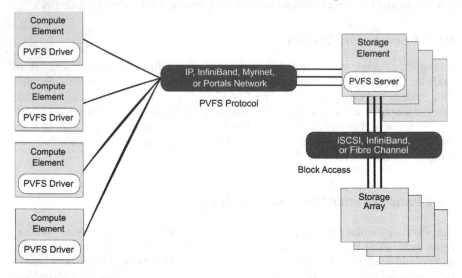

Fig. 8.6. PVFS architecture

PVFS employs a layered software architecture. Separating key functionality such as network access, storage organization, request processing, and data pipelining into components facilitates experimentation with new approaches and porting to new architectures. For example, new networking implementations only require approximately 5000 lines of C code, a modest level of effort to move to a new platform.

8.5.2.2 Fault Tolerance

The PVFS architecture eliminates storage of any critical file system data on clients, meaning that clients may appear and disappear without interrupting file system service. This is an important characteristic for a file system intended for use at very large scale. This characteristic is also a significant departure from the common PFS approach of leveraging locking to enforce consistency and performing client-side caching to hide latency. In these systems, heartbeat mechanisms must be used to detect client failures and reclaim resources, and data may be lost, if write-back caching is allowed.

As an artifact of this design decision, PVFS does not cache data on clients—there is no mechanism in PVFS for maintaining consistency of such data. This means that PVFS clients always see network latency when performing I/O operations, and operations are not aggregated on their behalf by PVFS (they may be aggregated at some other software layer, such as within the stdio library or MPI-IO). PVFS does cache some metadata, such as the distribution of PVFS files. Because this data does not change during the lifetime of a PVFS file, this data may be safely cached without impacting semantics. This limited caching eliminates the need to constantly contact the metadata server during I/O, therefore avoiding a potential bottleneck.

8.5.2.3 Application Interfaces

Another way in which PVFS caters to efficient access from very large numbers of clients is through its application interfaces. PVFS exposes file and directory references (handles) through its API, allowing application processes to exchange and reuse these values within the context of a parallel application. This facility can be very useful when many processes are sharing a single file. In this case, one process can perform the directory traversal in order to map a file name into a handle. Once this process has the handle, the process can use a scalable broadcast algorithm to distribute the handle to other processes, avoiding a storm of metadata operations from the individual processes.

PVFS also provides efficient mechanisms for describing noncontiguous data access. Noncontiguous accesses occur whenever a client moves data between more than one memory or file region. This is a common occurrence in scientific workloads. For example, extracting a subarray from a large multi-dimensional array is a noncontiguous operation because it requires pulling many small regions, pieces of array rows, out of a larger array.

For irregular access patterns, PVFS allows an arbitrary list of byte ranges in memory and file to be described. The PVFS system will manage movement of data described by these lists as a single operation. This feature minimizes the impact of network latency by aggregating as much data as possible into a single operation. For regular access patterns, PVFS can do even better. The PVFS API allows the user to describe regularity in a concise manner, reducing the size of the description of the I/O that must take place. The language for describing these accesses is similar to MPI datatypes (Gropp et al. 1999), and it includes primitives for vectors and block indexed regions, among others.

While these capabilities are all exposed in a user library, more often users take advantage of these features through the use of MPI-IO calls. The ROMIO MPI-IO implementation leverages these features to provide one of the most efficient MPI-IO implementations to date (Thakur et al. 1999).

8.5.2.4 Consistency Semantics

Commercial PFSes implement POSIX consistency semantics [IEEE/ANSI 1996]. These semantics mandate atomicity of contiguous I/O operations and guarantee that changes to a file are immediately made visible to other processes.

When an access falls on a single server, these semantics are relatively easy to implement—the server can simply order access locally. When an access spans multiple servers, however, things are more complicated because there are multiple resources that must be coordinated. As mentioned above, most PFSes use locking to solve this problem: clients must obtain a lock on the relevant contiguous region prior to reading or writing. Without such coordination, changes may be made in different orders on different servers, or a reader might see only some of the results of a concurrent write operation.

Scientific codes tend to operate in a write-only or read-only mode. When writing, these codes tend to not write to the same bytes; they don't have time to write things twice! As a result, these codes do not require the strict semantics of POSIX, and in fact enforcing these semantics only imposes unnecessary overhead. With this awareness of target applications, and keeping in mind the desire to allow clients to come and go at will, the PVFS team chose to support a more relaxed set of file access semantics. These semantics are identical to POSIX for accesses that do not touch the same bytes, but allow for undefined results when the same bytes are written concurrently or read while they are being written.

8.5.2.5 Similar File Systems

The PVFS design is similar to more recent systems that adopt an object storage model, such as the Lustre file system from Cluster File Systems.

8.5.3 The Google File System (GFS)

The Google File System is a custom distributed file system developed by Google for use in Google's distributed, data-intensive applications. While discussed in a number of publications (Ghemawat et al. 2003, Dean and Ghemawat 2004), GFS has not been made available to the larger community at the time of writing.

GFS is a relevant case study in our context because it illustrates the advantages of building a custom solution, tailored to the access patterns and needs of a particular set of commercial applications. In particular, the designers of GFS attempted to maximize productivity of users of the file system, maintain high performance and availability, and minimize cost.

Google is known for using commodity components in order to reduce hardware costs (Barroso et al. 2003). The GFS team followed this same approach, using commodity processors and storage as the underlying infrastructure for GFS file systems. One artifact of this decision is that storage devices are only accessible on a single server—shared storage is not a commodity at this time. Because of the number of components that Google uses to support its services, failures are commonplace. Since storage devices are only accessible on one server in the GFS system, managing redundant storage will be the responsibility of the GFS software, and recovering from failures must be rapid and automatic.

8.5.3.1 Architecture

GFS installations consist of a single *master* that manages metadata and a collection of *chunkservers* that are responsible for storing file data. These are implemented as user-space processes running on commodity hardware. Files are split into *chunks*, which are collections of 64 Mbytes of data that may be referenced by a unique 64-bit chunk handle. The large chunk size was chosen to match application access patterns and to reduce the overhead of metadata management and chunk discovery.

The master manages all file system metadata, including the name space, permissions, information mapping from files to chunks on chunkservers, and chunk locations (including replicas), and it keeps this metadata in memory for fast access. Of this information, all but the chunk locations are also stored persistently in an on-disk log that is replicated on other systems, so that the current state can be restored in the event of a failure. The chunk locations are determined by polling the chunkservers at startup or when a chunkserver joins the file system. Once the master is aware of chunkservers and their respective chunks, the master ensures that it has an up-to-date list via heartbeat messages. Because the master has comprehensive knowledge of the chunkservers, it has all the information necessary to make decisions on subsequent chunk placement and replication, and all these decisions are made at the master.

Once a client has determined from the master what chunks must be accessed to perform I/O, it directly contacts the relevant chunkservers. Chunkservers are simple entities that provide read and write access to file chunks. Chunks are stored as files on a local file system on the server.

8.5.3.2 Fault Tolerance

GFS is unique among the file systems discussed here in that it provides fault tolerance through managing data replicas on independent servers, rather than relying on shared, fault tolerant storage units. When writing, a client first obtains from the master a list of chunkservers holding the primary and any secondary copies of the chunk to be modified. When modifications are being made to a chunk, the master assigns the role of primary server to one of the replica holders. This distributes responsibility for coordination of writes and allows for greater overall throughput.

Once the client has this list, it pushes its data out to these chunkservers. The client chooses an order of chunkservers, and data is pipelined through these servers until all chunkservers have all data. Once all chunkservers have notified the client that they have received the changes, the client notifies the primary that these changes should be committed to storage. The primary assigns a number to this set of changes that is used to order this set with respect to any other ongoing changes.

It then passes a `message to the replicas notifying that they should commit these changes in the same order. Once all replicas have committed the change, the client is notified that the write is complete.

As time goes on, replicas may disappear because a chunkserver becomes disconnected from the network, a disk dies, or some other failure occurs. The master tracks the location of all replicas in the system, and when the number of replicas for a given file falls below a low-water mark, re-replication is scheduled. This re-replication is performed by sending a message to a new chunkserver requesting that it clone the chunk from an existing replica. This same mechanism is used to rebalance replicas across chunkservers.

The master state is also replicated. All metadata changes are stored in a log, and an approach similar to the one used in chunk modification is used: log updates are committed on all replicas before considering a change complete. These replicas serve as read-only copies of the metadata, allowing clients performing reads to spread their metadata workload over a larger number of servers. In the event that the current master dies, a new one is started by system monitoring infrastructure. Meanwhile, read-only operations to metadata can continue, allowing limited access to the FS while the new master is started.

To prevent the log from growing too large, the master's complete state is checkpointed occasionally. In this way a new master can rapidly determine the current file system state and begin servicing operations.

8.5.3.3 Application Interfaces

The GFS system provides two methods for "mutating" a file. The first is a normal write operation that places data at a specified location in the file. The second is a record append operation that puts data at the end of a file and is designed for use with concurrent processes performing appends.

The write operation provides a convenient interface for making serial changes to a file, but the results of this type of operation are undefined for concurrent access to the same regions. This is similar to the PVFS write semantics. In order to operate concurrently and produce well-defined output, most applications using GFS instead write files through the use of the record append operation. This type of mutation can result in regions of undefined data between the successfully written records, resulting from padding or duplicate records.

The use of the record append mutation for storing data in the applications has a larger impact on the Google application suite. In order to differentiate valid records from padding and partial records in files, writers include additional data in their records, such as checksums. Duplicates are identified through the use of unique tags on records, when necessary. The functionality for managing most of this additional work has been encapsulated in an I/O library that is shared by applications using GFS, but porting a new application to use GFS might require dealing specifically with these unique semantics.

8.5.3.4 Consistency Semantics

Atomicity of namespace operations is enforced by the single master. This makes for a simple implementation, but this also places a limit on the rate at which namespace operations may be completed.

We have already discussed some of the unique consistency semantics of GFS. In addition to those, the presence of replicas in the system adds the possibility of different clients seeing different contents for the same chunks under certain circumstances. Chunk locations are cached by clients, with timeouts on cached values and flushing on file close imposed to limit the opportunity for inconsistent views. Because most GFS applications mutate files using record appends, inconsistencies tend to appear in the form of records that are incomplete or not visible to particular clients. Applications reading records from files that are being generated as they read must be coded to deal with this possibility.

8.5.3.5 Similar File Systems

The most similar file system to GFS is the Hadoop Distributed File System (HDFS), part of the Apache Hadoop project [Hadoop]. HDFS is also designed to run on commodity hardware, manages metadata from a single metadata node, and breaks files up into large (64MB) blocks that are distributed on multiple nodes.

While different from GFS in that it relies on specialized hardware and presents a POSIX interface, the PanFS file system from Panasas is similar in that fault tolerance is provided by storage of error correcting data on independent storage units, rather than using shared storage as in the MPFS and PVFS cases.

8.5.4 pNFS

pNFS is unique among the PFS case studies in this chapter. It is not a specific file system implementation from a vendor or research group, but rather a standard for how to integrate parallel I/O into the ubiquitous NFS file system protocol. pNFS is currently under review by the Internet Engineering Task Force (IETF) and expected to be finalized in 2008. It is currently included as one of the principle extensions in the NFSv4.1 draft specification.The basic NFSv4 protocol without pNFS support has already been standardized (Shepler et al. 2003). NFSv4 is a single server network file system protocol based on experiences from NFSv2 and NFSv3. Improvements in the new protocol include integration of strong security, file locking, and a mount protocol. These features were available with previous versions of NFS but only as external components. NFSv4 also improves access and performance over the Internet, adds compound operations to improve efficiency, and adds read and write delegations to improve cache semantics. Finally, and importantly for pNFS, the NFSv4 protocol includes a mechanism for adding extensions to the protocol. Extensions do not compromise backwards compatibility.

pNFS is an extension that expands the NFSv4 protocol by separating the data access path from the metadata and control protocol. This allows file system clients to read and write file data in parallel without being limited by a single server bottleneck. However, they still leverage the NFSv4 protocol for the majority of file system metadata operations. pNFS therefore takes advantage of the well known semantics and portability of NFS without sacrificing raw data throughput for parallel I/O. pNFS does not dictate how the data path is implemented. It can be implemented for a variety of back end devices, including SAN storage arrays, OSDs, or even completely independent PFSes.

8.5.4.1 Architecture

Figure 8.7 illustrates the architecture of pNFS. As in standard NFSv4, there is an NFS driver on each client compute element and a single server for all metadata traffic. However, each client compute element and the NFSv4 server directly access file data information through a separate protocol.

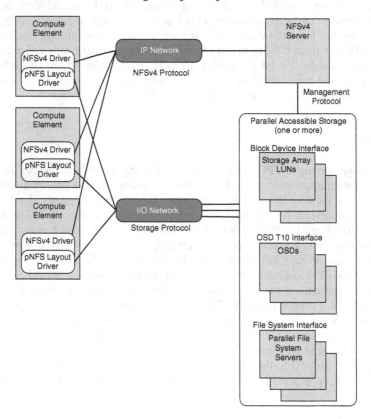

Fig. 8.7. pNFS architecture

This file data is stored on either a SAN storage array, a set of OSDs, a PFS, or some other back end storage. It is also possible for a combination of these components to be used in the same environment. The I/O networks connecting the clients to the storage devices may be implemented using any interconnect technology. It could be the same IP network as is used for NFSv4 protocol traffic, or it could be a separate dedicated network such as a fibre channel SAN. The server must implement a management protocol to exchange information with the storage device.

Access to the storage devices is managed using *layouts*. A layout in this context is an abstract representation of how a file region is stored on the back end devices. The layout format will be different depending on the type of storage device used. They are described in greater detail in the next subsection. Support for a given layout format is provided by a *layout driver* that is installed on each client compute element. This layout driver handles the data transfer path for NFSv4. The same core NFSv4 driver implementation and NFSv4 server implementation can be reused regardless of the back end storage type and layout format.

8.5.4.2 Layouts

The previous subsection defined a pNFS layout as an abstract representation of how a particular file region is stored. This representation can vary considerably depending on the storage technology used. The pNFS protocol therefore treats layouts as opaque objects rather than specifying their format. The NFSv4 client and NFSv4 server pass layout information without inspection or modification. Interpretation of the layout is left to the layout driver and the management protocol used by the server. pNFS implementations must define a standard interface for adding new layout drivers.

A typical layout will include four components. The first is a list of devices that are used to store the file. These devices are represented using numerical identifiers for brevity. The pNFS client can use a GETDEVICEINFO server request to resolve device identifiers into complete information. Examples of device information include volume labels for data available on SAN LUNs or hostname and port information for data stored on separate file servers. The second component of the layout will describe exactly what parts of the storage devices are being used. Examples include block offsets or file names. A third component of a layout is access control information. This is used to provide permission to access the specified storage objects. Finally, the layout will specify an aggregation scheme that defines how data is to be distributed across the devices. A common aggregation scheme is to simply stripe the data in regular intervals.

8.5.4.3 Layout Requests

The pNFS protocol defines three principle request types for exchanging layout information between clients and servers. The first is a LAYOUTGET request. This is used by the client to request layout information for a particular file region. The server is allowed to return layout information for a region larger than the client requested. For example, some pNFS implementations may use concise layouts that can easily describe an entire file at once. LAYOUTGET may be issued as a separate request after a file is opened, or it may be issued at the same time using an NFSv4 compound operation. The latter approach is an optimization that reduces latency by combining two requests into a single protocol message. The second principle layout request is LAYOUTRETURN. LAYOUTRETURN is used by a client to indicate to a server that it is no longer using a particular layout. This may be performed when a file is closed. The final request type is LAYOUTCOMMIT. This request is used by a client to commit a modified layout to the server. LAYOUTCOMMIT is useful for layout drivers that need to modify the layout when writing data. For example, a layout driver may elect to allocate new blocks as part of a write operation.

The preceding request types all assume that the pNFS client is in charge of controlling when and how a layout is used. However, the pNFS server also has the ability to actively participate. This is done using a CB_LAYOUTRECALL callback request to the client. CB_LAYOUTRECALL can be used by a server to revoke a layout that a client has previously acquired. Implementations may use CB_LAYOUTRECALL as a mechanism to maintain consistency if a layout is modified while in use or if a file is deleted. The storage devices should return an error to the client if it attempts to access storage in spite of a CB_LAYOUTRECALL callback.

8.5.4.4 Implementations

Several storage vendors have expressed interest in pNFS implementations. Panasas, Network Appliance, EMC, IBM, and Sun are all members of the IETF pNFS committee. pNFS is also being supported by the research community as well. One of the first pNFS prototype implementations was developed by the Center for Information Technology Integration (CITI) at the University of Michigan (Hildebrand and Honeyman 2005). The CITI implementation uses a PVFS file system as its storage mechanism.

Several factors should aid in the adoption of pNFS in the future. It is a natural fit for many current vendor file systems. The MPFS case study presented previously in this chapter is one example of a vendor file system with several architectural similarities to pNFS. Another factor is that pNFS is backwards compatible with NFSv4. If a particular file system client does not support pNFS (or the appropriate layout driver) then it can fall back to standard NFS access through the centralized NFSv4 server. This is a powerful interoperability feature because NFS is one of the most widely deployed network file system protocol in the world. Finally, the fact that pNFS reuses existing NFSv4 components for metadata and control should enable rapid implementation of pNFS support for new storage systems.

8.6 Conclusion

This chapter has covered the role that parallel file systems play in CDI Grids and discussed four specific examples of parallel file system options, ranging from commercial offerings to custom systems tailored to application needs. We have outlined how CDI workflows use the capabilities of PFSes and discussed some of the challenges in designing and building these systems to be effective in CDI Grid environments.

Storage systems are a quickly changing area. The amount of data being generated and processed in CDI Grids is growing at a rapid pace, and petabyte storage systems are appearing on the scene. These new deployments are using thousands, if not tens of thousands, of disks in concert. At these scales, disk failures are common. Because drives are growing in capacity faster than in bandwidth, the process of rebuilding when these failures occur is taking ever longer, prompting research into better systems for maintaining redundancy in disk arrays.

At the same time, by creating a common client-side interface that all vendors will support, advances such as pNFS offer the promise of simpler deployments and greater choice for storage system consumers. This will help to level the playing field in the commercial storage arena, and it should engender broader adoption of parallel file systems into a variety of new domains.

While groups investigate new approaches to mitigating drive failures, the cost of deploying high-availability solutions is pushing the storage community to adopt storage system models that minimize the use of SAN technologies. As we saw in the GFS case study, it is possible to build reliable storage systems that use unreliable, commodity storage components underneath. From a cost perspective this is very appealing, but questions still remain on how to create usable, general-purpose storage solutions using this model.

8.7 Exercises

1. Compare the primary file data path for two of the PFS case studies. How would this impact the performance requirements of hardware used in conjunction with the file systems?
2. Describe three best practices to consider when developing an application to perform efficiently on a PFS. This could include both how the I/O is performed as well as how the data format is organized.
3. What are the two most popular interfaces for parallel applications to use for performing I/O?
4. Compare how each of MPFS, PVFS, GFS, and pNFS utilize distributed locking in their designs.

8.8 References

Barroso L, Dean J, Holzle U (2003) Web search for a planet: The Google cluster architecture. In: IEEE Micro, vol. 23, issue 2, pp 22-28.

Culler D, Singh J, Gupta A (1999) Parallel Computer Architecture: A Hardware/Software Approach. Morgan Kaufmann, San Francisco, CA.

Dean J, Ghemawat S (2004) MapReduce: Simplified data processing on large clusters. In: OSDI'04, 6th Symposium on Operating Systems Design and Implementation, Sponsored by USENIX in cooperation with ACM SIGOPS, pp 137–150.

EMC Corporation (2006) Deploying Celerra MPFSi in high-performance computing environments. EMC White Paper.

Fridella S, Jiang X, Black D (2003) Elements of a scalable network file system protocol. In: NFS Extensions for Parallel Storage Workshop.

Ghemawat S, Gobioff H, Leung S (2003) The Google File System. In: ACM SIGOPS Operating Systems Review Volume 37, Issue 5, pp 29-43.

Gropp W, Lusk E, Skjellum A (1999) Using MPI: Portable Parallel Programming with the Message-Passing Interface. MIT Press, Cambridge, MA.

The Hadoop Distributed File System, http://lucene.apache.org/hadoop/hdfs_design.html.

Hildebrand D, Honeyman P (2005) Exporting storage systems in a scalable manner with pNFS. In: Proceedings of the 22nd IEEE - 13th NASA Goddard (MSST2005) Conference on Mass Storage Systems and Technologies, Monterey, California.

IEEE/ANSI Std. 1003.1 (1996) Portable operating system interface (POSIX) part 1: System application program interface (API) [C Language].

Message Passing Interface Forum (1997) MPI-2: Extensions to the Message-Passing Interface.

Patterson D, Gibson G, Katz R (1988) A case for redundant arrays of inexpensive disks (RAID). In: Proceedings of the ACM SIGMOD International Conference on Management of Data, pp 108-116.

Purakayastha A, Ellis C, Kotz D, Nieuwejaar N, Best M (1995) Characterizing parallel file-access patterns on a large-scale multiprocessor. In: Proceedings of the Ninth International Parallel Processing Symposium. pp 165-172.

Schroeder B, Gibson G (2007) Disk failures in the real world: What does an MTTF of 1,000,000 hours mean to you? In: 5th USENIX Conference on File and Storage Technologies.

Shepler S, Callaghan B, Robinson D, Thurlow R, Sun Microsystems, Inc., Beame C, Hummingbird Ltd. Eisler M, Noveck D, Network Appliance, Inc. (2003) Network File System (NFS) version 4 protocol. Network Working Group RFC 3530, Internet Engineering Task Force.

Thakur R, Gropp W, Lusk E (1999) On implementing MPI-IO portably and with high performance. In: Proceedings of the Sixth Workshop on I/O in Parallel and Distributed Systems, Atlanta, Georgia, pp 23-32.

Welch B, Halevy B, Goodson G, Black D, Adamson A (2005) pNFS operations. Internet Engineering Task Force Internet-Draft.

9 Performance Modeling of Enterprise Grids

Doug L. Hoffman[1], Amy Apon[2], Larry Dowdy[3], Baochuan Lu[2], Nathan Hamm[3], Linh Ngo[1], and Hung Bui[2]

[1] *Acxiom Corporation*
Conway, AR, USA

[2] *Department of Computer Science, University of Arkansas at Fayetteville*
Fayetteville, AR, USA

[3] *Department of Computer Science, Vanderbilt University*
Nashville, TN, USA

9.1 Introduction and Background

Modeling has long been recognized as an invaluable tool for predicting the performance behavior of computer systems. Modeling software, both commercial and open source, is widely used as a guide for the development of new systems and the upgrading of exiting ones. Tools such as queuing network models, stochastic Petri nets, and event driven simulation are in common use for stand alone computer systems and networks. Unfortunately, no set of comprehensive tools exists for modeling complex distributed computing environments such as the ones found in emerging grid deployments. With the rapid advance of grid computing, the need for improved modeling tools specific to the grid environment has become evident. This chapter addresses concepts, methodologies, and tools that are useful when designing, implementing, and tuning the performance in grid and cluster environments.

9.1.1 Performance Modeling

Typically, performance modeling is used to predict the impact of changes to a computer system, whether the system is a traditional monolithic computer or an enterprise grid system consisting of a collection of independent computers. A model can be used to predict the impact of system changes and various "what-if"

Y. Chan et al. (eds.), *Data Engineering*, International Series in Operations
Research & Management Science 132, DOI 10.1007/978-1-4419-0176-7_9,
© Springer Science+Business Media, LLC 2010

scenarios. Modeling tools can be useful in planning upgrades for system owners and can be a powerful sales tool for a vendor. Several kinds of "what-if" scenarios may be of interest. For example, a performance evaluator may be interested in predicting the response time or utilization of the system for scenarios such as adding 50% more load, increasing the number of processors by 10%, replacing single core processors by dual core upgrades, the failure of 5% of the nodes, expanding disk storage by a factor of 3, increasing memory by 2GB/node, changing the scheduling algorithm, deploying additional service nodes to ease the burden on a particular grid service that is overloaded, or switching to a faster network interconnect. Quality of Service (QoS) and Service Level Agreements (SLAs) can also be predicted by the model prior to system deployment. Vendors of traditional computing platforms have long had modeling tools and experimental test-bed environments available to assist in sizing new systems, however, applying these tools and developing new performance prediction tools to enterprise grid systems brings a new set of challenges (Shan et al. 2003).

Enterprise grids consist of collections of commodity computers, as shown in Fig. 9.1. Users submit jobs using a batch scheduling systems or other client software (Bode et al. 2000, Epema et al. 1996, Lifka 1995, Platform 2006). Application processes are assigned to some number of whole computers, individual processors, or cores (often loosely called "nodes") on the system. In a typical batch delivery system, such as the Acxiom CDI environment described in the introductory chapter of this section, an application holds the nodes exclusively until it completes, at which time the nodes are released for use by a newly scheduled application. Under these conditions, the resource usage characteristics of the application such as the number of nodes, run time, cpu usage, and wait time, are well known or easily obtained. From these characteristics, reasonable performance models can be constructed.

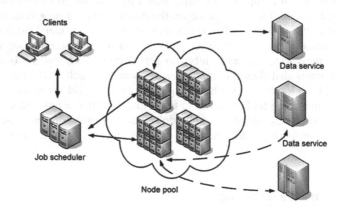

Fig. 9.1. Simplified View of an Enterprise Grid

Performance modeling in High Performance Computing (HPC) environments tends to concentrate on the characteristics of a specific algorithm or application mapped onto a limited range of specialized hardware components. This form of modeling can also be useful in a grid environment but, by itself, is not sufficient to capture the full complexity of an enterprise grid. In contrast to HPC environments, enterprise grids are more often used for High Throughput Computing (HTC). HTC favors many simultaneous processing jobs running concurrently, under an ever changing mix of resource usage patterns. HTC environments also tend to have a more Service Oriented Architecture (SOA) where at least part of a job's processing takes place on nodes providing common data services also as shown in Fig. 9.1. If not sized properly, these shared service nodes can bottleneck the entire HTC grid. Thus, HTC grids present a more complex computational environment than is usually found in the HPC world.

9.1.2 Capacity Planning Tools and Methodology

In a distributed computing environment such as that found in an enterprise grid system, the challenges of capacity planning are magnified by the scale and variability of the applications and components. It is essential for business planning purposes to identify the resource needs of client applications at the time that a grid computing system is being designed, configured, and deployed. Resource needs must also be continually reevaluated throughout the lifetime of the system as the demands on the system evolve (Wolski et al. 1999).

Capacity planning proceeds in a series of six steps as illustrated in Fig. 9.2. In Step 1, the performance of the current system is measured. Performance data collected includes trace files of submission, start, and completion times of all jobs. Also included are the hardware and software resources required by each job such as the number of processor nodes and the number and name of specific data services. These measurements form a *feature vector* for each job submitted to the system

---

1. Collect measurement data of the system hardware (e.g. node speeds, memory capacities) and of the system workload (e.g., job requirements, job dependencies, shared services).

2. Characterize the workload into a concise, representative, and understandable description.

3. Develop a baseline model using a modeling technique or tool such as simulation, analytic queuing models, or Petri nets.

4. Validate the output of the baseline model against measured performance metrics such as response times, throughput, and availability.

5. Develop prediction models by altering characteristics of the workload or system, such as the number of available nodes or the arrival rate of jobs.

6. Validate the prediction models.

Fig. 9.2. The Six Step Capacity Planning Process

In Step 2, workload characterization techniques are used to identify homogeneous classes of jobs that place similar resource demands on the system. This creates a description of the workload that is much smaller in size and with less complexity than the measurement data: a concise workload model that can be input into a simulation or an analytic model. Homogeneous workload classes are also used to identify patterns and trends in the data as a function of time.

In Step 3, a baseline model is constructed, typically using simulation but possibly including analytic, queuing, or Petri net models. In Step 4, the baseline model is calibrated and validated by comparing it against the measured performance data to verify that it accurately represents the real system. If the model is not considered to be accurate enough then Steps 1-4 may be repeated.

In Step 5, future workloads and projected new system acquisitions or upgrades are hypothesized. Future workloads may be calculated by using trend analysis on the characterized workload. Using the hypothesized new system environment, the model is used to predict future performance. In Step 6 (if possible), these prediction models are validated against the measured performance of the new system environment as it evolves over time.

The model produces various performance metrics for the grid, including node utilizations, job response times, and system throughput. The role of the model is to abstract and capture the primary characteristics of the system and to help assess whether the expected workload response times and throughputs will likely be met by the grid design. Alternative design scenarios created by varying any combination of the system features can be evaluated and compared on the basis of the output from the model analysis. Since the required objective of the system, such as a Service Level Agreement (SLA) for the response time of applications, can be specified, the model results can be used for business value analysis. For instance, the model can be used to assess whether or not a new client's workload can be handled with existing hardware without violating the SLAs of current clients (Czajkowski et al. 2004).

Capacity planning is an art with a well established history, encompassing experimental design, measurement, and analysis techniques. A model is a useful tool for providing insight for capacity planning, but the actual performance of an enterprise grid depends on complex and subtle interactions between factors including the number and types of resources, workload intricacies, memory management schemes, job scheduling policies, pipelining techniques, and caching policies (Hamscher et al. 2000). The remainder of this chapter is organized around the six step capacity planning process shown in Fig. 9.2. Section 9.2 discusses the primary aspects of measurement collection and preliminary data analysis (Step 1). Section 9.3 provides a detailed treatment of workload characterization (Step 2). Baseline model construction and modeling tools (Step 3) are presented in Section 9.4. The remaining steps of baseline model validation, prediction model construction (i.e., "what-if" scenarios), and prediction model validation (Steps 4, 5, and 6) are illustrated in a case study presented in Section 9.5. The chapter concludes with a summary in Section 9.6.

9.2 Measurement Collection and Preliminary Analysis

The initial step in the capacity planning process is to collect workload measurement data and then to perform preliminary analysis on it. Preliminary analysis of the collected data not only provides insight into the user behavior and the load it puts on the actual system but also reveals the significant features to be selected for workload characterization. The workload data is typically a workload trace file that has been acquired from the enterprise grid job scheduler and monitoring system (David 2006, Legrand et al. 2004, Massie et al. 2004). An example trace file is shown in Fig. 9.3.

	A	B	C	D	E	F	G	H	I
1	Job ID		DOW	submit date	hour	minute	start datetime	stop datetime	nodes
2	01719395	HIVEGRID	Tue	3/1/06	0	2	3/1/06 0:02	3/1/06 5:40	1
3	01721185	HIVEGRID	Wed	3/1/06	5	9	3/1/06 5:09	3/1/06 5:40	4
4	01721823	HIVEGRID	Wed	3/1/06	9	42	3/1/06 9:42	3/1/06 10:02	1
5	01722187	RECORDOP	Tue	3/1/06	0	42	3/1/06 0:46	3/1/06 2:53	10
6	01722787	HIVEGRID	Tue	3/1/06	0	5	3/1/06 0:05	3/1/06 0:08	16
7	01722788	HIVEGRID	Tue	3/1/06	0	8	3/1/06 0:09	3/1/06 0:09	1
8	01722831	HIVEGRID	Tue	3/1/06	0	2	3/1/06 0:02	3/1/06 0:03	1
9	01722838	HIVEGRID	Tue	3/1/06	0	4	3/1/06 0:04	3/1/06 0:04	1
10	01722839	HIVEGRID	Tue	3/1/06	0	5	3/1/06 0:05	3/1/06 0:08	16
11	01722840	HIVEGRID	Tue	3/1/06	0	8	3/1/06 0:09	3/1/06 0:09	1
12	01722842	HIVEGRID	Tue	3/1/06	0	6	3/1/06 0:06	3/1/06 0:09	4
13	01722845	HIVEGRID	Tue	3/1/06	0	7	3/1/06 0:07	3/1/06 0:08	2
14	01722848	HIVEGRID	Tue	3/1/06	0	9	3/1/06 0:09	3/1/06 0:17	1
15	01722849	HIVEGRID	Tue	3/1/06	0	18	3/1/06 0:52	3/1/06 0:55	16
16	01722850	HIVEGRID	Tue	3/1/06	0	55	3/1/06 0:56	3/1/06 0:56	1
17	01722851	HIVEGRID	Tue	3/1/06	0	9	3/1/06 0:09	3/1/06 0:49	2
18	01722852	RECORDOP	Tue	3/1/06	0	11	3/1/06 0:53	3/1/06 0:55	2
19	01722853	HIVEGRID	Tue	3/1/06	0	20	3/1/06 0:46	3/1/06 0:46	1
20	01722861	HIVEGRID	Tue	3/1/06	0	35	3/1/06 0:53	3/1/06 0:53	1
21	01722862	HIVEGRID	Tue	3/1/06	0	53	3/1/06 0:53	3/1/06 0:57	16
22	01722863	HIVEGRID	Tue	3/1/06	0	57	3/1/06 0:57	3/1/06 0:57	1
23	01722865	HIVEGRID	Tue	3/1/06	0	47	3/1/06 0:48	3/1/06 0:52	16
24	01722866	HIVEGRID	Tue	3/1/06	0	52	3/1/06 0:52	3/1/06 0:54	1
25	01722867	HIVEGRID	Tue	3/1/06	0	52	3/1/06 0:52	3/1/06 0:53	1
26	01722868	HIVEGRID	Tue	3/1/06	0	43	3/1/06 0:46	3/1/06 0:47	1
27	01722869	HIVEGRID	Tue	3/1/06	0	46	3/1/06 0:46	3/1/06 0:47	1
28	01722870	HIVEGRID	Tue	3/1/06	0	47	3/1/06 0:48	3/1/06 0:51	16
29	01722871	HIVEGRID	Tue	3/1/06	0	51	3/1/06 0:51	3/1/06 0:51	1
30	01722875	HIVEGRID	Tue	3/1/06	0	48	3/1/06 0:49	3/1/06 0:49	1
31	01722876	HIVEGRID	Tue	3/1/06	0	49	3/1/06 0:49	3/1/06 0:52	16
32	01722877	HIVEGRID	Tue	3/1/06	0	53	3/1/06 0:53	3/1/06 0:53	1
33	01722881	HIVEGRID	Tue	3/1/06	0	50	3/1/06 0:51	3/1/06 0:51	1

Fig. 9.3. Example of a Workload Trace File

This trace file was produced from the job scheduler and monitoring system running on the enterprise grid at Acxiom Corporation. The entire trace file contains 27 fields. Nine of them are shown in Fig. 9.3. The fields shown are typical of those produced by commercial and open source job scheduling and monitoring systems, and include the job ID, and job type (or category), the submit time as date, hour, and minute, the job start date and time, the completion date and time, and the number of nodes used by the job. Other fields that may appear in typical trace files include the memory usage, the number of records or bytes read, and the job priority. From this sample raw data, several workload characteristics can be determined for each job. These are extracted into a feature vector for each job.

For example, the feature vector for the job described on line 2 might be as simple as:

$$[1,3,338,1]$$

Here, the first field represents the type of job that it is (i.e., 1=HIVEGRID, 2=RECORDOP), the second field represents the day of the week that the job was submitted (i.e., 1=Sunday, 2=Monday, etc.), the third field represents the duration of the job in minutes (i.e., the difference between 00:02 and 05:40), and the fourth field represents the number of grid nodes required by the job. Using this same set of features, the feature vector for the job described on line 5 would be:

$$[2,3,131,10]$$

By performing such a preliminary data analysis, various patterns in job behavior can be extracted. For example, in the above trace, the jobs described on lines 6, 10, 15, 21, 23, and 28 are all quite similar since they are all HIVEGRID jobs, submitted on a Tuesday, executing on 16 nodes for 3-4 minutes. This indicates a particular class of jobs, or a representative job type, that may be appropriate to characterize for the simulation or analytical modeling engines. This example also illustrates potential, yet common, inconsistencies in collected data measurements, as evidenced by lines 2 and 3 since 3/1/06 cannot be both Tuesday and Wednesday. (In fact, it is Wednesday.) Understanding and adjusting for any inconsistencies found in the collected measurement data is also an important component of the preliminary analysis step.

9.3 Workload Characterization

One goal of capacity planning is to identify trends in usage patterns that can be used to forecast an expected user load at some time in the future, and this is difficult to do without some understanding of what is a typical, or average, usage pattern for the system (Feitelson 2006). A second goal is to create a realistic model of the system using input data from the real system. Both of these tasks require constructing a concise description of a known workload based upon performance trace data and other information about the execution environment. The trade-off in this process, known as *workload characterization*, is between complexity and predictive power. While the original trace data (i.e., the *natural workload*) contains very detailed information about the user load that is placed on the enterprise grid system, it is very difficult to construct a prediction workload from the trace data alone. Factors such as the number of nodes requested by a particular job, the overall run time, and the amount and rate of data read or written may not vary uniformly over a measurement period (Nitzberg et al. 2004). Typically, a *synthetic workload model* is constructed as an abstraction of the actual workload. The goal is to create a synthetic workload model that is as concise as possible while also being as close statistically to the actual workload as possible.

A critical step in workload characterization is identifying the set of features that will be used in the workload model. The model should include as many features from the actual workload as possible in order not to omit any important factors, but be simpler than the actual workload. Example features include the number of nodes required, runtime, number of records read, the job type, memory requirements, network bandwidth demands, processor needs, and software service requirements. Different systems are characterized by different features. Choosing which features to include in a representative workload model depends on the nature of the specific system, what parameters are actually available, and the purpose of the underlying performance study. In selecting the features, it is important that they be as statistically independent as possible. If multiple features correlate closely they should be combined or one eliminated from the feature set, due to redundancy. For example, if jobs come in three types and each type always corresponds to the same required node count then either node count or job type should be eliminated. The features that are chosen make up the feature vector.

After the features for the workload model are chosen, the measurement data are organized according to the feature vector. That is, the actual workload is described by the set of values that include all of the selected features for each of the jobs in the system, where each job is described by its feature vector.

In workload characterization, jobs are clustered into groups, or classes, of jobs so that the variability within the classes is lower than that of the entire data set. The job classes are generally defined by the average values for the class of the entries in the feature vector. These average values will provide input parameters to a system model. Various workload characterization techniques may be applied to an enterprise grid capacity planning system. Two techniques, K-means clustering (Robinson et al. 2006) and hierarchical workload characterization are described in this section.

The K-means clustering technique considers all of the features together when clustering jobs into classes, whereas the hierarchical workload characterization technique considers the features serially. Both techniques have been used historically in capacity planning studies. Informally, the difference between the two algorithms can be described by considering how the algorithms may be applied to the sample jobs illustrated as points on the graph in Fig. 9.4.

Figure 9.4 illustrates a graph of several sample jobs that are described with two job features, the number of nodes and the run time. In the sample data, a job can use 2, 4, or 8 nodes, with varying run times. If both features are considered together in the clustering, as in K-means clustering, then visually the jobs appear to first fall naturally into two classes as described by the solid ovals. However, if the features are considered sequentially, with the number of nodes considered first, then the jobs are first classified in this example into three classes as described by the dashed rectangles. In either case, the jobs can be further classified into more classes using either K-means clustering or hierarchical clustering. The four double circles show classes that might result by further clustering with either algorithm. If continued long enough, the two techniques will always result in the same set of classes—with every job in a separate class of its own. The art of modeling lies in finding the minimum number of classes that adequately describe the data.

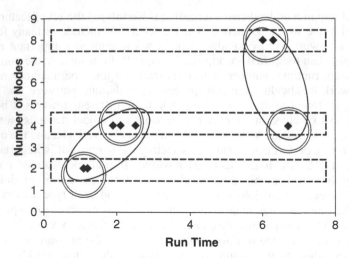

Fig. 9.4. Sample Job Data with Two Features

9.3.1 K-means Clustering

The K-means clustering algorithm finds k distinct classes of jobs, or clusters, when given a specific workload data set. The process begins by identifying the desired number of clusters, k, and a set of k initial starting points for the midpoint, or centroid, of each cluster. A centroid is defined as the point whose coordinates are obtained by computing the average of each of the coordinates (i.e., feature values) of the points of the jobs assigned to the cluster. Formally, the K-means clustering algorithm consists of the following steps.

1. Choose a number of desired clusters, k.
2. Choose k starting points to be used as initial estimates of the cluster centroids. These are the initial starting values.
3. Examine each point (i.e., job) in the workload data set and assign it to the cluster whose centroid is nearest to it.
4. When each point is assigned to a cluster, recalculate the new k centroids.
5. Repeat steps 3 and 4 until no point changes its cluster assignment, or until a maximum number of passes through the data set is performed.

The feature vector of the job can be thought of as a point in an M-dimensional space, where M is the number of features. Like other clustering algorithms, K-means requires that a distance metric between points be defined. This distance metric is used in step 3 of the algorithm given above. A common distance metric is the Euclidean distance. Given two sample points, p_i and p_j, each described by their feature vectors, $p_i = (F_{i1}, F_{i2}, \ldots, F_{iM})$ and $p_j = (F_{j1}, F_{j2}, \ldots, F_{jM})$, the distance, d_{ij}, between p_i and p_j is given by:

$$d_{ij} = \sqrt{\sum_{m=1}^{M} (F_{im} - F_{jm})^2} \qquad (9.1)$$

If the features being used in the feature vector have different relative values and ranges, the distance computation may be distorted since features with large absolute values tend to dominate the computation. To mitigate this, it is common for the feature values to be scaled in order to minimize distortion.

There are several different methods that can be used to scale data. The method used in the examples in this chapter is z-score scaling. Z-score scaling normalizes data values using the mean and standard deviation of each feature set. The z-score equation is:

$$F_{im}^* = \frac{F_{im} - \mu_m}{\sigma_m} \qquad (9.2)$$

where F_{im} is the value of the mth feature of the ith job (i.e., the data point), μ_m is the mean value of the mth feature, and σ_m is the standard deviation of the mth feature. Thus, before the algorithm is applied, the original data set is scaled, using the z-score scaling technique, where the feature mean is subtracted from the feature value and then divided by the standard deviation of that feature (i.e., F_{im} is replaced by its scaled value F_{im}^*). This technique has the effect of normalizing the workload features so that no single feature dominates in the clustering algorithm.

The number of clusters to be found, along with the initial starting point values are specified as input parameters to the clustering algorithm. Given the initial starting values, the distance from each (z-score scaled) sample data point to each initial starting value is found using equation (9.1). Each data point is then placed in the cluster associated with the nearest starting point. New cluster centroids are calculated after all data points have been assigned to a cluster.

Suppose that C_{im} represents the centroid of the mth feature of the ith cluster. Then,

$$C_{im} = \frac{\sum_{j=1}^{n_i} F_{i,jm}^*}{n_i} \qquad (9.3)$$

where $F_{i,jm}^*$ is the mth (scaled) feature value of the jth job assigned to the ith cluster and where n_i is the number of data points in cluster i. The new centroid value is calculated for each feature in each cluster. These new cluster centroids are then treated as the new initial starting values and steps 3-4 of the algorithm are repeated. This continues until no data point changes the clusters or until a maximum number of passes through the data set are performed.

Given a clustered workload, an error function can be defined that describes how much error (or difference) there is between all of the jobs in the workload and their respective cluster centroids. In this study, the error function used is the sum of the distances that each point is from its cluster's centroid. Assuming that there are k clusters, the error function (E_k) is defined as:

$$E_k = \sum_{i=1}^{k} \sum_{j=1}^{n_i} \sum_{m=1}^{M} \left(F_{i,jm}^{*} - C_{im} \right)^2 \tag{9.4}$$

where $(F_{i,jm}^{*} - C_{im})^2$ is the distance measure between a data point and the cluster centroid to which it is assigned.

Typically, to determine the optimum number of clusters for a particular workload, the k-means clustering algorithm is run on the sample data set for a range of possible clusters, say, from $k = 1$ to 10. At the end of each run, the error value E_k is calculated using equation (9.4). These error values are then plotted on a graph against the number of clusters. As the number of clusters k increases, it is reasonable to expect that the value of E_k decreases, since increasing the number of cluster centroids to choose from makes it is more likely that any given job will be assigned to a cluster with a closer centroid. The final number of clusters in the data set is chosen by examining and selecting the "knee" of the E_k curve. For example, consider the generic E_k curve shown in Fig. 9.5. Here the knee occurs when $k = 4$. Significant reduction in E_k occurs when going from $k=1$ to $k=4$. However, reducing E_k further by increasing the number of clusters beyond 4 is minimal. To summarize, the algorithm is executed with different numbers of potential clusters, k. The E_k curve is constructed and the value of k at the curve's knee determines the optimal number of clusters for the data set.

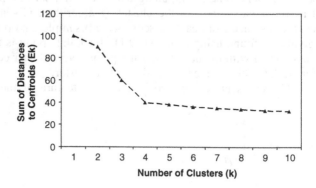

Fig. 9.5. Generic E-Curve

Determining the optimal number of clusters is often based on the experience of the modeler and illustrated the "art" of workload modeling. Often the decision is subjective and based on trial and error.

9.3.1.1 Starting Point Selection

In this section, a simple example is used to illustrate the fact that choosing different starting point values in the K-means clustering technique can lead to different clusters with different error values. First, consider a workload with a single feature. Suppose that the feature values range from 1.0 to 5.0 and that there are seven samples at 1.0, one sample at 3.0, and one at 5.0. Figures 9.6 and 9.7 show the results of running the K-clustering algorithm on the data set when trying to find two clusters. Figure 9.6 shows the two clusters that are found when the initial starting points are 1.7 and 5.1. Eight data points are placed in the first cluster, with a centroid value of 1.25. The second cluster consists of one data point, with a centroid value of 5.0. The error function value is $E_t = 3.5$.

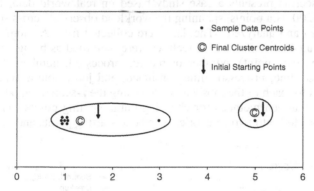

Fig. 9.6. Starting Points Example 1a

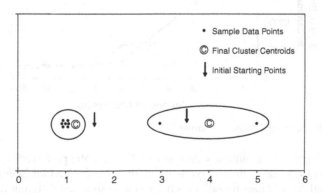

Fig. 9.7. Starting Points Example 1b

Figure 9.7 shows the two clusters that are found when the initial starting points are 1.5 and 3.5. With these starting points, one cluster consists of the seven data points with a centroid value of 1.0 and the other cluster consists of two data points with a centroid value of 4.0. This clustering leads to an error function value or $E_2 = 2.0$. This simple example illustrates that the selection of starting point values is important when trying to determine the best representation of a workload. In comparing Figs. 9.6 and 9.7 to determine which of the two clusterings is "better," a case can be made that a tight cluster is centered on 1.0, with the other two data points being outliers. This is captured in the second (i.e., Fig. 9.7) clustering and also results in a lower E_2 value. Thus, lower values of E_k are taken as better clustering representations.

9.3.1.2 K-means Analysis Example

As a further example of the use of K-means clustering to select workload job categories, this section presents a case study based on real world data. In this case study, over 4200 data points, spanning the workload observed across several days, were collected and analyzed. The data were collected from Acxiom's enterprise grid computing environment. Five features were identified as being descriptive of each job (i.e., data point): number of records processed, number of processors used, response time, processor time consumed, and job resource type. Each of these features for each of the jobs was scaled using the z-score method.

A total of fourteen methods for choosing initial starting points were analyzed. These methods fell into two categories: synthetic starting points and actual sample starting points.

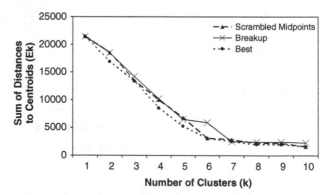

Fig. 9.8. Synthetic/Actual Sample Comparison

Figure 9.8 presents a summary comparison between the preferred actual sample method (*breakup*), the preferred synthetic method (*scrambled midpoints*), and the "best" overall error values found at each k when all fourteen different methods are considered. For example, *scrambled medians* could have found the lowest error value for k=3 clusters, *breakup* could have found the lowest error value for k=4 clusters, and *random* could have found the lowest error value for k=5 clusters. Based on Fig. 9.8, *scrambled midpoints* (marginally) outperforms *breakup* and never seems to deviate far from the best curve. Based on the study data, *scrambled midpoints* is the preferred method for choosing initial starting values for the K-means clustering algorithm.

9.3.2 Hierarchical Workload Characterization

In contrast to K-means workload characterization, hierarchical workload characterization classifies the jobs according to features that are considered one at a time. This technique is particularly effective when the values in the feature that is being considered are discrete and the number of possible values is relatively small. An example of a feature that may have this characteristic is the number of nodes required by the application in the enterprise grid system.

Even when the jobs fall naturally into classes based on some discrete criteria, just as with K-means clustering, a decision may need to be made concerning the number of classes that is most descriptive. Table 9.1 shows a set of jobs that have been classified into 13 classes based on the number of nodes used by each job along with the average arrival rate and service rate of the job. Some jobs classes, such as the class requesting 11 nodes in Table 9.1, have a relatively small number of arrivals during the measurement period, resulting in a very low arrival rate. This low arrival rate in proportion to the arrival rate in the other classes is difficult to model accurately in a discrete event simulation. It is preferable to combine this job class with another job class.

Table 9.1. Original Hierarchical Classes Based upon Number of Nodes

Number of Nodes	Arrival Rate (jobs/hr)	Service Rate (jobs/hr)	Number of Jobs
1	13.70	10.27	9862
2	6.39	12.96	4598
4	4.67	3.90	3361
5	0.26	3.17	186
6	0.34	23.47	245
8	0.21	2.16	150
10	0.88	1.59	631
11	0.01	8.04	7
12	3.58	4.61	2578
15	0.44	1.30	317
16	5.68	2.21	4089
20	0.71	1.58	510
30	0.03	0.87	23

Table 9.2 illustrates the same job data, only classified into just six classes based on the number of required nodes. The jobs requiring 10, 11, and 12 nodes, respectively, have been placed into a class that requires an average of 12 nodes and the arrival and service rates are calculated based on the aggregate measurements of all jobs placed into that class. Other classes with low arrival rates have also been combined. It is possible to create a discrete event simulation model with more accuracy, with higher confidence, and using fewer calculations with the classes as described in Table 9.2 compared to the classes as described in Table 9.1. The use of a smaller number of classes reduces complexity, makes it easier to ask "what-if" types of questions, and facilitates the development of a workload that can be used in a prediction model.

Table 9.2. Modified Hierarchical Classes Based upon Number of Nodes

Number of Nodes	Arrival Rate (jobs/hr)	Service Rate (jobs/hr)	Number of Jobs
1	13.70	10.27	9862
2	6.39	12.96	4598
4	4.67	3.90	3361
5,6,8 (8)	0.81	11.47	581
10, 11, 12 (12)	4.47	4.02	3216
15, 16, 20 (16)	6.86	2.08	4939

With hierarchical workload characterization the process often includes aggregating two or more small classes into a larger class based on the number of jobs in the small class and the similarity of the values of the feature used in the classification. The resulting classes may vary depending on how this decision is made.

9.3.3 Other Issues in Workload Characterization

No standard technique exists for defining the set of important features or for the process for defining workload classes from the measurement data of an enterprise grid system. In the HPC environment, the Parallel Workloads Archive (Parallel workload archive 2006) employs a standard format to archive a collection of parallel workloads. The format is used for both real and synthetic workloads, and it attempts to accommodate all important fields. This archive contains workloads from production parallel supercomputers, such as NASA Ames iPSC/860, SDSC DataStar, CTC SP2, and the LANL CM-5. These parallel workload models can be improved in various ways to make them more descriptive for enterprise grid systems. For example, the format can be extended to include additional resources such as memory and I/O, and to include information about shared services in enterprise grid systems.

Two categories of parallel workload models are often defined in the HPC setting. A *rigid job* model creates a sequence of jobs with arrival time, required number of processors, and runtime as three example features characterizing each job (Lublin and Feitelson 2003). This model represents applications that are fine-tuned for a specific parallel machine and configuration. For example, if a parallel program is design for 32 processors, assigning more processors to it will yield little benefit. A *flexible job* model provides total computation and a speed up function (e.g., an execution "signature" indicating that doubling the number of processors causes the application to run 1.5 times faster) as features characterizing each job. This model can be used to represent flexible applications where the applications can be run on a different number of processors.

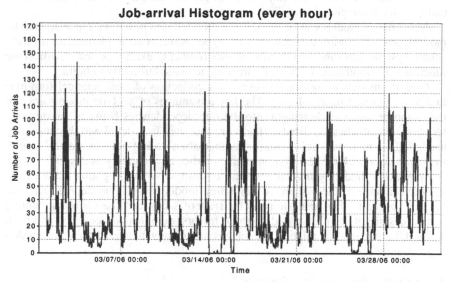

Fig. 9.9. A Typical Job Arrival Pattern in an Enterprise Grid

While both K-means clustering and the hierarchical workload clustering tend to groups jobs together that have a feature value or values that are "close" to the mean for the class, neither of these techniques describes the distribution of the values of all the jobs in the class. For example, the 1-node class shown in Table 9.1 above has an arrival rate of 13.7 jobs per hour over the measurement period. However, these jobs could have arrived uniformly spaced over the measurement period, or could have come all at one time, or could be spaced according to a statistical arrival process. Figure 9.9 illustrates a typical arrival pattern for an enterprise grid. In this figure, the number of arrivals for every thirty minute time segment is graphed over a five day period. The graph shows that the number of arrivals depends on the work hours of the employees of the enterprise. The number of arrivals increases during the peak operating times of the day, and falls off during the non-peak operating times of the night. Unless this pattern of arrivals is captured in the workload description, the model may not be as accurate as required. Various statistical techniques, such as the use of heavy-tailed or hyperexponential distributions (Riska et al. 2002), have been used to model the burst patterns in workload arrivals and service times.

9.4 Baseline System Models and Tool Construction

Once performance data about the system and its workload are collected and characterized into a concise manageable representation, a baseline system model can be constructed (See Fig. 9.2, Step 3). Such performance models are often embedded within a more global modeling tool environment.

Performance models can be broadly categorized into prototype models, analytic models, and simulation models. A prototype model is an implementation of the actual system software and hardware environment, except perhaps with some functionality simulated. Prototypes are very accurate but costly to build.

Analytic models represent a system as a collection of mathematical formulae that have a closed form solution. The key advantages of analytic models are that they capture and provide insight into the interdependencies between various system components, but the disadvantages are that they lack detail and, because they are based on mathematical assumptions that often do not hold in the real world, they may not match the real system characteristics as accurately as desired.

Simulation modeling involves writing custom software programs that emulate the performance of the system. A simulation model can be very detailed and can be more accurate than analytic models. Tradeoffs between the various modeling techniques are often made based on three factors: complexity, accuracy, and cost. Table 9.3 compares the relative advantages and disadvantages of the three modeling techniques.

Table 9.3. Modeling Technique Tradeoffs

Model	Advantages	Disadvantages
prototype	very accurate	very expensive
analytic	insight to component interdependencies	lack of detail, may not match real system closely
simulation	high-level detail, more accurate than analytic models	more expensive to develop than analytic models, do not match real system as closely as a prototype

9.4.1 Analytic Models

Analytic performance models capture the fundamental aspects of a computer system and relate them to each other using mathematical formulae and computational algorithms. The mathematical basis of analytic models, such as queuing network models and Petri net models, is Markov state space modeling.

A Markov model is a probabilistic process over a set of states and state transitions. The defining characteristic of Markov models is that they are memoryless, which means knowing the current state alone is sufficient. That is, if the system is in a particular state, then the history of previous states visited is irrelevant when determining which state the system will go to next. Also, the length of time that the system is in a particular state is irrelevant. The only important aspect is the current state. For example, suppose there is currently a job running on a processor. If the system is memoryless then the probability that the job completes at some future time t is independent of how long the job has already been running.

Since the exponential distribution is the only continuous distribution that is memoryless, Markov models assume that the time spent between relevant events, such as job interarrival times and job service times, is exponentially distributed. Markov models of multi-class systems that use a First Come First Serve (FCFS) or priority scheduling policy are more complex because these policies depend on the order of specific job arrivals, which must then be included in the state information of the models. Also, since exponential assumptions of job interarrival times and job service times are often not satisfied in enterprise grid systems (e.g., uniform or Gaussian assumptions may be more accurate, or these times may be dependent on the time of day), the output values of a purely analytic model such as device utilization and response time may not match measured values from the real system very accurately.

The construction of a Markov model involves three steps: state space enumeration, state transition identification, and parameterization. Given a Markov model with N states and N desired unknowns (i.e., the steady state probability of being in each state) along with N linear equations, solving the model is a straightforward linear algebra problem. However, this illustrates another difficulty in using purely analytic models for enterprise grid systems. Though conceptually simple, in any reasonably sized real-world system, it is possible for the number of states to be so large that solving the model becomes computationally intractable. Due to this problem of state space explosion, even when analytical models can be used to describe the overall system structure, simulation is often used as the underlying model solution technique. Markov models are best used for the evaluation of high-level tradeoffs when the system size is small and detailed accuracy is not as important as finding answers quickly.

9.4.1.1 Queueing Networks

A Queueing Network (QN) model is a collection of interconnected queues, each of which consists of a waiting line and a resource that services user requests. Customers in the network arrive at a queue, wait in line until they reach the head of the line, and then spend a statistically determined amount of time being serviced before moving on to another (probabilistically determined) queue. QN models are used to approximate real queueing systems and can be analyzed mathematically. Figure 9.10 depicts such a queue.

Fig. 9.10. A Simple Queueing System

A queue in a QN model is defined by the resource type and queueing discipline utilized. Possible resource types include load independent (where the service rate is independent of the number of customers at the queue), load dependent (where the service rate depends on the number of customers present), and delay center (where there is no waiting time, mimicking the effect of an infinite number of servers). Some well-known queueing disciplines are First Come First Served (FCFS), Last In First Out (LIFO), priority, round robin, and processor sharing. Brief descriptions of these disciplines are given below:

- First Come First Served—customers are served one at a time in the order in which they arrive, independent of the specific customer class.
- Last In First Out—customers are served as soon as they arrive, with any customer that is preempted resuming its service upon completion of the later arriving customer.
- Priority—customers with higher priority are (preemptively) served first.
- Round Robin—customers are served cyclically by assigning equal time slices (i.e., quantum) uniformly to each customer, ignoring customer priority.
- Processor Sharing—customers share the processor equally, with n customers present each receiving $1/n^{th}$ of the processor. (Processor sharing is the limit of round robin as the time quantum approaches zero. FCFS is the limit of round robin as the time quantum approaches infinity.)

Customer classes can be either open or closed, depending on whether the number of customers (jobs) in a system changes over time or remains fixed. The classification of a QN model depends on its customer classes: the QN model is open if all its customer classes are open, closed if all classes are closed, and mixed if some classes are open and some are closed.

The input parameters of a QN model are broken into two groups: workload intensity and service demand. Workload intensity is defined in different terms for different workload classes. For example, arrival rates are used for open classes and customer populations are used for closed classes. The service demand of a given customer class on a resource is defined as the average service time required by the customer per visit to the resource times the average number of visits that the customer makes to the resource. The outputs of a QN model are performance metrics, such as the utilization of resources, system throughput, and user response time. The output depends on the performance metrics of interest for a particular study. One approach to obtain performance metrics from QN models is operational analysis (Denning and Buzen 1978), which establishes relationships among measurable quantities (operational variables) and known system data. Measurable quantities include the length of the observation period, the number of resources in the system, and the total number of requests completed. From these measurable quantities, a set of derived quantities can be obtained, which are used for defining the operational laws (Menascé et al. 1994):

- S_i: mean service time per completion at resource i;

- U_i: utilization of resource i;

- X_i: throughput (i.e., completions per unit time) of resource i;

- $_i$: arrival rate at resource i;

- X_0: system throughput;

- V_i: average number of visits per request to resource i.

- D_i: average demand of a customer placed on device i. $D_i = V_i S_i$.

- N: average number of customers in the system.

- R: average system response time.

- Z: average think time per customer.

- K: number of resources in the system.

The operational laws are summarized in Table 9.4.

Table 9.4. Operational Laws

Operational Laws	Definitions
Utilization Law	$U_i = S_i \times X_i$
Service Demand Law	$D_i = V_i \times S_i = \dfrac{U_i}{X_i}$
Forced Flow Law	$X_i = V_i \times X_0$
Little's Law	$N = R \times X_0$
Interactive Response Time Law	$R = \dfrac{N}{X_0} - Z$

Little's Law describes the fundamental long-term relationship between throughput, response time and the number of customers in a system in steady state. Little's law requires few assumptions as long as customers are not destroyed or created. It can be applied to any "black box" within a system, which may contain an arbitrary set of components. If R is the average time customers spent in the box (i.e., response time) and X_o is the departure rate from the b), then N is the average number of customers in the box.

Using the operational laws, an upper bound on throughput and a lower bound on response time can be determined through bounding analysis. The bounding behavior of a system is determined by its bottleneck resource, which has the highest utilization because it receives the highest service demand (Menascé et al. 1994). Equations 9.5 and 9.6 give the upper bound for throughput and lower bound for response time, respectively.

$$X_0 \leq \min\left[\frac{1}{\max\{D_i\}}, \frac{N}{\sum_{i=1}^{K} D_i}\right] \qquad (9.5)$$

$$R \geq \max\left[N \times \max D_i, \sum_{i=1}^{K} D_i\right] \qquad (9.6)$$

Building a QN model helps understand the nature of the workload and helps determine what kind of data to collect. The most important goal is to predict performance, primarily by identifying the sources of contention.

Queueing networks can be used to model a wide range of complex systems. For example, a multi-tier Internet application is modeled as a network of queues by Urgaonkar, et al. (2005). Each application tier is represented by a queue, employing a processor sharing (PS) queueing discipline. Each session in the multi-tier Internet application is modeled by a job, which passes through the tier queues while being serviced. At each queue, jobs either make a transition to the preceding queue or to a delay center, which models user think times.

Typical model inputs for this type of system include workload characteristics of various classes: visit ratios, service times, and think times measured on a per-class basis. Given the average service times, visit ratios, think times, and number of concurrent sessions (population size), this type of system can be solved with Mean Value Analysis (MVA) (Menascé et al. 2004). MVA accepts single values for model inputs, such as the service demands for different devices, and computes single values for system performance measures, such as the mean response time and mean processor utilization. Given the predicted workload of an application, a model can be used to determine the capacity needed to keep system response time below a desired target SLA.

As with analytic models, QN models have their limitations. When dealing with complex real-world systems, classic queueing theory is often too mathematically restrictive to model a system exactly. This restriction arises when the underlying theoretical assumptions do not accurately reflect the real system. Sometimes these differences can be safely ignored or approximated because they are not statistically significant. However, other times they can cause a model to behave differently than the system it is supposed to represent. A major limitation of the model described above is its inability to model resources held simultaneously by multiple tiers. For more complex systems, where resource sharing must be modeled in greater detail, other modeling techniques must be used. A popular tool used under such circumstances is a Petri Net.

9.4.1.2 Petri Nets

Petri nets provide a descriptive way of modeling details about the system that may be difficult to capture with just simulation code alone. The CPN Petri net tool package (CPN tools 2007) provides a framework for building a Petri net model of a system. The process of constructing the actual Petri net model using CPN is analogous to the process of constructing a simulation model using a simulation package. In both cases, the primary components of the system and the communication connections between them are identified and represented using a modeling language associated with the tool. The Petri net provides capacity planners with a visualization of the enterprise grid, which benefits the modeling process.

Figure 9.11 shows a Petri net model used to describe the use of shared services in an enterprise grid system. On the left side of the diagram, a job generator is used to periodically create job tokens. The time between job creations in the Petri net model is determined by the average job inter-arrival time, an input parameter that is determined by the workload characterization phase. The top middle part of the diagram models the acquisition of the required number of nodes and the required number of shared service "certificates." For each shared resource there is a finite number of certificates that are used to regulate the demand placed on the resource. Each job must acquire a number of certificates for each service it utilizes prior to execution. Since the number of certificates is limited, they act as a throttling mechanism for the associated shared resources.

The lower portion of the diagram models the job flow as each job progresses through the system using processors, shared services, and data records. As shown in the Petri net diagram, a generated job is placed into the job queue, where it waits to acquire the necessary resources before being launched by the scheduler. After the required nodes and shared service certificates are acquired, a job starts and then waits in another queue until the required data records become available. In this model, record locks are acquired after a job has been launched, which is logically different from acquiring nodes and certificates. This is a characteristic of the enterprise grid environment being modeled since nodes and shared services are acquired and reserved before accessing the database records.

The Petri net shows how jobs requiring shared services in the enterprise grid can be modeled. Once started, a job acquires the necessary records from a shared database and is then categorized as a Type I or Type II job. Type I jobs bypass all shared services, perform necessary computations on the acquired records, and then terminate.

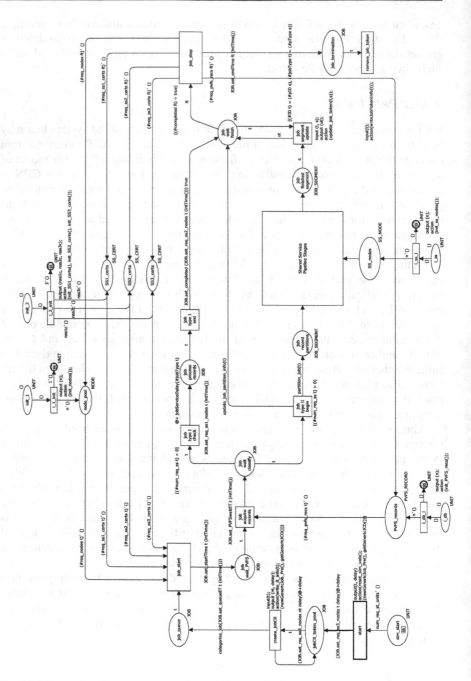

Fig. 9.11. Petri Net of an Enterprise Grid with Shared Services

Type II jobs are broken into a number of segments that is determined by a record block factor. The larger the block factor, the smaller the number of generated segments. Thus, a larger block factor means each segment will spend more time at each required shared service, in general. Each segment then flows through a series of pipeline stages, each representing the use of a specific shared service. Once all the job segments finish using all of the necessary shared services, the job terminates and returns its nodes and its shared service certificates.

The Petri net also illustrates how nodes are held exclusively by the jobs during the time period that they execute. The use of shared services is regulated by the acquisition of shared service certificates by each job. The certificates serve as a guarantee that the required shared services will be available when needed. These certificates regulate the number of jobs that are allowed to start, providing an operating threshold that prevents shared service overload. Thus, certificates provide a form of flow control through the shared service clusters.

At a given shared service, a job segment waits until the required number of shared service nodes is available. The shared service nodes are different from the nodes acquired before a job starts, where the former are used solely for executing shared services and the latter are assigned exclusively to the job. Thus, once launched, a job may have to wait for shared services due to other launched jobs or due to other segments in the same job. There is often a one-to-one relationship between shared service certificates and shared service nodes. This implies that one shared service certificate corresponds to (within the pipeline) acquiring one shared service node. Other mappings can be implemented and this feature adds flexibility to the overall net structure. While the modeling of shared services is possible using simulation alone, the Petri net assists a system modeler in defining this feature of the grid system.

The limitations of Markov models and QN models lie in their lack of detail and computational requirements. The limitation of Petri nets is their complexity. Though more capable than the other models described, Petri nets require more time to implement. For each of these techniques, software is available to aid the process of model creation.

9.4.2 Simulation Tools for Enterprise Grid Systems

A system simulation can either be written with or without using one of a number of available simulation tools. SimGrid (Legrand et al. 2003), GridSim (Buyya and Murshed 2002), and CPN Tools (CPN Tools 2007) are three tools that are available and appropriate for the modeling of enterprise grid systems.

SimGrid provides core functionalities for the simulation of distributed applications in heterogeneous distributed environments. In SimGrid, a resource is described by a name and related performance metrics. For a processor, the metrics include computational speed and availability; for a network link, available bandwidth and latency. SimGrid models time-shared resources by their latency (i.e., time to access the result) and service rate, which can be constants or vary according to collected traces (i.e., a series of time-stamped values). The load of the resources can be injected as constants or from real traces. These traces can be used to simulate background activities on time-shared resources.

GridSim is a discrete event simulation toolkit built on SimJava (Howell and McNab 1998) for the modeling and simulation of distributed resource management and scheduling for grid computing. It is designed after SimGrid to investigate scheduling issues in grid systems with a focus on grid economy based scheduling disciplines. Scheduling in GridSim involves notions of resource ownership, end-users, and brokers that discover resources and allocate them to end users. GridSim is a higher level simulator that is designed to study the interplay between scheduling decisions made by distributed brokers. GridSim models both system-centric and user-centric scheduling policies. If a user has a proprietary or customized resource broker, the scheduling policy can be optimized to accommodate the broker's requirements.

CPN Tools is another discrete event simulation environment that allows creation, specification, modification, simulation, and analysis of high level Petri nets, namely Colored Petri Nets (CPNs). A CPN is constructed from the system architecture, job flow description, and workload characterization. Jobs are represented by tokens and places are used to simulate the resource pool, execution states, and other workflow components. Job tokens contain all the data necessary to be propagated through the net. Transitions are used to time and sequence token propagation, as well as ensure necessary operating conditions and constraints are fulfilled. Unlike SimGrid and GridSim, CPN Tools does not provide any built-in functionality for particular modeling environments and the modeler is left to construct a custom CPN. To produce a large, flexible modeling environment for a distributed computing environment, a modeler usually needs to incorporate their own custom scripting and data analysis tools.

All of these tools require a significant level of programming skill to use effectively. They also do not provide support for all phases of the model development process. To address this, an integrated environment has been developed for doing model based capacity planning studies. This package, the Integrated Capacity Planning Environment (ICPE), is described in detail via an example capacity planning case study.

9.5 Enterprise Grid Capacity Planning Case Study

A joint research project was conducted by researchers from the University of Arkansas, Vanderbilt University, and Acxiom Corporation with a mission to specify, design and develop an integrated capacity planning environment for enterprise grid systems. This capacity planning study is based on performance data from an enterprise grid system used for large-scale data processing and made available by Acxiom Corporation. The enterprise grid architecture studied is a fully integrated production enterprise grid infrastructure for information-intensive applications.

This case study describes experiences in applying performance analysis techniques to Acxiom's enterprise grid system (Lu 2006). As a result of the capacity planning study, a standard format for the measurement trace files was adopted for both the measurement data and the simulation results. Several workload characterization techniques were compared and a repeatable, hierarchical workload characterization technique was adopted. The inclusion of both a Java-based simulation model and a Petri net model allowed the two models to be cross-validated against each other.

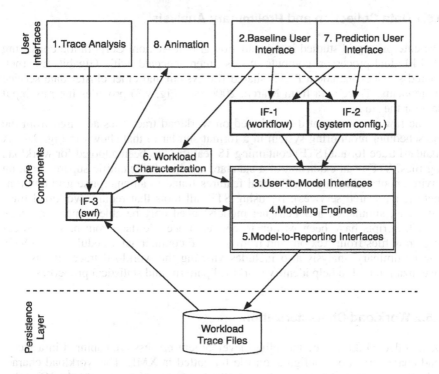

Fig. 9.12. Architecture of the Integrated Capacity Planning Environment (ICPE)

The tools used are integrated into a single environment with a graphical user interface through which enterprise grid capacity planning studies can be conducted in a streamlined fashion. The architecture of the Integrated Capacity Planning Environment (ICPE) is shown in Fig. 9.12. The toolkit is divided into three primary sections: 1) the user interfaces where ICPE interacts with the capacity planners, 2) the core components which contain the primary modeling engines, and 3) the persistence layer where all workload trace files and reports are archived. Figure 9.12 also illustrates the data and command flow between the ICPE components. Each component is functional as an independent module, providing greater flexibility in the modeling process. For example, modeling engines other than Java-based simulators or Petri nets could be used to drive simulations. Together,

the components form an integrated environment that provides a streamlined capacity planning process.

The ICPE proved to be useful at each of the steps of the capacity planning
process. The remainder of this section describes the Case Study using the six steps
of the capacity planning process as shown in Fig. 9.2.

9.5.1 Data Collection and Preliminary Analysis

The enterprise grid studied is a production grid at Acxiom Corporation consisting
of 140 dual-processor compute nodes interconnected with Gigabit Ethernet.
Shared services include a PVFS shared file system and other cluster data service
components. Trace data from March, 2006 (see Fig. 9.3) provides the raw input
data for the study.

The raw measurement data is based on workload trace files acquired from the
job scheduler monitoring system in a format similar to that shown in Fig. 9.4. A
standard trace format (STF) containing 18 features has been adopted for workload
log files. STF is an extension of a standard used in the scientific supercomputing
environment and includes additional features found in an enterprise grid environment (e.g., shared services). By using STF, all tools that require workload trace
data (e.g., simulation and Petri net models) need only be able to parse a single
format. Scripts have been written to convert trace file data from native sources
(e.g., raw files from Acxiom and from the LSF commercial schedulers) into STF.
The preliminary analysis also includes viewing the workload trace file using a
visualization tool to help identify workload patterns and statistical properties.

9.5.2 Workload Characterization

Data collected during the modeling development process are captured in a workload characterization configuration file formatted in XML. The workload characterization process produces a summary file that can be viewed using the ICPE display GUI. This summary file shows the tree structure of the hierarchical
characterization process. The display frame of the GUI is split into two panes: a
tree view and a table view. In the tree view pane, starting with the result of the
highest level process, the user can choose to go deeper into the tree and see the
subclusters created from the partial output of the current clusters. The table section
contains summary information of the chosen cluster such as the average, minimum, and maximum values of the features utilized. It also contains the summary
information of all the sub-clusters generated by this cluster. Figure 9.13 shows a
screen shot of the tree and table sections of the workload characterization frame in
the GUI.

In the preliminary analysis step of the capacity planning process, measurement
data are loaded into the ICPE environment from STF formatted trace files. After a
trace file is loaded, the GUI trace view component displays the file's header information. A variety of graphing options are provided to display the arrival behav-

ior and the statistical properties of the trace. These displays provide insight into what features and clustering algorithms are most appropriate for workload characterization.

In the workload characterization step of ICPE, users load a configuration file and guide the desired workload characterization process. Results are presented to the user in a detailed tree view showing the characteristics of the job classes. At the same time, the configuration is updated with the latest workload characterization information. When used in simulation mode, this enables a simulation to be executed immediately. A set of predefined graphs is provided to visualize the simulation results.

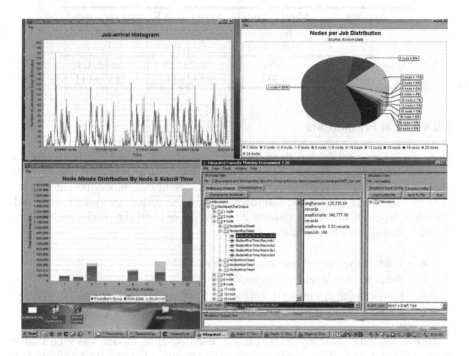

Fig. 9.13. Screen Shot of the ICPE User Interface

9.5.3 Development and Validation of the Baseline Model

In order to draw meaningful conclusions, the simulation model must be validated. Model correctness is validated by running a number of short simulations and comparing the resulting simulated system behavior with manually calculated results. Then, trace driven simulation runs are used to validate the model's accuracy by comparing performance metrics (e.g., queue lengths) from the simulation against actual measurements.

Because the simulation is driven by a non-deterministic workload, no single observation can provide a reliable indication of the system performance. Therefore, the sample mean of multiple run observations is used as a better estimator of system performance. The quality of the estimator is determined by establishing statistical confidence intervals for each metric.

For the example study, two batches of simulations were run for 60 and 90 simulated days, respectively. Each batch consisted of 29 individual runs with different random seeds. As shown in Table 9.5, the aggregated average values for the two performance metrics from simulations are close to that of the measured data.

Table 9.5. Validation Results.

Metrics (average)	Measurement Results (seconds)	Simulation Results (seconds) 95% Confidence Interval	
		60 days	90 days
Wait Time	558	562±108	563±104
Response Time	1333	1332±117	1437±111

9.5.4 Model Predictions

Once the baseline model has been validated, a "what-if" phase begins, where the model is used to answer or provide insight into questions of interest to the capacity planner. In order to investigate different future conditions, model parameters are modified to reflect anticipated future changes in the system or system workload. Different types of questions require different changes to the model parameters. Typical what-if questions might include:

- What is the current capacity of the system?
- What service levels are customers experiencing?
- How can the system performance be improved?
- Under what load will the system run out of capacity?

In this capacity planning study, the validated baseline model was modified to answer the question, "How many nodes will be required to meet the specified Service Level Agreement (SLA) if the job intensity increases?" The SLA in this case specifies that the average queuing delay be no more than 10 minutes. Figure 9.14 is a graph of the results obtained from the prediction model by varying the arrival intensity to represent a linearly increasing workload. An arrival intensity of 1.1 means that there are ten percent more jobs for all job classes (i.e., a multiplication factor of 1.1).

Multiple simulation runs were performed for each projected arrival intensity while varying the node count from 120 to 170. The curve shown in the graph represents the minimum number of nodes for which the average queuing time is no more than 10 minutes. In other words, the graph shows the minimum number of nodes required to meet the SLA for overall job arrival intensity factors from 1.0 to 1.6.

Given a designated number of nodes in the system, this graph also indicates the maximum arrival intensity the system can sustain while meeting the SLA. As expected, as the arrival intensity increases, the number of nodes required to meet the SLA also increases. For example, as the workload increases by 60% (i.e., as the workload intensity increases from 1.0 to 1.6), the number of nodes needed to meet the SLA increases from 120 to 163 (i.e., a 36% increase). It is interesting to note that a 60% increase in workload can be handled by only a 36% increase in the amount of resources.

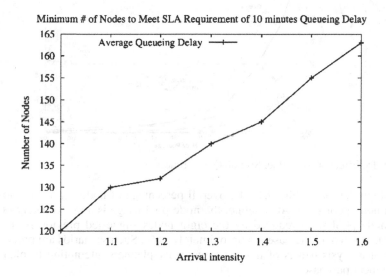

Fig. 9.14. Example Case Study Results

A variant "what-if" scenario is: *What is the effect of varying the number of processing nodes in the node pool?* Here the initial size of the node pool is varied from 100 to 200 nodes, in increments of 10. The SLA is a maximum waiting/queueing time of 15 minutes. The effect on queue time is shown in Fig. 9.15.

The bold line indicates the overall average queue time and the black dot on this line at 128 nodes marks the baseline average queue time of 7.82 minutes. As the number of processing nodes (node pool size) increases, the average job queue time decreases. An overall queue time of approximately 40 minutes is expected when the node pool size is 100 nodes and a queue time of nearly zero is expected as the node pool size approaches 200.

The regular black lines in Fig. 9.15 indicate the queueing times observed by each of the six individual workload classes. In order to maintain an SLA of 15 minutes for overall queue time, it is necessary to maintain a node pool size of approximately 120 nodes. Therefore, the node pool size can be reduced by approximately eight nodes, to 120, and still meet a 15-minute queue time SLA for the overall average. However, notice that at the baseline, a 15-minute SLA is not met for the class C16 jobs. The node pool must be increased to approximately 140 nodes if all job class queue times are required to meet such an SLA.

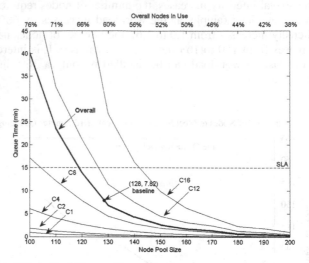

Fig. 9.15. Effect of Node Pool Size on Queue time

Along the top of Fig. 9.15 the overall percentage of nodes in use is shown for each node pool size. At baseline, the node pool usage is approximately 60%. If the node pool were reduced by the eight nodes suggested previously, the node pool usage would increase to approximately 66%. Such scenarios are precisely the type of analysis that is of interest to capacity planners attempting to plan future equipment purchases.

In this capacity planning study, the model was not compared with the actual performance of the system as it evolved over time, though this type of analysis is quite common. Long term predictions can provide an extra level of validation, helping to confirm that the workload model and the system description are robust enough to accurately forecast future conditions. However, if the characteristics of the system or the workload vary over time it may not be possible to validate long term performance predictions. If more hardware, with different performance characteristics, is added to the grid, the model may no longer accurately represent the system. Similarly, changing the balance among job types may lead to behaviors not captured by previous baseline data, again invalidating the model. The cautious modeler must constantly reassess the assumptions represented by the model in question. A model is at best a reasonable approximation of the real-world system it represents. If the system changes, the modeling process must be reevaluated.

9.6 Summary

This chapter presents a modeling paradigm and an introduction to several tools for enterprise grid system capacity planning. This approach consists of several phases: preliminary analysis, workload characterization, and system modeling. K-means clustering and hierarchical workload characterization are described as techniques for workload characterization.

Special emphasis is placed on using the ICPE toolkit (available on the Internet at http://sourceforge.net/projects/icpe/). The case study presented illustrates the modeling paradigm and demonstrates the usefulness of the toolkit. A six step modeling methodology is described and demonstrated from the initial data collection step through the final validation step. The methodology and toolkit have been successfully used on grids in both commercial and academic settings.

At Acxiom Corporation, a model has been used to plan future purchases of equipment and also to justify reallocation of existing resources. At the University of Arkansas, a modeling study has been performed to help select the most effective proposal for a new computing cluster. In both cases, the cost of modeling proved much less than the benefits it provided. As computer systems grow more complex human intuition regarding system performance becomes less reliable and modeling becomes a necessity.

9.7 Exercises

1. Collect sample data from a grid system and analyze it. Is the data consistent? Are there distinct classes apparent in the workload? What features would you use to characterize the data?
2. Suppose that Job 1 requires 4 seconds of CPU time, 2 seconds of disk time, and 10 MB of memory. That is, Job 1's feature vector is (4,2,10). Likewise, suppose that Job 2 and Job 3 have feature vectors of (2,6,2) and (4,0,4), respectively. Suppose the goal is to group the three jobs into two clusters. Use the K-means clustering algorithm to determine the two clusters.
3. Considering the same data as in the previous exercise. Use hierarchical workload characterization to determine two classes. What decisions do you have to make? What missing information might help you make better decisions? Do you get the same sets of jobs as with K-means clustering?
4. Reconsider exercise 2. Does the answer depend upon the initial starting points chosen? Justify by selecting various starting points and then generalize the observations.
5. Reconsider exercise 2 again. Does the answer depend upon the scaling technique selected for the individual feature values? Justify by selecting various scaling techniques and then generalize the observations.
6. Often, and unlike the previous exercises, the number of workload classes is unknown a priori. Given the following workload feature vector measurements, how many clusters would be identified and what are they?

$$(1, 3, 1, 2),$$
$$(2, 1, 5, 4),$$
$$(2, 0, 2, 2),$$
$$(3, 4, 2, 2), \text{ and}$$
$$(20, 1, 8, 2).$$

7. Prove, disprove, or make as convincing an argument as possible, that the K-means algorithm always converges.

9.8 References

Bode B, Halstead DM, Kendall R, Lei Z, Jackson D (2000) The portable batch scheduler and the Maui scheduler on Linux clusters. In: ALS'00 the 4th Annual Linux Showcase & Conference. USENIX Association, California, pp 27-34.

Buyya R, Murshed M (2002) GridSim: a toolkit for the modeling and simulation of distributed resource management and scheduling for Grid computing. J concurrency and computation: practice and experience 14(13-15):1175-1220.

CPN tools (2007) http://www.daimi.au.dk/CPNTools/.

Czajkowski K, Foster I, Kesselman C, Tueckce S (2004) Grid service level agreements: Grid resource management with intermediaries. In: Grid resource management: state of the art and future trends. Kluwer Academic Publishers, Norwell, pp 119-134.

David T (2006) Parallel Workload Archive http://www.cs.huji.ac.il/Labs/parallel/workload/

Denning P and Buzen J (1978) The operational analysis of queueing network models, ACM Comput. Surv., 10(3):225-261.

Epema DHJ, Livny M, Dantzig R, Evers X, Pruyne J (1996) A worldwide flock of Condors: load sharing among workstation clusters. In: Future generation computer systems. Elsevier Science Publishers B.V., Amsterdam, pp 53-65.

Feitelson DG (2006) Workload modeling for computer systems performance evaluation. (unpublished).

Hamscher V, Schwiegelshohn U, Streit A, Yahyapour R (2000) Evaluation of job-scheduling strategies for Grid computing. In: Proceedings of the first IEEE/ACM international workshop on Grid computing. Springer-Verlag, London, pp 191-202.

Howell F, McNab R (1998) SimJava: A discrete event simulation library for Java. In: First international conference on web-based modeling and simulation. Society for computer simulation international.

Legrand A, Marchal L, Casanova H, (2003) Scheduling distributed applications: The SimGrid simulation framework. In: Proceedings of the third IEEE international symposium on cluster computing and the Grid (CCGrid'03). IEEE computer society, Washington DC, pp 138-145.

Legrand I, Newman H, Voicu R, Cirstoiu C, Grigoras C, Toarta M, Dobre C (2004) MonALISA: An agent based, dynamic service system to monitor, control and optimize grid based applications. In: Proceedings of computing in high energy and nuclear physics (CHEP 2004).

Lifka DA (1995) The ANL/IBM SP scheduling system. In: Proceedings of the workshop on job scheduling strategies for parallel processing. Springer-Verlag, London, pp 295-303.

Lu B, Apon A, Dowdy L, Robinson F, Hoffman D, Brewer D (2006) A case study in Grid performance modeling. In: Proceedings of parallel and distributed computing. pp 607-615.

Lublin U, Feitelson DG (2003) The workload on parallel supercomputers: modeling the characteristics of rigid jobs. J Parallel Distrib Comput 63:1105-1122.

Massie ML, Chun B, Culler DE (2004) The Ganglia distributed monitoring system: design, implementation and experience. J Parallel Comput 30:817-840.

Menascé D, Almeida V, Dowdy L (1994) Capacity Planning and Performance Modeling: From mainframes to client-server systems. Prentice Hall.

Menascé D, Almeida V, Dowdy L (2004) Performance by Design: Computer Capacity Planning by Example. Prentice Hall.

Nitzberg B, Schopf JM, Jones JP (2004) PBS pro: Grid computing and scheduling attributes. In: Grid resource management: state of the art and future trends. Kluwer Academic Pulishers, Norwell, pp 183-190.

Platform (2006) Load Sharing Facility http://www.plateform.com.

Riska A, Diev V, Smirni E (2002) Efficient fitting of long-tailed data sets into hyperexponential distributions. In: Proceedings of global telecommunications conference. pp 2513-2517.

Robinson F, Apon A, Brewer D, Dowdy L, Hoffman D, Lu B (2006) Initial starting point analysis for K-means clustering: a case study. In: Proceedings of the 2006 conference on applied research in information technology. Acxiom Laboratory for Applied Research, Conway.

Shan H, Oliker L, Biswas R (2003) Job superscheduler architecture and performance in computational grid environments. In: Proceedings of the 2003 ACM/IEEE conference on supercomputing. IEEE Computer Society, Washington, pp 44-58.

Urgaonkar B, Pacifici G, Shenoy P, Spreitzer M, Tantawi A (2005) An analytical model for multi-tier internet services and its applications. SIG-METRICS Perform. Eva. Rev., 33(1):291-302.

Wolski R, Spring NT, Hayes J (1999) The network weather service: a distributed resource performance forecasting service for metacomputing. J Future Generation Computer Systems, 15(5-6): 757-768.

10 Delay Characteristics of Packet Switched Networks

Qiang Duan

Department of Information Science and Technology,
The Pennsylvania State University Abington College
Abington, PA, USA

10.1 Introduction

The rapid growth of the Internet, along with the availability of powerful computers and high-speed networks as low-cost commodity components, is changing the way people do computing and manage information. These new technologies have enabled the utilization of a wide variety of geographically distributed computational resources, including computers, storage systems, data sources, and special devices, as a unified resource. This new paradigm is popularly termed "grid" computing. The federation of highly distributed heterogeneous resources to deliver high-performance computational services is a key feature of grid computing. Computer networks form the basis for resource sharing across geographically distributed sites and many grid applications require the underlying networks guarantee certain levels of delay performance. Currently all computer networks are essentially packet switched networks that forward data in packets. Therefore, the delay performance achieved by packet switched networks contributes an important element of the end-to-end delay performance of grid applications. Understanding the delay performance characteristics of packet switched networks greatly facilitates delay performance analysis of grid computing systems and this is particularly important to grid applications with low latency requirements.

Traffic flows generated from distinct sources merge together and compete with each other to access available bandwidth from the outgoing links at the packet switches. Most network control operations are eventually carried out at packet switches. Therefore, traffic control mechanisms in packet switches play one of the most crucial roles in network delay performance. The packet switches discussed here are general networking devices that forward data packets from their arrival points to their destination points. A packet switch could be an IP router that forwards IP packets or an Ethernet switch that forwards Ethernet frames.

Y. Chan et al. (eds.), *Data Engineering*, International Series in Operations
Research & Management Science 132, DOI 10.1007/978-1-4419-0176-7_10,
© Springer Science+Business Media, LLC 2010

The switching fabric structure and queuing scheme employed in a packet switch are the two most significant factors on switch delay performance. Typical switching fabric structures include a shared transmission medium-based structure, a shared memory-based structure, and a crossbar-based structure. Among these structures, the crossbar-based structure is the most attractive one for building high-speed packet switches due to its parallel packet forwarding capability. Queuing schemes for packet switches include output queuing (OQ), input queuing (IQ), virtual output queuing (VOQ), and combined input and output queuing (CIOQ). The OQ scheme achieves an optimal delay performance but is not feasible for high-speed switches due to its implementation complexity. The recently developed buffered crossbar switching architecture employs a crossbar-based switching fabric and the CIOQ scheme, which is expected to be one of the dominating switch architectures in high-speed networks due to its ability to achieve good delay performance with reasonable complexity. In this chapter we develop models and techniques for analyzing delay performances of both OQ switches and buffered crossbar switches. The delay performance characteristics of these two types of switches are also compared with each other in this chapter.

The rest of this chapter is organized as follows. First, the general packet switch organization, typical switching fabric structures, and queuing schemes are described. The second section provides the technical backgrounds for understanding the modeling and analysis developed in later sections. The third and fourth section, respectively, develop the models and techniques for analyzing delay performances of OQ switches and buffered crossbar switches. The delay performance characteristics of buffered crossbar switches are compared with those of OQ switches in the fifth section. The last section summarizes the chapter.

10.2 High-Speed Packet Switching Systems

10.2.1 Packet Switched General Organization

The organization of a generic packet switch with N inputs and N outputs (referred to as an $N{\times}N$ switch) is illustrated in Fig. 10.1. This switch consists of a set of input modules X_i ($i=1,2,..., N$), a set of output modules Y_j ($j=1,2,..., N$), and a switching fabric. Network traffic consisting of streams of packets assigned to multiple classes enters the switch at input modules, which examine individual packets to determine their destined outputs and traffic classes. The switching fabric forwards packets from their arrival input modules to their destined output modules.

Packets in computer networks generally have variable lengths, but high-speed packet switches typically use a short fixed-length internal packet as the switching unit. Switch input modules perform packet fragmentation to generate fixed-size internal packets, and output modules reassemble internal packets back to the original packets. The time interval for receiving one internal packet at an input module is called a *time slot*. Since essentially all packet switches have an identical transmission rate for both input and output modules, a time slot is also the time interval in which an output module can process one packet. In this chapter, the term *packet* refers to the fixed-size internal packet.

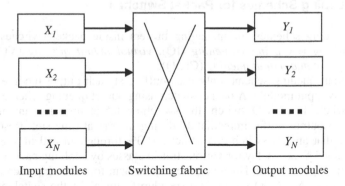

Input modules   Switching fabric   Output modules

Fig. 10.1. The organization for a generic packet switch.

Switching fabric structure and the buffer management mechanism (typically called the queuing scheme) are the two factors that have the most significant impact on switch performance. We discuss them in the following two sub-sections.

10.2.2 Switching Fabric Structures for Packet Switches

Switching fabric structures can be classified into three categories: *shared medium-based* structures, *shared memory-based* structures, and *crossbar-based* structures (Turner and Yamanaka 1998).

The shared medium-based switching fabrics use a bus or ring connected to all I/O ports as the transfer medium between inputs and outputs. The shared memory-based switching fabrics have a central memory that can be accessed by all input and output modules. Both the shared medium-based and the shared memory-based structures suffer a scalability problem which makes switching fabric complexity grow with the switch size at an unacceptable rate. For an $N{\times}N$ switch, the bandwidth of the shared medium or memory has to be at least N times of the I/O port rate. This requirement makes switch implementation very expensive when either the switch size N is large or the I/O port rate is high. Therefore these two kinds of structures are not suitable for large capacity switches.

The crossbar-based switching fabric is composed of a set of horizontal lines and vertical lines. Each horizontal line is connected to an input module and each vertical line is connected to an output module. There is a crosspoint between each horizontal line and each vertical line. The two lines are connected when the crosspoint between them is closed; thus creating a path between a pair of input-output modules. The crossbar-based structure allows multiple data transfers to take place simultaneously between disjoint input/output module pairs. This structure is scalable because the bandwidth of crossbar does not increase with the switch size. It is a promising switching fabric structure for high-speed switches due to its parallel packet forwarding capability.

10.2.3 Queuing Schemes for Packet Switches

Typical queuing schemes for managing buffers inside packet switches include *output queuing* (OQ), *input queuing* (IQ), *virtual output queuing* (VOQ), and *combined input and output queuing* (CIOQ).

The output queuing scheme only uses buffers at each output module with no buffer at any input module. A packet switch using output queuing scheme is called an OQ switch. In an OQ switch, the switching fabric forwards any incoming packet to an output buffer immediately during its arrival time slot. Research results show that an OQ switch can achieve 100% throughput and may guarantee upper-bounded packet delay for various traffic classes by applying packet scheduling at each output module. However, the requirement for achieving such desirable properties in an $N \times N$ OQ switch is a speedup factor N for the switching fabric. This means that the bandwidth of the switching fabric and the output buffers must be at least N times of the I/O port rate.

The input queuing scheme uses buffers only at each input module and no buffers at any output module. A packet switch using an input queuing scheme is called an IQ switch. The switching fabric of an IQ switch operates at the same rate as input ports and will not increase with the switch size. Therefore, IQ switches are more scalable than OQ switches. However, because there are no buffers at the output module, if there are multiple packets heading to the same output module, in each time slot only one of them can be forwarded through the switching fabric and all others are blocked at their arrival input modules. This causes the *head of line (HOL) blocking* problem in IQ switches if input buffers are FIFO queues. In this situation, if the first packet in an input queue is blocked, all packets in this queue are also blocked even if their destined output modules are available. This problem significantly limits the achievable throughput of IQ switches.

Virtual output queuing scheme provides a solution to HOL blocking in IQ switches. VOQ scheme uses separated logical queues at input modules, one for each output port. A packet switch using virtual output queuing scheme is called a VOQ switch. It has been proven that VOQ switches can achieve 100% throughput by applying suitable matching algorithms (Mekkittiul and McKeown 1998). Such algorithms determine which input modules can transfer a packet to which output modules in each time slot. However, without output buffers, IQ switches and VOQ switches can only transfer one packet to an output module in each time slot. This implies that packet scheduling cannot be applied at output modules to control the bandwidth and delay performance for different traffic classes, which limits the abilities of these types of switches to control bandwidth and delay performances for traffic flows.

The combined input and output queuing scheme uses buffers at both input and output modules, and a switch that employs this queuing scheme is called a CIOQ switch. Buffers at output modules enable a CIOQ switch to transfer multiple packets to the same output module in each time slot. A switch is said to have a speedup factor of K if up to K packets can be transferred from any input module to any output module in each time slot. It has been proven that a CIOQ switch using a switching fabric without internal buffers and with a speedup factor of two can achieve equivalent delay performance as an OQ switch does (Chuang et al. 1999).

Buffered crossbar switch is a recently developed switching architecture that employs a crossbar-based switching fabric and a variation of CIOQ scheme. There are buffers at each crosspoint of the crossbar switching fabric, which comprise a set of distributed queues for output modules. Due to its potential to achieve high-performance with reasonable implementation complexity, the buffered crossbar switch is expected to be one of the dominant switching architectures for high-speed networks (Yoshigoe and Christensen 2003).

10.3 Technical Background

10.3.1 Packet Scheduling in Packet Switches

One of the most well-studied packet scheduling algorithms is *Generalized Processor Sharing* (GPS) (Parekh and Gallager 1993). A GPS server with N flows is characterized by N positive real numbers, φ_1, φ_2, ..., φ_N, one for each flow, where φ_i can be called the *weight* of the flow f_i. Let $W_i(t_1, t_2)$ be the amount of service offered to the flow f_i in the time interval $(t_1, t_2]$ and $W(t_1, t_2)$ be the total amount of service provided by the server in the same time period. A flow is called backlogged at time t if a positive amount of that flow's traffic is queued at time t. A GPS server is working conserving and if the flow i is continuously backlogged in the time interval $(t_1, t_2]$, then $\dfrac{W_i(t_1,t_2)}{W_j(t_1,t_2)} \geq \dfrac{\varphi_i}{\varphi_j}$ holds for all j=1, 2, ..., N. Intuitively GPS is a server model that offers each backlogged flow the amount of service that is in proportion to the weight of the flow.

Any flow at a GPS server is guaranteed an amount of service no less than its reserved share of the server capacity; that is, if the flow f_i is continuously backlogged during the time interval $(t_1, t_2]$, then

$$W_i(t_1,t_2) \geq \frac{\varphi_1}{\varphi_s} W(t_1,t_2) \qquad (10.1)$$

where $\varphi_s = \sum_{j=1}^{N} \varphi_j$ and φ_i / φ_s is called the reserved share for the flow f_i. Suppose the flow is constrained by a leaky bucket with parameters (P_i, ρ_i, σ_i) and assigned a service rate $r_i \geq \rho_i$, the GPS server guarantees this flow a worst-case packet delay

$$D_{\max} = \sigma_i / r_i .$$

(10.2)

A GPS server is an ideal fluid model that cannot be implemented in practical packet systems. The Weighted Fair Queuing (WFQ) scheduling algorithm (Zhang 1995) approximates the GPS server by serving packets in an increasing order of the packet's *finish time* in the GPS system. A WFQ server guarantees that the departure time of any packet from a WFQ server will not be later by more than one packet transmission time than the departure time of the same packet from the GPS server.

Let d_{WFQ}^k and d_{GPS}^k denote the departure time of the k-th packet of a flow f_i from the WFQ server and the GPS server respectively. Let L_{max} denote the maximal packet length, and r_i and r denote the service rate assigned to the flow f_i and the total service rate of the server, respectively. Then it can be shown that

$$d_{WFQ}^k - d_{GPS}^k \le L_{\max} / r .$$

(10.3)

Thus, the WFQ algorithm guarantees a upper-bounded packet delay as follows:

$$D_{\max}^{WFQ} \le \sigma_i / r_i + L_{\max} / r .$$

(10.4)

That is, the delay bound provided by the WFQ algorithm to a flow is within one packet transmission time of the delay bound guaranteed by the GPS server to the same flow.

Let $W_{GPS}(0, \tau)$ and $W_{WFQ}(0, \tau)$ denote respectively the amount of service offered to a flow by a GPS server and by a WFQ server in the time interval $(0,\tau]$. It can be proven that

$$W_{GPS}(0,\tau) - W_{WFQ}(0,\tau) \le L_{\max} .$$

(10.5)

That is, the amount of service received by any flow in any time interval τ from a WFQ server will not be less than that received from a GPS server by more than one packet. Due to its bandwidth and delay guarantee capabilities, WFQ is adopted by most practical packet switches.

10.3.2 Introduction to Network Calculus

This section gives an introduction to network calculus (Boudec and Thiran 2001), which forms the basis of delay performance analysis presented in the rest of this chapter.

The *arrival curve* and *service curve* are two basic concepts in network calculus. Let $R^{in}(t)$ denote the accumulated amount of arrival traffic for a flow at a server by time t. If

$$R^{in}(t) - R^{in}(s) \le A(t-s) \text{ for all } 0<s<t,$$

(10.6)

this flow is said to have an arrival curve $A(t)$. The arrival curve of a flow essentially gives an upper bound for the amount of arrival traffic of this flow in an arbitrary time interval.

Suppose the accumulated amount of service offered by a server to a flow by time t is $R^{out}(t)$. We say the server guarantees a service curve $S(t)$ for the flow if for any time $t \geq 0$ in a busy period of the server,

$$R^{out}(t) \geq R^{in}(t) \otimes S(t), \tag{10.7}$$

where the operator $\otimes$ is defined as $h(t) \otimes x(t) = \min_{s:0 \leq s \leq t} \{h(t-s) + x(s)\}$. The service curve for a flow describes the minimum amount of service that can be guaranteed to the flow within an arbitrary time interval.

The above definitions of arrival curve and service curve are in general forms. In practice, one is particularly interested in the arrival curves of traffic flows constrained by a *leaky bucket*, which is the most commonly used traffic regulator in real networks. The arrival curve for a leaky bucket regulated traffic flow can be expressed by

$$A(t) = \min\{Pt, \sigma + \rho t\}, \tag{10.8}$$

where P, ρ, and σ are respectively the peak rate, sustained rate, and the maximal burst size of this flow.

The *Latency-Rate (LR) server* (Stiliadis and Varma 1998) is a general server model for a broad range of packet schedulers that are widely applied in various packet switches, including Weighted Fair queuing (WFQ) and Weighted Round-Robin (WRR) schedulers. The service capacity offered by these LR-class schedulers to a traffic flow can be described by two parameters: the latency θ and the rate r. For a LR server that guarantees a latency θ and a service rate r to a flow, the service curve for the flow at this server can be represented as

$$S(t) = r(t - \theta). \tag{10.9}$$

Network calculus provides an effective tool for delay performance analysis. Given the arrival curve $A(t)$ and the service curve $S(t)$ for a flow, the maximum packet delay guaranteed to the flow can be determined from the maximum horizontal distance between the two curves A(t) and S(t). That is,

$$D_{max} = \max_{t:t>0}\{\min\{\Delta : \Delta \geq 0, A(t) \leq S(t+\Delta)\}\}. \tag{10.10}$$

Typically an end-to-end packet forwarding path in networks consists of multiple switches in tandem and the traffic control mechanism inside each packet switch typically consists of both input and output schedulers in tandem. Network calculus facilitates analyzing systems consisting of a series of tandem servers, which is a model for typical networking systems consisting of a series of data processing engines. Suppose a series of tandem servers respectively guarantee the services $S_1(t)$, $S_2(t)$, ..., $S_n(t)$ to a flow. Network calculus shows that the service curve guaranteed by the entire system to the flow is:

$$S(t) = S_1(t) \otimes S_2(t) \cdots \otimes S_n(t).$$ (10.11)

10.4 Delay Characteristics of Output Queuing Switches

10.4.1 Output Queuing Switch System

A block diagram of an $N{\times}N$ OQ switch is shown in Fig. 10.2. This switch has a set of input modules, X_i ($i=1, ..., N$), a set of output modules, Yj ($j=1, ..., N$), and a switching fabric. All buffers in an OQ switch are located in output modules. These output buffers could be organized as one logical queue for each traffic class. There is an output scheduler at each output module to decide the order in which packets depart this output module. By employing a suitable scheduling algorithm at each output scheduler, the OQ switch can guarantee the minimum bandwidth and the maximum packet delay for different traffic classes.

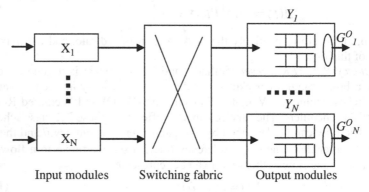

Fig. 10.2. Output queuing switch system

Because there is no buffer in either input modules or the switching fabric, any packet arriving at an OQ switch input port must be forwarded immediately through the switching fabric to its destined output buffer. This requires a speedup factor of N for the switching fabric, which means that the switching fabric must be able to forward up to N packets into each output module in one time slot. This also requires that the output buffer memory to be N times faster than the input port. Such requirements make the switch complexity increase significantly with the I/O port rate and the switch size N. Therefore, the OQ switch architecture suffers a scalability problem and is feasible only for medium capacity switches. However due to its ability to achieve 100% throughput and optimal delay performance, the OQ switch is often used by researchers as a reference model to represent the ideal case in switch performance analysis.

10.4.2 OQ Switch Modeling and Analysis

The traffic control system for a flow in an OQ switch is illustrated in Fig. 10.3. The X_i and Y_j are respectively the arrival input module and departure output module of the flow. The propagation delay between input and output modules is denoted by d_f. Since the output scheduler G_j^0 is the only server in the system, if d_f is ignorable, the service curve guaranteed by this system to the flow is equal to the service curve guaranteed by the output scheduler to the flow. Suppose the output scheduler is a latency-rate server with parameters (r_o, θ_o) for the flow, then the service curve guaranteed by the OQ switch to this flow is

$$S^O(t) = r_O(t - \theta_O).$$ (10.12)

Since the rate parameter of a LR-server service curve specifies the minimal amount of bandwidth offered to a flow by the server (Parekh and Gallager 1993), equation (10.12) implies that the minimal bandwidth guaranteed by the OQ switch to a flow is equal to the service rate allocated to the flow at the output scheduler.

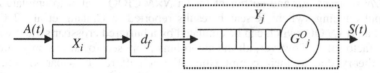

Fig. 10.3. The traffic control system for a flow in an OQ switch

Suppose the traffic flow is constrained by a leaky bucket with parameters (P, ρ, σ); that is, the flow has an arrival curve $A(t) = \min\{Pt, \sigma + \rho t\}$ By applying the network calculus delay analysis technique given in (10.10), we can obtain that the maximum packet delay for the flow is

$$D_{\max}^O = \theta_O + \left(\frac{P}{r_O} - 1\right)\frac{\sigma}{P - \rho}.$$ (10.13)

If the OQ switch employs the WFQ algorithm at each output scheduler, then the latency parameter guaranteed by the output scheduler for the flow will be $\theta_o = L(1/R + 1/r_o)$, where L and R are respectively the internal packet length and the switch I/O port rate. Therefore the maximum delay performance of the flow is

$$D_{\max}^O = L\left(\frac{1}{R} + \frac{1}{r_O}\right) + \left(\frac{P}{r_O} - 1\right)\frac{\sigma}{P - \rho}.$$ (10.14)

10.4.3 Output Queuing Emulation for Delay Guarantee

The essential approach of any scheduling algorithm for packet switches that guarantee delay performance for different flows is to control which packet is processed by the server in each time slot (Zhang 1995). This is equivalent to controlling the departure time of each packet from the switch.

The idea of emulating an OQ switch with another switch is to achieve a departure time for every packet in the switch that is identical to the time it would leave the OQ switch. If under any identical arrival traffic, a switch achieves an identical departure time for every packet as the departure time of the same packet from the OQ switch, this switch is said to *emulate* the OQ switch. Output buffer space is required in the switch for OQ emulation, so it applies only to combined input and output queuing (CIOQ) switches, including buffered crossbar switches. By emulating an OQ switch, all packets in a CIOQ switch get identical service orders at their output modules to what they would have in the OQ switch. Therefore, each traffic class achieves an identical delay performance as in the OQ switch.

Packet scheduling algorithms that can be used in a CIOQ switch for OQ emulation have been developed in Chuang et al. (1999). It is proven that a speedup factor of $2-1/N$ is necessary and sufficient for an $N \times N$ CIOQ switch to emulate an $N \times N$ output queuing switch. Research results reported in Chuang et al. (2003) shows that an $N \times N$ OQ switch can be emulated by a buffered crossbar switch with a speedup factor of 3. However, all the algorithms proposed so far are only interesting in theory due to their complexities. For a buffered crossbar switch, a speedup factor of 3 requires high crossbar bandwidth and very short crosspoint buffer access time; thus it may significantly increase the switch implementation cost, especially when the switch I/O port rate reaches a level of Gbps. Therefore, more practical approaches for delay performance guarantee in buffered crossbar switches must be sought. The modeling and analysis given in the rest of this chapter will show that a buffered crossbar switch may achieve almost identical delay performance as an OQ switch does under certain conditions.

10.5 Delay Characteristics of Buffered Crossbar Switches

10.5.1 Buffered Crossbar Switch System

As shown in Fig. 10.4, an $N \times N$ buffered crossbar switch consists of N input modules, X_i $(i=1,2,..., N)$, N output modules, Y_j $(j= 1,2, ..., N)$, and a crossbar-based switching fabric with an internal buffer at each crosspoint. The buffer between the input module X_i and the output module Y_j is referred to as the *crosspoint buffer* M_{ij}.

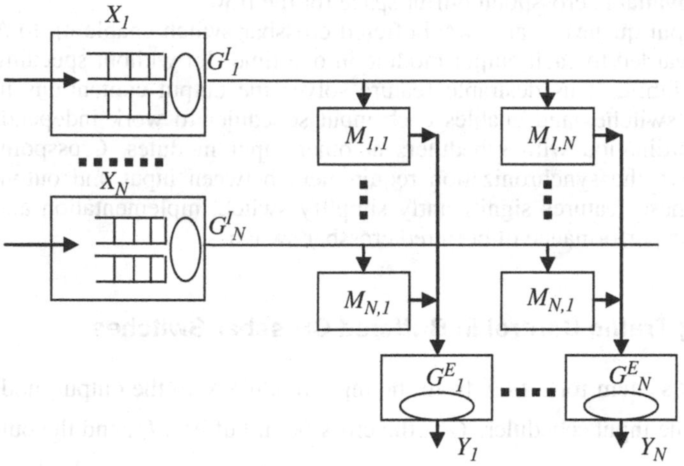

X_1
G^I_1
X_N
G^I_N
$M_{1,1}$ $M_{1,N}$
$M_{N,1}$ $M_{N,1}$
G^E_1 G^E_N
Y_1 Y_N

Fig. 10.4. Buffered crossbar switch architecture

The queuing scheme for buffered crossbar switch is a combination of Virtual Output Queue (VOQ) and Combined Input/Output Queue (CIOQ). Buffers at each input module are organized as one logical queue for each flow destined to each output port. All crosspoint buffers on the same vertical line of the switching fabric can be directly accessed from the output module connected with this vertical line. Therefore, these crosspoint buffers form a distributed output queue for this output module. For example, the crosspoint buffers M_{ij} $i=1,2,...,$ N, constitute an output queue for the output module Y_j. Each crosspoint buffer may also consist of multiple sub-queues, one for each flow, which are not shown in Fig. 10.4.

The traffic control system in a buffered crossbar switch consists of an input schedule at each input module, an output schedule at each output module, and a credit-based flow control mechanism between input modules and crosspoint buffers. The scheduler at the input module X_i is denoted as G^I_i and the scheduler at the output module Y_j is denoted as G^E_j. In each time slot, the input scheduler selects a logical queue at the input module from which a packet is forwarded into a crosspoint buffer. The output scheduler decides from which crosspoint buffer the output module can send a packet out in each time slot. Limited by hardware implementation technologies, crosspoint buffers inside the switching fabric have a relatively small buffer size. Therefore, a credit-based flow control mechanism is applied between input modules and crosspoint buffers to avoid losing packets due to crosspoint buffer overflow. Each flow is assigned a finite number of credits, which corresponds to the crosspoint buffer space allocated for this flow. The number of credits for the flow is decreased by one each time a packet of this flow is forwarded into the crosspoint buffer and increased by one whenever a packet is sent out from the crosspoint buffer. The input scheduler will not consider a flow as a scheduling candidate when the flow runs out of credits, which implies that currently there is no available crosspoint buffer space for the flow.

Distributed output queues in an $N \times N$ buffered crossbar switch enable up to N packets to be forwarded to each output module in one time slot without speeding up the switching fabric. This desirable feature solves the output contentions in buffered crossbar switches and enables each input scheduler to work independently without coordination with schedulers at other input modules. Crosspoint buffers also remove the synchronization requirement between input and output modules. All of these features significantly simplify switch implementation and greatly improve the performance of buffered crossbar switches.

10.5.2 Modeling Traffic Control in Buffered Crossbar Switches

The traffic control system for a flow from the input module X_i to the output module Y_j consists of the input scheduler, G_i^I, the cross-point buffer, M_{ij}, and the output scheduler, G_j^E. The total number of credits allocated to this flow is K. The input scheduler can only offer service to the flow when there are credits allocated to this flow available at the input port module. The amount of service offered to a flow by the input scheduler is determined by the combination of the input scheduling algorithm and the credit-based flow control. This is equivalent to having a controller C in front of the input scheduler to represent the influence of the credit-based flow control on the service offered to this flow. Therefore, traffic control in the switch can be represented as the closed loop system illustrated in Fig. 10.5.

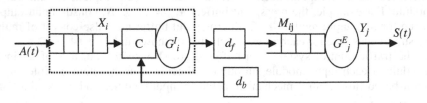

Fig. 10.5. The traffic control system for a flow in a buffered crossbar switch

It can be shown that the closed-loop traffic control system given in Fig. 10.5 can be modeled by a service curve-based open loop model shown in Fig. 10.6 (Duan et al. 2003). In this model, $S^I(t)$ and $S^E(t)$ are the service curves guaranteed by the input and output schedulers respectively, and $S^C(t)$ is the service curve guaranteed by the traffic controller C. The service curve for the traffic controller can be calculated as

$$S^C(t) = \min_{m \geq 0} \left\{ (S^G(t) + K)^M \right\} \tag{10.15}$$

where $S^G(t) = S^G(t) \otimes S^E(t) \otimes \delta(t - d_f - d_b)$, and $g^{(m)}$ denotes the $(m-1)$ folds of convolution of a function g. The service curve guaranteed by the entire switch traffic control system to the flow can be calculated by following the network calculus property of a tandem server system; that is,

$$S(t) = S^C(t) \otimes S^I(t) \otimes S^E(t) \otimes \delta(t - d_f - d_b) \tag{10.16}$$

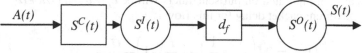

Fig. 10.6. Service curve-based model for traffic control in buffered crossbar switch

10.5.3 Delay Analysis for Buffered Crossbar Switches

The typical packet schedulers applied in practical packet switches, for example the Weighted Fair Queuing (WFQ) scheduler and the Weighted Round-Robin (WRR) scheduler, belong to the Latency-Rate server category that we discussed in the *Technical Backgrounds* section. Therefore, in our analysis for buffered crossbar switches we assume that the input and output schedulers are LR servers that both guarantee the service rate r to a flow and respectively guarantee the latencies θ_I and θ_E to the flow. That is, the service curve guaranteed to the flow by input and output schedulers are $S(t) = r(t - \theta_I)$ and $S(t) = r(t - \theta_E)$ respectively. Then the service curve guaranteed by the switch to the flow is related with the number of credits K allocated to the flow. It can be shown (Duan et al. 2003) that if $K \geq r(\theta_I + \theta_I + d_r)$ then the service curve guaranteed by the switch to the flow is

$$S(t) = r(t - \theta_\Sigma) \tag{10.17}$$

where $\theta = \theta_I + \theta_E + d_r$. Otherwise, if $K < r(\theta_I + \theta_I + d_r)$, then the service curve becomes

$$S(t) = r'(t - \theta_\Sigma) \tag{10.18}$$

where $r' = K / (\theta_I + \theta_E + d_r + d_b)$.

Equations (10.17) and (10.18) imply that the minimal amount of bandwidth guaranteed to a flow by a buffered crossbar switch is determined by both the service rate offered by the input and output schedulers and the number of credits allocated to the flow. The latter actually represents the cross-point buffer space allocated for the flow. If the number of allocated credits for a flow is at least the product of the offered service rate and the total round-trip latency of the credit circulation loop, the switch guarantees the flow a minimum bandwidth that is equal to the service rate offered by the input and output schedulers.

Suppose the flow has an arrival curve $A(t) = \min\{Pt, \sigma + \rho t\}$ and is guaranteed by the switch a service curve $S(t) = r(t - \theta)$, then by following (10.10) the delay upper bound for the flow can be determined as

$$D_{\text{max}}^{C} = \theta_{\Sigma} + \left(\frac{P}{r} - 1\right)\frac{\sigma}{P - \rho}. \tag{10.19}$$

If the switch employs the WFQ algorithm at each scheduler, then the latency parameters at both input and output schedulers will be $\theta_I = \theta_E = L(1/R + 1/r)$. Therefore the maximum packet delay for this flow is

$$D_{\text{max}}^{C} = 2L\left(\frac{1}{R} + \frac{1}{r}\right) + \left(\frac{P}{r} - 1\right)\frac{\sigma}{P - \rho}. \tag{10.20}$$

10.5.4 Numerical Examples

This section gives numerical examples to illustrate applications of the delay analysis techniques developed for buffered crossbar switches. Assume that a buffered crossbar switch has 1 Gb/s I/O port rate and employs the WFQ algorithm at each scheduler. Consider a traffic flow f consisting of a stream of video packets, which is constrained by a leaky bucket with parameters given in Fizek and Reisslein (2001); that is, the peak rate P=3.9 Mb/s, the sustained rate ρ=1.1 Mb/s, and the maximum burst size σ=143 kbits. Such a video traffic flow is selected in the examples because Internet video delivery is a typical multimedia application that requires an upper-bounded maximum packet delay.

Values of the maximum packet delay guaranteed to the flow f with various amounts of allocated bandwidth are calculated and the results are plotted in Fig. 10.7. Switches with a short (50 bytes) internal packet length and a longer (1000 bytes) internal packet length are examined. The first case is typical for switches in ATM networks while the second case is representative for switches in Ethernet networks. In Fig. 10.7 D_I and D_2 respectively denote the maximum packet delay in the switch with a short and a long packet length. From this figure we can see that for both cases the maximum packet delay decreases with the increase of allocated bandwidth. This means that the more bandwidth is available to a flow in a buffer crossbar switch, the better delay performance can be guaranteed to the flow. Comparison between D_I and D_2 shows that D_I is always less than D_2 in this example. This implies that the same flow achieves better delay performance in switches with a short internal packet length than in switches with a long internal packet length. That is, reducing internal packet length improves switch delay performance. This justifies that most high-speed packet switches used in practice cut long packets into a set of short internal switching units before forwarding them into the switching fabric. However, this will cause overhead for fragmentation and reassembly, therefore there is a tradeoff between QoS performance improvement gained from using short switching unit and the extra delay for packet reassembly.

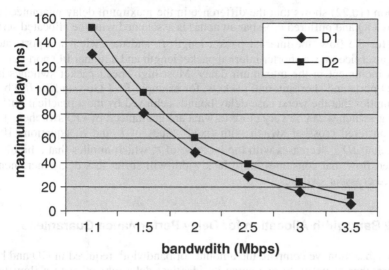

Fig. 10.7. Delay performance and available bandwidth in a buffered crossbar switch.

10.6 Delay Comparison of Output Queuing to Buffered Crossbar

10.6.1 Maximum Packet Delay Comparison

Suppose a flow f has a leaky bucket arrival curve with parameters (P, ρ, σ), and that the same amount of bandwidth is available to the flow in both OQ and buffered crossbar switches; that is $r = r_o$. Comparison between (10.13) and (10.19) shows that the difference in the maximum delay guaranteed by these two types of switches to the flow is

$$\Delta D_{\max} = D_{\max}^C - D_{\max}^O = \theta_\Sigma - \theta_O \tag{10.21}$$

Equation (10.21) shows that the maximum delay for the flow in the buffered crossbar switch is greater than that in the OQ switch. The increment is equal to the difference between the total traffic control latency of the buffered crossbar switch and that of the OQ switch.

Suppose both types of switches employ the WFQ algorithm at each packet scheduler, then with the same amount of bandwidth $\theta_I = \theta_E = \theta_O = L(1/R + 1/r)$. If the internal propagation delay d_f can be ignored, then from (10.21) we have

$$\Delta D_{\max} = L(1/R + 1/r). \tag{10.22}$$

Equation (10.22) shows that the difference in the maximum delay guaranteed to a flow by OQ and buffered crossbar switches is associated with the allocated service rate r for the flow, the internal packet length L, and the switch I/O port rate R. Given a service rate, a shorter internal packet length and a higher I/O port rate lead to less increment in the maximum delay. Most high-speed packet switches have fast I/O ports and short internal packets, for example $R>1$ Gb/s and $L<100$ bytes. This implies that the worst case delay bounds achieved by most practical buffered crossbar switches can be very close to what are guaranteed by OQ switches. For a given buffered crossbar switch with fixed values of L and R, equation (10.22) shows that ΔD_{max} decreases with the increase of r, which implies that a highly aggregated flow that consumes more bandwidth will suffer less delay increment in buffered crossbar switches.

10.6.2 Bandwidth Allocation for Delay Performance Guarantees

In this subsection we compare the amounts of bandwidth required in OQ and buffered crossbar switches to guarantee an identical delay objective to a flow f. Let D_{req} be the target packet delay upper bound for the flow. From equation (10.13) we derive the required bandwidth in an OQ switch to guarantee D_{req}, which is given by

$$r_{req}^{O} = \frac{P\sigma}{(P-\rho)(D_{req}-\theta_{O})+\sigma}. \tag{10.23}$$

Similarly from equation (10.19) we obtain that the required bandwidth in a buffered crossbar switch to guarantee the same D_{req} is

$$r_{req}^{C} = \frac{P\sigma}{(P-\rho)(D_{req}-\theta_{\Sigma})+\sigma}. \tag{10.24}$$

Suppose the same LR scheduling algorithm is employed by both types of switches, we can assume that the latency parameters guaranteed by input/output schedulers in the buffered crossbar switch and output schedulers in the OQ switch are equal; that is $\theta_{I}=\theta_{E}=\theta_{O}=\theta$. Thus, the bandwidth allocation increment is

$$\Delta r_{req} = r_{req}^{C} - r_{req}^{O} = \frac{(P-\rho)P\sigma\theta}{[(P-\rho)(D_{req}-2\theta)+\sigma][(P-\rho)(D_{req}-\theta)+\sigma]} \tag{10.25}$$

Equation (10.25) implies that more bandwidth is consumed in the buffered crossbar switch than in the OQ switch in order to guarantee the same delay objective. The increment in bandwidth requirement is a function of the target delay bound D_{req}, the flow traffic parameters (P, ρ, σ), and the scheduler latency parameter θ. For a given flow, the Δr_{req} is a decreasing function of D_{req}, which means that the tighter the delay objective is, the more bandwidth is required in the buffered crossbar switch than in the OQ switch.

Suppose both OQ and buffered crossbar switches employ the WFQ algorithm at each scheduler, then $\theta = L(1/R + 1/r)$. Thus,

$$r_{req}^O = \frac{P\sigma + L(P-\rho)}{(P-\rho)(D_{req} - L/R) + \sigma} \approx \frac{P\sigma + L(P-\rho)}{(P-\rho)D_{req} + \sigma} \qquad (10.26)$$

and

$$r_{req}^C = \frac{P\sigma + 2L(P-\rho)}{(P-\rho)(D_{req} - 2L/R) + \sigma} \approx \frac{P\sigma + 2L(P-\rho)}{(P-\rho)D_{req} + \sigma}. \qquad (10.27)$$

The above approximations can be made because the ratio L/R is ignorable for typical high-speed packet switches, where the internal packet length L is short and switch I/O port rate R is high. Then the bandwidth increment becomes

$$\Delta r_{req} = \frac{L(P-\rho)}{(P-\rho)D_{req} + \sigma}. \qquad (10.28)$$

Equation (10.28) shows that Δr_{req} is a decreasing function of D_{req} and an increasing function of L. This implies that buffered crossbar switches with the WFQ scheduling algorithm should use a short internal packet length to reduce the bandwidth allocation increment for achieving identical delay performances as OQ switches.

10.6.3 Numerical Examples

This section gives numerical examples to illustrate the performance comparison discussed in the previous section. Assume that both OQ and buffered crossbar switches apply the WFQ algorithm at each scheduler and have 1 Gb/s switch I/O port rate. We consider a video traffic flow constrained by a leaky bucket with parameters given in Fizek and Reisslein (2001): P=3.9 Mb/s, ρ=1.1 Mb/s, and σ=143 kbits.

The delay upper bounds guaranteed with various amounts of allocated bandwidth in OQ and buffered crossbar switches are given in Fig. 10.8. In this figure, D_{O1} and D_{C1} are respectively the maximum delay values guaranteed by the OQ and buffered crossbar switches, both of which have an internal packet length $L=50$ bytes; D_{O2} and D_{C2} are respectively the delay upper bounds guaranteed by the two types of switches with an internal packet length $L=1000$ bytes. This figure shows that D_{O1} and D_{C1} are almost indistinguishable, which means that delay upper bounds guaranteed by OQ and buffered crossbar switches with the same small internal packet size are almost identical to each other. We can also see from the figure that D_{O2} and D_{C2} are more distinct from each other, which implies that the difference in delay performances of the two types of switches increases with the internal packet length.

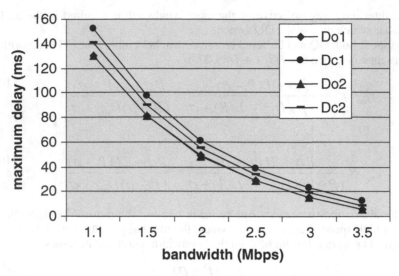

Fig. 10.8. Delay performance comparison between OQ and buffered crossbar switches

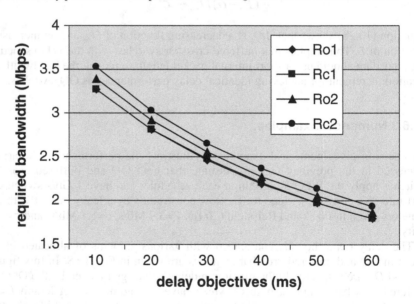

Fig. 10.9. Bandwidth allocation comparison between OQ and buffered crossbar switches

The relation between delay targets and required amounts of bandwidth in OQ and buffered crossbar switches is shown in Fig. 10.9. In this figure, r_{o1} and r_{c1} are respectively the required amounts of bandwidth in the OQ and buffered crossbar switches when $L=50$ bytes and r_{o2} and r_{c2} are respectively the required amounts of bandwidth in the two types of switches when $L=1000$ bytes. This figure shows that the difference between the required bandwidth r_{o1} and r_{c1} is almost ignorable, which means that the bandwidth allocation requirements for achieving an identical delay objective in the two types of switches are almost identical when the packet length is small. We can also notice from the figure that the difference between r_{o2} and r_{c2} is more than that between r_{o1} and r_{c1}, which implies that the difference in bandwidth allocation in the two types of switches increases with the internal packet length L.

10.7 Summary

This chapter studies the delay performance characteristics of packet switched networks. Specifically, models for traffic control in output queuing and buffered crossbar switches are developed and the techniques for delay performance analysis for these two types of switches are derived. Network calculus theory is applied as a basis for the analysis presented in this chapter. In the network calculus-based models, traffic control elements in packet switches, including packet schedulers and the credit circulation mechanism, are characterized by service curves. The amounts of traffic loaded on packet switches by traffic flows are described by their arrival curves.

Analysis results obtained in this chapter show that the delay performance achieved by a packet switch for a traffic flow is associated with multiple parameters, including the available bandwidth for the flow in the switch, the internal packet length used by the switch, and the characteristics of the traffic load of this flow. Given the traffic load of a flow, the more bandwidth available to the flow in the switch, the better delay performance can be achieved for the flow. With the same amount of bandwidth available to a flow, a shorter packet length helps the switch to achieve better delay performance for the flow. For buffered crossbar switches, another impact factor on the achievable delay performance for a flow is the crosspoint buffer space allocated to the flow. If the allocated buffer space is less than a certain threshold, the insufficient buffer will limit the service rate offered to the flow by input and output schedulers in the buffered crossbar switch; thus causing longer packet delay for the flow.

It has been proven by previous research that output queuing switches can achieve optimal delay performances for traffic flows. In this chapter, the delay performance characteristics of buffered crossbar switches are compared with those of output queuing switches. Comparison results show that if the internal packet length is short, a buffered crossbar switch is able to achieve almost identical delay performance as what an output queuing switch does, and the bandwidth consumption for achieving an identical delay objective is also approximately the same in the two types of switches.

Since the federation of highly distributed computing resources is a key feature of grid computing and the networking platform provides a foundation for building large scale grid infrastructures, the delay performance of packet switching networks play a significant role in the end-to-end delay performance that can be achieved by grid applications. The model and techniques discussed in this chapter provide some effective tools for analyzing network delay performance, which can contribute the delay performance analysis of the entire grid infrastructure.

10.8 Exercises

1. Why is the output queuing scheme not feasible for large capacity packet switches?
2. What is the head of line blocking problem and why does it limit the throughput of input queuing switches?
3. What is output queuing emulation and how can this technology support real-time traffic classes in buffered crossbar switches?
4. Describe the credit-based flow control mechanism in buffered crossbar switches and explain how this mechanism can prevent packet loss due to crosspoint buffer overflow.
5. Based on the performance analysis given in this chapter, explain why most buffered crossbar switches used in practice cut longer packets received at input modules into a sequences of internal packets with short packet length.

10.9 References

Boudec JL, Thiran P (2001) Network calculus: a theory of deterministic queuing systems for the Internet. Springer.

Chuang ST, Goel A, McKeown N, Prabhakar B (1999) Matching output queuing with a combined input/output-queued switch. J. IEEE Select. Areas Commun. 17: 1030–1038.

Chuang ST, Iyer S, McKeown N (2003) Practical algorithms for performance guarantees in buffered crossbar switches. Technical Report of Stanford University.

Duan Q, Li X, Zhang L (2003) Network calculus-based delay analysis for QoS provision in buffered crossbar switches. J. Interconnection Networks 4: 131–146.

Fizek FH, Reisslein M (2001) MPEG-4 and H.263 video traces for network performance evaluation. IEEE Network Magazine 15: 40–54.

Mekkittiul A, McKeown N (1998) A practical scheduling algorithm to achieve 100\% throughput in input-queued switches. In: Proc. IEEE INFOCOM'98, San Francisco, pp 792-799.

Parekh AK, Gallager RG (1993) A generalized processor sharing approach to flow control in integrated services networks: the single-node case. IEEE/ACM Trans. Networking 1: 344–357.

Stiliadis D, Varma A (1998) Latency-rate servers: a general model for analysis of traffic scheduling algorithms. IEEE/ACM Trans. Networking 6: 611–624.

Turner J, Yamanaka N (1998) Architectural choices in large scale ATM switches. IEICE Transactions E81-B: 120–137.

Yoshigoe K, Christensen KJ (2003) An evolution to crossbar switches with virtual output queuing and buffered cross points. IEEE Network Magazine, 17: 48–56.

Zhang H (1995) Service disciplines for guaranteed performance service in packet-switching networks. Proceedings of the IEEE 82: 1374–1398.

11 Knowledge Discovery in Textual Databases: A Concept-Association Mining Approach

Mutlu Mete [1], Nurcan Yuruk[2], Xiaowei Xu[3], and Daniel Berleant[2]

[1] Department of Computer Science, Texas A&M University-Commerce

[2] Department of Applied Science, University of Arkansas at Little Rock
Little Rock, AR, USA

[3] Department of Information Science, University of Arkansas at Little Rock
Little Rock, AR, USA

11.1 Introduction

The number of scientific publications is exploding as online digital libraries and the World Wide Web grow. MEDLINE, the premier bibliographic database of the National Library of Medicine (NLM), contains about 18 million records from more than 7,300 different publications dating from 1965; it is growing by about 400,000 citations each year. The explosive growth of information in textual documents creates great need for techniques for knowledge discovery from text collections.

Data mining, also known as knowledge discovery in databases, has been defined as the nontrivial extraction of implicit, previously unknown and potentially useful information from given data (Fayyad et al. 1996). Different techniques including clustering, classification and association rule mining have been used to extract knowledge from text collections.

Association rule mining, first introduced by Agrawal et al. (1993), can be summarized for our purposes here as follows. Suppose we have n tuples over a set A of attributes $A_1, A_2, A_3, \ldots A_n$. Each tuple represents a text passage. Each attribute represents a word, and the attributes are Boolean in the sense that a value of true indicates that the word is present in the passage and a value of false indicates that the word is not. Thus each tuple represents the bag of words associated with the passage. Let I and J be two disjoint subsets of attributes in A. We say that $I \rightarrow J$ is an association rule if the following two conditions are satisfied.

- Support: At least a fraction s of the tuples contain attributes I or J.

Y. Chan et al. (eds.), *Data Engineering*, International Series in Operations
Research & Management Science 132, DOI 10.1007/978-1-4419-0176-7_11,
© Springer Science+Business Media, LLC 2010

- Confidence: Among the tuples in which I appears, at least a fraction c also have J appearing in them.

The goal is to identify all valid association rules for a given relation. An attribute set is called a frequent item set if its attributes are in enough tuples. Frequent item sets form the basis of association rule mining. Exploiting the monotonicity property of frequent item sets (each subset of a frequent item set is as frequent or more), and using data structures that support counting, the set of all frequent item sets can be efficiently determined even for large databases. Different algorithms have been developed for that task, e.g. (Agrawal & Srikant 1994). Please see (Hipp et al. 2000) for a review of association rule mining.

Traditionally, association rule mining algorithms use the support-confidence framework to find interesting association rules in the following two steps.
- All itemsets that have support above the user specified minimum are generated. These itemsets are called the *large itemsets*.
- For each large itemset, all the rules that have a minimum confidence are generated as follows: for a large itemset X and any Y $\subset$ X, if support(X)/support(X-Y) $\geq$ *minimum_confidence*, then X-Y $\rightarrow$ Y is a valid rule.

The support-confidence framework cannot find association rules between rare items, i.e. items that do not satisfy the minimum support condition.

Recent works (Brin, Motwani & Silverstein 1997, Brin, Motwani & Ullman 1997, Liu et al. 1997, Morishita & Sese 2000) deal with finding rules based on other metrics besides support and confidence. In Brin, Motwani & Silverstein (1997), the authors mine association rules that identify correlations and consider both the absence and presence of items as a basis for generating the rules. In Brin, Motwani & Ullman (1997), the authors use support as part of their measure of interest of an association. However, when rules are generated, instead of using confidence, the authors use a metric they call conviction, which is a measure of implication and not just co-occurrence. In Liu et al. (1997), the authors present an approach addressing the rare item problem. In Omiecinski (2003), the authors also look at alternative measures of interest, named the gini index, entropy gain, and chi-squared.

Most recently, Omiecinski (2003) described all-confidence and bond as interestingness measures for association rules. These new measures are not based on support and can find dependence between item sets. Another advantage of these new measures is that they satisfy downward closure as support does. Therefore, there exist efficient algorithms to find association rules that satisfy the measures.

Although originally association rule mining was proposed for mining consumer purchasing patterns in retail stores, applications extend far beyond this specific setting. For example, Morishita & Sese (2000) applied association rule mining for genome mining. Association rule mining techniques are also used for classification (Liu et al. 1998) and clustering tasks (Beil et al. 2002).

The work most relevant work to this chapter is association rule mining based knowledge discovery in textual databases. Feldman & Dagan (1995), Feldman & Hirsh (1996), and Feldman et al. (1998) used an approach to association rule mining techniques for knowledge discovery in text collections based on statistical analysis for discovering associations among individual keywords assigned to texts. There is no description about how keywords were assigned to texts, suggesting that the assignment may be performed manually. Lin et al. (1998) used a similar technique. The main difference was that Lin et al. used key terms automatically extracted from text collections. Recently, Loh et al. (2000) proposed a concept based approach to text data mining. Their approach combines an automatic categorization step with a data mining step. Categorization identifies concepts presented inside texts. Data mining then discovers patterns by analyzing and relating concept distributions in the collection. Another classification step is then needed to create concept definitions.

In this chapter we use an *n-gram* based approach to extract concepts from textual databases. Our approach does not require a specific domain, unlike Weeber et al. (2001), who mapped sentences to predefined UMLS concepts.

Once concepts are extracted, we mine for associations in text collections. This is motivated by shortcomings of previous work which takes bags of words as input to the association rule mining algorithms, e.g. Agrawal & Srikant (1994), and finds associations among single isolated words. There are two pitfalls in that approach. One is that some concepts consist of multiple words. These multiple word concepts, such as *lung cancer,* cannot be found as a unit in the association rules. The other is that the number of associations is overwhelmingly large. This means that it is difficult to find interesting rules from such a large number of associations.

Attempts to mine rules using only single words appear to be rooted in the fact that they can introduce significant ambiguity, since it is the context within which word patterns appear that identifies the real meaning. We show examples in Table 11.1. For example, if a searcher is looking for information about lung cancer, the concept would be *lung cancer.* Instead of only single isolated words we permit multi-word concepts as input to the associate rule mining algorithm. Therefore, our approach is able to find associations among such concepts. This also reduces the number of associations. For example, if we use multi-word concepts as input we might find the rules "smoking → lung cancer" and "lung cancer → smoking." Using the single isolated words "lung" and "cancer," however, we might find the rules "smoking → lung," "smoking → cancer," "lung → cancer," "lung → smoking," "cancer → smoking," "cancer → lung," "smoking, lung → cancer," "smoking, cancer → lung," "cancer, lung → smoking," "cancer, smoking → lung," "lung, smoking → cancer," and "lung, cancer → smoking." In the second case there are twelve rules while with multi-word concept extraction only two rules would be found. In general, an isolated word based approach will generate many more redundant rules than a concept based approach.

Table 11.1. Isolated Words vs. Concepts

Isolated Words	Concepts
New	New York
Lung	Lung cancer
Data	Data mining

11.1.1 Graph Representation

To build on the concept associations that are extracted, a graph representation of them is useful because it shows indirect associations: if A and B are associated, and B and C are associated, then A and C are indirectly associated. This is not always obvious from a long list of associations, but is easily seen when associations are represented visually in a graph. These transitive associations can lead to new knowledge. For example, Hearst (1999) shows, when investigating causes of migraine headaches, that the following associations can be found:

- stress is associated with migraines
- stress can lead to loss of magnesium
- calcium channel blockers prevent some migraines
- magnesium is a natural calcium channel blocker
- spreading cortical depression (SCD) is implicated in some migraines
- high levels of magnesium inhibit SCD
- migraine patients have high platelet aggregability
- magnesium can suppress platelet aggregability

These transitive associations suggest that magnesium deficiency may play a role in some kinds of migraine headache.

11.2 Method

An experimental evaluation on real textual datasets was conducted. We compared our concept based approach with the isolated word based approach. Different interestingness measures were compared. Finally we show how the results can be used to generate a directed concept association graph.

11.2.1 Concept Based Association Rule Mining Approach

Our concept based text mining approach consists of three parts: concept extraction, concept association mining and concept association graph generation. They are described in the next sections respectively.

11.2.2 Concept Extraction

In general, it is well-known that the input heavily determines the quality of the outputs; *garbage in, garbage out* is a famous computer axiom meaning that if invalid data is entered into a system, the resulting output will also be invalid. Particularly in association rule mining, more accurate input produces more interesting rules that may lead to discovery of unknown associations. Instead of only single isolated words, concepts that are closely related multi-word groups that have semantic coherence seem more beneficial to use as inputs to association rules. The concept extraction approach we use here is different from usual concept extraction studies that focus on digging up the most representative words of documents. In such studies, e.g. Lewis (1992), finding common *themes* in a given document is the main objective and these common themes or patterns are considered as concepts. In this study we define and use concept in a different manner. Here, a concept is a single word or group of consecutive words that occurs frequently enough in the entire document collection. Each concept candidate was expected to satisfy a predefined support threshold equivalent to 10 occurrences, equal to the threshold used to prune the least frequent words during pre-processing.

We further elaborate our method for concept extraction as follows. It is necessary to pre-process the datasets before extracting the concepts. Only letters, digits, '/', and '-' were kept in words. Other pre-processing steps included stop word elimination, stemming, and pruning the least and most frequent words. Since the most frequent words can be an important part of a multi-word concept, and therefore removing them may lead to missing some meaningful rules, they are not pruned based on an upper threshold. Additional pre-processing performs stemming, which can affect concept extraction significantly. In general, stemming is finding the base form of the word to improve concept analysis. For instance, the stemmer converts both *addressing* and *addressed* words to the same stem term *address*. The Krovetz Stemmer (Krovetz 1993) was used for this purpose. After cleaning the raw dataset, it remains with only stemmed words that are frequent enough. We used an *n*-gram based approach for mining concepts. This approach needs two parameters *max_ngram_size* and *min_sup*. The former indicates the maximum number of words in a concept, and the latter is a frequency threshold for concepts.

One of the crucial steps that affect results is specification of key parameters. Assume that a dataset has a number of 4-gram concepts (i.e., concepts that are four words long). If *max_ngram_size* is set to 2, these concepts will be divided into two parts. Thus using a small *max_ngram_size* tends to both lose actual concepts, and also unnecessarily increase the number of concepts. It is also easy to see that the number of concepts can exceed the number of words in the original pre-processed dataset. Table 11.2 shows example textual data. The algorithm for extracting concepts consists of two steps. In the first step, candidate concepts are found, and then counted in order to check the support of each of them. The higher order *n*-grams are generated first in order not to split words apart from their neighbour. For each *n*, where *n* is the number of words in the concept, the algorithm passes over the dataset once. The result is a candidate concept table that will be used in the next step. In the second step, the concept candidates are pruned based on the threshold *min_sup*. All the candidates with less support than that are eliminated from the candidate table. The concepts in Table 11.3 show the IDs and supports for concepts extracted from the dataset shown in Table 11.2. Note that in Table 11.3 concept {B} does not appear because all of occurrences of B except in D5 are included in the 2-gram concepts {A B} and {C B} as shown in Table 11.2. Since the remaining B in D5 is not frequent enough to satisfy *min_sup*, it does not appear in Table 11.3. Also, since each occurrence of word E is contained in {C D E} or {E F}, there is no concept {E} in Table 11.3.

Table 11.2. Sample dataset with six documents and six words

Documents	Words
D_1	A B C D E F A
D_2	E F C B
D_3	A B E F
D_4	A C B F
D_5	C D C D E B A B
D_6	D A C D E C

Table 11.3. Concepts extracted using dataset from Table 11.2 with max_ngram_size = 3 and min_sup = 2

Concept_ID	Concept	Support
1	{C D E}	3
2	{A B}	3
3	{C B}	2
4	{E F}	2
5	{A}	3
6	{C}	2
7	{D}	2
8	{F}	2

After concept extraction each document is represented as a *bag of concepts*. Table 11.4 shows the *bag of concepts* representation for the original dataset in Table 11.2. We will use *bags of concepts* instead of bags of words as input for our next step of mining concept associations.

Table 11.4. Dataset from Table 11.2 with extracted concepts

Documents	Items
D_1	2 1 8 5
D_2	4 3
D_3	2 4
D_4	5 3 8
D_5	6 7 1 2
D_6	7 5 1 6

11.2.3 Mining Concept Associations

After concept extraction, each document is represented by a set of concepts. It is not the concepts themselves, but the associations between them that represent the knowledge buried in the documents that it is our goal to extract. One major difference between our approach and earlier methods is that we use multi-word concepts instead of single isolated words as items for association rule mining.

Because we are interested in the dependence between concepts in text, we decided to use all-confidence and bond as our measure of interestingness for association rules. We also compared these two measures with use of support and confidence measures for mining textual datasets to reveal differences in the two approaches. Our experimental evaluation will show that the rules generated using bond and all-confidence are more interesting and easy to examine than those generated using support and confidence.

11.2.4 Generating a Directed Graph of Concept Associations

The approach used to construct a directed concept association graph is not complicated. We need one pass over the rules generated previously. The method of generating a directed graph needs a confidence parameter *min_conf* to decide the type of line and the direction. The algorithm reads a rule and its confidence value. Each side of the association is created as a new node if it is not yet represented. If the confidence value is at least *min_conf*, the edge between two nodes is drawn as a solid line but otherwise a dashed line is used to show the weakness of the relation. It is clear that some rules that are paired (e.g. A → B and B → A) are read twice. In this case, the rule with the greater confidence value determines the direction of the edge. If both are equal, the edge will have two arrowheads. Also, if both confidence values of the pair of rules are smaller than *min_conf*, the edge between them will be a bidirectional dashed line. The directed graph of the dataset from Table 11.2 is shown in Figure 11.1 with *min_conf* = 0.6. It is obvious that directed graphs are more informative than undirected graphs. For example, the confidence values of 3 → 4 and 4 → 3 are both 0.5, smaller than *min_conf*, 0.6. Therefore, in Figure 11.2 the edge between {C B} and {E F} is a bidirectional dashed line. On

the other hand, the edge that connects {C} and {D} is a bidirectional solid line because their confidence values are equal and above *min_conf.*

Note how directed graphs highlight transitive rules that are otherwise obscured
in the result set. X → Y is a transitive rule if X implies Z, Z implies Y, and X does
not imply Y directly. For example, it is too time consuming to figure out that the
association between {C} and {A} can be interesting because {C} implies {C D E}
and {C D E} implies {A} but {C} does not imply {A} directly. More concretely,
based on the above discussions, directed graphs depict both direct associations between concepts as well as transitively justified indirect rules.

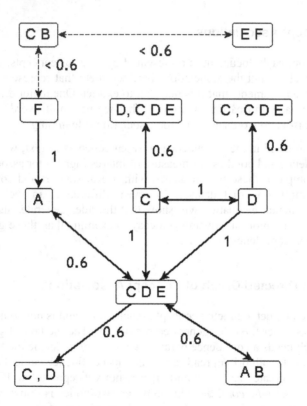

Fig. 11.1. Directed concept association graph based on dataset from Table 11.2.

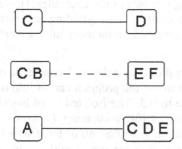

Fig. 11.2. Three sample of undirected concept association graph.

11.3 Experiments and Results

To demonstrate robustness and coherence of the approach, we chose two textual datasets. The first dataset, which we call PubMed-abstracts, consists of 9795 biomedical abstracts downloaded from (PubMed Central) with the keyword *mRNA*. For the second dataset, we did experiments with the (BioMed Central) text corpus that includes 4581 published articles of peer-reviewed biomedical research.

To show the effectiveness and efficiency of our algorithm, we look at the results in three different ways. Our first focus is to demonstrate how results from concept based association rule mining using multi-word phrases outperform the results from using only single words. Second, we must determine how to rate the *interestingness* of association rules that are extracted. For this purpose, we compare traditional support and confidence properties with new interestingness measures, *bond* and *all-confidence*, introduced in Morishita & Sese (2000). Finally, we evaluate our method for constructing concept association graphs - directed graphs for interesting concept associations based on the all-confidence property. A graph representation is employed to help users interpret the results and infer new rules.

11.3.1 Isolated words vs. multi-word concepts

In this section, we highlight the concept extraction technique that we have developed to generate accurate input to association rule mining algorithms. First, recall that in the case of single words, the number of association rules that is generated is considerably higher than when multi-word concepts are used. This large number of rules increases the human effort required to interpret them and identify the interesting ones. Our rule mining software is a modified version of the fast apriori implementation by Bodon (2003) and was run on a Sun machine with 4GB of physical memory.

Regarding PubMed-abstracts, using the traditional support and confidence interestingness measures, with a support threshold of 0.005 and a confidence threshold of 0.7, multi-word concept based rule mining produced only four rules. However, using isolated words caused the program to crash without yielding any rules. It started with 2105 frequent 1-itemsets and consumed all memory after generating 1,541,371 4-itemsets.

We tuned the support and confidence thresholds in order to decrease the number of frequent itemsets so that the process running the program can fit into memory. We set support to 0.007 and confidence to 0.5. The isolated word based approach returned 1,993,922 rules with the largest rule containing 11 words. The multi-word concept based approach produced only 5 rules, all of them with three words. All five seemed interesting. Certainly, five are manageable to interpret compared to 1,993,922 rules. From the isolated word based approach, 63,816 rules had a confidence value of 1.0, which was unexpected. A confidence value of 1.0 describes the strongest associations which therefore might be expected to be interesting. However, one can see that they are not actually meaningful and interesting by looking at the top 20 results shown in Table 11.5. Table 11.6 illustrates rules from the multi-word concept based approach. It is obvious that the concept based approach does not have redundant rules, while the word based approach does. For instance, the rules "transcription-polymerase → chain", "transcription-polymerase → chain, reaction" and "transcription-polymerase → reaction" in Table 11.5 are redundant.

Table 11.5. Top Association Rules from isolated words (support = 0.007, confidence = 0.5)

Rules	Support
method, conclusion, level, cell, expression → result	488
method, conclusion, effect, cell→result	469
rt-pcr, method, conclusion, cell→result	433
method, conclusion, decrease→result	406
reverse, chain, method, expression → reaction	390
reverse, chain, method, conclusion → reaction	381
objective, method, significant → result	381
objective, method, conclusion, significant → result	378
transcription-polymerase → chain	375
transcription-polymerase → chain, reaction	375
transcription-polymerase → reaction	375
background, method conclusion, study → result	374
objective, method, level → result	373
objective, method, conclusion, level → result	368
china, objective → result	361
method, conclusion, induce, cell → result	354
method, conclusion, level, protein, cell → result	346
method, conclusion, show, cell → result	345
line, human, study, mrna → cell	344
objective, method, conclusion, increase → result	340

Table 11.6. Association rules from concepts (support = 0.007, confidence = 0.5)

Rules	Support
vascular endothelial growth factor → vegf	124
cardiac → heart	89
background, method → result	88
induce apoptosis → apoptosi	78
apoptotic → apoptosi	71

11.3.2 New Metrics vs. the Traditional Support & Confidence

Table 11.7 is the summary of the results from the PubMed-abstracts dataset. They were acquired from multi-word concept based rule mining using the traditional support and confidence interestingness measure, the all-confidence measure, and the bond measure, respectively. It shows the total number of association rules for each interestingness measure.

Table 11.7. Number of association rules for support and confidence, all-confidence and bond

Threshold	Support (0.002) &Conf.	All Conf.	Bond
0.5	752	529	232
0.7	143	62	38
0.8	67	26	15
0.9	21	8	6
1.0	0	2	2

Initially, for both the PubMed-abstracts and BioMed Central datasets, *max_ngram_size* was defined as 4, so concept phrases up to four words long were sought, and *min_sup* was defined as 10, meaning the concept phrase appeared in at least ten documents. In the traditional model, for high support thresholds, such as 0.5 and 0.2, the software returned no rules. In order to make this model comparable with the new measures, we decreased the support threshold to 0.002, thus reducing the pruning effect of a high support as much as possible. The 0.002 value was determined by memory limitations because in case of an even lower threshold, 0.001, the memory needed for candidate generation greatly exceeded the available memory.

As noted in Morishita & Sese (2000), there is no certain relationship between the traditional and the new measures. From Table 11.7, it can be observed that the set of association rules is larger for the traditional measures but does not necessarily include all of the rules yielded by using bond or all-confidence. In the following we show some example rules from results obtained using the all-confidence measure with threshold value 0.5. Note that none of these rules are listed in the result set obtained using traditional interestingness measures (support = 0.002, confidence = 0.5). These example show that support pruning may cause some interesting rules to be lost in the pruning process. After each rule, a descriptive note with its source is attached to confirm the association.

• skin disease → psoriasis

... a chronic (long-lasting) *skin disease* of scaling and inflammation that affects 2 to 2.6 percent of the United States population, or between 5.8 and 7.5 million people. Although the disease occurs in all age groups, it primarily affects adults. It appears about equally in males and females. *Psoriasis* occurs when skin cells quickly rise from their origin below the surface of the skin and pile up on the surface before they have a chance to mature (Health Information).

• plasmodium → malaria

Four species of *Plasmodium* infect humans and cause *malaria* (College of Biological Sciences).

• spinal ligament → ectopic bone formation

... of the posterior longitudinal *ligament of the spine* (OPLL) is a common form of human myelopathy caused by a compression of the spinal cord by *ectopic ossification* of spinal ligaments (National Center for Biotechnology-A).

• vein wall → thrombu

Deep *vein thrombosis* (DVT), a form of venous thromboembolic disease, refers to the formation of a *thrombus* (blood clot) within a deep *vein*, commonly in the thigh or calf. Although venous thromboembolic disease can develop after any major surgery, people who have orthopaedic surgery on the lower extremities are especially vulnerable. Three factors contribute to formation of clots in veins:
Stasis, or stagnant blood flow through veins. This increases the contact time between blood and *vein wall* irregularities (Hospital for Special Surgery)...

When we compare the bond and all-confidence measures, the bond measure is more restrictive than all-confidence. With the same threshold value it returns fewer rules. Its result set is a subset of the results yielded by all-confidence using the same threshold. Nevertheless, by changing the threshold it is possible to obtain approximately the same set of rules. For example, experiments with the PubMed-abstracts dataset show that results from bond = 0.7 were the same as results using all-confidence = 0.8. Therefore, all-confidence and bond are equivalent in being able to find the most interesting rules. We show some rules generated by using bond and all-confidence for the BioMed Central dataset in Table 11.8.

Table 11.8. Number of association rules extracted from BioMed Central

Threshold		All Conf.	Bond
0.5	MF: 10	2968	626
	MF: 20	3141	285
0.7	MF: 10	226	120
	MF: 20	72	41
0.9	MF: 10	45	36
	MF: 20	20	18
1.0	MF: 10	32	23
	MF: 20	17	15

MF Minimum frequency threshold for concepts in dataset

11.3.2.1 Directed Graphs

Depending on the formal definition of bond and all-confidence, rules that are returned by these measures contain no information about direction of the association. After mining a sample dataset, Table 11.9 lists rules whose all-confidences are at least 0.5. Based on the aforementioned association rules, three examples of undirected graphs between some concepts are shown in Figure 11.2. Although graph representations of concept associations assist users to see relations quickly and easily, undirected graphs are less informative that one might like. Therefore, since each rule has a confidence value, we integrated the graph representation with the confidence value to give directions to edges.

Table 11.9. List of rules satisfying all-confidence=0.5 after concept mining of dataset from Table 11.2.

Rule	Confidence
8 → 3	0.5
3 → 8	0.5
8 → 5	1.0
5 → 8	0.6
7 → 6	1.0
6 → 7	1.0
7 → 6, 1	1.0
6 → 7, 1	1.0
1 → 7, 6	0.6
7 → 1	1.0
1 → 7	0.6
6 → 1	1.0
1 → 6	0.6
4 → 3	0.5
3 → 4	0.5
5 → 1	0.6
1 → 5	0.6
2 → 1	0.6
1 → 2	0.6
8 → 3	0.5
3 → 8	0.5
8 → 5	1.0
5 → 8	0.6

We further apply the traditional confidence metric to find the direction of each rule. Figures 11.3 to 11.6 are sample graphs that exhibit some interesting associations. The first two are constructed from the PubMed-abstracts dataset, and the last two are from the BioMed Central dataset. All the associations shown in the figures have all-confidence values greater than 0.5. Figure 11.5 shows interesting associations between *chlorthalidone* and the others. The dashed lines between concepts indicate weak confidence values (<0.6). The descriptive notes below explain the relationships between concepts in Figures 11.5 and 11.6 respectively.

- ALLHAT (Antihypertensive and Lipid-Lowering Treatment to Prevent *Heart Attack Trial*) was the largest antihypertensive trial and the second largest lipid-lowering trial and included large numbers of patients over age 65, women, African-Americans, and patients with diabetes, treated largely in community practice settings…This trial is comparing treatment of hypertension with a diuretic (*chlorthalidone*) against newer types of antihypertensives - an alpha-adrenoceptor blocker (*doxazosin*), an ACE inhibitor, and a calcium antagonist - in a high-risk patient group (all over 55 years with one or more cardiovascular disease (CVD) risk factors) (Information For Health Professionals).

- Osteoporosis is a significant public health problem associated with increased mortality and morbidity. Our aim in this cross-sectional study was to investigate the relationship between lifetime physical activity and_*calcium* *intake and bone mineral density (BMD)* and BMC (bone mineral content) in 42 regularly menstruating caucasian women (age 21.26+/-1.91 years, BMI 23.83+/-5.85). BMD and BMC at the lumbar spine (L2-L4), hip (femoral neck, trochanter, total), and total body were assessed by dual energy x-ray *absorptiometry* (DXA). (National Center for Biotechnology Information-B)

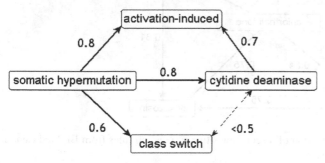

Fig. 11.3. Graph representation of a set of transitive association rules from PubMed (all-confidence = 0.5)

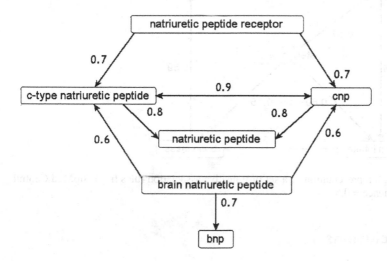

Fig. 11.4. Graph representation of a set of transitive association rules from PubMed (all-confidence = 0.5).

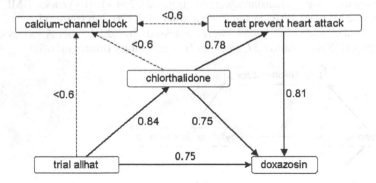

Fig. 11.5. Graph representation of a set of transitive association rules from BioMed Central with all-confidence = 0.6

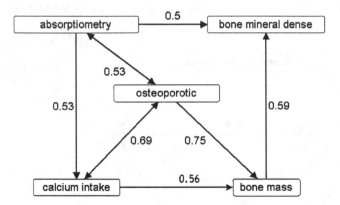

Fig. 11.6. Graph representation of a set of transitive association rules from BioMed Central with all-confidence = 0.5

11.4 Conclusions

In this chapter we explore a new approach for knowledge discovery from biomedical text databases. A concept is a keyword or multi-word phrase that describes the subject about which a user is seeking information. For example, if a searcher is looking for information about lung cancer, the concept would be *lung cancer*. Our goal is to extract interesting associations among concepts that co-occur within a text collection.

After concept extraction, the documents are each represented as a *bag of concepts*. It is not the concepts, however, but the associations between them that represent much of the knowledge buried in the documents. Our text data mining task is to dig out these buried associations as nuggets from text collections. One contribution of this chapter is the use of concepts as inputs for the associate rule mining algorithm. Another contribution is a graph representation of mined associations.

We evaluated our techniques by using two real textual datasets. The evaluation results show our system can automatically find interesting concepts and their associations from unstructured text data. The experimental results also show that our approach can significantly reduce the number of uninteresting associations. Considering the results from the real-world dataset we used, we conclude that the all-confidence measure is quite useful in generating interesting associations. Furthermore, the generated directed graph that is generated for concept associations not only shows the directed associations represented by association rules but also all transitive associations. The concept association graph can be used to infer new association rules. Therefore it can lead to the discovery of new knowledge from textual databases.

In the future, we will investigate other concept extraction algorithms for knowledge discovery from textual databases. We will also develop more efficient algorithms for generating concept association graphs.

11.5 Examples

As additional examples, we mine (Reuters-21578) Text Collection. Some interesting relations are visualized in Figures 11.7 and 11.8. Figure 11.7 depicts associations between a mining company, a union and others. Figure 11.8 shows interesting associations between *energy information administrate eia* and the others. The dashed line between *oil demand* and *gasoline demand* indicates weak confidence value. The concept *energy information administrate eia* contains also abbreviation *eia* for energy information administrate. The abbreviation *spr* stands for Strategic Petroleum Reserve in energy related news.

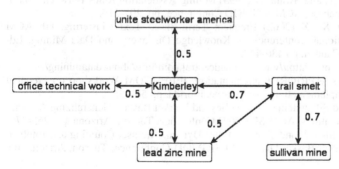

Fig. 11.7. Graph representation of a set of transitive association rules from Reuters-21578 Text Collection (all-confidence = 0.5)

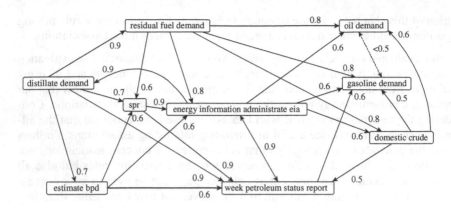

Fig. 11.8. Graph representation of a sample set of transitive association rules from Reuters-21578 Text Collection (all-confidence = 0.5)

11.6 Exercises

1. What is support and confidence of an association rule?
2. Formulate bond and all-confidence measures.
3. Discuss relations between all-confidence, bond, and support for a dataset.
4. What is a concept and how it is related to a n-gram?

11.7 References

Agrawal R and Srikant R (1994) Fast Algorithms for Mining Association Rules. 20th International Conference on Very Large Data Bases, Santiago de Chile, Chile, pp 487-499.

Agrawal R, Imielinski T, and Swami A (1993) Mining Association Rules Between Sets of Items in Large Database. ACM SIGMOD Conference, pp. 207-216.

Beil F, Ester M, and Xu X (2002) Frequent Term-Based Text Clustering. 8th ACM SIGKDD International Conference on Knowledge Discovery and Data Mining, Edmonton, Alberta, Canada, pp 436-442.

BioMed Central text corpus, http://www.biomedcentral.com/info/about/datamining/.

Bodon F (2003) A Fast APRIORI Implementation. IEEE ICDM Workshop on Frequent Itemset Mining Implementations, Melbourne, Florida, pp 56-65.

Brin S, Motwani R, and Silverstein C (1997) Beyond Market Basket: Generalizing Association Rules to Correlations. ACM SIGMOD Conference, Tucson, Arizona, pp. 265-276.

Brin S, Motwani R, Ullman J, and Tsur, S (1997) Dynamic Itemset Counting and Implication Rules for Market Basket Data ACM SIGMOD Conference, Tucson, Arizona, pp. 255-264.

College of Biological Sciences, http://www.biosci.ohio-state.edu/~parasite/plasmodium.html.

Fayyad U, Piatetsky-Shapiro G, and Smyth P (1996) Knowledge Discovery and Data Mining: Towards a Unifying Framework, Second Int. Conf. on Knowledge Discovery and Data Mining, Portland, OR, pp. 82-88.

Feldman R and Dagan I (1995) Knowledge Discovery in Textual Databases (KDT). First international conference on knowledge discovery (KDD'95), Montreal, pp 112-117.

Feldman R, and Hirsh H (1996) Mining Associations In Text In The Presence Of Background Knowledge. 2nd International Conference on Knowledge Discovery and Data Mining, pp. 343-346.

Feldman R, Dagan I, and Hirsh H (1998) Mining Text Using Keyword Distributions. Journal of Intelligent Information Systems: Integrating Artificial Intelligence and Database Technologies, 10(3), pp. 281-300.

Health Information Main Page, http://www.niams.nih.gov/hi/topics/psoriasis/psoriafs.htm.

Hearst MA (1999) Untangling Text Data Mining. 37th Annual Meeting of the Association for Computational Linguistics (ACL'99), University of Maryland, pp 3-10.

Hipp J, Guntzer U, and Nakhaeizadeh G (2000) Algorithms for Association Rule Mining – A General Survey and Comparison, ACM SIGKDD Explorations, Vol.2, pp. 58-64.

Hospital for Special Surgery, Orthopedic Surgery, http://orthopaedics.hss.edu/services/conditions/hip/dv_thrombosis.asp.

Information For Health Professionals http://allhat.sph.uth.tmc.edu.

Krovetz R (1993) Viewing Morphology as an Inference Process. 16th ACM SIGIR Conference, Pittsburgh, pp 191-202.

Lewis D (1992) An Evaluation Of Phrasal And Clustered Representations On A Text Categorization Problem. ACM-SIGIR Conference on Information Retrieval, Copenhagen, Denmark, pp 37-50.

Lin SH, Shih CS, and Chen MC (1998) Extracting Classification Knowledge of Internet Documents with Mining Term Associations: A Semantic Approach. 21st Annual International ACM SIGIR Conference on Research and Development in Information Retrieval, Melbourne, Australia, pp 241-249.

Liu B, Hsu W, and Ma YM (1998) Integrating Classification and Association Rule Mining. The Fourth International Conference on Knowledge Discovery and Data Mining (KDD-98), New York City, pp. 80-86.

Liu B, Hsu W, and Ma YM (1997) Mining Association Rules with Multiple Minimum Supports. The Fourth International Conference on Knowledge Discovery and Data Mining, pp. 337-341.

Loh S, Wives LK, and Oliveia JPM (2000) Concept Based Knowledge Discovery from Texts Extracted from the Web. ACM SIGKDD Explorations, vol. 2, pp. 29-40.

Morishita S and Sese J (2000) Traversing Itemset Lattices with Statistical Metric Pruning. In Proc. of the 19th ACM SIGACT-SIGMOD-SIGART Symposium on Principles of Database Systems,. ACM Press, pp. 226-236.

National Center for Biotechnology Information-A, retrieved from http://www.ncbi.nlm.nih.gov/entrez/query.fcgi?cmd=Retrieve&db=PubMed&dopt=Abstract&list_uids=9662402.

National Center for Biotechnology Information-B, retrieved from http://www.ncbi.nlm.nih.gov/entrez/query.fcgi?cmd=Retrieve&db=PubMed&list_uids=12150501&dopt=Abstract.

Omiecinski E (2003) Alternative Interest Measures for Mining Associations. IEEE Trans. Knowledge and Data Engineering, 15(1), pp. 57-69.

PubMed Central, retrieved from http://www.pubmedcentral.nih.gov/.

Reuters-21578 Text Categorization Text Collection retrieved from http://www.daviddlewis.com/resources/testcollections/reuters21578/.

Weeber M, Vos R, Klein H, de Jong-van den Berg LTW (2001) Using Concepts In Literature-Based Discovery: Simulating Swanson'S Raynaud Fish Oil And Migraine Magnesium Discoveries. Journal of American Society for Information Science and Technology; 52 (7), pp.548–557.

12 Mining E-Documents to Uncover Structures

Azita Bahrami

Department of Information Technology, Armstrong Atlantic State University, 11935 Abercorn Street, Savannah, GA 31419, USA

12.1 Introduction

An e-Document, D, coded in HTML is comprised of a body and a head. The body includes the contents of the e-document, and the head includes, among other things, metadata. In essence, an HTML e-document, D, is a triple (B, M, μ) Where,

B	(The body of D) is a non-empty finite set of primitive elements, e, where e can be a formal heading, an informal heading, a formal paragraph, an informal paragraph, a table, an image, or a hyperlink;
M= {E, I}	(The metadata section of D) where E is the set of explicit terms and I is the set of implicit terms; A term, τ, may be a token or a phrase;
μ	is a mapping function such that $\mu(\tau, B) = b$ where, $b \subset B$ and $\tau \in E$.

A term in the metadata section of an e-document is either *explicit* or *implicit*. The explicit terms (set E) are those whose descriptions constitute the body of the e-document, whereas the implicit terms (set I) are incidental and do not make up the body. For example, if "3NF" and "relational database" are two terms in the meta-data section of an e-document and the document covers the "normal forms" topic, then the "3NF" is an explicit term while the term "relational database" is an implicit one. If $(M \neq \varnothing)$ and $(E \neq \varnothing)$ then D is a *qualified* e-document.

The goal of this chapter is to investigate the mining of qualified e-documents to discover their physical and logical structures. The *physical* structure of a qualified e-document, D, refers to the primitive components of the body along with their boundaries. The *logical* structure of D refers to the subsets (segments) of B (along with their relationships) identified by the mapping function of μ. A segment, which describes an explicit term, may be composed of several paragraphs, tables, etc. scattered throughout the e-document's body. The discovery of physical and logical structures of an HTML document is a problem and knowing how to solve

Y. Chan et al. (eds.), *Data Engineering*, International Series in Operations Research & Management Science 132, DOI 10.1007/978-1-4419-0176-7_12, © Springer Science+Business Media, LLC 2010

it is of particular value to the users who seek: finer data granularity in the retrieval of web-based information; conceptual hierarchy within an e-document; semantic Web; Internet-based active learning; ontology; and e-learning, e-government, e-commerce, and e-military, to name a few.

To discover the physical and logical structures of an HTML document (D), one must mine the document in three steps: (1) Mine the body of D to discover the Physical Structure, (2) Mine the metadata section of D to discover the explicit terms using ontology, and (3) Mine the body of D to discover the logical structure of D using the explicit terms and the physical structure of D.

The organization of this chapter is as follow. A review of Related Research (section 12.2) followed by the explanation of the above three steps under the headings of Discovery of the Physical Structure (section 12.3), Discovery of the Explicit Terms Using Ontology (section 12.4), Discovery of the Logical Structure (section 12.5), and the discussion of Empirical Results and Conclusion (sections 12.6 and 12.7, respectively).

12.2 Related Research

A large number of research efforts on mining of e-documents have focused on the extraction of features from structured/unstructured HTML documents (Crescenzi et al. 2001; Garofalakis et al. 1999; Knoblock et al. 2000; Agichtein and Ganti 2004; Ford et al. 2005), but much smaller number has concentrated on discovering the logical structure of e-documents. Perhaps the work of Stojanovic et al. (2001) is the closest attempt to uncovering the logical structures of the body of a specific type of e-documents known as e-lessons. Their methodology works based on a premise that an e-document is presented as a *well-defined* XML document. The methodology, therefore, neither offers a solution for sloppy XML documents, nor for HTML documents, whether well-defined or not.

Uncovering the physical and logical structures of an e-document is advantageous in many areas including, but not limited to, data granularity in web-based information retrieval (Lin 2005; Lin 2007), discovery of the conceptual hierarchy within an e-document (Wang et al. 2003; Han and Kamber 2005), semantic Web (Berners-Lee et al. 2001; Peter et al. 2004), Internet-based active learning (Bahrami 2007; Bahrami 2006a), automation of ontology construction (Stoilos et al. 2005; Willem et al. 2005), and e-learning (Bahrami 2005; Bahrami 2006b).

As an example, let us look at the effects of this methodology on data granularity in a web-based information retrieval process. Searching W3 for a specific topic returns a list of e-documents. The search engine returns these documents because the requested topic appears in the e-documents' metadata sections. In other words, the search engine's job is to examine the metadata of numerous e-documents and return only the documents in whose metadata appear the requested topic. The inclusion of a topic in metadata constitutes an *explicit* term if about which some direct discussion is provided within the document. Otherwise, the inclusion of such topic in metadata constitutes an *implicit* term because within the document the term is mentioned only indirectly or not at all—their inclusion in the metadata section is solely for the purpose of maximizing the number of hits. Most search engines do a relevancy calculation of the found e-documents and rank them before returning the list to the user.

An explicit term (specifically discussed in the document) is likely to be mentioned in different sections of the document requiring the user to sift through the entire document to locate it. This cumbersome task is necessary because the e-document, as a whole, is the only granule the search engine can return. The reason is that no mechanism is used to divide an e-document into several granules and return only the relevant ones. Should the requested topic be an *implicit* term in the metadata, the user is not only faced with the time consuming task of reading the entire document, but also he/she has to endure the very frustrating experience of finding nothing about the requested topic. The question is: can this problem be solved? A set of mechanisms that can distinguish the explicit from implicit terms can solve the problem and would automatically locate the starting and ending positions of the topic's coverage in the document. This is possible once the logical structure of an e-document is unveiled.

12.3 Discovery of the Physical Structure

An e-document's body is comprised of n_e elements that include n_p paragraphs, n_h headings, n_t tables, and n_i images where ($n_p \geq 1$, $n_h \geq 0$, $n_t \geq 0$, $n_i \geq 0$ and $n_e = n_p + n_h + n_t + n_i$). Each element is analyzed further in the following sub-sections.

12.3.1 Paragraph

A paragraph is either formal or informal. A formal paragraph is a paragraph whose original designer/programmer has encased between the pairs of <p> and </p> tags. An informal paragraph, however, does not have paragraph tags. As a result, the following grammar is provided for the identification of the informal paragraphs. Note: a pair of curly braces is utilized to denote the non-terminal items in the grammar. The non-terminal *{Sentence}* below refers to any sentence in the English language.

$$\{Informal\ paragraph\} \rightarrow \{Begin\}\ \{Middle\}\ \{End\}$$
$$\{Begin\} \rightarrow
\ [
]^+ \mid </h_i> \mid </p> \mid <p>$$
$$\{Middle\} \rightarrow \{Sentence\}^+$$
$$\{End\} \rightarrow
\ [
]^+ \mid <p> \mid
\ <h_i>$$

Each paragraph, whether formal or informal, is identified by an identification number (PID), a starting position (PStart), and an ending position (PEnd). The paragraph identification number is constructed by the letter "P" followed by an order number (e. g. $P_1, \ldots, P_n$). If the entire body of an HTML e-document is considered as a long string of characters, then the positions of the first and the last characters of the paragraph, respectively, are the values for the PStart and PEnd.

12.3.2 Heading

A heading is either a word or a phrase, formal or informal. A formal heading is surrounded by a pair of <h$_i$> </h$_i$> tags (where $1 \leq i \leq 8$). An informal heading is not surrounded by the heading tags but for which the following grammar is provided with the convention that the non-terminal {A_word} and {A_phrase} refer to any word and any phrase in the English language.

> {Infomal_heading}→{Part1}{Bold_title}{Part2}|
>   {Part1}{Regular_title}{Part3}
> {Part1} →
 [
]$^+$ | </p>
> {Bold_title} → <b> {Regular_title} </b>
> {Regular_title}→{A_word} | {A_ phrase} | {A_numbered_word} |
>   {A_numbered_phrase}
> {A_numbered_word} → {Number}{A_word}
> {A_numbered_Phrase} →{Number} {A_phrase}
> {Number}→ {Simple_no} | {Simple_no}. | {Simple_no}
>   [.{Simple_no}]$^+$ {Simple_no} [.{Simple_no}]$^+$.
> {Simple_no} → {First_digit}{Digit}*
> {Part2} → {Part3}| , | : | . | - | --
> {Part3} →
[
]$^+$
> {Digit} → 0 | {First_digit}
> {First_digit} → 1 | 2 | 3| 4 | 5 | 6 | 7 | 8 | 9

Each heading is given an identification number (HID), starting position (HStart), and an ending position (HEnd) in the document. The heading identification number is denoted by the letter "h" followed by the heading level. There are eight heading levels of 1 through 8. HStart and HEnd are determined in the same way that PStart and PEnd are determined.

Headings of any level (1-8) can be either numbered or unnumbered. A formal numbered heading is the one for which the original designer has provided both a pair of heading tags and a title number. Example: <h$_1$> 1. Introduction </h$_1$>. A formal unnumbered heading has only the heading tags (<h$_1$> Introduction </h$_1$>).

An informal heading may also be numbered (example: 1. Introduction) or unnumbered (example: Introduction). The methodology used requires the assignment of heading tags (i.e. levels) to the informal headings.

12.3.2.1 Assigning Heading Levels to Informal Headings

A notation is used to express the *levels* of headings. The fewer sub-sections a heading has, the higher its level is, hence: 3.1>3.1.2. To further explain the notation, if there are three headings numbered 3.1, 3.2, and 3.1.1, the notations 3.1 > 3.1.1 and 3.1 = 3.2 are used to express that the heading with number 3.1 has a higher level than 3.1.1, and it has the same level as does the heading numbered 3.2. The same notations are used to express the levels among the formal tagged headings (e.g. h$_1$ > h$_2$).

Table 12.1. Possible combinations for the types of headings.

H	TH	NH	UH	Action
0	0	0	0	Practically Impossible
0	0	0	1	Practically Impossible
0	0	1	0	Practically Impossible
0	0	1	1	A(numbered heading) followed by B( )
0	1	0	0	Practically Impossible
0	1	0	1	A(tagged heading):
0	1	1	0	B( )
0	1	1	1	C( )
1	0	0	0	D( )
1	0	0	1	E( )
1	0	1	0	Headings are tagged through outlining techniques.
1	0	1	1	Practically Impossible
1	1	0	0	Heading numbers are dictated by the heading tags.
1	1	0	1	Practically Impossible
1	1	1	0	Heading numbers are dictated by the heading tags.
1	1	1	1	Practically Impossible

To assign heading levels to informal headings within an e-document, the type of existing heading formats within that document must be known (i.e. Tagged Heading, Numbered Heading, and Untagged-and-unnumbered Heading), because the assignment of headings depends on the mixture of existing headings. For example, if the e-document's body *does not have* a mixture of above heading formats, the body's heading format is a *homogenous* one; otherwise it is a *non-homogenous* heading format. To express it formally, an e-document's body has a homogeneous heading format if it satisfies one of the following conditions.

- All of the headings have heading tags and are numbered.
- All of the headings have heading tags and are unnumbered.
- All of the headings lack heading tags and are numbered.
- None of the headings are either numbered or have heading tags.
- No headings exist.

The assignment of heading levels to informal headings requires taking certain steps including a systematic study of all the possible combinations of heading formats in an e-document's body. Let us assume that we have four binary variables of Homogeneity (H), Tagged Heading (TH), Numbered Heading (NH), and Untagged-and-unnumbered Heading (UH). These variables have sixteen possible combinations displayed in Table 12.1. The values 1 and 0 represent "presence" and "absence" of a binary variable, respectively. Each combination requires an "Action" in order to be assigned proper heading levels, shown in Table 12.1. The details of each action are provided shortly.

Table 12.2. The Precedence Table for the informal unnumbered headings: (a) All of the headings are bold, (b) None of the headings are bold, and (c) Some of the headings are bold and the others are not.

Precedence Number	Pattern
1	
 [
]$^+$ {bold_title}
 [
]$^+$
2	
 [
]$^+${bold_title}
3	
 {bold_title}
4	
 [
]$^+$ {bold_title} (, | : | . | - | --)
5	
 {bold_title} (, | : | . | - | --)

a

Precedence Number	Pattern
1	
[
]$^+${regular_title}

]$^+$
2	
 [
]$^+$ {regular_title}[
]$^+$
3	
 {regular_title}

b

Precedence Number	Pattern
1	
 [
]$^+${bold_title}
[
]$^+$
2	
[
]$^+${regular_title}
[
]$^+$
3	
 [
]$^+${bold_title}
4	
 [
]$^+${ regular_title}
5	
 {bold_title}
6	
 { regular_title}
7	
 [
]$^+${bold_title} (, | : | . | - | --)
8	
 {bold_title} (, | : | . | - | --)

c

A *Precedence* table (Table 12.2) is used by some of these actions. This table is composed of three precedence sub-tables for the three cases when the headings are one of (a) bold, (b) regular, or (c) a combination of bold and regular. In any of the three precedence sub-tables, a precedence number is assigned to each row corresponding the row number. The precedence number 1 is the highest precedence.

The action **"Practically Impossible"** means that the combination can not happen in reality. As an example, let us look at the first row of the Table 12.1. Having zero values for the variables TH, NH, and UH means that no heading exists in the body of the document. Therefore, the body of the document has a homogenous heading format (based on the condition "e" of the homogeneity conditions). This conclusion contradicts the fact that H = 0, which means false. The zero value for H denotes that the body of the document *is not* homogenous.

Action A(T)

Let N_i and N_j be the two headings of type T (either numbered or tagged heading). If Ni

1. If a set of informal headings is placed above all of the T headings and the N_i is the first T heading in the document, then:
   a. Use the Precedence Table to assign precedence numbers (PN) to every member of the set.
   b. Assign the level of N_i to all informal headings starting with the highest PN and, accordingly, adjusting the assigned level to the other informal headings in the set.
2. If a set of informal headings is placed between the T headings (Ni and Nj), then:
   a. Use the Precedence Table to assign precedence numbers (PN) to every member of the set.
   b. If the level of $N_i > N_j$, then: Assign the level of N_j to all of the informal headings starting with the highest PN and, accordingly, adjusting the assigned level to the other informal headings in the set.
   c. If $N_i = N_j$, then: Assign the level of $N_i + 1$ to all of the informal headings starting with the highest PN and, accordingly, adjusting the assigned level to the other informal headings in the set.
   d. If $N_i < N_j$, then: Assign the level of $N_i - 1$ to all of the informal headings starting with the highest PN and, accordingly, adjusting the assigned level to the other informal headings in the set.
3. If a set of informal headings is placed bellow all of the T headings and the N_i heading preceding it is the last T headings in the document, then:
   a. Use the Precedence Table to assign precedence numbers (PN) to every member of the set.
   b. Assign the level of N_i to all of the informal headings starting with the highest PN and adjusting the assigned level to the other informal headings in the set.

End of Action A

Action B( )

Assign a heading tag to each numbered heading in accordance with the section level number accompanying the heading. For example, the numbered headings "1 α," "1.1 β," and "2γ," would become the tagged headings <h1> 1 α </h1>, <h2> 1.1 β </h2>, and <h1> 2 γ </h1>, respectively. The Greek letters of α, β, and γ, are headings texts. If there is a missing number in the sequence, an empty heading is created for it, which then is inserted in the body. For example, the numbered headings "1α," "1.1β," and "2.1γ" would become the tagged headings <h1> 1 α </h1>, <h2> 1.1 β </h2>, <h1> 2 $\emptyset$ </h1> and <h2> 2.1 γ </h2>.

End of Action B

Action C( )

Apply Action B to remove the problem resulting from the combination of numbered headings and tagged headings. Apply Action A(tagged heading) to remove

the problem resulting from the combination of unnumbered headings and tagged headings.
End of Action C

Action D( )
Let the title of the e-document, requested from the retrieval system, be α. Add the heading tags of <h1> α </h1> at the beginning of the e-document's body.
End of Action D

Action E( )
Assign PN to each informal heading using the Precedence Table. Assign the heading tag of <h_{PN}> ... </h_{PN}> to each informal heading.
End of Action E

12.3.3 Table

A table starts with the tag <table> and ends with the tag </table>. Each table is identified by an identification number, TID, a starting position, TStart, (the position of the first character of the tag <table>), an ending position, TEnd, (the position of the last character of the tag </table>). The table identification number is constructed by two letters of "TB" followed by an order number of (e. g. TB_1, . . ., TB_k). Each table may have a caption surrounded by caption tags, <caption> . . . </caption>. A caption usually starts with the word "Table" followed by at least one space and a table order number, all of which collectively are called Table-Ref (e.g. *Table 12.5*).

When a table in a paragraph is referenced for the first time, the paragraph is earmarked as the *owner* of the table and the table is the *gear* of the paragraph. (The Owner Identification, OID, is also a property of the table.) To determine the owner of a table, there are four possible combinations attesting the existence of caption tags and Table-Ref within the caption. Each combination along with its prescribed action is shown in Table 12.3. The values 1 and 0 represent true and false, respectively.

Table 12.3. The four possible combinations indicating the existence of a caption, and a Table-Ref within the caption along with the prescribed actions for each.

Caption Exist	Caption has Table-Ref	Action
0	0	F1( )
0	1	Practically Impossible
1	0	F2( )
1	1	F3( )

Table 12.4. Phrases for establishing adjacency between a table and its owner paragraph: Tables (a) and (b) are, respectively, located above and below the owner paragraph.

Phrase	Phrase
"above Table"	"following Table"
"Table above"	"Table below"
"Table displayed above"	"Table displayed below"
"Table presented above"	"Table presented below"
"Table shown above"	"Table shown below"
a	b

Action F1( )

Two cases can happen: The owner paragraph is either (a) immediately located above the <table> tag or (b) immediately located below the </table> tag. If neither case (a) nor case (b) is true, then the table is an orphan and is ignored. In case (a) the presence of one of the phrases shown in Table 12.4.a establishes the ownership of the paragraph. In case (b) the presence of one of the phrases shown in Table 12.4.b establishes the ownership of the paragraph.
End of Action F1.

Action F2( )

Three cases can happen: (a) the owner paragraph is immediately located above the <table> tag, (b) the owner paragraph is immediately located below the </table> tag, or (c) the owner paragraph is not adjacent to the table. In case (a) the presence of one of the phrases shown in Table 12.5.a establishes the ownership of the paragraph. In case (b) the presence of one of the phrases shown in Table 12.5.b establishes the ownership of the paragraph. In case(c) the presence of one of the phrases shown in Table 12.5.c establishes the ownership of the paragraph.
End of Action F2.

Action F3( )

Three cases of (a), (b), and (c) can happen exactly in the same way mentioned for Action F2( ) of which the cases (a) and (b) are handled exactly in the same way but the case (c) is handled differently. That is, in case (c) the presence of one of the phrases shown in Table 12.5.c or Table-Ref is used to establish the ownership.
End of Action F3.

12.3.4 Image

An image is included in the body using the tag <img src = "*fn*"> where the image source reference *filename* (*fn*) is the pathname to a .jpg or .gif file. The *owner* of an image is the paragraph that includes the image tag while the image is the *gear* of the paragraph. If the image is a value for one of a table's cells, then the owner of the table is the owner of the image as well.

Each image is identified by an identification number, IID, a starting position, IStart, (the position of the first character of the image tag), an ending position, IEnd, (the position of the last character of the image tag), and an owner identification (OID). Image identification number is constructed by the letters of "IM" followed by an order number (e. g. $IM_1, \ldots, IM_u$).

Table 12.5. The phrases for establishing the ownership of a paragraph when the caption exists but the Table-Ref does not: (a) the table is located above the paragraph, (b) the table is located below the paragraph, and (c) the table and its owner are not adjacent.

Phrase
"above Table"
"Table above"
"Table displayed above"
"Table presented above"
"Table shown above"
The phrase "Table of" followed by the caption (e.g. Table of Salary)
A caption followed by the word "Table" (e.g. Customer Table)

a

Phrase
"above Table"
"Table above"
"Table displayed above"
"Table presented above"
"Table shown above"
The phrase "Table of" followed by the caption (e.g. Table of Salary)
A caption followed by the word "Table" (e.g. Customer Table)

b

Phrase
The phrase "Table of" followed by the caption (e.g. Table of Salary)
A caption followed by the word "Table" (e.g. Customer Table)

c

12.3.5 Capturing the physical structure of an e-document

The physical structure of an e-document is captured in four tables of Primitive Elements Look-up (PEL), Grouped Elements Look-up (GEL), Clustered Elements Look-up (CEL), and Cleaned Clustered Elements Look-up (CCEL). The look-up tables are constructed through the applications of the algorithms LOOK-UP, GROUPED-LOOK-UP, PARTITION, and AUDITOR, respectively. The algorithm LOOK-UP delivers the type, starting position, ending position, and owner of each primitive element of the body. The algorithm locates the headings (formal and informal), paragraphs (formal and informal), tables, and images in the body of the e-document. Once located, their starting and ending positions along with their types are recorded and the paragraphs that own the tables and figures are identified (i.e. the paragraphs in which the tables/images have been referred to for the first time).

The algorithm GROUPED-LOOK-UP integrates the tables and figures with their owners and removes the redundant "owned primitives." That is, if a table/image is immediately located before/after the paragraph that owns it, the start/end position of the paragraph is changed to include the table/image. In other words, the paragraph is extended to include its gear. After such extension, the gear's record in PEL becomes a redundant one and is removed. In the case that the table/image is not adjacent to its owner, its record in PEL is appended to the record of the owner. Should the table/image be surrounded by its owner, its record in PEL is redundant and is removed.

The algorithm PARTITION is a recursive algorithm that partitions an e-document's body based on the headings' levels. In other words, this algorithm determines the starting and ending positions of every heading's boundary (territory).

The algorithm AUDITOR cleans CEL to reflect the rightful ownership of the out-of-boundary elements. When a paragraph and its gear are physically located within the boundaries of two different headings (e.g. h1 and h'1), the gear located within the boundary of h'1 is considered to be part of the h1 boundary and not the h'1 boundary. Therefore, the gear's record is appended to the boundary of h1 creating a hole in the h'1 because, logically, the gear is not within the h'1 boundary.

Algorithm LOOK-UP
Input: The entire body of an e-document as a long string of characters, STR, and an empty Primitive Elements Look-up (PEL) table, with four columns of Type, Start, End, and Owner.
Objective: Building the Primitive Elements Look-up (PEL) table for the e-document.
Step1- Repeat while (a formal or an informal heading exists)
Identify the beginning and ending of the heading in STR, assign a heading number to it, and insert (HID, HStart, HEnd, "") as a record into PEL;
Step2- Repeat while (a formal or an informal paragraph exists)
Identify the beginning and ending of the paragraph in STR, assign a paragraph number to it, and insert (PID, PStart, PEnd, "") as a record into PEL;
Step3- Repeat while (a table exists)
Identify the beginning and ending of the table in STR, assign a table number to the table, identify the owner of the table, and insert (TID, TStart, TEnd, and the OID) as a record into PEL;
Step4- Repeat while (an image exists)
Identify the beginning and ending of the image tag in STR, assign an image identification number to the image, identify the owner of the image, and insert (IID, IStart, IEnd, and the OID) as a record into PEL;
Step 5- End;

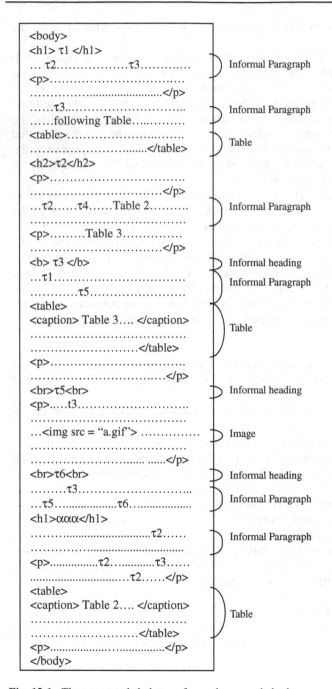

Fig. 12.1. The annotated skeleton of an e-document's body.

Example: The e-document of Figure 12.1 (in the form of a skeleton) is given. The formal and informal paragraphs, the headings, the tables, and the images are shown in the figure. The Primitive Elements Look-up (PEL) table is shown in Table 12.6. The skeleton of the e-document, after applying the LOOK-UP algorithm, is shown in Figure 12.2.

Table 12.6. The Primitive Elements Look-up (PEL) table for Figure 12.1.

Type	Start	End	Owner
h1	5	20	
h2	900	910	
h2	2618	2638	
h3	4605	4645	
h3	5600	5650	
h1	6610	6640	
P1	25	200	
P2	205	598	
P3	600	798	
P4	925	1600	
P5	1603	2115	
P6	2122	2612	
P7	2640	3100	
P8	3643	4598	
P9	4653	5596	
P10	5653	6600	
P11	6650	7341	
P12	7350	9380	
P13	9903	10000	
TB1	800	898	P3
TB2	9382	9900	P5
TB3	3105	3638	P6
IM1	4700	4715	P9

Algorithm GROUPED LOOK-UP

Input: The PEL table with four columns of Type, Start, End, and Owner. An empty Grouped Elements Look-up (GEL) table with three columns of Type, Start, and End.

Objective: Integrating the owner paragraph and its gear for building the Grouped Elements Look-up (GEL) table for the e-document.

Step 1- Make a copy of PEL in GEL;

Step 2- Repeat for all rows in GEL;

    If $(row_i .OID \neq \emptyset)$

        Then If $(row_i.Start > OID.Start)$ & $(row_i.End < OID.End)$

            Then Remove row_i;

    If $(row_i$ is the next element to OID)

        Then If $(row_i$ is below OID)

            Then OID.End = row_i.End; remove row_i;

            Else OID.Start = row_i.Start; remove row_i;

If (row$_i$ is not the next element to OID)

Then insert the record <row$_i$.Start, row$_i$.End> into OID; remove row$_i$;

//all of the OID records are sorted by Start attribute in ascending order.

Step 3- GEL = Project GEL for Type, Start, and End attributes.

Step 4- End;

The Grouped Elements Look-up (GEL) table produced by the execution of the algorithms GROUPED LOOK-UP is shown in Table 12.7 for the e-document of Figure 12.1.

A close study of the GEL table asserts that some rows have more than one pair of Start-End. This situation occurs because the table and its owner are not necessarily physically adjacent to each other.

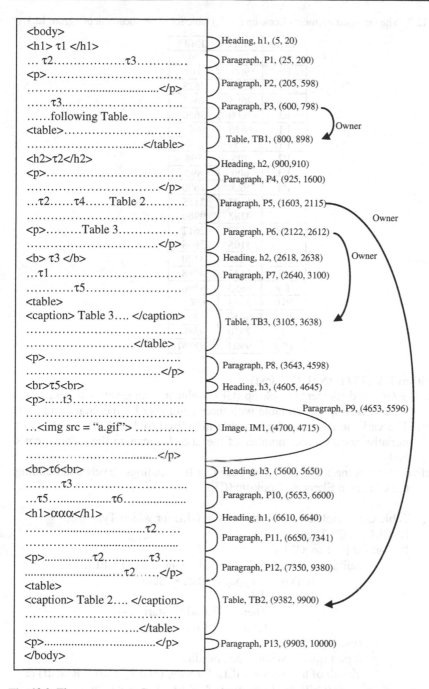

Fig. 12.2. The annotated skeleton of e-document in Figure 12.1 after the application of LOOK-UP algorithm indicating the body elements, starting and ending positions, and owners.

Table 12.7. The Grouped Elements Look-up (GEL) table for the e-document of Figure 12.1.

Type	Start	End
h1	5	20
h2	900	910
h2	2618	2638
h3	4605	4645
h3	5600	5650
h1	6610	6640
P1	25	200
P2	205	598
P3	**600**	**898**
P4	925	1600
P5	**1603**	**2115**
	9382	**9900**
P6	**2122**	**2612**
	3105	**3638**
P7	2640	3100
P8	3643	4598
P9	**4653**	**5596**
P10	5633	6600
P11	6650	7341
P12	7350	9380
P13	9903	10000

Algorithm PARTITION (i, GE, last)

Input: The Grouped Elements Look-up (GEL) table and an empty Clustered Elements Look-up (CEL) table with three columns of Type, Start, and End. The variable i is an index variable initialized to 1 and the variable *last* initially has the order number of the last character in the e-document's body.

Objective: Partitioning the e-document based on the headings' levels and building the Clustered Elements Look-up (CEL) table.

Step1.   Table GEL_1 includes all of the rows in GEL for which Type = h_i;
If $(GEL1 \neq \varnothing)$ Then:
Repeat for j = 1 to $|GEL_1|$;
        Build a new record, R, for CEL using row_j of GEL_1:
                R.Type = $Type_j$; R.Start = $Start_j$
                If j < $|GEL1|$
                        Then   R.End = $Start_{j+1}$ -1;
                        Else   R.End = Last;
        Insert R into CEL;
        // partitioning within each heading
        K= all of the rows in GEL_1 for which $(GEL_1.Start > R.Start)$ &
                $(GEL_1.End \leq R .End)$ & (GEL. Type = "h.");
        If $(k \neq \varnothing)$

Step 2. End;
          Then   i = i + 1; Invoke PARTITION (i+1, K, R.End);

The Clustered Elements Look-up (CEL) table produced by the execution of the algorithms PARTITION for the e-document of Figure 12.1 is shown in Table 12.8. The skeleton of the e-document after the application of PARTITION algorithm is shown in Figure 12.3.

Table 12.8. The Clustered Elements Look-up (CEL) table for the e-document of Figure 12.1.

Type	Start	End
h1	5	6609
h2	900	2617
h2	2618	6609
h3	4605	5599
h3	5600	6609
h1	6610	10000

Table 12.8 does not display the gear of the paragraph located within a heading boundary different from the one the paragraph itself resides. That is, paragraph 6 (P6) has two pairs of Start-End: (2122-2612) and (3105-3638) within two different h2 boundaries, Table 12.7 and Figure 12.3. The first h2 in Table 12.8 with the boundary of (900-2617) and the second h2 in the same table with boundary of (2618-6609) cover the first and the second Start-End pairs of P6, respectively. This is because P6 and its gear are spread over two headings. Such a problem is remedied by adding the *second Start-End pair* (3105-3638) of P6 to the *first h2 boundary* and subtracting the same pair from the *second h2 boundary*. As a result, the first h2 boundary changes from (900-2617) to ((900-2617) and (3105-3638)) and the second h2 boundary changes from (2618-6609) to ((2618-3104) and (3639-6609)).

The reason for not adding the *first pair* of P6 to the *second h2 boundary*, instead, and subtracting the same pair from the *first h2* boundary is that the first Start-End pair of P6 represents the location of the *paragraph itself* whereas the second Start-End pair represents the location of the *paragraph's gear*. The details of the process described above are provided by the following algorithm.

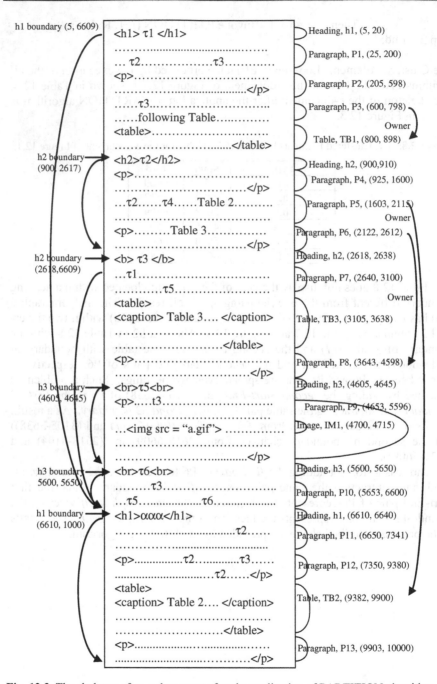

Fig. 12.3. The skeleton of an e-document after the application of PARTITION algorithm.

Algorithm AUDITOR
Input: The CEL and GEL tables. An empty Cleaned Clustered Elements Look-up
      (CCEL) table with three columns of Type, Start, and End.
Objective: Cleaning the CEL to reflect the elements' ownerships and generate the
      Cleaned Clustered Look-up (CCEL) table.
Step 1- Copy CEL into CCEL;
Step 2- Table TEMP includes all of the rows of GEL, which have two or more
        pairs of Start-End. Make a new row out of every pair in TEMP. The
        type for the new row is the same as the type for the original row.
Step 3. Repeat for every two rows, row_i and row_j, in TEMP where,
        $row_i.type = row_j.type$
                Repeat for every row, row_k, in CCEL;
                        If ($row_i.Start \geq row_k.Start$) & ($row_i.End \leq row_k.Start$) &
                        ($row_j.Start > row_k.End$)
                    Then   Append <$row_j.Start, row_j.End$> to row_k;

                        If ($row_i.Start < row_k.Start$) & ($row_j.Start \geq row_k.Start$)
                        & ($row_j.End \leq row_k.End$)
                    Then   Append <$row_k.Start, row_j.Start-1$> to row_k;
                            Append <$row_j.End +1, row_k.End$> to row_k;
                            Remove <$row_k.Start, row_k.End$>;
Step 4. End;

The result of applying the above algorithm for cleaning the CEL is illustrated in
Table 12.9.

Table 12.9. The Cleaned Clustered Elements Look-up (CCEL) table for the e-document of
Figure 12.1.

Type	Start	End
h1	5	6609
h2	900	2617
	3105	3638
h2	2618	3104
	3639	6609
h3	4605	5599
h3	5600	6609
h1	6610	9380
	9903	10000

12.4 Discovery of the Explicit Terms Using Ontology

To mine an e-document's metadata section, the following are used: (a) a *stemmer*
that was developed for this purpose (Bahrami 2007) based on the work of (Porter
1980) and (b) the *ontology* whose evolution is underway by another group of re-

of researchers (Cassel 2007). The stemmer and the ontology are briefly described in the next two subsections.

12.4.1 The Stemmer

If the affix (prefix and suffix) of a given token is removed, the remainder of the token is the *stem* of that token (Porter 1980). The stemmer was developed by Carey (Carey 2007) to perform suffix stripping rather than affix stripping. The suffix stripping allows for differentiating between the tokens such as "communication" and "miscommunication" so that after stemming, the former becomes "communicate" whereas the latter becomes "miscommunicate." Had the affix stripping been used, both would be stemmed to "communicate" causing semantic chaos. However, the stems "communicate" or "miscommunicate' can further be truncated to "communicat" and "miscommunicat." For example, truncating "communicate" to "communicat" allows for the inclusion of other possible tokens such as "communicating," "communicate," "communicates," "communication," "communicator," and "communicators." Also, the following changes were made to the algorithm to speed up the processing of large documents.

- Apply the First-Rule-Fit. That is, when a token fits a stemming rule, the resulting stem should not be challenged for further reduction.
- Handle *Problem Tokens*. That is, special-treat certain tokens such as *"this"* and *"that,"* which would otherwise become stemmed to "thi" and "tha."
- Apply the *Truncation Rule*. That is, truncate the last character in the stem to make its search meaningful.

12.4.2 The Ontology

The ontology used in this chapter is an up-to-date version of the ontology that is under construction by Lillian Cassel and her team (Cassel 2007). This ontology is coined ONTOLOGY Project and is supported in part by, ACM, IEEE, the Open University of the Netherlands, and the National Science Foundation. The ontology in its current form has 121 general subjects and each subject serves as the root of a single subject-tree. Conceptually, within each general subject there are a set of major topics that can be identified as "TOP." All of the "TOP"s of a given subject can be considered as the second level of the tree. Under each "TOP" there would be a set of sub topics, "SUB." Each "SUB" has its own subtopics, "SUBSUB," and each SUBSUB has its own subtopics, "SUBSUBSUB." This conceptual structure can continue until the leaves are reached.

The naming convention easily lends itself to a tree structure. For example, the TOP topic of the "File organization" in the ontology, Figures 12.4, has the tree structure of Figure 12.5, called TOP-tree.

```
TOP File organization
SUB Sequential
SUB Hashed
SUBSUB Hash cluster
SUB Indexed
SUBSUB Indexing techniques
SUBSUBSUB B-tree based indexing
SUBSUBSUBSUB Dynamic, multilevel indexes
SUBSUBSUB Hash-based indexing
SUBSUB Indexing challenges
SUBSUBSUB Files with dense index
SUBSUBSUB Files with variable length records
```

Fig. 12.4. The Ontology content for the "TOP" topic of the "File organization."

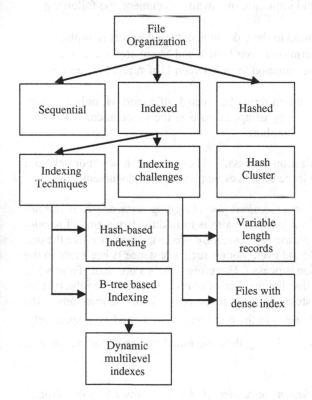

Fig. 12.5. The "TOP" tree structure of the topic "TOP" in Figure 12.4.

12.4.3 Discovery Process

A metadata section, M, of an e-document is defined as a non-empty set of:
M = {T} $\cup$ {F} where,
T is a set of tokens, T = {t_1 ... t_n}, and |T| $\geq$ 0,
F is a set of phrases, F = {f_1 ... f_m}, and |F| $\geq$ 0,
f_i = {t'_1 ... t'_k | t'_i is a token, k $\geq$ 2}, and
t_i and f_j are called *terms* (for 0 < i $\leq$ n and 0 < j $\leq$ m).

Let τ_i represent any term (t_i or f_i) and let term τ_i be a node in a TOP-tree, the *Upper Equivalence set*, U, of τ_i includes all of the nodes that are located on the path from root to τ_i. The *Lower Equivalence set*, L, of τ_i includes all of the nodes in the sub-tree for which τ_i is the root. The node τ_i itself is not included in either of the sets. For example, the Upper and Lower Equivalence sets of the node "Indexing Techniques" in Figure 12.5 are: U = {"File Organization," "Indexed"} and L= {"Hash-based Indexing," "B-tree based Indexing," "Dynamic, multilevel indexes"}.

To identify the explicit and implicit terms in an e-document, the following rules are applied:

- If a term, τ_i, is not found in the e-document, then the term is implicit.
- All of the common terms between U of τ_i and M are implicit terms.
- If there is at least one common term between L of τ_i and M then τ_i is implicit.
- Among all of the common terms between L of τ_i and M, only the ones with the highest frequency of appearance in the e-document's body are explicit and the rest are implicit.

Let the phrase f_i be "normalization process." The stems of f_i are "normal" and "process." Let the following three sentences be parts of an e-document:

1. *"The collection of specifications for designing software is a normal process."* Explanation: When the aim is to find the two stems of *normal* and *process* for the phrase *normalization process*, a sentence like the one above will also be found even though such a sentence is irrelevant to the phrase "normalization process." Therefore, this is a problem. To solve it, it may be assumed that the number of blank spaces between the two tokens, matching the stems, in the e-document is B and the locations of the first and the second stems in the e-document are ℓ_1 and ℓ_2, respectively.

   If ℓ_1 + Length (stem$_1$) + B = ℓ_2, then the found phrase is not the same as the phrase f_i.

2. *"The normalized relations have already been approved for processing."* Explanation: Although, both stems appear in the sentence but the distance between the two is too great. Consequently, the search result is false. The question is what is an acceptable distance? To answer this

question, not only the stem of a given token should be identified, but also the size of the truncated suffix should be identified: Size = Length (token) – Length (stem). The distance less than (Size + Th_1) is an acceptable distance, where Th_1 is a threshold value decided by the user.

3. *"The relations that are in the BCNF have already gone through the process of normalization."*
Explanation: In this case, the locations of the stems are in reverse order and there is a conjunction, "of". Such a search result is true.

In order to support the above cases, the suffix size of each stem is also noted. If the suffix size is equal to zero, the token and its stem are the same. The details of applying the above rules are given in the following algorithm.

Algorithm RECOGNIZE

Input: An e-document in HTML retrieved from the Internet. The metadata section of this e-document has a set of terms that are a mixture of tokens and phrases. The assumption is that the terms are divided into a set of tokens $T = \{t_1, ..., t_n\}$ and a set of phrases $F = \{f_1, ..., f_k\}$

Objective: Determining the list of explicit and implicit terms in the metadata.

Step 1- Stem T and F and use the stemmed members of T to create TS set and use the stemmed members of F to create FS set.

Step 2- Compare the members of the set TS against the contents of the document and if they do not appear in the document, remove them from the set. Call the resulting set TS_{in};

Step 3- Remove those tokens from T whose stems are not in TS_{in} and call the new set T_{core};

Step 4- Compare the members of FS against the contents of the document and if they do not appear in the document, remove them from the set. Call the resulting set FS_{in}. Check the existence of FS members in the document through the following convention. A phrase in FS is made up of, for example, three stemmed tokens of tf_1, tf_2, and tf_3;

    a- Locate tf_1 in the document and make the set ℓ_1 out of all of the positions in which reside the instances of tf_1;

    b- Repeat the process for tf_2 and tf_3 and generate sets of ℓ_2 and ℓ_3, respectively. Examine ℓ_1, ℓ_2, and ℓ_3, to determine whether the phrase— that is made up of tf_1, tf_2, and tf_3— is in the document by checking the location of each token in the sequence of tokens;

Step 5- Remove those phrases from F whose stems are not in FS_{in} and call the new set F_{core};

Step 6- Check members of the set F_{core} against the ontology. If a member, f_m, is found, then build its U_{fm} and L_{fm} sets;

    a- If $(U_{fm} \cap T_{core} \neq \varnothing)$
then remove $(U_{fm} \cap T_{core})$ from T_{core};

b- If $(U_{fm} \cap F_{core} \neq \varnothing)$

then remove $(U_{fm} \cap F_{core})$ from F_{core};

c- If $((L_{fm} \cap T_{core} \neq \varnothing) \parallel (L_{fm} \cap F_{core} \neq \varnothing))$ then remove f_m from F_{core}.

Step 7- Check members of the set T_{core} against the ontology. If a member, t_m, is found, then build its U_{tm} and L_{tm} sets.

a- If $(U_{tm} \cap T_{core} \neq \varnothing)$ then remove $(U_{tm} \cap T_{core})$ from T_{core};

b- If $(U_{tm} \cap F_{core} \neq \varnothing)$ then remove $(U_{tm} \cap F_{core})$ from F_{core};

c- If $((L_{tm} \cap T_{core} \neq \varnothing) \parallel (L_{tm} \cap F_{core} \neq \varnothing))$ then remove t_m from T_{core}.

Step 8. Explicit terms in metadata are EXP = $\{T_{core} \cup F_{core}\}$ and Implicit terms in metadata are IMP = $\{(T \cup F) - EXP\}$;

Step 9. End.

12.5 Discovery of the Logical Structure

To discover the logical structure of an e-document, the e-document's segments containing each explicit term are identified and the relationships among the segments are determined.

12.5.1 Segmentation

This is a process that takes an e-document's body and divides it into a number of segments in such a way that each segment is considered as the contents of one of the metadata's explicit terms, $(\mu (\tau, B) = b$ where, $b \subset B$ and $\tau \in E$.)   The algorithm MAP provides such segmentation. A tem's segment is comprised of a collection of paragraphs and headings in which the term occurs. Regardless of the number of paragraphs and headings in a segment, when p_j is within the boundary of h_i, the record of p_j is ignored.

Algorithm MAP

Input: The entire body of an e-document as a long string of characters, STR, the set of explicit terms in the metadata section of the e-document, E = $\{\tau_1, \ldots, \tau_n\}$, the GEL table, the CCEL table , and an *empty map*, Q, with four columns of Term, Type, Start, and End.

Objective: Building the map of the e-document.

Step 1- Repeat for every τ_i in E;

Find all of the stemmed occurrences of τ_i in STR.

Repeat for each occurrence of τ_i;

Use the Start position of the Occurrence (SO) in STR to find an entry in the GEL table such that entry.Start $\leq$ SO $\leq$ entry.End;

Insert record $< \tau_i$, Type, Start, End $>$ into Q;

Step 2- Sort Q by attribute Start in ascending order;

Step 3- For any two rows (i and j) in Q

    If ((term$_i$ = term$_j$) & (type$_i$ = type$_j$))

        Then   Delete one of the rows;

    If ((term$_i$ = term$_j$) & (type$_i$ = "h.") & (type$_j$ ≠ "h."))

        Then   Delete row j;

    If ((term$_i$ = term$_j$) & (type$_i$ and type$_j$ are adjacent paragraphs))

        Then   Insert into Q the record:

                                  <term$_i$, Min(Stat$_i$, Start$_j$), Max(End$_i$, End$_j$)>

                Delete both rows;

Step 4- Using CCEL, update Start and End of the rows in Q with the type = "h.";

Step 5- End;

The outcomes of the steps 3 and 4 are shown in Tables 12.10 and 12.11, respectively.

Table 12.10. The outcome of the algorithm MAP after the completion of Step 3 for the e-document of Figure 12.1.

Term	Type	Start	End
τ1	h1	5	20
τ2	h2	900	910
τ4	P5	1603	2115
		9382	9900
τ3	h2	2618	2638
τ5	h3	4605	4645
τ6	h3	5600	5650

In order for Q to be used in the next section, two rules of integration are needed to integrate the rows with multiple pairs of (Start-End):

- If row.type = "h.," then the smallest Start value and the largest End value among all of the pairs of the row are served as *Integrated Start* (IS) and *Integrated End* (IE).
- If row.type = "P.," then the actual Start and End of the paragraph "P." act for the row, respectively, as the Integrated Start and Integrated End for the row.

Table 12.11. The final Map Q for the e-document of Figure 12.1.

Term	Type	Start	End
τ1	h1	5	6609
τ2	h2	900	2617
		3105	3638
τ4	P5	1603	2115
		9382	9900
τ3	h2	2618	3104
		3639	6609
τ5	h3	4605	5599
τ6	h3	5600	6609

It is obvious that IS and IE for those rows with only one pair of (Start-End) are the same as their Start and End, respectively. The IS and IE for every row of Q is shown in Table 12.12.

Table 12.12. The Map Q of the e-document with IS and IE for each row.

Term	Type	Start	End	IS	IE
$\tau 1$	h1	5	6609	5	6609
$\tau 2$	h2	900	2617	900	3638
		3105	3638		
$\tau 4$	P5	1603	2115	1603	2115
		9382	9900		
$\tau 3$	h2	2618	3104	2618	6609
		3639	6609		
$\tau 5$	h3	4605	5599	4605	5599
$\tau 6$	h3	5600	6609	5600	6609

12.5.2 Segments' Relationships

In order to discuss the segments' relationships, the terms *encompassing* and *encompassed* are defined and an algorithm for delivering the logical structure of the e-document is discussed. If s_i and s_j are the segments of the terms τ_i and τ_j, respectively, and if s_j is completely inside s_i, then s_i is an *encompassing* segment and s_j is an *encompassed* segment. The terms τ_i and τ_j are also, respectively, referred to as encompassing and encompassed terms. The algorithm STRUCTURE establishes hierarchical relationships among segments of all of the explicit terms produced by algorithm MAP. The task is accomplished by identifying the encompassing and encompassed segments. The hierarchical relationship may be presented in the form of a tree whose root is the e-document itself. Each encompassing segment in the tree is the parent of its encompassed segments

Algorithm STRUCTURE
Input: An e-document and its Q with IS and IE for all rows.
>   An empty Logical Structure (LS) table in which each row has six attributes of encompassing term (GTerm), encompassing term Starting position (GStart), encompassing term Ending position (GEnd), encompassed term (DTerm), encompassed term Starting position (DStart), and encompassed term Ending position (DEnd).

Objective: Identifying the logical structure of the e-document.
Step 1- Sort Q by the attribute IS in ascending order;
Step 2- Repeat for $i = 1$ to $|Q|-1$;
>   Repeat for $j = i+1$ to $|Q|$;
>   If (for rows i and j in Q, $IS_i < IS_j$ & $IE_i \geq IE_j$)
>   Then   If (there is a row, k, in LS in which $DTerm_k = Term_j$)
>   Then   Remove row k from LS;
>   Append $<Term_i, IS_i, IE_i, Term_j, IS_j, IE_j>$ to LS;

Step 3- Remove rows from LS for which DTerm is unique and GTerm is empty;

Step 4- If (there is a row, row_w, in Q for which $term_w$ = "τ.") &

        ("τ." is not an encompassing or encompassed term)

    Then   Append < "e-Document", "", "", $term_w$, IS_w, IE_w > to LS;

Step 5- If (there is a row, row_z, in Q for which $term_z$ is not an encompassed term)

    Then   Append < "e-Document", "", "", $term_z$, IS_z, IE_z > to LS;

Step 6- Sort LS by GStart attribute in ascending order;

Step 7- Replace the GStart and DStart for each term, "τ.", and use the Start value(s) recorded in Q;

    Replace the GEnd and DEnd for each term and use the End value(s) recorded in Q;

Step 8- End;

Table 12.13. The Logical Structure (LS) table produced for the e-document of Figure 12.1 in Step 6 of the STRUCTURE Algorithm.

GTerm	GStart	GEnd	DTerm	DStart	DEnd
e-Document			τ1	5	6609
τ1	5	6609	τ2	900	3638
τ1	5	6609	τ3	2618	6609
τ2	900	3638	τ4	1603	2115
τ3	2618	6609	τ5	4605	5599
τ3	2618	6609	τ6	5600	6609

Table 12.14. The Final LS table for the e-document of Figure 12.1.

GTerm	GStart	GEnd	DTerm	DStart	DEnd
e-Document			τ1	5	6609
τ1	5	6609	τ2	900 3105	2617 3638
τ1	5	6609	τ3	2618 3639	3104 6609
τ2	900 3105	2617 3638	τ4	1603 9382	2115 9900
τ3	2618 3639	3104 6609	τ5	4605	5599
τ3	2618 3639	3104 6609	τ6	5600	6609

The outcome of step 6 and the final outcome of the above algorithm are shown in Tables 12.13 and 12.14, respectively. Table 12.14 can easily be converted into a tree structure. The root of the tree is named "e-Document." For each row in Table 12.14, the DTerm is the child of the GTerm. The result of this conversion is shown in Figure 12.6. Each node of the tree represents an explicit term along with its starting and the ending positions in the e-document. An explicit term may have more than one pair of (Start-End).

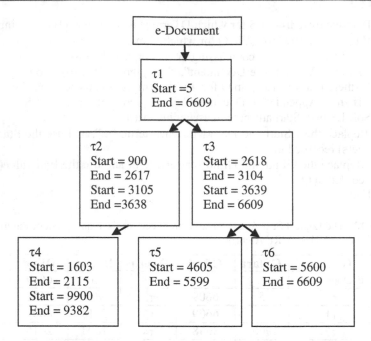

Fig. 12.6. The tree representation of the logical structure of the e-document in Figure 12.1.

With regard to Figure 12.6, two assumptions can be made:
1. There is a new term τ7 residing in the same paragraph (P5) in which τ4 is resided.
2. τ4 has a child (τ8) with start and end positions of "s" and "e", respectively.

Considering these assumptions, it is obvious that τ4 and τ7 are siblings as which result τ8 is the child of both τ4 and τ7. This means that Figure 12.6 is no longer a tree. Instead, it is now a lattice.

12.6 Empirical Results

Three sets of twenty e-documents were randomly chosen from a retrieved pool of e-documents from the World Wide Web using Google search engine. The e-documents were about a variety of subject matters contained in the ontology.

Table 12.15 shows the average number of primitive elements (formal and informal headings and paragraphs, images, and tables) for every set along with the total average of the three sets. The physical structures of all three sets of the e-documents were identified with 100% accuracy.

Table 12.15. The discovered average numbers of the primitive elements in all three sets of e-documents.

Set of Documents	Average # of Headings		Average # of Paragraphs		Average # of Images	Average # of Tables
	Informal	Formal	Informal	Formal		
1	12.3	5.2	22	41.4	7	5.6
2	4.5	5.8	15.8	28	2.4	8.3
3	6	8.4	30.2	25.7	12.4	11.1
Total	22.8	19.4	68.0	95.1	21.8	25.0
Average	7.6	6.47	22.67	31.7	7.27	8.3

The metadata section of each e-document was *manually* examined and the lists of explicit and implicit terms were identified. A total of 213, 248, 312 terms were included in the three sets of 20 documents. The distributions of the terms are shown in Table 12.16.

Table 12.16. The number of explicit and implicit terms in the three sets of documents.

Set of Documents	# of Explicit terms	# of Implicit terms	Total
1	144	69	213
2	161	87	248
3	221	91	312

The same process was completed again, this time using the methodology presented in this chapter. The quality of the automated process for each set is shown in Table 12.17 and the summarized version of it is presented in Table 12.18. Based on this data, the automated process is able to accurately identify 76% of the combined explicit and implicit terms.

Table 12.17. Quality of the automated process.

Set of Documents	Term	Automatically Identified Term		
		Explicit	Implicit	Total
Set 1	Explicit (Manually)	129	15	144
	Implicit (Manually)	36	33	69
Set 2	Explicit (Manually)	150	11	161
	Implicit (Manually)	37	50	87
Set3	Explicit (Manually)	198	23	221
	Implicit (Manually)	64	27	91

When the mining is done manually, 100% of combined explicit and implicit terms can be identified. From the found *explicit* terms, the logical structure of the document can be uncovered. However, when the mining is done automatically, 76% of the combined explicit and implicit terms can correctly be identified and from such identification the logical structure of the e-document can be uncovered with 76% accuracy. The reader should note, however, that the automatic identification of explicit terms is more successful than the identification of the implicit terms. To be more specific, on average 91% of explicit terms and 45% of implicit terms can correctly be identified. Incidentally, the identification of the explicit-and-implicit terms with 76% accuracy is inconsequential to discovery of the logical structure of an e-document, because automatic discovery of the logical structure of e-documents is based on the explicit terms (91%) and not the implicit terms (45%).

Table 12.18. Summarized quality of the automated process.

Set of Documents	% of Correctly Identified Explicit and Implicit Terms	Explicit Terms Predictive Value	Implicit Terms Predictive Value
Set 1	76	0.9	0.48
Set 2	81	0.93	0.57
Set 3	72	0.90	0.30
Average	76	0.91	0.45

12.7 Conclusions

A number of algorithms are provided that collectively are able to mine an HTML e-document for the purpose of unveiling its physical structure as a prelude to discovering its logical structure by the use of explicit terms of the metadata identified through the ontology. The results in Table 12.17 testify to the effectiveness of the methodology with 91% accuracy. This is particularly valuable to the users who seek: finer data granularity in the retrieval of web-based information; conceptual hierarchy within an e-document; semantic Web; Internet-based active learning; ontology; and e-learning, e-government, e-commerce, and e-military, to name a few.

12.8 Exercises

1. Apply algorithm LOOK-UP and build the Primitive Elements Look-up (PEL) Table for the following e-document.

|← —————————— 90 characters ——————————→|
```
<html>
    <head><title>Dependencies in Relational Databases</title>
        <meta name="description" content="A brief description of the dependencies in re-
        lational databases>
        <meta name="keywords" content="relational database, data model, operational
        anomaly, updating anomaly, functional dependency, FD, full functional depend-
        ency, MVD, multivalued dependency, JD, join dependency, normalization proc-
        ess, normal forms, trivial MVD, non-trivial MVD, trivial multivalued dependency,
        non-trivial multivalued dependency lossless join, lossy join">
    </head>
    <body><font face = Helvetica">
        <h1><font color="blue"> Operational Anomalies</font></h1>
```
◄ 8 ► `<p>`Let us look at the relation Project presented as a table (Table 1). The first
chars tuple of this relation is interpreted as "John works on the research project PR1 and
the budget for the PR1 is 250K. If the first tuple is updated as "John PR1 300K",
then the relation loses its integrity because it generates inconsistency in the PR1
budget (tuples 1 and 3). This is known as an updating anomaly.`</p>`
There are other types of anomalies that can easily undermine the integrity of a relation. To explain it further, we first introduce three types of dependencies and
then address the dependency problem.`<br><br>`
```
        <table boarder = 2>
          <caption><b>Table 1.</b> Representation or relation Project.</caption>
            <tr><th>Researcher</th><th>Project</th><th>Budget  </th> </tr>
            <tr> <td> John</td> <td> PR1 </td> <td> 230K </td></tr>
            <tr> <td> Kathy</td> <td> PR2 </td> <td> 280K </td></tr>
            <tr> <td> Paul</td> <td> PR1 </td> <td> 230K </td></tr>
        </table>
        <h2> Functional Dependency (FD)</h2>
```
`<p>`Let X and Y be two attributes of relation R. Y is `<i>`functionally`</i>` depend-
ent on X iff any two tulpes, t1 and t2, that agree on their values of X also agree on
their values of Y. If X is a composite attribute and Y is functionally dependent on
the entire X and not a subset of X then Y is `<i>`fully functionally`</i>` dependent
on X.`</p><br>`

```
        <h2> Multivalued Dependency (MVD) </h2>
```
Let us look at two different cases: (1) X and Y are two attributes in Relation R
such that X and Y make the entire attributes of R and (2) X, Y, and Z are three attributes in Relation R such that X, Y, and Z make the entire attributes of R. (In
both cases X, Y, and Z can be composite attributes.) In case 1, if there are more
than one tuple, t1 and t2, in R such that t1[X] = t2[X] and t1[Y] != t2[Y], then Y
has multivalue dependency on X.`<br><br>`

`<p>`In case 2, let t1 and t2 be two tuples in R such that t1[X] = t2[X]. Let t3 and
t4 be two new tuples built out of t1 and t2 using the following rules: (a) t1[X] =
t2[X] = t3[X] = t4[X], (b) t3[Y] = t1[Y] and t3[Z] = t2[Z], and (c) t4[Y] = t2[Y]
and t4[Z] = t1[Z]. If t3 and t4 are in R, then Y has multivalue dependency on X.
The MVDs in case 1 and 2 are trivial MVD and non-trivial MVD, respectively.

```
        <h2>Join Dependency (JD)</h2>
```
`<p>`Let P1, . . ., Pn be n projections of relation R. Attributes in Pi are a subset of
attributes in R. Let U = P1 Join P2 Join . . . Join Pn. If U = R, then the JD of P1,
. . ., Pn holds true in R. `</p><br>`
`<b>` `<font color="green">` Revisiting the Dependency Problem `</b>` `<br><br>`
`<p>` Relation R is given. If all the non-key attributes of R fully functionally de-
pendent on the primary key of R and all the existing MVDs in R are trivial and all
JDs hold true in R, then R is free of operational anomalies.
```
    </body>
</html>
```

2. Apply Algorithm GROUPED and build the Grouped Elements Look-up (GEL) table for the e-document in question 1.
3. Build the CEL and CCEL tables for the e-document of question 1 using SEGMENT and AUDITOR algorithms, respectively.
4. Use the ontology to determine the explicit and implicit terms in the metadata section of the e-document presented in question 1.
5. Using Map algorithm, create the map of e-document in question 1. Upon Completion of each of the steps 3 and 4, show the results. Then, include IS and IE columns in the results found in Step 4.
6. Build the Logical Structure (LS) table of the e-document of question 1 by using algorithm STRUCTURE.
7. Display the logical structure of the e-document of question 1 in a tree structure.
8. What are the uses of discovering physical and logical structures of an e-document?
9. Can physical structure of an e-document be used instead of its logical structure? Explain why.
10. Can the following approach be used as an alternative for determining the explicit and implicit terms? Explain why.

    In response to a query, N e-documents are returned with N sets of metadata, one per document. The union and intersection of the N sets are K_u and K_i, respectively. The terms in K_i make up the set of explicit terms and the terms in $K_u - K_i$ make up the implicit terms.

11. If an e-document does not have a metadata section, how can its logical structure be uncovered?

12.9 Acknowledgments

I would like to extend my special thanks to Mr. Clinton Carey for his coding of the explicit and implicit terms identification.

12.10 References

Agichtein E and Ganti V (2004) Mining Reference Tables for Automatic Text Segmentation. Proceedings of the 10th ACM SIGKDD International Conference on knowledge Discovery and Data Mining (KDD'04), Kim W, Kohavi R, Gehrke J, and DuMouchel W (eds.), Seattle, WA. pp. 20-29.
Bahrami A (2005) A Framework for Development and Management of E-Lessons in E-Learning. Proceedings of 2005 International Conference on Web Information Systems and Technologies (WEBIST'05), Cordeiro J, Pedrosa V, Encarnacão B, and Filipe J (eds.), Miami, Florida, USA, pp. 504-509.

Bahrami A (2006) Integration of Active Learning in E-Lessons. Proceedings of 2006 International Conference on E-Learning (ICEL'06), Remenyi D (ed.), Montreal, Canada, pp. 13-21.

Bahrami A (2006) Structural Discovery of E-lessons, Proceedings of the 2006 International Conference on E-Learning, E-Business, Enterprise Information Systems, E-Government, and Outsourcing (EEE'06), Arabnia H (ed), Las Vegas, Nevada, USA, pp. 3-9.

Bahrami A (2007) An L-Tree Based Analysis of E-lessons. Proceedings of the 2007 International Conference on Information Technology: New Generation (ITNG'07), Latifi S (ed.), Las Vegas, Nevada, pp. 329-334.

Bahrami A and Carey C (2007) Ontology-Based Identification of Explicit and Implicit Metadata Terms. Proceedings of the 2007 International Conference on E-Learning, E-Business, Enterprise Information Systems, E-Government, and Outsourcing (EEE'07), Arabnia H and Bahrami A (eds.), Las Vegas, Nevada, USA, pp. 210-214.

Berners-Lee T, Hendler J and Lassila O (2001) The Semantic Web, online journal of Scientific American, http://sciam.com/.

Carey C (2007) A System for the Efficient Storage and Retrieval of Term Relevant E-Lessons. Masters Project, Armstrong Atlantic State University, Savannah, Georgia, May 2007.

Cassel L "The Ontology Project" (2007) http://what.csc.villanova.edu/twiki/bin/view/Main/OntologyProject.

Crescenzi V, Mecca G, and Merialdo P (2001) RoadRunner: Towards Automatic Data Extraction from Large Web Sites. Proceedings of 27th International Conference on Very Large Data Bases, Roma, Italy, pp. 109-118.

Ford C, Chiang C, Wu H, Chilka R, Talburt J (2005) Text Data Mining: A Case Study. Proceedings of the 2005 International Conference on Information Technology: Coding and Computing (ITCC-2005), Srimani P K (ed), Las Vegas, Nevada, pp. 122-127.

Garofalakis M N, Rastogi R, Shim k (1999) SPIRIT: Sequential Pattern Mining with Regular Expression Constraints. Proceedings of 25th International Conference on Very Large Data Bases (VLDB'99), Atkinson M P, Orlowska M E, Valduriez P, Zdonik S B, Michael L. Brodie M L (eds.), Edinburgh, Scotland, UK, pp. 223-234.

Han J and Kamber M (2005) Data mining, Concepts and Techniques, Morgan Kaufmann Publishers, 2nd ed.

Knoblock C A, Lerman K, Minton S, and Muslea I (2000) Accurately and Reliably Extracting Data from the Web: A machine Learning Approach. IEEE Data Engineering Bulletin, 23 (4):33-41.

Lin T Y (2005) Granular computing: examples, intuitions and modeling Proceedings of the 2005 IEEE International Conference on Granular Computing (GrC 2005), Hu X, Liu Q, Skowron A, Lin T Y, Yager R R, Zhang B (eds.), Beijing, China, pp. 40-44.

Lin T Y (2007) Granular Computing and Modeling the Human Thoughts in Web Documents. Proceedings (Lecture Notes in Computer Science) of the 12th International Fuzzy Systems Association World Congress (IFSA'07), Patricia Melin P, Castillo O, Aguilar L T, Kacprzyk J, Pedrycs W (eds.), Cancun, Mexico, pp.263-270.

Peter. F. Patel-Schneider P F, Hayes P, and Horrocks I (2004) OWL web ontology language: Semantics and abstract syntax. W3C Recommendation, http://www.w3.org/TR/owl-semantics/, 2004.

Porter M F (1980) An algorithm for Suffix Stripping. Program, 14(3), pp.130-137, 1980.

Stoilos G, Stamou G, and Kollias S (2005) String Metric for Ontology Alignment. Proceedings (Lecture Notes in Computer Science) of the International Semantic Web Conference (ISWC'05), Gil Y, Motta E, Benjamins V R, and Musen M (eds.), Galway, Ireland, pp. 623-637.

Stojanovic L, Staab S, and Studer R (2001) Knowledge Technologies for the semantic Web. Proceedings of the WebNet2001-World Conference on the WWW and Internet, Lawrence-Fowler W A, Hasebrook J (eds.), Orlando, Florida, pp. 1174-1183.

Wang Q, Wang X, Zhao M, and Wang D (2003) Conceptual hierarchy based rough set model. Proceedings of the 2003 International Conference on Machine Learning and Cybernetics, Vol. pp. 402-406.

Willem Robert Van Hage, Sophia Katrenko, Guus Schreiber, "A Method to Combine Linguistic Ontology-Mapping Techniques", Proceedings (Lecture Notes in Computer Science) of the International Semantic Web Conference (ISWC'05), Yolanda Gil, Enrico Motta, V. Richard Benjamins, and Mark Musen (eds.), Galway, Ireland, pp. 732-744.

13 Designing a Flexible Framework for a Table Abstraction

H. Conrad Cunningham [1], Yi Liu [2], and Jingyi Wang [3]

[1] *Department of Computer and Information Science, University of Mississippi, University, MS 38677 USA*

[2] *Department of Electrical Engineering and Computer Science, South Dakota State University, Brookings, SD 57007 USA*

[3] *Acxiom Corporation, 1001 Technology Drive, Little Rock, AR 72223 USA*

13.1 Introduction

In a provocative essay from the mid-1980s, Brooks asserts that "building software will always be hard" because software systems are inherently complex, must conform to all sorts of physical, human, and software interfaces, must change as the system requirements evolve, and are inherently invisible entities (Brooks 1986). A decade later Brooks again observes, "The best way to attack the essence of building software is not to build it at all" (Brooks 1995). That is, software engineers should reuse both software and, more importantly, software designs.

The concept of software family (Parnas 1976) is one of the responses to the need for software reuse. Parnas (1976) defines a *software family* as "a set of programs with so many common properties that it is worthwhile to study the set as a group." Thus, by developers analyzing and exploiting the "common aspects and predicted variabilities" (Weiss and Lai 1999) among the members of a software family, the resulting software system can be constructed to reuse code for the common parts and to enable convenient adaptation of the variable parts

Y. Chan et al. (eds.), *Data Engineering*, International Series in Operations
Research & Management Science 132, DOI 10.1007/978-1-4419-0176-7_13,
© Springer Science+Business Media, LLC 2010

(Cunningham et al. 2006a). Some writers use the terms *frozen spot* to denote a common aspect of the family and *hot spot* to denote a variable aspect of the family (Pree 1995; Schmid 1996).

A *software framework* (Johnson and Foote 1988) is a form of software family. A framework is "a generic application that allows different applications to be created from a family of applications" (Schmid 1999). In general, a framework represents the skeleton of a system that can be customized for a particular purpose. The frozen spots embody the overall structure of the framework (that is, the overall design) and are reused by the entire family of applications. In the context of an object-oriented language, frozen spots are expressed as a set of abstract and concrete classes that collaborate to embody the solutions to problems in the application domain. The hot spots are represented by the abstract classes, which can be extended to provide customized implementations of the variable aspects of a family. A specific set of implementations of the hot spots yields a member of the software family.

A framework is a system that is designed with generality and reuse in mind. *Software design patterns* (Gamma et al. 1995; Buschmann et al. 1996), which are well-established solutions to program design problems that commonly occur in practice, are intellectual tools for achieving the desired level of generality and reuse (Cunningham et al. 2006a). They are the building blocks for reusing designs. Building a software framework for a family is more costly than building a single application, but a well-designed framework can yield considerable benefit if many members of the family eventually need to be constructed.

In software design it is always important to specify precisely what a software artifact is to do. This is especially important in software frameworks, where the implementations of the hot spots vary from one application to another and are not usually developed at the same time nor by the same team as the framework itself. Framework designers must specify interfaces that do not change regardless of which implementation is "plugged in" to a hot spot. The specification should guide the users of the framework to provide appropriate implementations of the hot spots. Parnas and his colleagues (Parnas 1978; Britton et al. 1981) call this an *abstract interface* because it gives the assumptions that are common to all implementations. Meyer's Design by Contract (Meyer 1992, 1997; Mitchell and McKim 2002) method provides an effective formal technique for specifying the expected behaviors of abstract interfaces.

This chapter shows how commonality and variability analysis, software design patterns, and Meyer-like formal design contracts can be applied in the design of a small Java software framework for building implementations of the Table Abstract Data Type (ADT). A previous paper (Cunningham and Wang 2001) presents an earlier version of the framework design developed in a careful, but ad hoc manner. This chapter expands on that work by revisiting the design from the perspective of commonality and variability analysis, improving the formal specifications, specifying additional framework features, and examining how the framework can evolve.

The Table ADT represents a collection of records that can be accessed by the unique keys of the records. The framework design should encompass a wide range of possible implementations of the Table ADT—simple array-based data structures in memory, B-tree file structures on disk, perhaps even structures distributed across a network. By approaching this as a family, the goal is to be able to assemble a Table implementation by selecting the combination of record access structures and storage structures to meet a specific application need.

The design process first analyzes the Table ADT as a family and then takes advantage of several well-known software design patterns to structure the framework. The commonality/variability analysis (in particular, the desire to decouple the record access mechanism from the storage mechanism) suggests a hierarchical structure based on the Layered Architecture (Buschmann et al. 1996; Shaw 1996) and Interface (Grand 1998) design patterns. Given the layered architecture, the Bridge and Proxy patterns (Gamma et al. 1995; Grand 1998) then suggest how to organize the interactions among the various layers. The Iterator pattern (Gamma et al. 1995; Grand 1998) is also helpful; it provides a systematic mechanism for accessing groups of records. The Template Method, Strategy, Decorator, and Composite patterns (Gamma et al. 1995; Grand 1998) provide standard structures for plugging variable components into the framework. Furthermore, as the framework evolves, it follows the general development path documented by the Evolving Frameworks system of patterns (Roberts and Johnson 1998).

The rest of the chapter is organized as follows. Section 13.2 briefly describes the requirements of the Table ADT and applies commonality and variability analysis to recognize the frozen spots and hot spots of the Table ADT framework. Section 13.3 briefly introduces the technique of using formal design contracts, which is applied in the specification of the interface design in the sections that follow. Section 13.4 applies Layered Architecture design pattern to build the top-level framework architecture. Sections 13.5, 13.6, and 13.7 apply several patterns to the design of interfaces among the different layers. Section 13.8 describes a utility module needed by the lower levels of the architecture. Section 13.9 applies the Iterator pattern to enhance the framework design. Section 13.10 illustrates the patterns of evolving frameworks that can be adopted into the Table framework design. Section 13.11 discusses the related work and Section 13.12 gives a conclusion.

13.2 Analysis of the Table ADT

The Table ADT is an abstraction of a widely used set of data and file structures. It represents a collection of records, each of which consists of a finite sequence of data fields. The value of one (or a composite of several) of these fields uniquely identifies a record within the collection; this field is called the *key*. For the purposes here, the values of the keys are assumed to be elements of a totally ordered set. The operations provided by the Table ADT allow a record to be stored and retrieved using its key to identify it within the collection.

In (Cunningham and Wang 2001), Cunningham and Wang consider the design of the Table framework to have the following requirements:

1. It must provide the functionality of the Table ADT for a large domain of client-defined records and keys.

2. It must support many possible representations of the Table ADT, including both in-memory and on-disk structures and a variety of indexing mechanisms.

3. It must separate the key-based record access mechanisms from the mechanisms for storing records physically.

4. All interactions among its components should only be through well-defined interfaces that represent coherent abstractions.

5. Its design should use appropriate software design patterns to increase reliability, understandability, and consistency.

In building a framework, it is important to separate the concerns. The designers must separate the frozen spots, the aspects common to the entire family members, from the hot spots, the aspects specific to one family member. Furthermore, they must separate the various common and variable aspects from each other and consider them somewhat independently (Cunningham et al. 2006a). Commonality and variability analysis (Coplien et al. 1998; Weiss and Lai 1999) is a means of identifying the frozen spots and hot spots. The analysis produces commonalities, a list of assumptions that are true to all the members of the family, and variabilities, a list of assumptions that are true for only some members of the family. Thus, frozen spots and hot spots are chosen on the basis of commonalities and variabilities, respectively. In this chapter, the commonalities and variabilities of the Table ADT are examined based on the requirements of the Table ADT and the prototype implementations (Wang 2000).

The requirements stated above mix concerns in the framework design—commonalities, variabilities, and non-functional aspects of the design and code. These need to be more cleanly separated than is done in (Cunningham and Wang 2001). Requirements 1 and 2 describe functional requirements of the family, which are our primary concerns here. Requirements 3 and 4 express desired characteristics of the framework. Requirement 5 suggests characteristics of the design process. By analyzing the functional requirements, we identify one primary commonality, i.e., frozen spot, as follows:

1. All clients of the framework use the Table ADT's key-based access methods to the collections of records stored in table. (Requirement #1)

We also identify five variabilities, i.e., hot spots, as follows:

1. *Variability in the keys.* Clients of the Table framework can define the keys using many different data structures. (Requirement #1)

2. *Variability in the records.* Clients of the Table framework can define the records using many different data structures. (Requirement #1)

3. *Variability in the external representation of the record state.* For tables stored on external devices, it must be possible to store the state of a record accurately on the external device and restore it to memory when needed. This process may vary somewhat depending upon the nature of the record and the external device. (Requirements #1 and #2)

4. *Variability in the indexing mechanisms.* Different customizations of the Table framework can use different algorithms for indexing the records. (Requirement #2)

5. *Variability in the storage mechanisms.* Different customizations of the framework can use different mechanisms for storing the records. (Requirement #2)

The hot spots #1 and #2 are not completely independent of each other. However, to separate the concerns, we choose to separate the variabilities of keys and records into two different hot spots. Hot spot #3 is a bit subtle, but the need for this variability should be clear as we proceed with the design.

Following the design method outlined above, the framework should allow the five variabilities to be realized independently from each other, which has an implication for the architecture of the Table framework. Before we proceed further, let's look a bit more at the use of formal design contracts for specifying software behaviors.

13.3 Formal Design Contracts

Design by Contract is a design approach developed by Meyer (Meyer 1992, 1997). It is motivated by an analogy with a contract in business. In the business setting a contract defines an agreement between a supplier and a client:

1. The supplier must satisfy certain obligations, such as providing the product the client ordered, and expects certain benefits, such as the client paying the established price for the product.

2. The client must satisfy certain obligations, such as paying the supplier the established price for the product, and expects the benefits, such as getting the product.

3. Both the supplier and the client must satisfy certain obligations that apply to all contracts, such as laws and regulations.

Meyer (Meyer 1992, 1997) adopts the concepts of "client," "supplier" and "contract" into object-oriented design. Building upon earlier work on program verification (Hoare 1969), information hiding (Parnas 1972), data abstraction (Hoare 1972), and abstract data types (Guttag 1977), Meyer introduces logical assertions to describe the contract between the clients (users) of an abstract data type (ADT) and the suppliers (i.e., developers) of the ADT. In Meyer's approach to object-oriented design and programming, an ADT is normally represented by a class. The key assertions are of three types: preconditions, postconditions, and invariants.

Preconditions and postconditions are assertions attached to each operation of an ADT. A *precondition* expresses requirements that any call of the operation must satisfy if it is to be correct. A *postcondition* expresses properties that are ensured in return by the execution of the call. If the precondition is not satisfied, the operation is not guaranteed to return a correct value or to even return at all. For example, an operation to delete a record from a collection might have a precondition requiring that a record with that key exists and a postcondition requiring that it no longer be an element of the collection.

An *invariant* is a constraint attached to an ADT that must hold true for each instance of the ADT whenever an operation is not being performed on that instance. In object-oriented design, this type of invariant is often called a *class invariant*. For example, in the Table ADT, an invariant might state that the table must *not* have more than one record with a particular key. The invariant gives a condition that must be satisfied to maintain the integrity of the table.

In the client-supplier context,

- a client must satisfy the obligation (the precondition) of an operation to expect to receive the benefit (the postcondition) of getting a correct result from the operation,

- a supplier must satisfy the obligation to make the postcondition of the operation hold upon return whenever the precondition of the operations is satisfied by the call,

- both the client and the supplier must maintain certain properties, the invariants.

In specifying the design of the interfaces of the Table framework, we not only need to give the method signatures (i.e., parameters and return type) but also to express their semantics (i.e. behaviors), using preconditions and postconditions for each method and invariants for the ADT as a whole (Cunningham and Wang 2001).

The simple application of Design by Contract is not by itself sufficient for formal proofs of correctness of the desired properties of framework applications. The concrete classes that implement hot spots in a framework must, of course, preserve the general expectations of the framework specification, that is, they should be behavioral subtypes (Liskov and Wing 1994) of the abstract classes they extend. However, the concrete implementations exhibit richer behaviors than the minimum required by the framework specification. Thus extended techniques are needed to handle these richer behaviors (Soundarajan and Fridella 2000; Hallstrom and Soundarajan 2002). Nevertheless, simple design contract techniques are still quite useful in helping designers explore and refine the requirements and framework designs.

13.4 Layered Architecture

The overall architecture of the Table framework should embody the frozen spot and, as much as possible, separate the concerns related to each hot spot into an independent component. That is, it should hide the implementation of each hot spot within a separate component, behind a well-defined interface. To use the terminology from Parnas' information-hiding approach to modular software design, the implementation details for a hot spot should be a "secret" of the component that is hidden behind an appropriate "abstract interface" (Parnas 1972; Britton et al. 1981; Cunningham et al. 2004).

Clearly, there is a mix of high- and low-level issues among the hot spots. Clients can define their own key (hot spot #1) and record (hot spot #2) structures and then call the table (frozen spot) to store the records. The table implementation may use some key-based record access mechanism (hot spot #4) paired with some storage structure (hot spot #5).

This mix of high- and low-level issues suggests a hierarchical architecture based on the *Layered Architecture* pattern (Buschmann et al. 1996; Shaw 1996). When there are several distinct groups of services that can be arranged hierarchically, this pattern assigns each group to a layer. Each layer can then be developed independently. A layer is implemented using the services of the layer below and, in turn, provides services to the layer above. In the simplest version of this pattern, services in a layer cannot directly call upon services defined more than one layer down. It cannot directly call services defined in a layer above except using specific *call-backs* that it is supplied in calls from the higher level.

As shown in Fig. 13.1, we can define three layers in the Table framework design. From the top to the bottom these include:

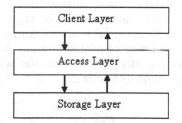

Fig. 13.1. Applying the *Layered Architecture* pattern

Client Layer. This layer consists of the client-level programs that use the table implementation in the layer below to store and retrieve records. Clients of the Table framework implement the user-defined data types for keys and records, which are the variabilities expressed by hot spots #1 and #2.

Access Layer. This layer must provide client programs key-based access to the records in the table. It uses the layer below to store the records physically. Implementations of this layer provide the data structures and algorithms for indexing the records, which is hot spot #4. The interface to this layer represents the frozen spot.

Storage Layer. This layer must provide facilities to store and retrieve the records from the chosen physical storage medium. Implementations of this layer provide the data structures and algorithms for storing the records, for example, a structure in the computer's main memory or a random-access file on disk. The layer expresses hot spot #5.

For example, suppose we want a simple indexed file structure with an in-memory index that uses an array-like relative file to store the records on disk (Folk et al. 1998). The implementation of the index would be part of the Access Layer; the implementation of the relative file would be in the Storage Layer. A program that uses the simple indexed file structure would be in the Client Layer.

What about hot spot #3? This hot spot involves the ability to represent a "record" in an external form suitable for storage on some physical storage medium (e.g., rendering it as a sequence of bytes). So, on the surface, it would seem that this would be a structure defined by the Client Layer that is passed through the Access Layer to the Storage Layer, where a call-back to the implementation of the structure in the client may take place. However, a closer examination reveals a more complicated situation. The client's keyed-record may itself consist of a hierarchy of structures, each of which needs to be converted to the external form independently. For some implementations of the Access Layer, a physical record to be stored by the Storage Layer might consist of a group of client keyed-records (e.g., a B-tree node or a hash-table bucket) or it might consist of auxiliary information about the access structure that needs to be made persistent. Because hot spot #3 does not fit cleanly into any of the layers, we place the needed abstraction in a utility module called the Externalization Module.

The various layers and modules need to be kept independent from one another. Thus, following the fundamental *Interface* design pattern (Grand 1998), we define each layer in terms of a set of related Java interfaces and require that interactions among the layers use only the provided interfaces. Next, let us examine the design of the each layer and its interfaces.

13.5 Client Layer

The design of the *Client Layer* must enable the Access Layer to access client-defined keys and records and should avoid requiring unnecessary programming to use common data types.

13.5.1 Abstract Predicates for Keys and Records

As much as possible, clients (i.e., users) of the table implementations should be able to define their own key (hot spot #1) and record structures (hot spot #2). The internal details of the different types of records and keys, which are implemented in the Client Layer, must be hidden from the Access and Storage Layers. However, the specification of the Access Layer depends upon certain assumptions about the nature of the records and keys. In specifying the operations for the interfaces in this and other layers, we express key features of the keys and records as abstract predicates (Meyer 1997) to make these assumptions more explicit. These are called *abstract* because they are used for specification only; they do not represent functions that are to be built as executable code. The precise definition of these predicates depends upon the particular implementations used in this layer. The abstract predicates associated with the Client Layer are

- `boolean isValidKey(Object key)` that is true if and only if `key` is an element of the set of meaningful keys supported by the client's key class.

- `boolean isValidRec(Object rec)` that is true if and only if `rec` is an element of the set of meaningful records supported by the client's keyed record class.

13.5.2 Keys and the Comparable Interface

As stated earlier, clients of the table implementations should be able to define their own record and key structures (hot spot #1). However, any implementation of the Table ADT must be able to extract the keys from the records and compare them with each other. Thus we restrict the records to objects from which keys can be extracted and compared using some client-defined total ordering.

The built-in Java interface `Comparable` is sufficient to define the functionality of the keys. Any class that implements this interface must provide a public method `compareTo`, which is defined to have the signature and semantics (design contract) as defined below.

To state logical and mathematical expressions in specifications, this chapter uses a Java-influenced notation. The symbol `&&` denotes logical conjunction ("and"), `||` denotes the logical disjunction (inclusive "or"), `!` denotes negation, $\Rightarrow$ denotes logical implication ("if-then"), and `==` denotes equality. The symbol $\forall$ denotes universal quantification ("for all") and $\exists$ denotes existential quantification ("there exists"). For mathematical sets, we use braces { and } to list the elements explicitly, $\cup$ to denote union, $-$ to denote set subtraction, $\in$ to denote membership, and $\emptyset$ to denote the empty set. In appropriate contexts, pairs of parentheses (and) denote tuple formation. In postconditions, the variable **result** refers to the value returned by a function method call and the prefix **#** attached to a variable denotes the value at the time the method was called. Unless a new value is explicitly assigned to a variable in the postcondition, its value must not be changed by the method call.

The description and design contract (pre- and postconditions) for the `compareTo` method are as follows:

- `int compareTo(Object key)` that compares the associated object (`this`) with argument `key` and returns -1 if `key` is greater, 0 if they are equal, and 1 if `key` is less.
  Pre: `isValidKey(this) && isValidKey(key)`
  Post: `result == (if this < key then -1`
                 `else if this == key then 0`
                 `else 1)`

Clients can use any existing `Comparable` class for their keys or implement their own.

13.5.3 Records and the Keyed Interface

To enable keys to be extracted from records, we introduce the Java interface `Keyed` to represent the type of objects that can be manipulated by a table (hot spot #2). We model the `Keyed` abstraction as having an abstract attribute `key`. Any class that implements this interface must implement the method `getKey`, which has the following description and design contract:

- `Comparable getKey()` that extracts the key from the associated record (`this`).
  Pre: `isValidRec(this)`
  Post: `(result == this.key) && isValidKey(result)`

An alternative design for handling the keys and records might be to allow the client to use any Java objects and then to supply appropriate objects that encapsulate the key-extraction and key-comparison operations—developed in accordance with the *Strategy* design pattern (Gamma et al. 1995; Grand 1998). This alternative might enable changes to these operations to be done more dynamically but at the loss of some type safety and of the ability to use the classes in the API that implement the `Comparable` interface. With the approach taken in this section, clients can, if needed, construct wrapper classes that implement the `Comparable` and `Keyed` interfaces and encapsulate the actual key and record objects. This use the *Adapter* design pattern (Gamma et al. 1995; Grand 1998) enables clients to utilize a wide range of pre-defined objects as keys or records as needed.

13.5.4 Interactions among the Layers

The Client Layer thus consists of the Comparable and Keyed interfaces and the abstract predicates isValidKey and isValidRec (all of which are part of the framework) and the concrete classes that implement the interfaces (which are part of the customization of the framework for some specific application). The encapsulation of the key and record implementations in the Comparable- and Keyed-implementing classes, respectively, thus enable the Access Layer to use the client-defined keys and records without knowing the specifics of their implementation. A table implementation in the Access Layer can use the getKey method of the Keyed interface to extract keys from the client-defined records and can then use the compareTo method of the Comparable interface to compare the client-defined keys.

13.6 Access Layer

The design of the *Access Layer* must provide the Client Layer programs key-based access to a collection of records (frozen spot), enable diverse implementations of the indexing structures (hot spot #4), and support diverse storage structures in the Storage Layer. The primary abstraction of the Access Layer is the Table ADT.

13.6.1 Abstract Predicates for Tables

In the specifications in this section, we use the following abstract predicates to capture assumptions the Table ADT makes about the environment:

- isValidKey(Object key) and isValidRec(Object rec) which are defined in the Client Layer to identify valid keys and records.

- isStorable(Object rec) which is defined in the Storage Layer to identify records that can be stored.

The specifications of other interfaces may also depend upon assumptions about the integrity of a Table ADT instance. We thus introduce the abstract predicate:

- boolean isValidTable(Table t) that is true if and only if t is a valid instance of Table (i.e., satisfies all the design contracts below).

13.6.2 Table Interface

We model the collection of records by the variable table, which is a partial function from the set of keys defined by the type Comparable to the set of records defined by the type `Keyed`. For convenience, we use the variable `table` to denote either the function or the corresponding set of key-record pairs.

Now, we can define the Table ADT as a Java interface that includes the following ADT invariant and public methods. In English, the *invariant* can be stated:

> *All stored keys and records in the* `table` *are valid and capable of being stored on the chosen external device, and the records can be accessed by their keys.*

Stated more formally, the invariant is:

```
(∀k,r : r == table(k) : isValidRec(r)
                && isStorable(r) && k == r.getKey())
```

The Table ADT has mutator (i.e., command or setter) operations with the following descriptions and design contracts:

- `void insert(Keyed r)` inserts the `Keyed` object `r` into the table.
  Pre: `isValidRec(r) && isStorable(r) &&`
     `!containsKey(r.getKey()) && !isFull()`
  Post: `table == #table ∪ {(r.getKey(),r)}`

- `void delete(Comparable key)` deletes the `Keyed` object with the given `key` from the table.
  Pre: `isValidKey(key) && containsKey(key)`
  Post: `table == #table - {(key,#table(key))}`

- `void update(Keyed r)` updates the table by replacing the existing entry having the same key as argument `r` with the argument object.
  Pre: `isValidRec(r) && isStorable(r) &&`
     `containsKey(r.getKey())`
  Post: `table == (#table -`
                `{(r.getKey(),#table(r.getKey()))} )`
          `∪ {(r.getKey(),r)} )`

The `Table` ADT has accessor (i.e., query or getter) operations with the following descriptions and design contracts:

- `Keyed retrieve(Comparable key)` searches the table for the argument `key` and returns the `Keyed` object that contains this key.
  Pre: `isValidKey(key) && containsKey(key)`
  Post: `result == #table(r.getKey())`

- `boolean containsKey(Comparable key)` searches the table for the argument `key`.
  Pre: `isValidKey(key)`
  Post: `result == defined(#table(key))`

- `boolean isEmpty()` checks whether the table is empty.

Pre: `true`
Post: `result == (#table == ∅)`

- `boolean isFull()` checks whether the table is full.
  Pre : `true`
  Post: `result ==` (`#table` implementation has no free space to
  store a new record)

- `int getSize()` returns the size of the table.
  Pre: `true`
  Post: `result == cardinality(#table)`

Note that there are several tacit assumptions being made. Having `getSize` return an integer means that the size of the table must be finite, but it is not necessarily bounded. Of course, for unbounded tables `isFull` would always need to return the value `false`. The contracts for the methods other than `getSize` do not preclude the definition of an infinite size table (e.g., with some ranges of key values having records that are generated by a function as needed). However, the behavior of `getSize` would need to be defined for infinite tables. Also a class that implements an infinite table would need to provide a constructor or additional methods for setting up techniques for calculated records that are not explicitly inserted into the table.

13.6.3 Interactions among the Layers

The Access Layer thus consists of the `Table` interface and the `isValidTable` abstract predicate (which form part of the framework itself) and the concrete classes that implement `Table` (which are part of a customization of the framework to create a specific member of the family). Concrete classes that implement the `Comparable` and `Keyed` interfaces are part of the Client Layer. The interactions between the Client Layer and the Access Layer occur as follows:

- The Client Layer calls the Access Layer using the `Table` interface.

- The Access Layer calls back to the Client classes that implement the `Keyed` and `Comparable` interfaces to do part of its work.

In the design of the Access Layer, the only constraint placed upon the storage mechanism is that the records inserted into the table are capable of being stored and retrieved reliably (i.e., satisfy `isStorable`). Thus the design of the Access Layer enables client-defined keys and records, diverse record access mechanisms, and diverse storage mechanisms. Next, let us examine the Storage Layer and its interface.

13.7 Storage Layer

The *Storage Layer* provides facilities to store records to and retrieve records from a physical storage medium. It encapsulates hot spot #5 and, hence, must enable a diverse range of physical media. Of course, this layer must also support client-defined records in the Client Layer and diverse record-access mechanisms in the Access Layer. It should also enable the access structures in the Access Layer to be stored on the physical media and decouple the implementations in the layers above from the physical media as much as possible.

13.7.1 Abstract Predicate for Storable Records

The specifications of the Access Layer and the Storage Layer interfaces depend upon certain assumptions about the nature of records that can be stored on the physical storage media. In specifying the operations, we express key features of the media in terms of an abstract predicate to make these assumptions more explicit. The predicate defined by the Storage Layer is:

- `boolean isStorable(Keyed rec)` that is true if and only if `rec` can be stored on the storage medium being used with the implementation of the `table`.

13.7.2 Bridge Pattern

To define the interfaces between the Access and Storage layers, we adopt a structure motivated by the Bridge and Proxy design patterns (Gamma et al. 1995; Grand 1998) to achieve the desired degree of decoupling and collaboration. We also take into account both the expected characteristics of the storage media and the expected needs of the implementations of the `Table`'s indexing mechanisms.

The *Bridge* design pattern is useful when we wish to decouple the "interface" of an abstraction from its "implementation" so that the two can vary independently (Gamma et al. 1995; Grand 1998). In this design (as shown in Fig. 13.2), the "interface" is the `Table` abstraction in the Access Layer, which provides key-based access to a collection of records; the "implementation" is the `RecordStore` abstraction in the Storage Layer, which provides a physical storage mechanism for records. These two hierarchies of abstractions collaborate to provide the table functionality. At the time a table is created, any concrete `Table`-implementing class can be combined with any concrete `RecordStore`-implementing class.

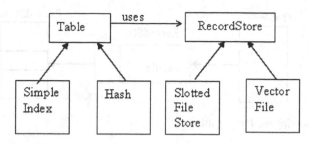

Fig. 13.2. Applying the *Bridge* pattern

We assume that a storage medium abstracted into the `RecordStore` ADT consists of a set of physical "slots." Each slot has a unique "address," the exact nature of which is dependent upon the medium. A program may allocate slots from this set and release allocated slots for reuse. There may, however, be restrictions upon the characteristics of the records acceptable to the storage medium. For example, if a random-access disk file is used, it may be necessary to restrict the record to data that can be written into a fixed-length block of bytes.

There are many possible implementations of `Table` in the Access Layer— such as simple indexes, balanced trees, and hash tables. Any `Table` implementation must be able to allocate a new slot, store a record into it, retrieve the record from it, and then deallocate the slot when it is no longer needed. The `Table` must be able to refer to slots in a medium-independent manner. Moreover, most implementations will need to treat these slot references as data that can be stored in records and written to a slot. For example, the nodes of a tree-structured table are "records" that may be stored in a `RecordStore`; these nodes must include "pointers" to other nodes, that is, references to other slots.

13.7.3 Proxy Pattern

Because we cannot expose the internal details of the `RecordStore` to the Access Layer, we need a medium-independent means for addressing the records in the `RecordStore`. The approach we take is a variation of the *Proxy* design pattern (Gamma et al. 1995; Grand 1998).

The idea of the Proxy design pattern is to use a proxy object that acts as a surrogate for a target object. When a client wants to access the target object, it does so indirectly via the proxy object. Since the target object is not accessed directly by the client, the exact nature and location, even the existence, of the target object is not directly visible to the client. The proxy object serves as a "smart pointer" to the target object, allowing the target's location and access method to vary.

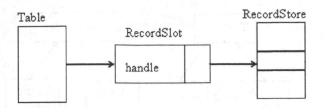

Fig. 13.3. Applying the *Proxy* pattern

In this design, we define the `RecordSlot` abstraction to represent the prox-
ies for the slots within a `RecordStore`. As shown in Fig. 13.3, these two abstractions collaborate to enable the Access Layer to store and retrieve records in a
uniform way, no matter which storage medium is used. Because of the need to
write the slot references themselves into records as data, we also assign an integer
"handle" to uniquely identify each physical slot in a `RecordStore`. Since multiple `RecordStore` instances may be in use at a time, each `RecordSlot` also
needs a reference to the `RecordStore` instance to which it refers.

13.7.4 RecordStore Interface

We can now specify the `RecordStore` and `RecordSlot` interfaces. The model
for the semantics of these ADTs includes two sets. The set `alloc` denotes the set
of slot handles that have been assigned to `RecordSlot` instances. The set
`store` is a partial function from the set of valid handles to the set of storable objects. For convenience, the set `unalloc` is used to denote the set of valid but unallocated handles, that is, the complement of the set `alloc`. The constant
`NULLHANDLE` represents a special integer code that cannot be assigned as a valid
slot handle; it is neither in `alloc` nor `unalloc`. Here we assume that `Re-
cordStore` is finite, but unbounded in size.

We define the `RecordStore` ADT as a Java interface that includes the following ADT invariant and public methods. In English, the *invariant* can be
stated:

*All records in the `store` are capable of being stored on the selected medium
and the stored records can be accessed by their handles.*

Stated more formally in logic, the invariant is:

```
(∀ h, r : r == store(h) : isStorable(r)) &&
(∀ h :: h ∈ alloc == defined(store(h)))
```

The `RecordStore` ADT has operations with the following descriptions and design contracts:

- `RecordSlot newSlot()` allocates a new record slot and returns the
  `RecordSlot` object.
  Pre: true
  Post: result.getContainer() == this &&
        result.getRecord() == NULLRECORD &&
        result.getHandle() ∉ #alloc &&
        result.getHandle() ∈ alloc ∪ {NULLHANDLE}

- `RecordSlot getSlot(int handle)` reconstructs a record slot us-
  ing the given `handle` and returns the `RecordSlot`.
  Pre: handle ∈ alloc
  Post: result.getContainer() == this &&
        result.getRecord() == #store(handle) &&
        result.getHandle() == handle

- `void releaseSlot(RecordSlot slot)` deallocates the allocated
  record `slot`.
  Pre: slot.getHandle() ∈ alloc ∪ {NULLHANDLE} &&
       slot.getContainer() == this
  Post: alloc == #alloc - {slot.getHandle()} &&
        store == #store -
                  {(slot.getHandle(),slot.getRecord())}

Note that, to support a wide domain of variability in implementation, the pa-
rameterless `newSlot` method allows lazy allocation of the handle and, hence, of
the associated physical slot. That is, the handle may be allocated here or later upon
its first use to store a record in the `RecordStore`. For this method, we set the
value of a new slot to be `NULLRECORD`.   This constant denotes an inert, empty
record implemented according to the *Null Object* design pattern (Woolf 1998;
Grand 1998). That is, `NULLRECORD` has the same interface as the other records
returned by `getRecord` (below) except that it has no data associated with it and
the operations have no effect. According to Woolf, "the Null Object encapsulates
the implementation decision to do nothing and hides those details from its collabo-
rators" (Woolf 1998). It sometimes avoids a situation where a caller must take a
special action to capture error returns from operations.

13.7.5 RecordSlot Interface

The `RecordSlot` interface represents a proxy for the physical record "slots"
within a `RecordStore`. The semantics of its operations are, hence, stated in
terms of the effects upon the associated `RecordStore` instance. We model the
`RecordSlot` ADT as having two abstract attributes, the `container` which is a
reference to the associated `RecordStore` and the integer `handle`.

We thus define the `RecordSlot` ADT as a Java interface that includes the following ADT invariant and public methods. In English, the *invariant* can be stated:

The handle of a `RecordSlot` object denotes a slot of the `store` that has been allocated, unless it has the value NULLHANDLE.

Stated more formally in logic, the invariant is:

> getHandle() ∈ alloc ∪ {NULLHANDLE}

The `RecordSlot` ADT has operations with the following descriptions and design contracts:

- `void setRecord(Object rec)` stores the argument object `rec` into this `RecordSlot`.
  Pre: `isStorable(rec)`
  Post: Let `h == getHandle()`:
  >   (h ∈ #alloc ⇒ store == (#store −
  >   {(h,#store(h))}) ∪ (h,rec)})
  >   && (h == NULLHANDLE ⇒
  >   (∃ g : g ∈ #unalloc :
  >   alloc == #alloc ∪ {g} &&
  >   store == #store ∪ {(g,rec)}))

  Note that this allows the allocation of the handle to be done here or already done by the `newSlot` method of `RecordStore`.

- `Object getRecord()` returns the record stored in this `RecordSlot`.
  Pre: `true`
  Post: Let `h == getHandle()`:
  >   (h ∈ #alloc ⇒ result == #store(h)) &&
  >   (h == NULLHANDLE ⇒ result == NULLRECORD)

- `int getHandle()` returns the handle of this `RecordSlot`.
  Pre: `true`
  Post: `result == this.handle`

- `RecordStore getContainer()` returns a reference to the `RecordStore` with which this `RecordSlot` is associated.
  Pre: `true`
  Post: `result == this.container`

- `boolean isEmpty()` determines whether the `RecordSlot` is empty (i.e., does not hold a record).

Pre: true
Post: result == (getHandle() == NULLHANDLE ||
               getRecord() == NULLRECORD)

Note that getRecord returns the inert NULLRECORD object if no record has been stored in the slot. Also note that isEmpty returns true for either an unallocated handle or the NULLRECORD being stored in the slot.

13.7.6 Interactions among the Layers

The Storage Layer consists of the RecordStore and RecordSlot interfaces and the abstract predicate isStorable (all of which are part of the framework) and the concrete classes that implement the interfaces (which are part of an application of the framework). A Table implementation in the Access Layer calls a RecordStore implementation in the Storage Layer to get RecordSlot object. The Access Layer code then calls RecordSlot to store and retrieve its records. If needed, a RecordSlot object calls back to a Record implementation in Access Layer. The Record interface is part of the Externalization Module, which we examine in the next section.

The design of the RecordStore and RecordSlot abstractions and the use of slot handles give the Storage Layer the capability to be implemented using a diverse group of physical media, including both main memory and on-disk structures. These interfaces provide operations with sufficient functionality and make the functionality available in manner that is independent from the actual physical medium used. The combination of these interfaces and the Record interface in the Externalization Module (defined in the next section) enable the Storage Layer to be decoupled from the layers above and for the Access Layer to store a wide range of information in the Storage Layer.

13.8 Externalization Module

How can the RecordSlot mechanism store the records on and retrieve them from the physical slots on the storage medium? This is an issue because the records themselves are defined in the layers above and their internal details are, hence, hidden from the RecordStore. For in-memory implementations of RecordStore this is not a problem; the RecordStore can simply clone the record (or perhaps copy a reference to it). However, disk-based implementations must write the record to a (random-access) file and reconstruct the record when it is read. So, once we allow diverse physical media, we have to handle the external byte presentation of record state (hot spot #3).

The solution taken here is similar to what is done with the `Keyed` interface. We introduce a `Record` interface with three user-defined methods with the following design contracts:

- `void writeRecord(DataOutput out)` writes this record to stream `out`.
  Pre: `true`
  Post: suffix of stream `out` == this record's state encoded as
                     byte sequence

- `void readRecord(DataInput in)` reads this record from stream `in`.
  Pre: `true`
  Post: this record's state == prefix of stream `in` decoded from
                     byte sequence

- `int getLength()` returns the number of bytes in the external representation of this record (e.g., that will be written by `writeRecord`).
  Pre: `true`
  Post: `result` == number of bytes in external representation of this
                     record

The `Record` interface must also satisfy a *State Restoration Property*, defined as follows:

If, for some `Record` object, a `writeRecord` call is followed by a `readRecord` call with the same byte sequence, the observable state of the `Record` object will be unchanged.

The concrete implementations of the `Record` interface appear in either the Client Layer for client-defined records or in the Access Layer for "records" used internally within a `Table` implementation. The Storage Layer calls the `Record` methods when it needs to read or write the physical record. The code in the `Record`-implementing class does the conversion of the internal record data to and from a stream of bytes. The `RecordStore` and `RecordSlot` implementations are responsible for routing the stream of bytes to and from the physical storage medium.

The framework design using the `Record` interface takes a low-level approach to handling the conversion of user-defined records to the desired external form. It requires that the users provide facilities for translating their records to/from a sequence of bytes by having the records themselves implement the `Record` interface. An alternative would be to encapsulate this functionality within an externalization object developed in accordance with the Strategy pattern (Gamma et al. 1995). Methods of the externalization object could access the fields of the user's record to create the needed external form and vice versa. This access might be direct using accessor methods the user record provides or it might be indirect using reflection. Taking this approach further, the Storage Layer might be parameterized with other Strategy objects that convert from a device-independent form coming from the externalization object to the form actually stored on the physical device. Given that strict typing is not maintained when a record is externalized, this would be an acceptable, possibly more dynamic alternative to the approach using the `Record` interface. It would also better support external forms such as an XML representation. However, we opt for the simpler, low-level approach for the framework design in this chapter.

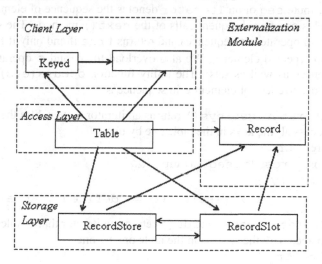

Fig. 13.4. Abstraction Usage Replationships

In summary, Fig. 13.4 shows the *use* relationships among the Client, Access, and Storage Layer and Externalization Module abstractions. The user program in the upper-level Client layer calls the Table ADT directly and the lower layers have callbacks to implementations of the `Keyed`, `Comparable`, and `Record` abstractions defined in the layers above.

13.9 Iterators

So far, we have specified the basic structure of the Table framework. More design patterns could be applied to enhance the design of the framework. This section illustrates how to apply the *Iterator* design pattern (Gamma et al. 1995; Grand 1998) in the Table framework. This design pattern enables the client code to access all the records in the table in some order without exposing the internal details of the table implementations. The interface `Iterator`, defined in the Java API, provides a standard means for Java programs to support iterators. It includes method `hasNext` to check for the existence of another element and method `next` to return the next element. We can add several useful iterators and iterator-manipulating methods to the framework design.

13.9.1 Table Iterator Methods

As a convenience for clients of the table implementations, we add two iterator accessor methods, `getKeys()` and `getRecords()`, to the `Table` interface (defined in the Access Layer). Remember that the ADT invariant for `Table` must also hold as a precondition and postcondition for these operations.

Here we introduce new notation for describing the semantics of iterators. The abstract attribute `seq` of an `Iterator` denotes the sequence of elements that the iterator yields on any subsequent calls of the `next()` method. The suffix predicate `nodups` operates on sequences and returns `true` if and only if the sequence contains no repeated elements. We also overload the $\in$ and $\notin$ operators to work with sequences as well as sets. The utility function `occurs(e,s)` returns the number of occurrences of element `e` in sequence `s`.

- `Iterator getKeys()` returns an iterator that enables the client to access all the keys in the table one by one.
  Pre: `true`
  Post: `result.seq.nodups &&`
         `(∀ k ::`
            `k ∈ result.seq == defined(#table(k))`

- `Iterator getRecords()` returns an iterator that enables the client to access all the records in the table one by one.
  Pre: `true`
  Post: `result.seq.nodups &&`
         `(∀ r ::`
            `r ∈ result.seq == (∃ k :: r = #table(k))`

Similarly, we can add overloaded versions of the `insert` and `delete` methods that take appropriate iterators as arguments.

- `void insert(Iterator iter)` inserts the `Keyed` objects denoted by the iterator `iter` into the table.
  Pre: `iter.seq.nodups &&`
       `(∀ r : r ∈ iter.seq : isValidRec(r) &&`
         `isStorable(r) && !containsKey(r.getKey()))`
  Post: `table == #table ∪`
                   `{(r.getKey(),r) : r ∈ iter.seq }`

- `void delete(Iterator iter)` deletes the objects from the table whose keys match those returned by iterator `iter`.
  Pre: `iter.seq.nodups &&`
       `(∀ k: k ∈ iter.seq :`
          `isValidKey(k) && containsKey(k))`
  Post: `table == #table -`
                   `{(k,#table(k)) : k ∈ iter.seq }`

We note that the precondition of the `insert(Iterator)` method requires all elements yielded by the iterator to be absent from the table. In practice, this may be difficult to ensure for all calls. Alternative specifications might be to require that an insert of an existing key to either be ignored or result in an update operation, but these would make the iterator version behave differently than the non-iterator version of `insert`. A similar situation arises for `delete(Iterator)` because its precondition requires the presence of every key.

13.9.2 Input Iterators

The method `insert(Iterator)` is a convenient mechanism for loading a table with a sequence of items that come from a different format. We add the abstract base class `InputIterator` to enable users to conveniently create a class to read records from external files. The design of this class takes advantage of the Template Method design pattern.

The *Template Method* design pattern (Gamma et al. 1995; Grand 1998) is a quite useful pattern for building frameworks. Central to this pattern is an abstract class that provides a skeleton of the needed behaviors. The class consists of two kinds of methods:

Template methods are concrete methods that implement the shared functionality of the class hierarchy. They are not intended to be overridden by subclasses.

Hook methods are (often abstract) methods that provide "hooks" for attaching the functionality that varies among applications. Although hook methods may have a default definition in the abstract class, in general they are intended to be overridden by subclasses. A template method calls a hook method to carry out application-dependent operations.

The `InputIterator` class implements the Java `Iterator` interface, providing the required `Iterator` methods as template methods. It also includes two abstract hook methods that are called by the template methods:

- `boolean atEnd()` that returns `true` when the end of the input has been reached.

- `Object readNext()` that returns the next object in the input stream.

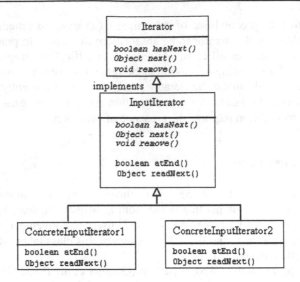

Fig. 13.5. Applying the *Template Method* pattern

A client who wishes to use this class must extend the `InputIterator` class, providing appropriate concrete definitions for the abstract methods. As shown in Fig. 13.5 the `InputIterator` is itself a small framework, with a hot spot concerning that nature of the source from which data objects are being read.

13.9.3 Filtering Iterators

Sometimes users need to transform the elements of one sequence into another. Some elements may need to be deleted and others kept. Sometimes a conversion operation needs to be applied to every element of a sequence. We can support these operations on iterators by introducing the `FilterIterator` class.

The `FilterIterator` class is a concrete class that implements the `Iterator` interface. Its constructor takes three arguments: an iterator, a selector, and a converter. Its implementation takes advantage of the Decorator and Strategy design patterns as shown in Fig. 13.6.

The *Decorator* design pattern extends the functionality of an object in a way that is transparent to the users of that object (Gamma et al. 1995; Grand 1998). A Decorator object is of the same type as the original object. It serves as a wrapper around the original object that provides enhanced functionality but it delegates part of its work to the original object. The `FilterIterator` is an iterator whose constructor takes another iterator as an argument; it uses the argument iterator as its source of data but selects and transforms the data that is returned by its `next()` method. The use of the Decorator design pattern thus allows a `FilterIterator` to provide enhanced functionality at any place that an `Iterator` is used.

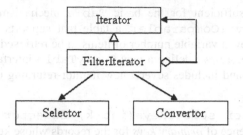

Fig. 13.6. Applying the *Strategy and Decorator* pattern

The *Strategy* design pattern abstracts a family of related algorithms behind an interface (Gamma et al. 1995; Grand 1998). The desired algorithm can be selected at runtime and plugged into the object that uses the algorithm. The selector and converter arguments of the `FilterIterator` are Strategy objects that encapsulate the selection and conversion algorithms, respectively. For example, the selector is an object of a class that implements the `Selector` interface. This interface requires that the class implement the method:

- `boolean selects(Object obj)` that returns `true` if and only if `obj` satisfies the chosen criteria.

The `FilterIterator` delegates the choice of which objects from its input sequence to keep to the `selects()` method of the selector object. The use of the Strategy design pattern enables the same `FilterIterator` object to be configured flexibly to have different behaviors as needed.

13.9.4 Query Iterator Methods

The `Table` abstraction defined in a previous section only provides access based on the unique, primary key of the record. Sometimes a client may want to access records based on the values of other fields. Unlike the primary key, these secondary key fields may not uniquely identify the record within the collection.

The framework can be readily extended to accommodate access on secondary keys as well as the primary key. We can, for example, define a `MultiKeyed` interface in the Client Layer that extends the `Keyed` interface with additional methods:

- `int getNumOfKeys()` that returns the number of keys supported by the associated record implementation

- `Comparable getKey(int k)` that extracts the key k from the record, where key 0 is the primary key

While it is sufficient for the basic `Table` mechanism to have a simple method `retrieve(Comparable)`, a table that supports access on multiple keys needs to allow a variable number of items to be retrieved for each secondary key value. Therefore, we define a new `QueryTable` interface that extends the `Table` interface and includes several new iterator-returning methods. These include:

- `Iterator selectKeys(int k, Selector sel)` that returns the sequence of *primary keys* for the records whose key k satisfies the selector `sel`

- `Iterator selectRecords(int k, Selector sel)` that returns the sequence of records whose key k satisfies selector `sel`

As a convenience, it is also useful to allow a query to be done using a combination of various primary and secondary key values. We can thus define two additional iterator methods:

- `Iterator selectKeys(Query q)` that evaluates the query q and returns the sequence of *primary keys* of all records that satisfy the query

- `Iterator selectRecords(Query q)` that evaluates the query q and returns the sequence of all records that satisfy the query

In this design, `Query` is the abstract base of a class hierarchy constructed according to the *Composite* design pattern (Gamma et al. 1995; Grand 1998). This hierarchy, shown in Fig. 13.7, represents the abstract syntax tree of the query commands. The primary operation of the `Query` classes is the method:

- `Iterator eval(QueryTable t)` that evaluates the query in the context of the `QueryTable` argument t and returns the primary keys from the table for records that satisfy the query

The concrete class `FieldSelector` is a leaf subclass of the `Query` Composite hierarchy. The class has two attributes, an integer to identify which key field of the multikeyed table is to be considered and a `Selector` Strategy object to determine what values of that (secondary or primary) key field are to be selected for inclusion in the result. When a simple query of this nature is evaluated (e.g., by the `selectKeys` method), the set associated with the resulting iterator consists of all the primary keys from the table for the records that satisfy the `FieldSelector`.

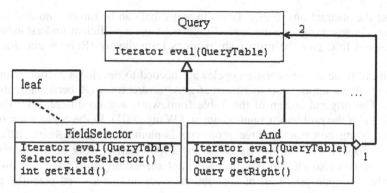

Fig. 13.7. Applying the *Composition* Pattern

Query also has several composite subclasses denoting operations to be performed. For example, the subclass And has two attributes, a left and a right child query. When an And query is evaluated by the selectKeys method, first the two sub-queries are evaluated recursively to get two sets of primary keys and then the intersection of the two sets is returned. Similarly, Or performs a union of the sets, Diff subtracts the set represented by the second argment from the first, and Xor constructs the symmetric difference of the two sets (i.e., elements in only one of the two sets).

The prototype implementation of the Table framework (Wang 2000) implements a flat query syntax with the same general semantics as described above. The QueryTable it implements has an index for each primary and secondary key.

13.10 Evolving Frameworks

The framework design described informally in this chapter is presented from the perspective of an *a priori* design approach for frameworks. Such an approach seeks to derive the framework using systematic analysis (Coplien et al. 1998; Weiss and Lai 1999) and generalization (Schmid 1999; Cunningham and Tadepalli 2006) techniques. In a more traditional approach, framework designs tend to evolve as their usage grows and the developers learn more about the application domain. This evolution often follows the steps documented in the *Evolving Frameworks* system of patterns (Roberts and Johnson 1998). The evolution of the different versions of the Table Framework also exhibits several of these *process patterns*.

13.10.1 Three Examples

In most nontrivial frameworks, it is not easy to come up with the right abstractions just by thinking about the problem. Domain experts typically do not know how to express the abstractions in their heads in ways that can be turned into designs for abstract classes; programmers typically do not have a sufficient understanding of the domain to derive the proper abstractions immediately (Roberts and Johnson 1998).

Often, three implementation cycles are needed to develop a sufficient understanding of the application to construct good abstractions (Roberts and Johnson 1998). The original design of the Table framework was no different despite the simplicity of the problem (Cunningham and Wang 2001). In the exploration of the design, Wang constructed three prototype implementations of RecordStore and two implementations of Table (Wang 2000). Earlier work designing similar Table libraries also yielded insight. Each implementation effort gave new insights into what an appropriate set of abstractions were and uncovered potential problems.

13.10.2 Whitebox Frameworks

As this framework is defined so far, the Table framework is a pure *whitebox framework* (Johnson and Foote 1988; Fayad et al. 1999). In general, a whitebox framework consists of a set of interrelated abstract base classes. Developers implement new applications by extending these base classes and overriding methods to achieve the desired new functionality. The implementers must understand the intended functionality and interactions of the various classes and methods. Such frameworks are flexible, extensible and easy to build, but they are difficult to learn and use.

While whitebox frameworks rely upon inheritance to achieve extensibility, *blackbox frameworks* use object composition to support extensible systems (Johnson and Foote 1988; Fayad et al. 1999). Such frameworks define interfaces for components and allow existing components to be plugged into these interfaces. Appropriate components that conform to these interfaces are collected in a component library for ready reuse. Such frameworks can be easy to use and extend. However, they tend to be difficult to develop because they require the developers to provide appropriate interfaces for a wide range of potential uses.

13.10.3 Component Library

Once a basic whitebox framework is in place, the design usually evolves toward a blackbox framework by the addition of useful concrete classes to a component library (Roberts and Johnson 1998). The addition of concrete implementations of the Table and RecordStore abstractions thus is a natural next step in the evolution of the Table framework.

A prototype component library has been developed for an earlier version of Table framework design (Wang 2000). This component library provides three different implementations of the Storage Layer, in particular of the RecordStore interface:

- `VectorStore`, an implementation that stores the records in a Java Vector

- `LinkedMemoryStore`, an implementation that stores the records in a linked list

- `SlottedFileStore`, an implementation that stores the records in a relative file of fixed length blocks on disk and uses a bit-map to manage the blocks.

The component library also provides two implementations of the Access Layer, in particular of the `Table` interface:

- `SimpleIndexedFile`, an implementation that uses a simple sorted index in memory to support the location of records using keys (Folk et al. 1998)

- `HashedFileClass`, an implementation that uses a hash table to support the key-based access

In the prototype component library (Wang 2000), the `SimpleIndexedFile` component actually implements the `QueryTable` interface, the extended version supporting more complex queries.

13.10.4 Hot Spots

Even if one does attempt to identify some of the frozen and hot spots beforehand, experience in developing applications with a framework helps to identify more points of shared functionality and more points of variability. Once identified, the shared functionality (new frozen spots) can be incorporated into the framework as concrete classes or as concrete methods of abstract classes. The points of variability (new hot spots) can be incorporated into the framework as abstract hook methods that are refined via inheritance (e.g., using the Template Method pattern). Alternatively, hot spots can be implemented by delegation to classes that encapsulate the required functionality (e.g., using the Strategy and Decorator patterns).

In the Table framework, the input iterator extension is an example of new functionality that might be added to the framework as a result of user experience. Users of the framework discover that they are frequently writing new iterator classes to wrap different data sources. This suggests that a new frozen spot, the `InputIterator` Template Method class, be added to the framework. The hook methods of this class represent a hot spot that can be defined by subclassing the `InputIterator` class.

13.10.5 Pluggable Objects

In early versions of an evolving framework, there is the tendency to have large-grained hot spots implemented in a whitebox fashion using inheritance. As the framework is used, it is sometimes discovered that almost the same subclass is being repeatedly implemented. The solution is to implement the common parts of these subclasses as a concrete class and parameterize it so that the variable aspects can be "plugged in" as an argument to the constructor or some setter method.

In the Table framework, the filtering iterator extension is another example of new functionality that might be added to the framework as a result of user experience. Users of the framework discover that they are frequently selecting a subset of the items in the table using a standard iterator and then performing some transformation on each selected item. This suggests a new frozen spot, the `Filter-Iterator` concrete decorator class, be added to the framework, with two new hot spots for the selection and conversion functions. The hot spots are implemented as Strategy objects passed as arguments to the constructor.

The Evolving Frameworks patterns include several other steps that the development of long-lived frameworks may take: the gradual inclusion of many useful, fine-grained objects to eventually enable a fully blackbox framework to be constructed and the development of visual builders and language-oriented tools to assist clients to use the framework to develop and test new applications. The Table framework has not yet evolved to the point where these patterns have been used.

13.11 Discussion

A key requirement in the framework design presented in this chapter is the separation of the key-based access mechanisms, represented by the `Table` interface, from the physical storage mechanisms for the records, represented by the `RecordStore` interface. This idea is inspired, in part, by Sridhar's YACL C++ library's approach to B-trees (Sridhar 1996), which separates the B-tree implementation from the NodeSpace that supports storage for the B-tree nodes. The design extends Sridhar's concept with the `RecordSlot` abstraction, which is inspired, in part, by Goodrich and Tamassia's Position ADT (Goodrich and Tomassia 1998). The Position ADT abstracts the concept of "place" within a sequence so that the element at that place can be accessed uniformly regardless of the actual implementation of the sequence.

This chapter's approach generalizes the NodeSpace and Position concepts and systematizes their design by using standard design patterns. The Layered Architecture and Bridge patterns motivate the design of the `RecordStore` abstraction and the Proxy pattern motivates the design of the `RecordSlot` mechanism. The result is a clean structure that can be described and understood in terms of standard design patterns concepts and terminology. Careful attention to the semantics of the abstract methods in the various interfaces helps us allocate responsibility among the various abstractions in the framework and helps us decide what functionality can be supported across many possible implementations.

Framework design involves incrementally evolving a design rather than discovering it in one single step. Historically, this evolution is a process of examining existing designs for family members, identifying the frozen spots and hot spots of the family, and generalizing the program structure to enable reuse of the code for frozen spots and use of different implementations for each hot spot. This generalization may be done in an informal, organic manner as the Patterns for Evolving Frameworks (Roberts and Johnson 1998) or it may be done using systematic techniques such as *systematic generalization* (Schmid 1996, 1999) and *function generalization* (Cunningham and Tadepalli 2006; Cunningham et al. 2006b).

Schmid's methodology seeks a way to identify the hot spots a priori and construct a framework systematically. It identifies four steps for construction of a framework: (1) creation of a fixed application model, (2) hot spot analysis and specification, (3) hot spot high-level design, and (4) generalization transformation. In Schmid's approach, the fixed application model is an object-oriented design for a specific application within the family. Once a complete model exists, the framework designer analyzes the model and the domain to discover and specify the hot spots. The hot spot's features are accessed through the common interface of the abstract class. However, the design of the hot spot subsystem enables different concrete subclasses of the base class to be used to provide the variant behaviors.

Function generalization (Cunningham and Tadepalli 2006; Cunningham et al. 2006b) is another systematic approach. Instead of generalizing the class structure for an application design as Schmid's methodology does, the function generalization approach generalizes the functional structure of an executable specification to produce a generic application. It introduces the hot spot abstractions into the design by replacing concrete operations by more general abstract operations. These abstract operations become parameters of the generalized functions. That is, the generalized functions are higher-order, having parameters that are themselves functions. Such functions can be expressed in functional programming languages, such as Haskell (Peyton Jones 2003), and also in newer, multiparadigm languages such as Scala (Odersky et al. 2006) and application languages such as Ruby (Thomas et al. 2005). After generalizing the various hot spots of the family, the designers can use the resulting generalized functions to define a framework in an object-oriented language such as Java.

The Table framework presented here was originally developed in a somewhat organic fashion but did utilize software design patterns systematically (Cunningham and Wang 2001). This chapter revisits that work from the standpoint of more careful commonality/variability analysis. Future work should examine the framework design using a more formally systematic technique such as function generalization and seek to evolve the framework design more toward a blackbox design.

13.12 Conclusion

This chapter describes how commonality/variability analysis, software design patterns, and formal design contracts are applied advantageously in the design of a small application framework for building implementations of the Table ADT. The framework consists of a group of Java interfaces that collaborate to define the structure and high-level interactions among components of the Table implementations. The key feature of the design is the separation of the Table's key-based record access mechanisms from the physical storage mechanisms. The systematic application of commonality/variability analysis and the Layered Architecture, Interface, Bridge, and Proxy design patterns lead to a design that is sufficiently flexible to support a wide range of client-defined records and keys, indexing structures, and storage media. The use of the Template Method, Strategy, Decorator, and Composite design patterns also enables variant components to be easily plugged into the framework. The Evolving Frameworks patterns give guidance on how to modify the framework as more is learned about the family of applications. The conscious use of these software design patterns increases the understandability and consistency of the framework's design.

13.13 Exercises

1. Suppose you wish to modify the Client Layer design to use comparison and extraction Strategy objects as described in Section 12.4.3. Discuss the impacts of these changes upon the Client and Access Layer designs.

2. Suppose you wish to modify the Table ADT to allow a (conceptually) infinite number of key-value pairs to be held in the table. How would you modify the specification? What new operations, if any, would you add? Suggest an implementation of such a table.

3. Suppose you wish to develop a new map operation (similar to what might be found in a functional programming language like Haskell or Lisp) in the Table ADT. A map operation takes a function and applies the function to every element of some data structure, leaving the modified element in the place of the previous element. Define the method map and give its design contract. What restrictions, if any, on the function must be made to ensure the integrity of the Table?

4. Suppose you wish to use a more general approach to externalization of the record's internal state than the low-level, byte-stream approach used in this chapter. (See the discussion in Section 12.8.) Give an alternative design and identify the impacts of this change upon the Externalization Module and other aspects of the framework.

5. Characterize the new hot spot(s) introduced into the `FilterIterator` abstraction. What are the variabilities? What design pattern is used to realize each variability?

6. The `InputIterator` uses the Template Method design pattern and the `FilterIterator` uses the Strategy design pattern. Investigate the literature on these patterns (Gamma et al. 1995; Grand 1998). What are the relative advantages and disadvantages of these two patterns as means for implementing variability for a hot spot?

7. Using the logical notation of this chapter, state the needed preconditions for the methods `int getNumOfKeys()` and `Comparable getKey(int)` of the `MultiKeyed` abstraction defined in Section 12.9.4.

8. Using the logical notation of this chapter, state appropriate design contracts for the `Iterator`-returning methods `selectKeys(int,Selector)` and `selectRecords(int,Selector)` of the `QueryTable` abstraction defined in Section 12.9.4.

9. Using the logical notation of this chapter, state appropriate design contracts for the `Iterator`-returning query methods `selectKeys(Query)` and `selectRecords(Query)` defined in Section 12.9.4. These can use the `eval(QueryTable)` method of the `Query` class hierarchy.

10. Using the logical notation of this chapter, state an appropriate design contract for the method `eval(QueryTable)` of the `Query` class hierarchy defined in Section 12.9.4.

11. Implement the framework and design an application.

    a. Develop a version of the Access Layer (i.e., `Table`) that uses an array in memory (or `Vector` or `ArrayList`) to create a sorted index of the keys.

    b. Develop a version of the Storage Layer that uses a Java `Vector` (or `ArrayList`) as the storage medium for the records.

    c. Pair the two programs developed in the previous two problems.

    d. Test the application with various kinds of keys and records.

12. Continue the programming exercise above and develop new components. Develop a version of the Access Layer that uses a hash table and pair it with the Storage Layer developed above.

13. Complete the design and implement an Access Layer based on a multikeyed table as defined by the `QueryTable` abstraction in Section 12.9.4.

14. The framework presented in this chapter mostly consists of large-grained components. Examine one of the detailed designs and implementations of the Access Layer from the previous three exercises. Suggest additional frozen

spots and hot spots in your design that will allow a useful finer-grained framework to be constructed by using more "pluggable objects."

15. Examine the Java API for stream and file input/output. Identify the hot spots in this framework. How are the hot spots implemented? What design patterns are used to structure the designs?

13.14 Acknowledgements

The preparation of an earlier version of this chapter was supported, in part, by a grant from Acxiom Corporation titled "An Acxiom Laboratory for Software Architecture and Component Engineering (ALSACE)." The authors thank Robert Cook and "Jennifer" Jie Xu for their suggestions for improvements to the paper (Cunningham and Wang 2001). We also thank the two anonymous reviewers, the editors, Chuck Jenkins, and Pallavi Tadepalli for their useful comments on this chapter. As this chapter was being revised, the first author benefited from discussions about various aspects of the framework design with Jenkins. Pallavi Tadepalli is a collaborator on the related function generalization research (Cunningham and Tadepalli 2006; Cunningham et al. 2006b) and Cuihua Zhang is involved with work on the educational aspects of software patterns and framework design (Cunningham et al. 2004, 2006a). This research also benefited from insights provided by projects completed by the first author's former students Wei Feng on relative files, Jian Hu on Table libraries, and Deep Sharma on B-tree libraries.

13.15 References

Britton KH, Parker RA, Parnas DL (1981) A procedure for designing abstract interfaces for device interface modules, In: Proceedings of the 5th International Conference on Software Engineering, pp 95-204.

Brooks FP Jr (1986) No silver bullet—Essence and accidents in software engineering, In: Information Processing, Elsevier Science, pp 1069-1076.

Brooks FP Jr (1995) "No Silver Bullet" refired, Chapter 17, In: The mythical man-month, Anniversary edn, Addison-Wesley.

Buschmann F, Meunier R, Rohnert H, Sommerlad P, Stal M (1996) Pattern-oriented software architecture: A system of patterns, Wiley.

Coplien J, Hoffman D, Weiss D (1998) Commonality and variability in software engineering, IEEE Software, vol 15, no 6, pp 37-45.

Cunningham HC, Wang J (2001) Building a layered framework for the table abstraction, In: Proceedings of the ACM Symposium on Applied Computing, pp 668-674.

Cunningham HC, Tadepalli P (2006) Using function generalization to design a cosequential processing framework, In: Proceedings of the 39th Hawaii International Conference on System Sciences, IEEE, 10 pages.

Cunningham HC, Zhang C, Liu Y (2004) Keeping secrets within a family: Rediscovering Parnas. In: Proceedings of the International Conference on Software Engineering Research and Practice (SERP), CSREA Press, pp 712-718.

Cunningham HC, Liu Y, Zhang C (2006a) Using classic problems to teach Java framework design. Science of Computer Programming, vol 59, pp 147-169.

Cunningham HC, Liu Y, Tadepalli P (2006b) Framework design using function generalization: A binary tree traversal case study. In: Proceedings of the ACM SouthEast Conference, pp 312-318.

Fayad ME, Schmidt DC, Johnson RE (1999) Application frameworks, In: Fayad ME, Schmidt DC, Johnson RE (eds) Building application frameworks: Object-oriented foundations of framework design, Wiley, pp 3-27.

Folk MJ, Zoellick B, Riccardi G (1998) File structures: An object-oriented approach with C++, Addison Wesley.

Gamma R, Helm R, Johnson R, Vlissides J (1995) Design patterns: Elements of reusable object-oriented software, Addison Wesley.

Goodrich MT, Tomassia R (1998) Data structures and algorithms in Java, Wiley.

Grand M (1998) Patterns in Java, vol 1, Wiley.

Guttag JV (1977) Abstract data types and the development of data structures, Communications of the ACM, vol 20, no 6, pp 396-404.

Hallstrom J, Soundarajan N (2002) Incremental development using object-oriented frameworks: A case study, Journal of Object Technology, Special issue TOOLS USA 2002, vol 1, no 3, pp 189-205.

Hoare CAR (1969) An axiomatic basis for computer programming, Communications of the ACM, vol 12, no 10, pp 45-58.

Hoare CAR (1972) Proofs of correctness of data representations, Acta Informatica, vol 1, pp 271-281.

Johnson RE, Foote B (1988) Designing reusable classes, Journal of Object-Oriented Programming, vol 1, no 2, pp 22-35.

Liskov B, Wing J (1994) A behavioral notion of subtyping, ACM Transactions on Programming Languages and Systems, vol 16, pp 1811-1840.

Mitchell B, McKim J (2002) Design by contract, by example. Addison-Wesley.

Meyer B (1992) Applying design by contract. IEEE Computer, pp 40- 51.

Meyer B (1997) Object-oriented software construction, second edn, Prentice Hall PTR.

Odersky M, Altherr P, Cremet V, Dragos I, Dubochet G. Emir B, McDirmid S, Micheloud S, Mihaylov N, Schinz M,. Stenman E, Spoon L, Zenger M (2006) An overview of the Scala programming language, second edn, LAMP-REPORT-2006-001, Ecole Polytechnique Federale De Lausanne (EPFL), 20 pages.

Parnas DL (1972) On the criteria to be used in decomposing systems into modules, Communications of the ACM, vol 15, no 12, pp 1053-1058.

Parnas DL (1976) On the design and development of program families, IEEE Transaction on Software Engineering, vol SE-2, pp 1-9.

Parnas DL (1978) Some software engineering principles. Infotech State of the Art Report on Structured Analysis and Design, Infotech International, 10 pages, 1978. Reprinted in: Hoffman DM, Weiss DM (eds) (2000) Software fundamentals: Collected papers by David L. Parnas, Addison-Wesley.

Peyton Jones S (2003) Haskell 98 language and libraries: The revised report, Cambridge University Press.

Pree W (1995) Design patterns for object-oriented software development, Addison-Wesley.

Roberts D, Johnson R (1998) Patterns for evolving frameworks, In: Martin R, Riehle D, Buschmann F (eds) Pattern languages of program design 3, Addison-Wesley, pp.471-486.

Schmid HA (1996) Creating applications from components: A manufacturing framework, IEEE Software, vol 13, no 6, pp 67-75.

Schmid HA (1999) Framework design by systematic generalization, In: Fayad ME, Schmidt DC, Johnson RE (eds) Building application frameworks: Object-oriented foundations of framework design, Wiley, pp 353–378.

Soundarajan N, Fridella S (2000) Framework-based applications: from incremental development to incremental reasoning, In: Proceedings of the 6th Interantional Confernce on Software Reuse (ICSR), LNCS 1844, Springer-Verlag, pp 100-116.

Shaw M (1996) Some patterns for software architecture, In: Vlissides JM, Coplien JO, Kerth NL (eds), Pattern languages of program design 2, Addison Wesley.

Sridhar MA (1996) Building portable C++ applications with YACL, Addison-Wesley.

Thomas D, Fowler C, Hunt A (2005) Programming Ruby: The pragmatic programmer's guide, second edition, The Pragmatic Bookshelf.

Wang J (2000) A flexible Java library for table data and file structures, Technical Report UMCIS-2000-07, Department of Computer and Information Science, University of Mississippi.

Weiss DM, Lai CTR (1999) Software product-line engineering: A family-based software development process, Addison-Wesley.

Woolf B (1998) Null object. In: Martin R, Riehle D, Buschmann F (eds), Pattern languages of program design 3, Addison-Wesley, pp. 5-18.

14 Information Quality Framework for Verifiable Intelligence Products

Hongwei Zhu[1] and Richard Y. Wang[2]

[1] College of Business and Public Administration, Old Dominion University Norfolk, VA, USA

[2] MIT Information Quality Program, Massachusetts Institute of Technology Cambridge, MA, USA

14.1 Introduction

Organizations have been increasingly investing in technology to collect and process vast volumes of data. Even so, they often find themselves stymied in their efforts to effectively use the data to improve business processes and to make better decisions. This difficulty is often caused by information quality issues within the organization and other related organizations.

The government is not immune to the problems of IQ. In response, many government agencies in the U.S. have begun to establish IQ policies and guidelines as part of their effort in practicing Enterprise Architecture (EA) to improve collaboration and information sharing across the Community.

In particular, the intelligence community (IC) gathers and analyzes a large amount of information from a variety of sources to produce intelligence products for decision makers and policy makers. It is imperative that these intelligence products are of highest quality. From raw inputs to final intelligence products, there are often many processes involved. In addition to the quality of final intelligence products, another important aspect of quality is the *verifiability* of the final intelligence products: how is the conclusion derived, from what sources? In this chapter we will illustrate the need for verifiability and propose to develop a solution towards Verifiable Intelligence Products (VIP). We will use the term *information quality* (IQ) and *data quality* interchangeably in the rest of the chapter.

This chapter presents an effort to improve IQ within the broader IC EA initiative. Its motivation can be illustrated by a hypothetical example (Fig. 14.1) adapted

Y. Chan et al. (eds.), *Data Engineering*, International Series in Operations
Research & Management Science 132, DOI 10.1007/978-1-4419-0176-7_14,
© Springer Science+Business Media, LLC 2010

from "A Compendium of Analytic Tradecraft Notes" issued by the Directorate of Intelligence of the Central Intelligence Agency (CIA Directorate of Intelligence, 1997).

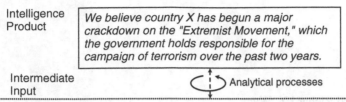

Intelligence Product

> *We believe country X has begun a major crackdown on the "Extremist Movement," which the government holds responsible for the campaign of terrorism over the past two years.*

Intermediate Input   Analytical processes

The Army has been ordered to support the police in cleaning out *Extremist* strongholds (*direct information*), according to special intelligence (*sourcing*). The President of X reportedly is using last week's attack on a shopping center in a working-class neighborhood to justify calling upon the Army to close down the terrorist campaign (*indirect information*). according to a reliable clandestine source (*sourcing*). The pro-government press reports (*sourcing*) the *Extremists* cannot match Army firepower and are taking high casualties (*indirect information*). A US Embassy observer reports (*sourcing*) seeing Army trucks deliver more than 100 prisoners, some badly wounded, to the Central Prison (*direct information*). According to country X police officials (*sourcing*), these were part of the 1,000 *Extremists* rounded up so far in the crackdown (*indirect information*). CIA's "Country X Terrorism Chronology" indicates this is the first time the Army has been used against the *Extremists* since the terrorism campaign began in 1993 (*data*).

Integration, cleansing, mining processes

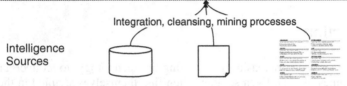

Intelligence Sources

Fig. 14.1. From Intelligence Information to Intelligence Product

A statement in an intelligence product is shown in the top of Fig. 14.1. It is derived from the intermediate input shown in the middle of Fig. 14.1 via certain analytical processes. The intermediate input is obtained from various sources, shown in the bottom of Fig. 14.1, using such techniques as information integration/extraction, information retrieval, data cleansing, and data mining. Two questions the customers of the intelligence product may ask are:

- How good is the statement (i.e., what is the overall quality of the product)?
- How is the statement derived (i.e., what are the sources and procedures that lead to the statement)?

The first question concerns with quality assessment of the intelligence product. The second question concerns with the capability of verifying sources and explaining processes of intelligence production. We will develop an information quality framework to address both questions. The framework integrates key findings from two decades of information quality research and adapts them to take into account of the characteristics of the IC. Specifically, we propose to develop a comprehensive and systematic set of metrics for measuring the quality of intelligence products. We also propose to develop techniques for tracing the sources and production processes involved in producing the final intelligence products.

The rest of this chapter is organized as follows. Section 14.2 provides background information about the production of intelligence products and key findings in IQ research. Section 14.3 discusses IQ challenges faced by the IC. Section 14.4 presents a proposed solution. Section 14.5 concludes the chapter.

14.2 Background

14.2.1 Production Process of Intelligence Products

Intelligence production is a dynamic and iterative process, as illustrated in Fig. 14.2. Below we describe the major steps involved.

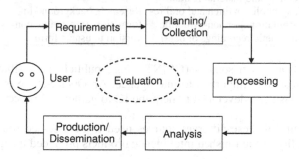

Fig. 14.2. Intelligence Production Process (adapted from Krizan 1999)

Requirements
Intelligence customers often express their needs using their own terminology. Such needs are converted to intelligence requirements understood within the IC. This is often done by asking the five-W questions: Who, What, When, Where, and Why. Sometimes the intelligence requirements can be characterized using a taxonomy of problems (Jones 1995) that classifies problems into five categories: simplistic, deterministic, moderately random, severely random, and indeterminate. The expected quality of products varies amongst products that deal with different types of intelligence problems. A method for describing IQ is needed.

Planning and Collection
Sometimes the intelligence at hand is sufficient to meet the customer requirements and no extra intelligence needs to be collected. This requires the ability of knowing what information is available. Search technology and information retrieval tools can be helpful. At other times, intelligence collection is necessary; in this case the collection phase of the intelligence process involves several steps:

translation of the intelligence need into a collection requirement, definition of a collection strategy, selection of collection sources, and information collection.

There are four types of sources that the IC primarily uses. Their characteristics and intended uses are summarized in Table 14.1.

Table 14.1. Characteristics of Intelligence Information Sources (Clauser and Weir 1975)

Source	Collection Disciplines and Source Attributes	Analytic Use
People	HUMINT; subject-matter experts, professional researchers, information specialists, eyewitnesses or participants	Transfer of first-hand knowledge, referral to other sources
Objects	IMINT; physical characteristics of equipment, materials, or products, such as texture, shape, size, and distinctive markings	Basis for emotive but objective reporting on composition, condition, origin, or human purpose
Emanations	MASINT, SIGINT; detectable phenomena given off by natural or manmade objects; electromagnetic energy, heat, sound, footprints, fingerprints, and chemical and material residues	Scientific and technical analysis
Records	IMINT, SIGINT; symbolic (written and oral reports, numerical tabulations) or non-symbolic (images, electro-magnetic recordings of data)	Research, background information, translation, conversion to usable form

Recently, information from open sources (OSINT) (e.g., publicly accessible websites) has become increasingly important to intelligence. An Open Source Information System (OSIS) has been developed to help the IC to gather and process intelligence information.

The quality and reliability of these different sources need to be assessed routinely to determine the quality of the finished intelligence products produced using these sources.

Processing

This is the process that transforms raw data to intelligence information. Processing methods vary depending on the form of the collected information and its intended use. One important procedure is information collation, which organizes the information into a usable form, adding meaning where it was not evitable in the original. Collation includes gathering, arranging, and annotating related information; drawing tentative conclusions about the relationship of "facts" to each other and their significance; evaluating the accuracy and reliability of each item; grouping items into logical categories; critically examining the information source; and assessing the meaning and usefulness of the content for further analysis. Collation reveals information gaps, guides further collection and analysis, and provides a framework for selecting and organizing additional information (Mathams 1995). It is important that no bias is introduced in the selection and interpretation of information during collation. The information must be evaluated to determine whether it will be used in the rest of the intelligence production process (Harris 1989).

Analysis

Three levels of analysis are often conducted for different customer requirements (Krizan 1999):

- *Describe*: fully describe the phenomenon under study, accounting for as many relevant variables as possible.
- *Explain*: thoroughly explain the phenomenon through interpreting the significance and effects of its elements on the whole.
- *Estimate*: provide synthesis and effective persuasion about the situation.

These different levels of analysis are better known as "intelligence food chain" within the IC (Davis 1995):

- *Facts*: verified information related to an intelligence issue (for example: events, measured characteristics).
- *Findings*: expert knowledge based on organized information that indicates, for example, what is increasing, decreasing, changing, or taking on a pattern.
- *Forecasts*: judgments based on facts and findings and defended by sound and clear argumentation.
- *Fortunetelling*: inadequately explained and defended judgments.

The mnemonic "Four Fs Minus One" may serve as a reminder of how to apply this criterion. Whenever the intelligence information allows, and the customer's validated needs demand it, the intelligence analyst will extend the thought process as far along the Food Chain as possible, to the third "F" but not beyond to the fourth (Krizan 1999).

Commonly used methods for analysis include opportunity analysis (Davis 1992), linchpin analysis (Davis 1995), and analogy (Clauser and Weir 1975). It is important that no misperceptions and bias are introduced during analysis.

Production and Dissemination

This is the process of creating the finished intelligence products in any medium usable by the customers and delivering the products to intended customers. Product content and tone often need to be adjusted according to the level of expertise of the customer. Caution needs to be exercised to avoid misinterpretation by intended customers as well as incidental customers. Feedback from customers should be collected to continuously improve intelligence products (Hulnick 1988).

14.2.2 Current IQ Practices in the IC

Within the Central Intelligence Agency, and the IC in general, the Kent doctrine has been widely adopted for quality assurance in intelligence analysis. As enumerated by Frans Bax and discussed in (Davis 2002), the doctrine consists of nine aspects:

- Focus on Policymaker Concerns
- Avoidance of a Personal Policy Agenda

- Intellectual Rigor
- Conscious Effort to Avoid Analytic Biases
- Willingness to Consider Other Judgments
- Systematic Use of Outside Experts
- Collective Responsibility for Judgment
- Effective communication of policy-support information and judgments
- Candid Admission of Mistakes

In addition to the doctrine, the IC relies on customer feedback to evaluate the quality of intelligences products. The evaluation framework presented in (Brei 1996) uses six criteria to evaluate the products of the sub-processes of the production process:

- *Accuracy*: All sources and data must be evaluated for the possibility of technical error, misperception, and hostile efforts to mislead.
- *Objectivity*: All judgments must be evaluated for the possibility of deliberate distortions and manipulations due to self-interest.
- *Usability*: All intelligence communications must be in a form that facilitates ready comprehension and immediate application. Intelligence products must be compatible with a customer's capabilities for receiving, manipulating, protecting, and storing the product.
- *Relevance*: Information must be selected and organized for its applicability to a customer's requirements, with potential consequences and significance of the information made explicit to the customer's circumstances.
- *Readiness*: Intelligence systems must be responsive to the existing and contingent intelligence requirements of customers at all levels of command.
- *Timeliness*: Intelligence must be delivered while the content is still actionable under the customer's circumstances.

This framework suggests a 2-dimentional evaluation matrix as shown in Table 14.2 to be used to assess the quality of interim and finished intelligence products.

Table 14.2. Evaluation Matrix for Intelligence Product

	Needs Definition	Collection	Processing	Analysis	Production
Accuracy					
Objectivity					
Usability					
Relevance					
Readiness					
Timeliness					

The Kent doctrine and the evaluation matrix, when systematically applied, should provide a means to ensure that the intelligence products are of high quality. However, there are still areas where we can improve.

14.2.3 Relevant Concepts and Methods of IQ Management

The Total Data Quality Management (TDQM) framework (Madnick and Wang 1992) has been widely adopted and proven to be effective in practice. The framework consists of a set of concepts and methods for describing, measuring, and improving information quality. Our preliminary investigation indicates that the following concepts and methods are relevant to the IC:

- Multiple dimensions of IQ
- Treating information as a product and IP-Map (a methodology for describing and optimizing information manufacturing process)
- PolyGen – a model for maintaining data lineage and useful IQ attributes
- Quality Entity Relationship (QER) – a conceptual modeling technique to incorporate quality in conceptual data model

14.2.3.1 TDQM Framework

The TDQM framework advocates continuous data quality improvement through cycles of *Define, Measure, Analyze,* and *Improve* (Madnick and Wang 1992). The framework extends the Total Quality Management (TQM) framework for quality improvement in manufacturing domain (Deming 1982; Juran and Godfrey 1999) to the domain of data.

Define. It has been found effective to define data quality from consumer's point of view as *fitness for use* (Strong et al. 1997). Further research identified the dimensions of data quality (Wang and Strong 1996). These dimensions are organized in four categories, as shown in Table 14.3. Intrinsic data quality denotes the quality that data inherently has. Accessibility and representational data quality emphasizes the role of systems that store, process, and deliver data to the consumers. Contextual data quality highlights that data quality must be considered within the context of the task at hand (e.g., imagery data with a certain resolution may be sufficient for one task but insufficient for another).

Table 14.3. Data quality categories and dimensions

Category	Dimensions
Intrinsic DQ	Accuracy, Objectivity, Believability, Reputation
Accessibility DQ	Accessibility, Access security
Contextual DQ	Relevancy, Value-added, Timeliness, Completeness, Amount of data
Representational DQ	Interoperability, Ease of understanding, Concise representation, Consistent representation

Measure. A comprehensive data quality assessment instrument has been developed for use in research as well as in practice to measure data quality in organizations (Lee et al. 2002). The instrument operationalizes each dimension into four to five measurable items; appropriate functional forms are applied to these items to determine the score of each dimension (Pipino et al. 2002). The instrument can be adapted to accommodate specific organizational needs.

Analyze. The measurement results are interpreted at this step. The analysis determines the dimensions that need improvement and the root causes of data quality problems. Gap analysis techniques (Lee et al. 2002) can be used to reveal the data quality perception gaps between different dimensions and between different roles of data production process. The three major roles are data collectors, data custodians, and data consumers (Lee and Strong 2004).

Improve. At this step, actions are taken to change data values directly or, more appropriately, change the processes that produce the data. The latter approach is more effective as discussed in (Wang 1998; Wang et al. 1998), where steps towards managing information as a product are provided. In addition, technologies mentioned earlier such as PolyGen and Quality-ER can be applied as part of the continuous improvement process.

14.2.3.2 Treating information as Product and IP-Map

To effectively improve IQ, an organization should treat information as a product instead of a byproduct. An information product (IP) needs to conform to specifications and to meet consumer expectations.

To operationalize the notion of "information as a product", we need to model the information manufacturing process. Many modeling methods for information manufacturing systems have been developed. Almost all of these lack the ability to systematically represent the manufacturing processes. The proposed information product map (IP-MAP) method can systematically model the manufacture of an IP (Shankaranarayan et al. 2003; Shankaranarayan and Wang 2007). The IP-MAP is an extension of the Information Manufacturing System (IMS) proposed earlier. This representation offers several advantages:

- It allows the IP manager to visualize the most important phases in the manufacture of an IP and identify the critical phases that affect its quality.
- Using this representation, IP managers will be able to pinpoint bottlenecks in the information manufacturing system and estimate the time to deliver the IP.
- Based on the principles of continuous improvement for the processes involved, the IP-MAP representation would not only help identify ownership of the processes at each of these phases but would also help in implementing quality-at-source.
- The representation would permit IP managers to understand the organizational (business units) as well as information system boundaries spanned by the different processes / stages in the IP-MAP.
- It permits the measurement of the quality of the IP at the different stages in the manufacturing process using appropriate quality dimensions.

14.2.3.3 PolyGen

Intelligence analysis is often accomplished using information contained in heterogeneous/distributed databases. In this environment, data consumers often need to know not only the sources of information, but also the intermediate sources that helped in composing the information. The PolyGen model (Wang and Madnick 1990) has been developed to answer the questions "where did the data come from" and "which intermediate sources were used to derive the data." The PolyGen model is named for its multiple (poly) source (gen) perspective. It uses a data source tagging mechanism to identify sources. The model has both a data structure and a query answering mechanism to help objectively determine the quality of the data. Follow on research has developed methods for managing data lineage of semi-structured data such as XML (Buneman et al. 2001) and implemented data lineage management as a part of the query processing engine (Widom 2005).

14.2.3.4 QER

QER is an extension to Entity-Relationship model to capture data quality requirements in the design phase. As illustrated in (Wang et al. 1993), this extension can capture data quality requirement as meta-data at the individual data element level. Furthermore, the querying system can be extended to allow for efficient process of data quality meta-data (Wang et al. 1995). A recent extension to QER can be found in (Jiang et al. 2007). The QER method is important to the IC and can be incorporated into the IC-wide Enterprise Architecture efforts.

14.3 IQ Challenges within the IC

In the Introduction and Background sections, we presented a motivating example concerning information quality and information lineage and related these issues to a range of IQ challenges faced by the IC. In this section, we review these challenges to provide a better understanding of the issues addressed by the research.

14.3.1 IQ Issues in Intelligence Collection and Analysis

Intelligence collection and analysis is an inexact science at best. Accurate results often require data from multiple sources or data that has been collected over time and then integrated to develop a final product. Critical elements of data may reside in the databases of multiple IC organizations. There are major problems with intelligence that must be addressed. A few of these include:

- Incompleteness. IC organizations usually cannot collect all necessary information because of the obstacles created by the adversaries. Also, it is often difficult to validate the collected information. To address this challenge, the IC attempts to collect from multiple sources to corroborate the facts.
- Inconsistency. Information from multiple sources sometimes points to different answers. It is difficult to determine which information is correct and which is false.

- Uncertainty and validity. The adversaries often execute deception operations. It can be difficult to determine if collected information is the true fact or deception.
- Source identification. A problem that has been an issue in human intelligence (HUMINT) collection is the same source providing the same information to multiple collection organizations. When integrated, it appears that we have multiple sources that corroborate the facts. Worse, if the source is not trustworthy, he/she may pass invalid information to each organization. Also, the source may be passing information solely for the purpose of advancing a personal objective that may or may not be an objective of the IC.

These problems directly affect the quality of finished intelligence products. To a certain extent, these problems are related to the ability (or lack thereof) of identifying the actual sources of information and the quality of information. For example, in the case of inconsistent information, we can give more weight to information from sources of higher reliability. If we know the true source of information, we can avoid the problem of mistaking a single source as multiple sources in the case of HUMINT collection. In addition, we also need to consider the process of intelligence production since error can be introduced at any point of the process.

14.3.2 Other IQ Problems

In addition to the issues in the areas of intelligence collection and analysis, there are several other IQ problems within the IC. Some of the areas of concern are:
- The problem of maintaining the quality of information for which there is a known authoritative source. One example is personnel data for members of the IC organizations. The quality of this information must be maintained as it is entered into an IC directory to support information sharing among IC organizations. Faulty or duplicate data can result in denial of access to information critical for individuals to do their jobs or improper access that can compromise the data.
- The problem of maintaining the quality of information developed from the analysis of multiple sources of intelligence. Once a fact has been determined it must be recognized and maintained consistently by the members of the IC. Fairly simple areas like ensuring embassy locations are properly maintained can help eliminate political embarrassments and unwanted loss of life as happened in Serbia.
- The problem of maintaining consistency and timeliness of information as existing information is revised and updated. At times what is known (or thought) to be true is discovered to need modification. An IC organization may recall the information or publish modifications. These must be accurately disseminated to the other IC organizations and used to modify their internal databases.

As the IC expands its information sharing, information exchanges and collaborative analysis, IQ areas like those above must be addressed.

14.3.3 IQ Dimensions Related to the IC

The various issues discussed above can be understood from the 16 dimensions of IQ. The dimensions are general enough to be used across sectors. However, when they are applied to the IC, specific considerations need to be taken into account because of certain unique characteristics of the IC. Table 14.4 summarizes the IQ dimension definitions (Wang and Strong 1996; Kahn et al. 2002) and the specific considerations of the IC (Mosier 2005).

Table 14.4. IQ Dimensions and IC Considerations (adapted from Kahn et al. 2002; Mosier 2005)

Dimension	Definition	IC Considerations
Accessibility	The extent to which data is available, or easily and quickly retrievable.	This has been shown to be a major deficiency across the IC. Not explicitly identified by the definition, but import to the IC, is knowledge of existence of the information.
Amount of Information	The extent to which the volume of data is appropriate for the task at hand.	Difficult to guarantee. Information can be overloaded in certain cases and extremely insufficient in other cases.
Believability	The extent to which data is regarded as true and credible.	This is an extremely important dimension for the area of collection and analysis. It addresses the deception and false information areas.
Reputation	The extent to which information is highly regarded in terms of its source or content.	Information gathered from imagery usually has a high reputation, especially when multi-spectral analysis is done. Information from SIGINT is considered accurate, but may always be a deception. HUMINT is sometime suspected by the consumers.
Completeness	The extent to which information is not missing and is of sufficient breadth and depth for the task at hand.	Challenging because of difficulties in collection. The potential for IQ processes to determine the level of completeness could be a major area of investigation.
Concise Representation	The extent to which data is compactly represented	
Consistent Representation	The extent to which the data is presented in the same format.	Major efforts in this area through IC standardization efforts.
Ease of Operations	The extent to which data is easy to operate on and apply to different tasks.	

Free-of-Error	The extent to which data is correct and reliable.	Very important, but hard to ensure in the collection area because of deception and other factors.
Interpretability	The extent to which data is in appropriate languages, symbols, and units and the definitions are clear.	Increasingly important as IC organizations begin to share information.
Objectivity	The extent to which data is unbiased, unprejudiced, and impartial.	An important area for analysis within the IC. Intelligence products that contain the analyst bias can lead to potential disaster.
Relevancy	The extent to which data is applicable and helpful for the task at hand.	
Security	The extent to which data access to data is restricted appropriately to maintain its security.	Of major importance to the IC.
Timeliness	The extent to which data is sufficiently up-to-date for the task at hand.	In the IC it is critical to get the time sensitive information to the people who need it in time.
Understandability	The extent to which data is easily comprehended.	
Value Added	The extent to which data is beneficial and provides advantages from its use.	This is an area where further investigation could lead to insights into how data integrated from multiple sources add value to a final product.

14.4 Towards a Proposed Solution

In this section we propose a solution to address the questions raised in the motivating example: (1) determining the quality of intelligence products; and (2) being able to verify the sources and processes that lead to the final intelligence product. The two issues are related: the quality of the final product is determined by the quality of all original and intermediate sources. At each stage of the production process, the quality of the products needs to be evaluated. Conversely, as we trace the production process of an intelligence product, we want to examine the quality of intermediate products in the process. Thus the proposed solution consists of two components: (1) a set of metrics for assessing the quality of information products throughout the production process; and (2) a mechanism for enabling the verifiability of intelligence products.

14.4.1 IQ Metrics for Intelligence Products

The IC produces a variety of intelligence products for different purposes. To assure the quality of intelligence product and to continuously improve product quality, it is necessary to establish IQ metrics for these products. The metrics will provide a means of monitoring product quality over time and optimizing resources for quality improvement. At the minimum, the metrics will consist of the six attributes that have been used within the IC: accuracy, objectivity, usability, relevant, readiness, and timeliness (Brei 1996). The metrics can be further extended to include the 16 IQ dimensions (Wang and Strong 1996).

Establishing systematic metrics for each individual intelligence product is costly and inefficient. The inefficiency can be avoided if we can appropriately categorize the products, in which case we establish a set of metrics for each category of products. Garst (1989) suggests categorizing intelligence products according to the *subject* and the intended *use* (See Table 14.5).

Table 14.5. Categories of Intelligence Products

By Subject	By Use
Biographic	Research
Economic	Current
Geographic	Estimative
Military	Operational
Political	Scientific and Technical
Sociological	Warning
Scientific and Technical	
Transportation and Communications	

A product covering a certain subject is often used for different purposes or uses. For example, a *military* analysis can be used for *operational* purposes and for *research* purposes. The quality requirements for different purposes are often different. Therefore, a set of quality metrics should be established for each use of a particular category of products. We propose a quality metrics system in the form a 3-dimentional matrix, as illustrated in Fig. 14.3.

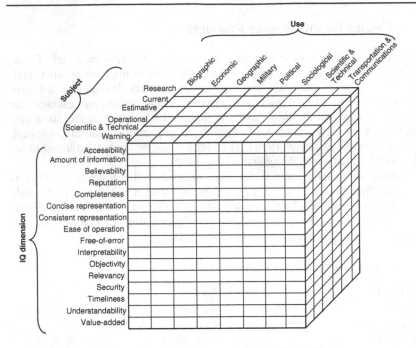

Fig. 14.3. Metrics for Intelligence Products and their Different Uses

For purposes of benchmarking and quality management, every intelligence product can be measured according to the quality metrics that correspond to the *subject* and the *use* of the product.

The specific objective of this research task is to verify, and help the IC to implement, the quality metrics system. Specifically, we need to:

- determine if the categorization mechanism is appropriate
- determine what quality dimensions are appropriate
- define each selected quality dimension and design instrument for measurement
- validate the instrument and verify the overall quality metrics system

14.4.2 Verifiability of Intelligence Products

Within the Intelligence Community (IC), it is desirable that the statements in a finished intelligence product are verifiable. In the ensuring discussion, we call these statements *conclusions*. A careful examination of this criterion reveals that there are three kinds of verifiability:

- Capability to show the information source and the analytical processes that lead to the conclusions. We call this capability *traceability*.

- Capability to show whether the information from the source reflects the real world situation, i.e., whether the information reflects an objective fact of the real world.
- Capability to show whether the information from the source reflects the actual perceptions about a real world situation. That is, suppose different entities have different perceptions about a fact, the information represents the true perception of each entity.

This study focuses on the *traceability* aspect of *verifiability*. The other two aspects rely on traceability. Because not all information is used for analysis, traceability will help to reduce cost of verifying information validity in terms of real world state or the perceived states.

14.4.3 Objectives and Plan

The primary objective of this study is to develop a methodology that can help improve the quality of the finished intelligence product. Specifically, the methodology will enable the IC to:

- include quality indicators in the finished intelligence products to provide an objective verifiable level of confidence about the conclusions; and
- allow consumers and analysts to trace the sources and the analytical processes that lead to the conclusions.

Appropriate quality indicators can help the consumers to avoid misinterpretation of the finished intelligence products. Traceability is an important mechanism for improving the quality of the finished intelligence products. With traceability, the IC can diagnose the entire production process to pinpoint the elements that cause intelligence failure, identify the bottlenecks that need further improvement, and optimize resources to improve the overall efficiency of intelligence production.

The investigation is driven by the following set of questions:

- Does the existing intelligence production process capture information that would enable traceability? Is it done systematically or in an ad-hoc fashion?
- Suppose the existing production process systematically captures information for traceability, is it done manually? How long would it take to trace from a conclusion to the sources of information that contribute to the conclusion?
- To what extent can computerization of the provision of traceability information help improve quality and productivity?
- How do we provide information to derive quality indicators in finished intelligence products?

We propose three tasks to address the issues raised by the questions:

- Investigate the existing process to identify the opportunities for quality improvement.

- Develop a methodology of enabling traceability and the provision of quality indicators in finished intelligence products.
- Verify the methodology through proof-of-concept prototyping.

Investigation of Existing Process

We propose to identify several cases to hand-simulate the existing process of intelligence production. The simulation results will allow us to identify the opportunities of modifying the process to improve the quality of finished intelligence products. It also provides the baseline information for benchmarking the effectiveness of the methodology that we will develop.

Several important questions to ask include:

- Given a finished intelligence product, does the consumer know the level of confidence in the conclusions?
- If the consumer asks for a confidence level, how much effort is involved to give a good answer?
- Can confidence level be quantified? Or what are the best ways of describing confidence level?
- If the consumer would like to know how a conclusion is derived, how much effort is involved in identifying the sources and analytical processes that lead to the conclusion?
- How is traceability information captured? Explicitly and systematically, or the opposite?
- Is the traceability information easy to query and manipulate? By hand or using computer tools?

Methodology for Traceability and Quality Indicators

We propose to develop the methodology by adapting the TDQM framework and its relevant concepts and methods identified earlier to fit the specific needs of the IC.

The methodology will be applied to the set of cases identified in the preceding step to hand-simulate the improved process. The results should allow us to estimate the costs and benefits of the proposed changes to the existing process. We anticipate that the benefits will outweigh the costs, hence demonstrating the feasibility of applying the methodology to the IC.

Similar questions can be asked to determine the capability of traceability and providing quality indicators in the finished intelligence products.

Tool Development

Certain tasks of the proposed methodology can be assisted with software tools. For example, the methodology requires the storage and manipulation of traceability information. To assist with this task, we plan to create a suite of tools for visualizing production process and processing data quality related information.

14.5 Conclusion

The IC has been following the Kent doctrine in its quality assurance practice. While helpful, the doctrine operates at a very high level and heavily relies on an analyst's experience to ensure the quality of finished intelligence products. The existing evaluation framework only partially captures quality dimensions that concern the end users.

The IC can improve the quality of its intelligence products by incorporating an effective IQ framework. After reviewing the TDQM framework, we discussed the relevance of the framework with the IC's quality enhancement efforts. We also identified several concepts and methods useful to the IC. The proposed solution focuses on two areas: 1) developing comprehensive quality metrics for the IC; and 2) developing a methodology and a set of technologies to enable verifiability of intelligence products.

With the proposed solution, we anticipate that intelligence production process will become more visible to the end consumers, and the quality of the products can be examined more easily. Consequently, the finished intelligence products will be more useful because the users can easily assess the confidence level of the produces and use the products more appropriately.

Future work will evaluate the proposed solution to identify areas for enhancement, e.g., incorporating entity resolution methods (Talburt et al. 2005; Wang and Madnick 1989) to improve quality of information from multiple sources. Since we have only focused on the traceability aspect so far, future work will develop mechanisms to facilitate the improvement of the validity aspects.

14.6 Exercises

1. Briefly describe the TDQM framework and discuss how it can be applied to the IC as it tries to improve the quality of intelligence products.
2. Explain the concept of Verifiable Intelligence Product and discuss why it is important especially when complex processes and algorithms (e.g., data mining) are used to produce the final intelligence product.
3. Survey the literature and summarize your findings about techniques and products that enable traceability of information products.

14.7 References

Brei WS (1996) Getting Intelligence Right: The Power of Logical Procedure. Occasional Paper #2, Joint Military Intelligence College (JMIC).
Buneman P, Khanna S, Tan WW (2001) Why and Where: A Characterization of Data Provenance. In Jan Van den Bussche and Victor Vianu, editors, *International Conference on Database Theory*, pages 316-330. Springer, LNCS 1973.

CIA Directorate of Intelligence (1997) A Compendium of Analytic Tradecarft Notes. http://www.au.af.mil/au/awc/awcgate/cia/tradecraft_notes/contents.htm

Clauser JK, Weir SM (1975) Intelligence Research Methodology, An Introduction to Techniques and Procedures for Conducting Research in Defense Intelligence. Defense Intelligence School.

Deming WE (1982) Out of the Crisis. MIT Press, Cambridge, MA.

Davis J (1992) The Challenge of Opportunity Analysis. Intelligence Monograph. CSI 92-003U, Center for the Study of Intelligence.

Davis J (1995) Intelligence Changes in Analytic Tradecraft in CIA's Directorate of Intelligence. CIA Directorate of Intelligence.

Davis J (2002) The Sherman Kent Center for Intelligence Analysis. Vol. 1, No. 5, CIA.

Directorate of Intelligence, Central Intelligence Agency (1997) A Compendium of Analytic Tradecrafts Notes. Vol. 1.

Garst RD (1989) Components of Intelligence. In A Handbook of Intelligence Analysis (Ed, Garst, R. D.), Defense Intelligence College, Washington, D.C., pp. 1-32.

Harris G (1989) Evaluating Intelligence Evidence. In A Handbook of Intelligence Analysis (Ed, Garst, R. D.), Defense Intelligence College, Washington, DC, pp. 33-48.

Hulnick AS (1988) Managing Intelligence Analysis: Strategies for Playing the End Game. International Journal of Intelligence and CounterIntelligence, 2(3), 321-343.

Jiang L, Borgida A, Topaloglou T, Mylopoulos J (2007) Data Quality by Design: A Goal-Oriented Approach. The 12th International Conference on Information Quality, 249-263.

Jones MD (1995) The Thinkers Toolkit: 14 Powerful Techniques for Problem Solving. Three Rivers Press, New York.

Juran J, Godfrey AB (1999) Juran's Quality Handbook 5th Ed. McGraw-Hill, New York, NY.

Kahn BK, Strong DM, Wang RY (2002) Information Quality Benchmarks: Product and Service Performance. Communications of the ACM, 45(4): 184-192.

Krizan L (1999) Intelligence Essentials for Everyone. Occasional Paper #6, Joint Military Intelligence College.

Lee Y, Strong D (2003-4) Knowing-why about Data Processes and Data Quality. Journal of Management Information Systems, 20(3), 13-39.

Lee Y, Strong D, Kahn B, Wang Y (2002) AIMQ: a methodology for information quality assessment. Information & Management 40, 133-146.

Madnick S, Wang RY (1992) Introduction to Total Data Quality Management (TDQM) Research Program. TDQM-92-01, Total Data Quality Management Program, MIT Sloan School of Management.

Mathams RH (1995) The Intelligence Analyst's Notebook. In Strategic Intelligence: Theory and Application (Eds, Dearth, D. H. and Goodden, R. T.), JMITC, Washington, DC, pp. 77-96.

Mosier D (2005) Data/Information Quality in Intelligence Community. SAIC Whitepaper.

Pipino L, Lee Y, Wang. R (2002) Data quality assessment. Communications of the ACM 45, 4, 211-218.

Shankaranarayan G, Ziad M, Wang RY (2003) Managing Data Quality in Dynamic Decision Environment: An Information Product Approach. Journal of Database Management, 14(4), 14-32.

Shankaranarayan G, Wang RY (2007) IPMAP Research Status and Direction. The 12th International Conference on Information Quality, 500-517.

Strong DM, Lee YW, Wang RY (1997) Data Quality in Context. Communications of the ACM, 40(5), 103-110.

Talburt J, Morgan C, Talley T, Archer K (2005) Using Commercial Data Integration Technologies to Improve the Quality of Anonymous Entity Resolution in the Public Sector. 10th International Conference on Information Quality, Cambridge, MA, 133-142.

Wang RY (1998) A Product Perspective on Total Data Quality Management. Communications of the ACM, **41**(2), 58-65.

Wang RY, Kong HB, Madnick SE (1993) Data Quality Requirements Analysis and Modeling. In Proceedings of the 9th International Conference of Data Engineering, 670-677.

Wang RY, Lee YW, Pipino LL, Strong DM (1998) Manage Your Information as a Product. Sloan Management Review, **39**(4), 95-105.

Wang RY, Madnick SE (1989) The Inter-database Instance Identification Problem in Integrating Autonomous Systems. In Proceedings of the 5th International Conference on Data Engineering, 46-55.

Wang RY, Madnick SE (1990) A PolyGen Model for Heterogeneous Database Systems: The Source Tagging Perspective. In Proceedings of the 16th VLDB Conference, Brisbane, Australia, 519-538.

Wang RY, Reddy M, Kon H (1995) Toward Quality Data: An Attribute-based Approach. Decision Support Systems, **13**(3-4), 349-372.

Wang RY, Strong DM (1996) Beyond Accuracy: What Data Quality Means to Data Consumers. Journal of Management Information Systems, **12**(4), 5-34.

Widom J (2005) Trio: A System for Integrated Management of Data, Accuracy, and Lineage. In Proceedings of the Second Biennial Conference on Innovative Data Systems Research (CIDR '05), Pacific Grove, California.

15 Interactive Visualization of Large High-Dimensional Datasets

Wei Ding[1] and Ping Chen[2]

[1] Department of Computer Science
University of Massachusetts Boston
Boston, MA, USA

[2] Department of Computer and Mathematical Sciences,
University of Houston Downtown
Houston, TX, USA

15.1 Introduction

Nowadays many companies and public organizations use powerful database systems for collecting and managing information. Huge amount of data records are often accumulated within a short period of time. Valuable information is embedded in these data, which could help discover interesting knowledge and significantly assist in decision-making process. However, human beings are not capable of understanding so many data records which often have lots of attributes. The need for automated knowledge extraction is widely recognized, and leads to a rapidly developing market of data analysis and knowledge discovery tools.

In spite of many advances from knowledge discovery and data mining area, the human eye-brain system remains the best existing pattern recognition device for information extraction, and human analysis and insight are still the most important way to interpret and utilize the knowledge obtained from automated data mining tools. Data visualization transforms data into direct views and plays a very important role in knowledge discovery. Data visualization is a rapidly expanding research area, and its techniques range from simple histogram plots to large 3D visual reality system.

15.1.1 Related work

Traditionally, many simple methods are designed to render small amount of data or statistical features of big datasets, such as histogram, pie chart, tree, etc. To

Y. Chan et al. (eds.), *Data Engineering*, International Series in Operations
Research & Management Science 132, DOI 10.1007/978-1-4419-0176-7_15,
© Springer Science+Business Media, LLC 2010

visualize more complex data, modern scientific visualization utilizes more advanced techniques. Visualization techniques, such as EXVIS (Grinstein et al. 1989), Chernoff Faces (Chernoff 1973), icons (Buja et al. 1996; Levkowitz 1996) and m-Arm Glyph (Pickett and Grinstein 1996), are called glyph-based methods (Ebert et al. 2000; Wenzel et al. 1988). Glyphs are graphical entities whose visual features, such as shape, orientation, color and size, are used to encode attributes of an underlying dataset, and glyphs are often used for interactive exploration of datasets (Enns 1990; Julesz and Bergen 1983; Wegenkittl et al. 1997; Wong and Bergeron 1997). Glyph-based techniques range from representation via individual icons to the formation of texture and color patterns through the overlay of many thousands of glyphs (Healey and Enns 1999; Triesman and Gormican 1988; Vlachos et al. 2002). Chernoff used facial characteristics to represent information in a multivariate dataset (Chernoff 1973). Each dimension of the dataset encodes one facial feature, such as nose, eyes, eyebrows, mouth, or jowls. Glyphmaker proposed by Foley and Ribarsky visualizes multivariate datasets in an interactive fashion (Foley and Ribarsky 1994; Ward 1994). Levkowitz described a prototype system for combining colored squares to produce patterns to represent an underlying multivariate dataset (Laidlaw et al. 1998). In (Levkowitz 1996) an icon encodes six dimensions by six lines of different colors within a square icon. Levkowitz et al. (Healey and Enns 1999) described the combination of textures and colors in a visualization system. The m-Arm Glyph by Pickett and Grinstein (Pickett and Grinstein 1996) consists of a main axis and m arms, and the length and thickness of each arm and the angles between each arm and main axis are used to encode different dimensions of a dataset. A glyph-based system for large high dimensional datasets is described (Chen et al. 2003). Here are some common shortcomings with the current visualization techniques:

- Lack of interaction with users to generate customized displays.
- Lack of integration with other data mining and knowledge discovery (KDD) tools. The goal of data visualization is to help data analysis and knowledge discovery. There are many successful techniques in KDD, and integration of these techniques will be a great benefit. In this paper we will show how clustering plays an important role in revealing interesting details of a dataset.
- Incapable to deal with large amount of data. Nowadays, a dataset can easily have millions or even billions of records. How can we visualize both local details and general overview of such datasets?
- Incapable to dynamically assign data dimensions to visual elements. Most existing methods use only one visual object to visualize one data record. When a record has lots of dimensions, the visual object becomes too complex (that is, many visual properties of this visual object have to be used) for human beings.

15.1.2 General requirements for a data visualization system

On one hand visualization is used to assist data analysis process, and it should be as automatic or intelligent as possible to minimize a user's workload. On the other hand, viewers should be able to fine tune the display manually as much as they want. A visualization system needs to transform data of different formats to visual components in a two-dimensional or three-dimensional space. An intelligent visualization process involves initial automatic analysis and rendering, and the following fine tuning and interaction with viewers. Generally a visualization system should satisfy the following requirements:

- Rendering a large dataset efficiently. As the collection and storage of data becomes more mature and cheaper, huge amount of data can be quickly accumulated, which requires that a visualization system displays data not only loyally, but also efficiently. With limited hardware resources, often approximation techniques have to be used to deal with a large dataset, and one of such methods called summary icons is discussed in Section 4.
- Rendering a high-dimensional dataset. High dimensional data is a serious challenge for any visualization system. Transforming high dimensional data to two-dimensional or three-dimensional space requires careful consideration, and such a transformation needs to be as intuitive as possible to reduce viewers' cognitive load. In Section 15.2.1.1 we give a systematic discussion on transforming data to visual elements.
- Dealing with complex data formats. Modern datasets often contain data of complex and different formats, such as numerical and categorical values. How to show them in a clear and coherent way is critical for a visualization system.

To satisfy these requirements, a visualization system needs to be interactive and have an open architecture for easy integration of other data analysis components. In the rest of this chapter, section 15.2 explains visualization process and some related problems. Section 15.3 describes general properties for an interactive visualization system. Section 15.4 discusses how to use summary icons to render large amount of data. Section 15.5 gives one case study based on a real oil exploration dataset, and conclusion is given in section 15.6.

15.2 Data Visualization Process

Data visualization is a graphic presentation of a dataset, with the goal of providing a viewer with a qualitative understanding of the embedded information in a natural and direct way. Graphic presentation involves the usage of visual objects and its elements. One visual element is one visual feature of a visual object. The visual objects (these objects are differentiated by their shapes and styles) could be: point, line, polyline, glyph, 2-D or 3-D surface, 3-D solid, image, text, etc. One visual object may have the following visual elements: color, location, shape/style, texture, size, orientation, position/motion, etc. We can divide visualization process into three stages:

- Data rendering (forward transformation) stage
- Backward transformation stage
- Knowledge extraction stage

15.2.1 Data Rendering Stage

The basic requirement for data rendering is that different values should be displayed differently, the more different the original values are, the more different they should look. There are two steps:

1. *Association step*: Associate data dimensions/columns with visual elements:

   $$F_a: D \bullet V, D = \{d_1, d_2, \ldots \ldots, d_n\}, V = \{v_1, v_2, \ldots \ldots, v_m\},$$

   where D is the set of n dimensions in a dataset, and d_i is the ith dimension in D; V is the space of m visual elements which include visual objects and their features, and v_j is the jth element in V.

   If n < m, some visual elements are shown but do not represent any information, and they unnecessarily attract the viewer's attention, so usually this case is undesirable.

   If n > m, at least one visual element need encode two or more data dimensions, which will make the display hard to understand, so this case is seldom used.

   If n = m, one visual element represents one dimension of a dataset. This case is used by most visualization methods. In the rest of this paper, we only consider this approach.

2. *Transformation step*: In this step we will choose a transformation function for each dimension-visual element pair which maps each value in that dimension to a member in that visual element domain. The transformation function can be expressed as:

   $$F_i: d_i \rightarrow v_i, (i=1, 2, \ldots \ldots, n)$$

   where d_i is the set of values of ith dimension, and v_i is the set of domain members of ith visual element.

Association and transformation steps are straightforward and it seems that we can make almost arbitrary choice. However, a visualization system is a human-computer system, which brings two constraints:

1. Human eyes can not distinguish very small visual differences, so a visualization system should not use very small visual differences to carry any information.
2. Human eyes have difficulty to handle a display with overwhelmingly rich visual features, which make understanding and extraction of information difficult and hurt the motivation of visualization.

These constraints require a visualization system designer to choose association and transformation functions carefully, and in next section we will discuss some details.

15.2.1.1 Choosing visual objects and features

Choosing visual features is very important to a visualization system. In human visual system some visual properties are processed preattentively, without the need for focused attention. Typically, tasks that can be performed on large multi-element displays in less than 200 milliseconds to 250 milliseconds are considered preattentive (Levkowitz 1996). Eye movements take at least 200 milliseconds to initiate, and random locations of the elements in the display ensure that attention can not be prefocused on any particular location, but usually they can be completed with very little effort. This means that certain visual information is processed in parallel by the low-level visual system. If we avoid feature conjunction which inhibits a user's low-level visual system, we can develop tools making use of preattentive vision, which can offer a number of important advantages:

- Visual analysis of preattentive tasks is rapid (within 200 milliseconds or less), accurate and relatively effortless.
- The time required for preattentive task analysis is independent of display size, so more data elements in a display will not increase the time required to analyze the display. This property is especially important in data mining field that usually involves huge amount of data.

15.2.1.2 Non-uniform data distribution problem

In this section we will discuss why a clustering step is necessary before data is visualized. Within a dataset, it is common that the data values are clustered along one or several dimensions, which means that data distribution is not uniform. The problem of non-uniform data distribution has to be handled for better visualization quality, which is shown by the following example.

Suppose there is a one-dimensional dataset, $\{1, 1, 1, 1, 1, 5, 10, 10, 100\}$, and we choose the color of icon "bar" to represent it, and our transformation function is:

- $\{value | 1 \leq value \leq 10\} \rightarrow$ dark gray
- $\{value | 11 \leq value \leq 20\} \rightarrow$ gray

- ... ...
- {value|91 ≤ value ≤ 100} → light gray

Fig. 15.1. The problem of non-uniform data distribution

The dataset will be visualized as Figure 15.1, although the visualization system can use ten different colors, most icons are blue because most data values fall into the interval [1, 10]. We can not tell the difference of these data values from the display, and such a visualization is less effective. We could use more colors, but too many colors may hurt visualization quality as we explained in Section 15.2.1.1. Instead, a better option is to find the data clusters first for each dimension i. For one-dimensional data clustering we have plenty of clustering algorithms to choose from, such as BIRCH (Zhang et al. 1996), Fractal Clustering (Barbara and Chen 2003), etc.

Let k_i be the number of clusters for the ith dimension, we divide v_i (set of members of ith visual element used to render i^{th} dimension) into k_i clusters, i.e.

$$v_i = \{v_{ij} \mid 1 \leq j \leq k_i\}$$

The transformation between the ith data dimension and its visual element will be determined according to the cluster which the data value belongs to. c_{ij} denotes the jth cluster of data in the ith dimension, and we have:

$$C_i = \{c_{ij}\} \, (1 \leq i \leq n, 1 \leq j \leq k_i)$$

where C_i is the set of clusters in dimension i, n is the number of dimensions in a dataset, k_i is the number of clusters in dimension i. We divide members in visual element V_i into k_i groups:

$$V_i = \{v_{ij}\} \, (1 \leq i \leq n, 1 \leq j \leq k_i)$$

where v_{ij} is a group of members in visual element i. Number of members in v_{ij} should be proportional to number of members of c_{ij}. For example, if we choose visual element "bar size", as shown in Figure 15.2, we could divide different sized bars into three groups, and each group has three members of visual element "bar size".

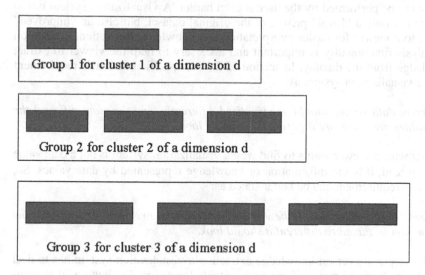

Group 1 for cluster 1 of a dimension d

Group 2 for cluster 2 of a dimension d

Group 3 for cluster 3 of a dimension d

Fig. 15.2. Members of "bar size" are divided into three groups with three members

The transformation between data dimensions and visual elements is:

$$F_{ij} \colon C_{ij} \rightarrow V_{ij} \; (1 \leq i \leq n, \, 1 \leq j \leq k_i)$$

With a clustering step we can assign members of visual elements more reasonably to data values, and a visualization system is able to reveal more information about a dataset.

15.2.2 Backward Transformation Stage

Viewers need to understand the association and transformation steps during the "data rendering" stage, and be able to reverse the transformed display and restore the original picture in their mind. Such a backward transformation process is done solely by human beings, so it cannot be too complex. This requirement makes a complex association or transformation in the "data rendering" stage infeasible, and it is why most visualization systems associate one visual element to only one data dimension.

15.2.3 Knowledge Extraction Stage

Rendering millions of icons is computationally expensive, and interpretation and analysis to be performed by the user is even harder. A visualization system has to provide not only a "loyal" picture of the original dataset, but also an "improved" picture to a viewer for easier interpretation and knowledge extraction. Integration of analysis functionality is important and necessary to help the viewer to extract knowledge from the display. In section 15.2.1 we specified the basic requirement about a visualization system as:

"Different data values should be visualized differently, and the more different the data values are, the more different they should look."

But what a viewer wants to find with a visualization system is not a data value itself. Instead, it is the information or knowledge represented by data values. So, the above requirement can be better stated as:

"Different information should be visualized differently, and the more different the information is, the more different it should look."

To help a viewer on knowledge extraction a visualization system has to deal with the problem of non-uniform knowledge/information distribution. It is common in some datasets or fields that a small difference of a value could mean a big difference, and the knowledge and information is not distributed uniformly within data values. A user would like a visualization system to be able to show these knowledge differences clearly. To be specific, the same difference in data values may not necessarily be rendered by identical difference in visual elements on the screen. Instead the difference representing more information should be displayed more significantly to get attention from a viewer. We give an example as follows. Suppose we have a one-dimensional dataset of human body temperatures,

{36.5, 37.0, 37.5, 38.0, 38.5, 39.0, 39.5, 40.0, 40.5, 41.0, 41.5, 42.0}

This dataset is uniformly distributed. We still use a bar's color to visualize the dataset, and after a clustering step our transformation function will map the values uniformly since the dataset has a uniform distribution:

- {value|36.0 ≤ value < 38.0} → light gray
- {value|38.0 ≤ value < 40.0} → gray
- {value|40.0 ≤ value ≤ 42.0} → dark gray

The dataset is visualized in Figure 15.3. The visualization system visualizes the data loyally. Both 40.0 and 42.0 are represented by dark gray, but as human body temperatures 40.0 and 42.0 could mean a difference of life and death, and this important information is lost. This example clearly shows how important it is to integrate domain knowledge in a visualization system. Such an integration can be achieved through interaction between viewers and a visualization system which will be discussed in next section.

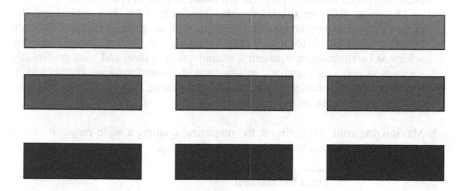

Fig. 15.3. The problem of non-uniform knowledge distribution

15.3 Interactive Visualization Model

In Figure 15.4 we give an interactive visualization model which has the following properties:

1. Interaction: From the example in Section 15.2.3, it is clear that integration of domain knowledge into a visualization system is very important due to the problem of non-uniform knowledge distribution. To a visualization system integration of domain knowledge can be achieved by choosing proper association function and transformation function during visualization process. However, there is no universal technique for all fields, datasets or users, and a visualization system should be interactive and provide a mechanism for views to adjust or change association and transformation functions during visualization process. Each dataset or field has to be studied individually and visualized interactively before its important information can be revealed, which can only be performed by domain experts. By interaction a viewer can guide a visualization system step by step to display what he is interested in more and more clearly.

2. Correctness: We propose the following criteria for correct visualization:

   a) If possible a visualization system should show different dimensions of a dataset differently through different visual objects or visual elements of one visual object.

b) The more different the values are, the more differently they should be rendered. Since we may not know the distribution of a dataset, assigning data values to visual elements/properties may not make full usage of available visual elements/properties, a clustering step is preferred.

c) The more different the information represented by data values are, the more differently they should be rendered. A distinguished visual difference between different information can help viewers better, which can be achieved by interaction between a visualization system and viewers. In this interaction process, viewers can fine-tune the transformation between data values and visual elements, and domain knowledge is obtained and reflected through a more customized display.

3. Maximizing rule: To optimize the rendering quality, a wide range of visual objects/elements should be used as default setting.

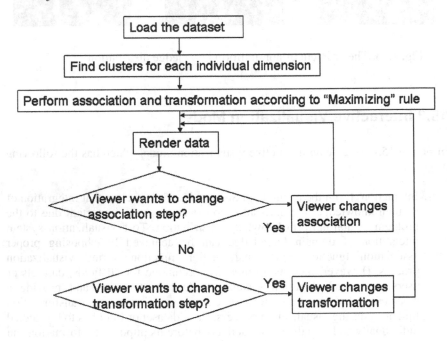

Fig. 15. 4. Interactive visualization system model

15.4 Utilizing Summary Icons

In this section we discuss how to render a large dataset effectively. The first option is to simply display all data records, but this approach has the following disadvantages:

1. Rendering a large number of icons at one time will make the icons indistinguishable;
2. Rendering a huge set is computationally expensive.

The second option to visualize a large amount of data is sampling. We can render only a sample of original dataset if:

1. A viewer specifies a value range for each dimension, only icons in this range can be displayed.
2. A viewer specifies the types of dimensions/icons to be displayed.
3. A viewer chooses a sampling rate and displays data records randomly.
4. A viewer uses some domain-related criteria, such as choosing data between two horizons in geophisical data.

However, sampling has the disadvantage of potentially missing infrequently occurring details of a dataset, which may be of user's interests. Also sampling cannot provide an overall picture of a dataset.

To display the local details and overall context of a dataset at the same time, we use summarization. We use "summary" icons to display summarized data for "uninteresting" parts of a dataset, and regular icons to display the "interesting" parts of a dataset which will show all details. One feature of a summary icon does not represent one field in a data record, instead it represents a statistical parameter (summary) of the fields from multiple underlying data records, such as sum, mean, median. By this way, we can build a hierarchical structure of icons as in Figure 15.5. An icon in low level represents only one record, and an icon in high level will be a summary of icons/records below it. The icons on the high level are more general, and they summarize information from a lot of records. The icons on the low level are more specialized or local, and they represent and visualize only one record. We show how to use summary icons in visualization by an example.

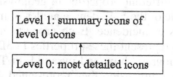

Fig. 15.5. Hierarchical structure of icons

We still use the one-dimensional human body temperature set we displayed in Figure 15.2. But we use summary icons to summarize some data values shown in Figure 15.6. The left figure in Figure 15.6 shows two level-one summary icons, the top bar represents the average of first three values and middle bar represents the average of values 4, 5, and 6. The right figure in Figure 15.6 uses one summary icon to represent the average of all data values in this set. Summarization can be very flexible, we can assign higher weights to regular icons which are more interesting, so they will be shown more significantly than summary icons, and it is easier for a viewer to notice these interesting data.

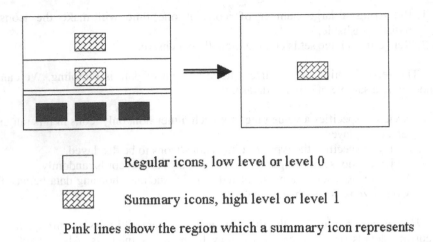

Regular icons, low level or level 0

Summary icons, high level or level 1

Pink lines show the region which a summary icon represents

Fig. 15.6. An example of summary icons

15.5 A Case Study

In this case study we visualize a large dataset that encodes multiple data fields at a single spatial location. This set of 12-dimensional geophysical data was obtained with man-made earthquakes to discover oil underground and recorded in nine files. Each file includes some headers and 6,172,871 one-dimensional records. These records are data samples of signals from 111 X 111 locations within 2 seconds after an explosion. The sampling rate is 4 milliseconds. Data, recorded in the 9 files, represents three different properties in geophysical science, which are interval velocity, amplitude of the 5-45 degree angles of incidence, and amplitude of the 35-55 degree angles of incidence. Each property has three dimensions (nine dimensions in total). To represent these properties in 3D space, we used three different 3D icons: parallelogram, box, and pyramid. In Table 15.1, we list features of each icon and the data dimension they represented. In Figure 15.7 six records are rendered for illustration purposes. We do not display any records with fast interval velocity equal to 0, and the number of records we need to show is reduced to 4,262,747. The loading time is 149 seconds. View rendering (move, rotate, zoom) can be done in real time. In Figure 15.8 we performed clustering for each data dimension and displayed data with summary icons, so a viewer can have a general idea about the data directly. If a user is interested in a specific area, he can drill to that area and have a detailed display similarly as Figure 15.7.

Icons	Visual features	Data dimensions
parallelogram		Interval Velocity
	size	Fast Interval Velocity
	orientation	Azimuth of the fast interval velocity
	color	(Fast-Slow) Interval Velocity
box		Amplitude of the 5-45 degree angles of incidence
	size	Large Amplitude Variation with Offset (AVO) Gradient
	orientation	Azimuth of the large AVO Gradient
	color	Azimuthal variation in the Gradient (Large minus small)
pyramid		Amplitude of the 35-55 degree angles of incidence
	size	Large Amplitude Variation with Offset Gradient
	orientation	Azimuth of the large AVO Gradient
	color	Azimuthal variation in the Gradient (Large minus small)

Table 15.1 Association between dimensions and visual elements

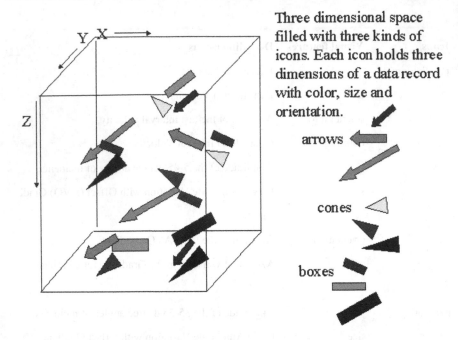

Three dimensional space filled with three kinds of icons. Each icon holds three dimensions of a data record with color, size and orientation.

arrows

cones

boxes

Fig. 15.7. A sample figure to visualize a twelve-dimensional dataset with six records. Each icon uses color, size and orientation to represent three dimensions of a data record, three icons located in the same position can represent nine dimensions of a data record, the position itself can encode three dimensions, so a group of three icons can represent twelve dimensions. In total there are six icon groups, which represent six records in the dataset.

In Figure 15.9 the viola reflector is shown as the gray-wire mesh grid, and the icon shown is the interval velocity icon, which holds three dimensions: fast interval velocity; azimuth of the fast interval velocity, and magnitude of the Vfast-Vslow interval velocity (the azimuthal variation of the interval velocity). A stress plume associated with a bend in the fault can be detected by a viewer right away.

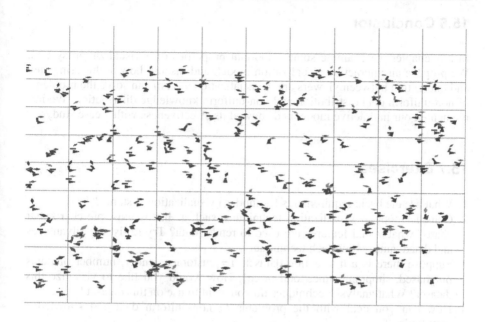

Fig. 15.8. A screen capture of the display which visualizes the samples of a dataset (Grids are drawn to help locate icons.)

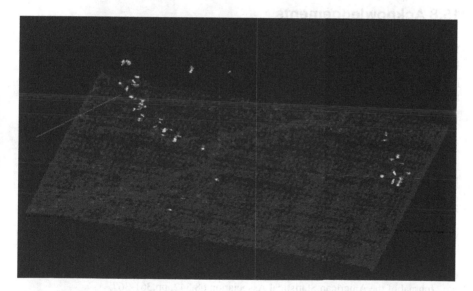

Fig. 15.9. A screen capture with a stress plume associated with a bend in the fault pointed out by the gray line

15.6 Conclusion

In this chapter we examine some important properties of a visualization system. We propose an interactive visualization model, and discuss how a clustering step and interaction between viewers and a visualization system can solve the problems of non-uniform data distribution and non-uniform knowledge distribution. We implemented our interactive model and showed its effectiveness with a case study.

15.7 Exercises

1. What are the basic requirements for modern visualization systems?
2. Consider popular visualization techniques, such as histograms, pie charts, bar charts, what visual features are used to render data? Try to list the advantages and disadvantages for each technique.
3. Suppose there is a transaction dataset, T={customer gender, number of items purchased, shopping time, total price}. How would you like to visualize this dataset? What analysis techniques do you want to use on this dataset?
4. How can you deal with the problems of non-uniform data and knowledge distribution?

15.8 Acknowledgements

We gratefully thank Devon Energy for permission to show their data. We thank Bob Vest and 3DSEIS software for being our 3D seismic interpretation software package. Also we would like to express our gratitude toward the referees who gave detailed and valuable suggestions for the improvement of this chapter.

15.9 References

Barbara D, Chen P (2003) Using Self-Similarity to Cluster Large datasets, Data Mining and Knowledge Discovery 7(2): 123-152.
Buja A, Cook D, and Swayne D F (1996) Interactive high-dimensional data visualization. Journal of Computational and Graphical Statistics 5, pp. 78-99.
Chen P, Hu C, Ding W, Lynn H. Yves S (2003) Icon-based Visualization of Large High-Dimensional Datasets, Third IEEE International Conference on Data Mining, Melbourne, Florida, November 19-22.
Chernoff H. (1973) The use of facesto represent points in k-dimensional space graphically. Journal of the American Statistical Association 68,342, pp.361-367.
Ebert D, Rohrer R, Shaw C, Panda P, Kukla D, Roberts D (2000) Procedural shape generation for multi-dimensional data visualization. Computers and Graphics, Volume 24, Issue 3, Pages 375-384.
Enns JT, (1990) Three-Dimensional Features that Pop Out in Visual Search. In Visual Search, Brogan, D., Ed., Taylor and Francis, New York, pages 37-45.

Foley J, Ribarsky W (1994) Next-generation data visualization tools. Scientific Visualization: Advances and Challenges, L. Rosenblum, Ed. Academic Press, San Diego, California, pages 103-127.

Grinstein GG, Pickett RM, Williams M (1989) EXVIS: An Exploratory Data Visualization Environment. Proceedings of Graphics Interface '89 pages 254-261, London, Canada.

Healey CG, Enns JT (1999) Large Datasets at a Glance: Combining Textures and Colors in Scientific Visualization. IEEE Transactions on Visualization and Computer Graphics, Volume 5, Issue 2.

Julesz B, Bergen JR (1983) Textons, the Fundamental Elements in Preattentive Vision and Perception of Textures. The Bell System Technical Journal 62, 6, pages 1619-1645.

Laidlaw DH, Ahrens ET, Kremers D, Avalos MJ, Jacobs RE, Readhead C (1998) Visualizing diffusion tensor images of the mouse spinal cord. Proceedings of Visualization '98, pages 127-134.

Levkowitz H (1996) Color Icons: Merging Color and Texture Perception for Integrated Visualization of Multiple Parameter, Proceedings of IEEE Visualization'91 Conference, San Diego, CA.

Pickett RM, Grinstein GG (1996) Iconographics Displays for Visualizing Multidimensional Data. IEEE Conference on Systems, Man and Cybernetics.

Triesman A, Gormican S (1988) Feature Analysis in Early Vision: Evidence from Search Asymmetries. Psychological Review 95, 1, pages 15-48.

Vlachos M, Domeniconi C, Gunopulos D, Kollios G, Koudas N, (2002) Non-Linear Dimensionality Reduction Techniques for Classification and Visualization. KDD '02, Edmonton, Canada.

Ward MO (1994) Xmdvtool: Integrating multiple methods for visualizing multivariate data. In Proceedings of Visualization '94, pages 326-333, October.

Wegenkittl R, Löffelmann H, Gröller E (1997) Visualizing the behavior of higher dimensional dynamical systems. Proceedings of the conference on Visualization '97, , Phoenix, Arizona, United States.

Wenzel EM, Wightman FL, Foster SH (1988) Development of a three-dimensional auditory display system. ACM SIGCHI Bulletin, v.20 n.2, pages 52-57.

Wong P, Bergeron R (1997) 30 years of multidimensional multivariate visualization, In G. M. Nielson, H. Hagan, and H. Muller, editors, Scientific Visualization Overviews, Methodologies and Techniques, Los Alamitos, CA.

Zhang T, Ramakrishnan R, Livny M (1996) BIRCH: An efficient data clustering method for very large databases. In SIGMOD'96, Montreal, Canada.

16 Image Watermarking Based on Pyramid Decomposition with CH Transform

R. Kountchev[1], M. Milanova[2], Vl. Todorov[3], and R. Kountcheva[3]

[1] Department of Radio Communications, Technical University of Sofia,
Boul. Kl. Ohridsky 8, Sofia 1000, Bulgaria

[2] Department of Computer Science, University of Arkansas at Little Rock,
Little Rock, AR, USA

[3] T&K Engineering Co., Mladost 3, POB 12, Sofia 1712, Bulgaria

16.1. Introduction

The new method for digital image watermarking, presented in this chapter, could be used for intellectual property right protection of digital still images of any kind (natural, scanned documents, computer graphics, etc.). The method is suitable for distance learning applications; access control for medical or biometric information in corresponding databases; detection of forgeries and illegal distribution of electronic or scanned documents; data hiding in medical, cartographic, and other images; authorized contents editing; etc.

The widely known methods for digital image watermarking are classified in the following major groups by Arnold et al. (2003), Barni and Bartolini (2004), Cox et al. (2002), Furht (2006), Katzenbeisser and Petitcolas (2000) and Tewfik (2000), as follows:

- In the spatial domain: Methods with LSB (Least Significant Bit) substitution, correlation methods, methods based on pseudorandom transforms (Error diffusion), spread spectrum systems, etc.

- In the frequency domain: Methods based on change of the amplitudes of selected spectrum coefficients, obtained using DCT, Wavelet, DFT, Fourier-Mellin or Hadamard transform with phase modulation of a part of the calculated coefficients, etc.

Since the phase modulation is more resistant than the amplitude one with respect to noises (i.e. – to forgery attempts), in accordance with Falkowski and Lim

Y. Chan et al. (eds.), *Data Engineering*, International Series in Operations
Research & Management Science 132, DOI 10.1007/978-1-4419-0176-7_16,
© Springer Science+Business Media, LLC 2010

(2000) and O'Ruanaidh et al. (1996), it has definite advantages and is accepted as a basic approach in this work.

In the new method, described below, the processed image is represented in the frequency domain by a spectrum pyramid and in the spatial domain - by the so-called "Inverse Difference Pyramid" (IDP). The pyramid's consecutive decomposition layers comprise the values of the Complex Hadamard Transform (CHT) coefficients. A new matrix investigated by Mironov, Kountchev and Mirchev (Mironov et al. 2007) is used for their calculation. Specific feature of the matrix is that it is arranged in accordance with the number of sign changes of the elements in its rows. The phases of the complex spectrum coefficients selected satisfying definite threshold and zone requirements are modified with the watermark data. The phase modification is limited up to several degrees (usually no more than 10). The Inverse Complex Hadamard Transform (ICHT) is then applied for all decomposition levels, and the watermarked image is obtained in the result.

16.2. Algorithm for multi-layer image watermarking

16.2.1. Resistant watermarking

The algorithm is aimed at the embedding of multi-layer resistant watermark in halftone or color bmp images. For this, the original image is presented with the matrix $[B(N)]$ of size $N \times N$ elements ($N = 2^n$); then, the matrix is transformed in a spectrum pyramid (SP), obtained with 2D Complex Hadamard Transform (2D-CHT) as investigated by Kountchev et al. (2003, 2005, 2006, 2007) and Kountchev, Todorov and Kountcheva (2007). The 2D-CHT is performed using a new, "ordered" complex Hadamard matrix. Unlike the natural matrix, this new one ensures higher concentration of the discrete spectrum energy in the low-frequency area (Mironov, Kountchev and Mirchev, 2007). The watermark embedding comprises the following steps:

Step 1: For the initial decomposition layer ($p = 0$), which corresponds with the top of the spectrum pyramid, the ordered 2D-CHT is calculated as:

$$[S_0'(2^n)] = [CH_0'(2^n)][B(2^n)][CH_0'(2^n)] \tag{16.1}$$

Here $[CH_0'(2^n)]$ is the ordered matrix of size $2^n \times 2^n$, used for the 2D-CHT of the processed image, and $[S_0'(2^n)]$ is the two-dimensional transform of same size, which represents its' discrete spectrum. The matrix $[CH_0'(2^n)]$ is defined using the natural complex Hadamard matrix $[CH_0(2^n)]$, the elements of which are calculated in accordance with the relation:

$$ch_0(t,q) = j^{tq} \, h_0(t,q) \quad \text{for } t, q = 0,1,..,2^n - 1, \tag{16.2}$$

where $j = \sqrt{-1}$, $h_0(t,q) = \begin{cases} 1 & \text{for } n=2; \\ (-1)^{\sum_{r=3}^{n} \left\lfloor \frac{t}{2^{r-1}} \right\rfloor \left\lfloor \frac{q}{2^{r-1}} \right\rfloor} & \text{for } n = 3,4,.., \end{cases}$ is the sign function

of the element (t,q) of the matrix $[CH_0(2^n)]$ for the SP layer $p = 0$, and $\lfloor \frac{*}{*} \rfloor$ is an operator, used for the calculation of the integer part obtained in result of the division. The ordered matrix $[CH_0'(2^n)]$ is obtained from the natural (not ordered) one $[CH_0(2^n)]$, rearranging it so that the number of sign changes $\Sigma_{sign}(q)$ of the elements in the row q to increase by one in every consecutive row, $(q+1)$. Then, for each $q = 0,1,..,2^n-1$ is performed:

$$1 + \Sigma_{sign}(q) = \Sigma_{sign}(q+1), \tag{16.3}$$

where:

$$\Sigma_{sign}(q) = \tfrac{1}{2} \sum_{p=0}^{2^n-2} |sign[ch_0'(p,q)] - sign[ch_0'(p+1,q)]|$$

For example, the corresponding CHT matrices for $n = 2$ ($N = 4$), defined in accordance with Eqs. (16.2) and (16.3), are:

$$[CH_0(2^n)] = \begin{bmatrix} 1 & 1 & 1 & 1 \\ 1 & j & -1 & -j \\ 1 & -1 & 1 & -1 \\ 1 & -j & -1 & j \end{bmatrix} \begin{matrix} \to 0 \\ \to 1 \\ \to 3 \\ \to 2 \end{matrix}, \quad [CH_0'(2^n)] = \begin{bmatrix} 1 & 1 & 1 & 1 \\ 1 & j & -1 & -j \\ 1 & -j & -1 & j \\ 1 & -1 & 1 & -1 \end{bmatrix} \begin{matrix} \to 0 \\ \to 1 \\ \to 2 \\ \to 3 \end{matrix}$$

At the matrices' right side is given the value of $\Sigma_{sign}(q)$ for q = 0,1,..,3. In this example, the matrix $[CH_0'(2^n)]$ is the ordered one. The transform $[S_0(4)]$, obtained with Eq. (16.1) using the matrix $[CH_0(4)]$, is:

$$[S_0(4)] = \begin{bmatrix} s_0(0,0) & s_0(0,1) & s_0(0,2) & s_0(0,3) \\ s_0(1,0) & s_0(1,1) & s_0(1,2) & s_0(1,3) \\ s_0(2,0) & s_0(2,1) & s_0(2,2) & s_0(2,3) \\ s_0(3,0) & s_0(3,1) & s_0(3,2) & s_0(3,3) \end{bmatrix}$$

In the case, when the relation presented with Eq. (16.1) is calculated with the matrix $[CH_0'(4)]$, the corresponding transform $[S_0'(4)]$ contains the same coefficients as $[S_0(4)]$, but a part of them are rearranged as follows:

$$[S_0'(4)]=\begin{bmatrix} s_0'(0,0) & s_0'(0,1) & s_0'(0,2) & s_0'(0,3) \\ s_0'(1,0) & s_0'(1,1) & s_0'(1,2) & s_0'(1,3) \\ s_0'(2,0) & s_0'(2,1) & s_0'(2,2) & s_0'(2,3) \\ s_0'(3,0) & s_0'(3,1) & s_0'(3,2) & s_0'(3,3) \end{bmatrix}=\begin{bmatrix} s_0(0,0) & s_0(0,1) & s_0(0,3) & s_0(0,2) \\ s_0(1,0) & s_0(1,1) & s_0(1,3) & s_0(1,2) \\ s_0(3,0) & s_0(3,1) & s_0(3,3) & s_0(3,2) \\ s_0(2,0) & s_0(2,1) & s_0(2,3) & s_0(2,2) \end{bmatrix}$$

In general, every spectrum matrix $[S_0'(2^n)]$ could be defined from the corresponding matrix $[S_0(2^n)]$, arranging its elements in accordance with the rule presented with Eq. (16.3).

Step 2: Low-frequency filtration of the spectrum matrix $[S_0(2^n)]$, in result of which, the retained spectrum coefficients are defined in accordance with the rule:

$$\tilde{s}_0(u,v) = l_0(u,v)s_0(u,v) = \begin{cases} s_0(u,v), & if \quad l_0(u,v)=1, \\ 0, & if \quad l_0(u,v)=0, \end{cases} \qquad (16.4)$$

where $s_0(u,v)$ are the coefficients of the transform $[S_0(2^n)]$, u and v are the corresponding discrete spatial frequencies from the 2D image spectrum in horizontal and vertical direction, and $l_0(u,v)$ are the elements of the binary matrix-mask $[L_0(2^n)]$ of size $2^n \times 2^n$, which is set in advance. This matrix is used for the selection of the high-energy coefficients $\tilde{s}_0(u,v)$ in the SP layer $p=0$. Usually, these are the low-frequency coefficients of the transform $[S_0(2^n)]$. For example, for $n = 2$ $(N = 4)$, the matrix-mask should be:

$$[L_0(4)] = \begin{bmatrix} 1 & 1 & 0 & 0 \\ 1 & 1 & 0 & 0 \\ 0 & 0 & 0 & 0 \\ 0 & 0 & 0 & 0 \end{bmatrix}$$

In this case, the retained coefficients are:

$$\tilde{s}_0(0,0) = s_0(0,0); \ \tilde{s}_0(0,1) = s_0(0,1); \ \tilde{s}_0(1,0) = s_0(1,0); \ \tilde{s}_0(1,1) = s_0(1,1).$$

The coefficients of $[S_0(2^n)]$, calculated using the matrix $[CH_0(2^n)]$ for the 2D-CHT, are defined in accordance with Eq. (16.1) by the relation:

$$s_0(u,v) = \sum_{i=0}^{2^n-1} \sum_{k=0}^{2^n-1} B(i,k) e^{j\frac{\pi}{2}(ui+vk)} h_0(u,i) h_0(v,k) \quad \text{for } u,v = 0,1,..,2^n\text{-}1, \qquad (16.5)$$

where $B(i,k)$ are the elements (pixels) of the matrix $[B(2^n)]$, which represents the original image.

For the calculation of the spectrum coefficients $s'_0(u,v)$ using the matrix $[CH'_0(2^n)]$, the coefficients are rearranged as illustrated above with the example for $N = 4$.

The basic functions of the 2D-CHT using the ordered matrix $[CH'_0(2^n)]$ ($n = 2$) are presented in Fig. 16.1.

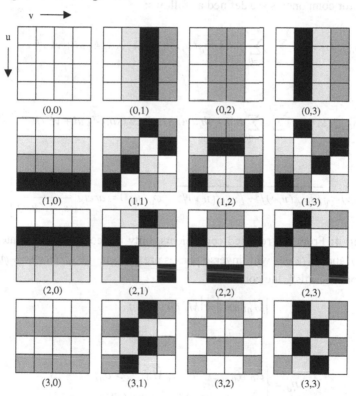

Fig. 16.1. Basic 2D-CHT functions with ordered matrix $[CH'_0(4)]$ of size $N = 4$

In this figure, the values $(+1)$ are presented as white; the values (-1) – as dark gray; the values $(+j)$ - as light gray; and the values $(-j)$, as black. The presented basic functions correspond with the spectrum coefficients $s'_0(u,v)$ of the transform $[S'_0(2^n)]$ for the SP layer $p = 0$ of the processed image $[B(2^n)]$. The basic images in Fig. 16.1 for the ordered 2D-CHT show, that for every retained coefficient $s_0'(u,v)$ there is another, complex-conjugated one $\tilde{s}_0'^*(u,v)$, defined by the relation:

$$s_0'(0,1) = s_0'^*(0,3), \ s_0'(1,0) = s_0'^*(2,0), \ s_0'(1,1) = s_0'^*(2,3)$$

Step 3: Every retained spectrum coefficient $\tilde{s}_0(u,v)$ defined by Eq. (16.5) is presented in vector form in correspondence with the relation:

$$\tilde{s}_0(u,v) = \tilde{s}_{0,Re}(u,v) + j\tilde{s}_{0,Im}(u,v) = \tilde{M}_0(u,v)e^{j\tilde{\varphi}_0(u,v)}. \tag{16.6}$$

The vector components are defined as follows:

$$\tilde{s}_{0,Re}(u,v) = \sum_{i=0}^{2^n-1} \sum_{k=0}^{2^n-1} B(i,k)h_0(u,i)h_0(v,k)\cos[\tfrac{\pi}{2}(ui+vk)], \tag{16.7}$$

$$\tilde{s}_{0,Im}(u,v) = \sum_{i=0}^{2^n-1} \sum_{k=0}^{2^m-1} B(i,k)h_0(u,i)h_0(v,k)\sin[\tfrac{\pi}{2}(ui+vk)] \tag{16.8}$$

$$\tilde{M}_0(u,v) = \sqrt{[\tilde{s}_{0,Re}(u,v)]^2 + [\tilde{s}_{0,Im}(u,v)]^2} \ ; \ \tilde{\varphi}_0(u,v) = arctg\left[\frac{\tilde{s}_{0,Im}(u,v)}{\tilde{s}_{0,Re}(u,v)}\right] \tag{16.9}$$

Step 4: From the retained coefficients, only the complex-conjugated couples $\tilde{s}_0(u,v)$ and $\tilde{s}_0^*(u,v)$ with inverse phases are chosen, i.e. $\tilde{\varphi}_0(u,v) = -\tilde{\varphi}_0^*(u,v)$, if their modules satisfy the condition:

$$\left|\tilde{M}_0(u,v)\right| = \left|\tilde{M}_0^*(u,v)\right| > \eta_0 \tag{16.10}$$

where:

$$\eta_0 = \begin{cases} \alpha_0 \tilde{M}_{0,max} & if \ \alpha_0 \tilde{M}_{0,max} > \delta_0, \\ \delta_0 & - \ \ \ in \ all \ other \ cases. \end{cases}$$

Here η_0 is a threshold, the value of which is calculated in accordance with Eq. (16.10); α_0 is a coefficient with value $\alpha_0 < 1$ (usually $\alpha_0 = 0.2$); $\tilde{M}_{0,max}$ is the value of the largest coefficient in the lowest SP layer; δ_0 is a positive threshold value (for example $\delta_0 = 0.1$). For smaller values of δ_0 the number of coefficients suitable for watermarking increases, but this can result in worse image quality.

Step 5: The consecutive bit $w_r(b_o)$ of the lowest watermark layer b_o is inserted in the phases of the selected couple of spectrum coefficients $\tilde{s}_0(u,v)$ and $\tilde{s}_0^*(u,v)$, which satisfy the condition in Eq. (16.10), in accordance with the relation:

$$\tilde{\varphi}_{0w_r}(u,v) = -\tilde{\varphi}_{0w_r}^*(u,v) = \begin{cases} \tilde{\varphi}_0(u,v) + \Delta_0 & if \quad w_r(b_0) = 1; \\ \tilde{\varphi}_0(u,v) - \Delta_0 & if \quad w_r(b_0) = 0, \end{cases} \tag{16.11}$$

where $\tilde{\varphi}_{0w_r}(u,v)$ and $\tilde{\varphi}_{0w_r}^*(u,v)$ are correspondingly the phases of the watermarked coefficients $\tilde{s}_{0w_r}(u,v)$ and $\tilde{s}_{0w_r}^*(u,v)$, and R_o is the number of the binary elements in the sequence $w_r(b_o)$, inserted in the SP layer $p = 0$. The parameter Δ_o is the angle for the layer $p = 0$, which sets the "depth" of the inserted watermark b and, together with $\alpha_{0,}$ defines its resistance against pirates' attacks and its transparency.

The sequence $w_r(b_o)$ is obtained in result of applying the operation "XOR" on every bit of the watermark and the corresponding bit of a pseudorandom sequence, which represents a secret (personal) or a public key used for the watermark encryption. In this case, the autocorrelation function of the sequence $w_r(b_o)$ is similar with a delta pulse. This requirement ensures high accuracy of the watermark detection and reliable watermark extraction.

Step 6: The pixels $\tilde{B}_{0w}(i,k)$ of the watermarked image $[\tilde{B}_{0w}(2^n)]$ are calculated for the SP layer $p = 0$, which approximates the matrix $[B(2^n)]$ of the original image. For this, using Eqs. (16.9) and (16.10), the complex coefficients of the watermarked transform $[\tilde{S}_{0w}(2^n)]$ are calculated in accordance with:

$$\tilde{s}_{0w_r}(u.v) = \begin{cases} \tilde{M}_0(u,v)e^{j\tilde{\varphi}_{0w_r}(u,v)} & if \; \tilde{M}_0(u,v)\sin\tilde{\varphi}_{0w_r}(u,v) \neq 0; \\ \tilde{M}_0(u,v)e^{j\tilde{\varphi}_0(u,v)} & - \quad\quad\quad in \; all \; other \; cases. \end{cases} \tag{16.12}$$

Then, on the rearranged matrix $[\tilde{S}_{0w}'(2^n)]$, the inverse 2D-CHT is applied in correspondence with the relation:

$$[\tilde{B}_{0w}(2^n)] = \tfrac{1}{4^n}[CH_0'(2^n)]^{*t}[\tilde{S}_{0w}'(2^n)][CH_0'(2^n)]^{*t} \tag{16.13}$$

Here, $[CH_0'(2^n)]^{-1} = \dfrac{1}{2^n}[CH_0'(2^n)]^{*t}$ is the inverse ordered CHT matrix of size $2^n \times 2^n$, elements of which are complex-conjugated with their corresponding elements of the transposed matrix $[CH_0'(2^n)]^t$. The elements of the natural complex-conjugated matrix $[CH_0(2^n)]^*$ are defined in accordance with Eq. (16.2) as follows:

$$ch_0^*(t,q) = j^{-tq} \, h_0(t,q) \text{ for } t, q = 0,1,..,2^n-1, \tag{16.14}$$

where $h_0(t,q)$ is the sign function of the element (t,q) of the matrix $[CH_0(2^n)]$.

Step 7: Calculation of the pixels $\tilde{B}_0(i,k)$ of the matrix $[\tilde{B}_0(2^n)]$, which approximates the original image $[B(2^n)]$ for the SP layer $p = 0$. For this, in accordance with Eqs. (16.4) and (16.5), the coefficients of the rearranged transform $[\tilde{S}_0'(2^n)]$ are calculated, and on it, inverse 2D-CHT is applied:

$$[\tilde{B}_0(2^n)] = \frac{1}{4^n}[CH_0'(2^n)]^{*t} \, [\tilde{S}_0'(2^n)][CH_0'(2^n)]^{*t}. \tag{16.15}$$

Together with the spectrum coefficients, retained in accordance with Eq. (16.4), in the matrix $[\tilde{S}_0'(2^n)]$, are included their corresponding complex-conjugated coefficients, creating this way a set of complex-conjugated couples.

Step 8: Calculation of the difference matrix for the SP layer $p = 0$:

$$[E_0(2^n)] = [B(2^n)] - [\tilde{B}_0(2^n)]. \tag{16.16}$$

Step 9: Using Eqs. (16.13) and (16.16), the watermarked image $[B_{0w}(2^n)]$ is calculated with watermark n_0, embedded in the SP layer $p = 0$:

$$[B_{0w}(2^n)] = [\tilde{B}_{0w}(2^n)] + [E_0(2^n)]. \tag{16.17}$$

Step 10: The difference matrix $[E_0(2^n)]$ is divided in 4 sub-matrices $[E_0^{k_1}(2^{n-1})]$ for $k_1 = 1, 2, 3, 4$, as follows:

$$[E_0(2^n)] = \begin{bmatrix} [E_0^1(2^{n-1})] & [E_0^2(2^{n-1})] \\ [E_0^3(2^{n-1})] & [E_0^4(2^{n-1})] \end{bmatrix} \tag{16.18}$$

In the next SP layer ($p = 1$), the watermark could be inserted in every difference sub-matrix $[E_0^{k_1}(2^{n-1})]$ for $k_1 = 1, 2, 3, 4$, applying the already described steps (1-9), which define the image watermarking in the layer $p = 0$.

Step 11: For the next SP layers: $p = 1, 2,.., P-1$ $(P \leq n-1)$ on the already obtained difference sub-matrix $[E_{p-1}^{k_p}(2^{n-p})]$, direct 2D-CHT is applied:

$$[S_p'^{k_p}(2^{n-p})] = [CH_p'(2^{n-p})][E_{p-1}^{k_p}(2^{n-p})][CH_p'(2^{n-p})] \text{ for } k_p = 1,2,..,4^p, \tag{16.19}$$

where $[CH_p'(2^{n-p})]$ is ordered CHT matrix of size $2^n \times 2^n$, and $[S_p'^{k_p}(2^{n-p})]$ is the transform of the difference sub-matrix $[E_{p-1}^{k_p}(2^{n-p})]$, which is of same size. The sub-matrices $[E_{p-1}^{k_p}(2^{n-p})]$ comprise the difference matrix $[E_{p-1}(2^n)]$, defined with the relation:

$$[E_{p-1}(2^n)] = [E_{p-2}(2^n)] - [\tilde{E}_{p-2}(2^n)] \text{ for } p = 1,2,..,P. \qquad (16.20)$$

Here, $[\tilde{E}_{p-2}(2^n)]$ is the approximating difference matrix, which contains the sub-matrices $[\tilde{E}_{p-2}^{k_{p-1}}(2^{n-p+1})]$ of size $2^{n-+1} \times 2^{n-+1}$ for $k_{p-1}=1,2,..,4^{p-1}$, obtained after quad-tree division of the matrix $[\tilde{E}_{p-2}(2^n)]$, i.e.:

$$[\tilde{E}_{p-2}(2^n)]=\begin{bmatrix} [\tilde{E}_{p-2}^{1}(2^{n-p+1})] & [\tilde{E}_{p-2}^{2}(2^{n-p+1})] & -- & [\tilde{E}_{p-2}^{2^{p-1}}(2^{n-p+1})] \\ [\tilde{E}_{p-2}^{2^{p-1}+1}(2^{n-p+1})] & [\tilde{E}_{p-2}^{2^{p-1}+2}(2^{n-p+1})] & -- & [\tilde{E}_{p-2}^{2^{p}}(2^{n-p+1})] \\ --- & --- & -- & --- \\ [\tilde{E}_{p-2}^{4^{p-1}-2^{p-1}+1}(2^{n-p+1})] & [\tilde{E}_{p-2}^{4^{p-1}-2^{p-1}+2}(2^{n-p+1})] & -- & [\tilde{E}_{p-2}^{4^{p-1}}(2^{n-p+1})] \end{bmatrix} \qquad (16.21)$$

Step 12: Each sub-matrix $[\tilde{E}_{p-2}^{k_{p-1}}(2^{n-p+1})]$ in Eq. (16.21) is defined with inverse 2D-CHT of the transform $[S_{p-1}'^{k_{p-1}}(2^{n-p+1})]$ for $k_{p-1} = 1,2,..,4^{p-1}$, i.e.

$$[\tilde{E}_{p-2}^{k_{p-1}}(2^{n-p+1})]=\frac{1}{4^{n-p+1}}[CH'_{p-1}(2^{n-p+1})]^{*t}[\tilde{S}_{p-1}'^{k_{p-1}}(2^{n-p+1})][CH'_{p-1}(2^{n-p+1})]^{*t} \quad (16.22)$$

Here, $[CH'_{p-1}(2^{n-p+1})]^{-1} = \frac{1}{2^{n-p+1}}[CH'_{p-1}(2^{n-p+1})]^{*t}$ is the inverse, ordered CHT matrix of size $2^{n-p+1} \times 2^{n-p+1}$, elements of which are complex-conjugated with the corresponding elements of the transposed matrix $[CH'_{p-1}(2^{n-p+1})]^{t}$. The elements of the natural complex-conjugated matrix $[CH_{p-1}(2^{n-p+1})]^{*}$ are defined in accordance with Eq. (16.2) as follows:

$$ch_{p-1}^{*}(t,q) = j^{-tq} h_{p-1}(t,q) \text{ for } t, q = 0,1,..,2^{n-p+1}-1,$$
$$(16.23)$$

where $h_{p-1}(t,q)$ is the sign function of the element (t,q) of the matrix $[CH_{p-1}(2^{n-p+1})]$ for the SP layer $p-1$.

The elements $[\tilde{S}_{p-1}'^{k_{p-1}}(2^{n-p+1})]$ are defined in accordance with the rule for retaining the transform spectrum coefficients $[S_{p-1}^{k_{p-1}}(2^{n-p+1})]$:

$$\tilde{s}_{p-1}^{k_{p-1}}(u,v) = l_{p-1}(u,v)s_{p-1}^{k_{p-1}}(u,v) = \begin{cases} s_{p-1}^{k_{p-1}}(u,v), & if \ l_{p-1}(u,v)=1, \\ 0, & if \ l_{p-1}(u,v)=0. \end{cases} \quad (16.24)$$

Here, $l_{p-1}(u,v)$ is an element of the binary matrix-mask $[L_{p-1}(2^{n-p+1})]$ for the layer p-1. In the matrix $[\tilde{S}_{p-1}^{\prime k_{p-1}}(2^{n-p+1})]$ are retained the complex-conjugated couples, defined by Eq. (16.24).

Step 13: The modules and the phases of the spectrum coefficients retained in accordance with Eq. (16.24) are calculated for the sub-matrices k_p in every SP layer:

$$\tilde{s}_p^{k_p}(u,v) = \tilde{s}_{p,Re}^{k_p}(u,v) + j\tilde{s}_{p,Im}^{k_p}(u,v) = \tilde{M}_p^{k_p}(u,v)e^{j\tilde{\varphi}_p^{k_p}(u,v)}, \quad (16.25)$$

where

$$\tilde{s}_{p,Re}^{k_p}(u,v) = \sum_{i=0}^{2^{n-p}-1} \sum_{k=0}^{2^{n-p}-1} E_{p-1}^{k_p}(i,k)h_p(u,i)h_p(v,k)\cos[\tfrac{\pi}{2}(ui+vk)], \quad (16.26)$$

$$\tilde{s}_{p,Im}^{k_p}(u,v) = \sum_{i=0}^{2^{n-p}-1} \sum_{k=0}^{2^{n-p}-1} E_{p-1}^{k_p}(i,k)h_p(u,i)h_p(v,k)\sin[\tfrac{\pi}{2}(ui+vk)], \quad (16.27)$$

$$\tilde{M}_p^{k_p}(u,v) = \sqrt{[\tilde{s}_{p,Re}^{k_p}(u,v)]^2 + [\tilde{s}_{p,Im}^{k_p}(u,v)]^2} , \ \tilde{\varphi}_p^{k_p}(u,v) = arctg\left[\frac{\tilde{s}_{p,Im}^{k_p}(u,v)}{\tilde{s}_{p,Re}^{k_p}(u,v)}\right] \quad (16.28)$$

Step 14: From the retained coefficients, only the complex-conjugated couples $\tilde{s}_p^{k_p}(u,v)$ and $\tilde{s}_p^{k_p*}(u,v)$ are selected, phases of which are inverse i.e. $\tilde{\varphi}_p^{k_p}(u,v) = -\tilde{\varphi}_p^{k_p*}(u,v)$. Together with this, their modules should satisfy the requirement:

$$\left|\tilde{M}_p^{k_p}(u,v)\right| = \left|\tilde{M}_p^{k_p*}(u,v)\right| > \eta_p \quad (16.29)$$

where

$$\eta_p = \begin{cases} \alpha_p \tilde{M}_{p,max}^{k_p} & if \ \alpha_p \tilde{M}_{p,max}^{k_p} > \delta_p, \\ \delta_p & - \quad in \ all \ other \ cases. \end{cases}$$

Here η_0 is a threshold, the value of which is calculated in accordance with Eq. (16.29); α_0 is a coefficient with value $\alpha_0 < 1$ (usually $\alpha_0 = 0.2$); $\tilde{M}_{p,max}$ is the value of the largest coefficient in the SP layer p; and δ_p is a positive threshold value (usually $\delta_p = 0.1$). For smaller values of δ_p the number of coefficients suitable for watermarking increases, but this usually results in worse image quality.

Step 15: Each consecutive bit $w_r(b_p)$ from the layer b_p of the watermark b is inserted in the phases of the couple of coefficients $\tilde{s}_p^{k_p}(u,v)$ and $\tilde{s}_p^{k_p*}(u,v)$ selected in accordance with Eq. (16.29) as follows:

$$\tilde{\varphi}_{pw_r}^{k_p}(u,v) = -\tilde{\varphi}_{pw_r}^{k_p*}(u,v) = \begin{cases} \tilde{\varphi}_p^{k_p}(u,v) + \Delta_p & \text{if} \quad w_r(b_p) = 1; \\ \tilde{\varphi}_p^{k_p}(u,v) - \Delta_p & \text{if} \quad w_r(b_p) = 0, \end{cases} \quad (16.30)$$

$$\text{for } r = 1,2,..,R_p,$$

where $\tilde{\varphi}_{pw_r}^{k_p}(u,v)$ and $\tilde{\varphi}_{pw_r}^{k_p*}(u,v)$ are the phases of the watermarked coefficients $\tilde{s}_{pw_r}^{k_p}(u,v)$ and $\tilde{s}_{pw_r}^{k_p*}(u,v)$, and R_p is the number of the binary elements from the sequence $w_r(b_p)$ for $r = 1,2,..,R_p$, inserted in the SP layer p. The parameter Δ_p is the angle, which sets the "depth" of the watermark layer b_p in the layer p, and together with α_p, defines its transparency and resistance against pirates' attacks. The sequence $w_r(b_p)$ is obtained in similar way, as it was performed with the watermark layer b_0 in the SP layer $p = 0$.

Step 16: Calculation of the elements $\tilde{E}_{p-1,w}^{k_p}(i,k)$ of the watermarked difference sub-matrix $[\tilde{E}_{p-1,w}^{k_p}(2^{n-p})]$ for the SP layer p, which approximates the difference sub-matrix $[E_{p-1,w}^{k_p}(2^{n-p})]$. In accordance with Eqs. (16.28) and (16.30), the transform coefficients $[\tilde{S}_{pw}^{k_p}(2^{n-p})]$ are calculated as follows:

$$\tilde{s}_{pw_r}^{k_p}(u,v) = \begin{cases} \tilde{M}_p^{k_p}(u,v)e^{j\tilde{\varphi}_{pw_r}^{k_p}(u,v)} & \text{if } \tilde{M}_p^{k_p}(u,v)\sin\tilde{\varphi}_{pw_r}^{k_p}(u,v) \neq 0; \\ \tilde{M}_p^{k_p}(u,v)e^{j\tilde{\varphi}_p^{k_p}(u,v)} & - \quad \text{in all other cases.} \end{cases} \quad (16.31)$$

Then, on the matrix $[\tilde{S}_{pw}^{\prime k_p}(2^{n-p})]$, inverse 2D-CHT (2D-ICHT) is applied in correspondence with the relation:

$$[\tilde{E}_{p-1,w}^{k_p}(2^{n-p})] = \frac{1}{4^{n-p}}[CH_p'(2^{n-p})]^{*t}[\tilde{S}_{pw}^{\prime k_p}(2^{n-p})][CH_p'(2^{n-p})]^{*t} \quad (16.32)$$

$$\text{for } k_p = 1,2,..,4^p$$

Step 17: Using Eqs. (16.13) and (16.32), the matrix of the watermarked image $[B_{p,w}(2^n)]$ is defined, and in it's layers b_p the corresponding watermark data are inserted:

$$[B_{p,w}(2^n)] = \begin{cases} [\tilde{B}_{0w}(2^n)] + [E_0(2^n)] & for & p=0; \\ [\tilde{B}_{0w}(2^n)] + \sum_{r=1}^{p} [\tilde{E}_{r-1,w}(2^n)] + [E_p(2^n)] & for & p=1,2,..,P-1. \end{cases} \quad (16.33)$$

Here, $[E_p(2^n)]$ is the so-called "residual" matrix, calculated in accordance with the relation:

$$[E_p(2^n)] = \begin{cases} [B(2^n)] - [\tilde{B}_0(2^n)] & for & p=0; \\ [E_{p-1}(2^n)] - [\tilde{E}_{p-1}(2^n)] & for & p=1,2,..,P-1. \end{cases} \quad (16.34)$$

The SP decomposition, presented with Eq. (16.33) describes the Inverse Difference Pyramid of the watermarked image. Every decomposition component is a matrix of size $2^n \times 2^n$, which corresponds with one of the SP layers $p=0,1,..,P-1$ and is obtained with 2D-ICHT.

The spectrum pyramid SP with total number of P layers comprises the following spectrum coefficients:

- In the initial (lowest) layer, $p = 0$ - all coefficients of the transform $[\tilde{S}_0(2^n)]$;

- In the next layers, $p = 1,2,..,P-1$ – all coefficients of the transforms $[\tilde{S}_p^{k_p}(2^{n-p})]$ for $k_p = 1,2,..,4^p$.

All SP coefficients, which satisfy the requirements of the conditions defined in Eqs. (16.10) and (16.29), are phase-watermarked in correspondence with Eqs. (16.11) and (16.30).

16.2.2. Resistant watermark detection

One of the main features when watermarking is concerned is the successful detection or extraction of the inserted watermarks. Here, the algorithm for watermark detection is presented.

The algorithm for multi-layer watermark detection is "blind", i.e. it does not require the use of the original image but needs the original watermark data only. For the detection, a part of the already described watermarking algorithm is used, in particular – steps 1 to 4 for the SP layer $p = 0$ and steps 11 to 14 – for the consecutive SP layers $p = 1, 2, . . , P-1$. This permits definition of all complex-conjugated couples of spectrum coefficients, which satisfy the requirements of the conditions in Eqs. (16.10) and (16.29) and are suitable for watermark embedding.

Step 1: In the processed SP layer p is checked up the availability of the corresponding layer b_p of the watermark b, which is one of a set of D watermarks known in advance. This check is based on the evaluation of the cross correlation coefficient's value $C_{m,b}(p)$ between layers b_p and m_p of the two watermarks, which could be used for watermarking of the coefficients $\tilde{s}_0(u,v)$ and $\tilde{s}_0^*(u,v)$ for $p = 0$ and $\tilde{s}_p^{k_p}(u,v)$ and $\tilde{s}_p^{k_p*}(u,v)$ - for $p = 1, 2,.., P\text{-}1$, in correspondence with Eqs. (16.11) and (16.30). The cross-correlation coefficient for the layer p is defined with the relation:

$$C_{m,b}(p) = \sum_{r=1}^{R_p} [\tilde{\varphi}_p^{k_p}(u,v) + \Delta_r(b_p)]\,\Delta_r(m_p) = A_m(p) + B_{m,b}(p) \qquad (16.35)$$

$$\text{for } m_p, b_p = 1,2,..,D_p,$$

where D_p is the number of the searched (known) watermarks for the layer b_p; $[\varphi_p^{k_p}(u,v) + \Delta_r(n_p)] = \tilde{\varphi}_{pw_r}^{k_p}(u,v)$ is the phase of the watermarked coefficient $\tilde{s}_{pw_r}^{k_p}(u,v)$ in the transform $[\tilde{S}_{pw}^{k_p}(2^{n-p})]$ for the layer p;

$$\Delta_r(b_p) = (-1)^{w_r(p)}\Delta_p = \begin{cases} +\Delta_p & \text{if } w_r(b_p) = 1; \\ -\Delta_p & \text{if } w_r(b_p) = 0, \end{cases} \text{for } r = 1,2,..,R_p; \qquad (16.36)$$

$w_r(b_p)$ is the bit r of the pseudorandom sequence with length R_p, which describes the layer b_p of the watermark b inserted in the layer p;

$$A_m(p) = \sum_{r=1}^{R_p} \varphi_p^{k_p}(u,v)\Delta_r(b_p), \quad B_{m,b}(p) = \sum_{r=1}^{R_p} \Delta_r(b_p)\Delta_r(m_p) \qquad (16.37)$$

For big values of R_p from Eq. (16.36) follows that $A_m(p) = \varphi_p^{k_p}(u,v)\sum_{r=1}^{R_p}\Delta_r(b_p) \approx 0$.

In case spectrum coefficients selected in accordance with conditions in Eqs. (16.11) and (16.30) are not watermarked, $\Delta_r(b_p) = 0$ and from Eq. (16.37) follows that $C_{m,b}(p) \approx 0$; if the coefficients are watermarked, we obtain the relation:

$$C_{m,b}(p) \approx \begin{cases} \sum_{r=1}^{R_p} [\Delta_r(m_p)]^2 = R_p\Delta_p^2 & \text{if } m_p = b_p; \\ \sum_{r=1}^{R_p} \Delta_r(m_p)\Delta_r(b_p) \approx 0 & \text{if } m_p \neq b_p. \end{cases} \qquad (16.38)$$

Step 2: The decision that the layer b_p of the watermark b has been detected can be taken if the following requirement is satisfied:

$$b_p = \begin{cases} Yes & if \quad [C_{m,b}(p)/R_p \, \Delta_p^2)] \geq \theta_p; \\ No & - \quad in \; all \; other \; cases. \end{cases} \qquad (16.39)$$

In this relation, θ_p is a threshold, set in advance for the layer p, the value of which is in the range $0 < \theta_p < 1$. The value of θ_p should satisfy the contradictory requirements: for minimum possibility to miss the inserted watermark and for false detection of the searched watermark b in the layer b_p.

Step 3: The decision for the detection of the multi-layer watermark b in the processed image is taken if the following requirement is satisfied:

$$b = \begin{cases} Yes, & if \; Watermark \, (b_p) \Rightarrow det\,ected \; for \; p=0,1,..,P\text{-}1, \\ No, & - \quad in \; all \; other \; cases. \end{cases} \qquad (16.40)$$

The block diagrams of the coder and decoder used for watermark insertion and detection for halftone still images in accordance with the presented algorithm are shown in Figure 16.2a, b.

The performance of the coder is presented with the block diagram in Fig. 16.2a, which comprises 3 main parts, i.e. - the processing in the decomposition layers: $p = 0, 1$ and P-1. The performance in the layer $p = 0$ comprises steps 1-10 of the presented algorithm, and the obtained results are written in blocks 2-12. Here, the elements $w_r(b_0)$ of the watermark for the lowest decomposition layer are inserted in the corresponding layer of the processed image. At the output of block 13, the difference matrix for the processed layer is obtained as well as at the output of block 8 – the watermarked matrix, which is the zero approximation of the input image. In the next part of the block diagram for the layer $p = 1$, steps 11-17 of the watermarking algorithm are performed. Here, the elements $w_r(b_1)$ of the watermark for the second decomposition layer are inserted in the corresponding layer of the processed image. At the output of block 27, the difference matrix for the processed layer is obtained as well as at the output of block 22 – the watermarked matrix, which is the approximation of the first difference matrix. The processing continues in a similar way for the next layers. In the last part, for layer $p = P$ - 1, the same steps (11-17) are performed again. At the output of block 45 the multi-layer watermarked image is obtained.

The block diagram of the decoder is in Fig. 16.2b. It comprises three main parts, corresponding to the processing in layers $p = 0$, $p = 1$ and $p = P$ - 1. In the first part, for the layer $p = 0$, steps 1-4 of the coding algorithm and steps 1 and 2 from the decoding algorithm are performed. At the input of block 46 the tested image is applied, which could be watermarked or original. At the output of block 50 in the part for $p = 0$, the lowest layer b_0 of the detected watermark is obtained. At the second output of the same part, one of the differences $E_{0w}(i,k)$ or $E_0(i,k)$, correspondingly – watermarked or not watermarked, is obtained. In the next main blocks – for layers $p = 1, 2,..., P$-1, similar operations are performed. At the output of block 82, the layers of the multi-layer watermark, detected in the tested image, are combined.

The same algorithm could be applied for color images, represented with the components Y, U, and V. In this case, it is enough to insert the watermark in the brightness component (Y) only.

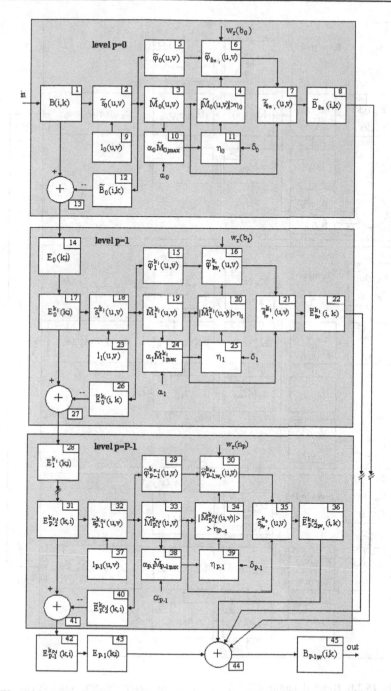

Fig. 16.2.a. Block diagram of the coder for watermark insertion in halftone images

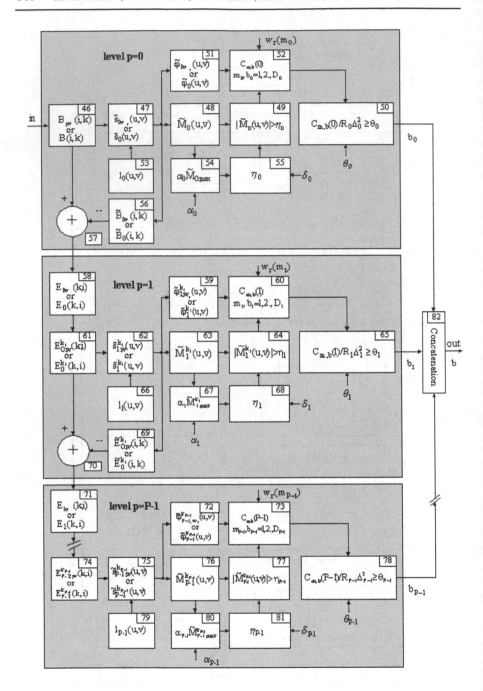

Fig. 16.2.b. Block diagram of the decoder for multi-layer watermark detection

The main advantages of the method for resistant watermarking are: the ability to insert data in the consecutive decomposition layers, the high transparency and resistance of the inserted watermark, the relatively low computational complexity, and the ability for "blind" watermark detection.

16.2.3. Fragile watermarking

The fragile watermark is inserted in the last SP layer ($p = P-1$). In accordance with the algorithm, only some of the real coefficients are watermarked. In Eq. (16.10) was proved that when $u = 2e$ and $v = 2f$, for $e, f = 1,2, ..$ are satisfied the conditions:

$$s(2e,2f) = M(2e,2f) \text{ and } \varphi(2e,2f) = 0, \tag{16.41}$$

i.e. the even spectrum coefficients are real numbers. The real spectrum coefficients in the SP layer $p=P-1$, retained in accordance with Eq. (16.24), are watermarked, changing their modules as follows:

$$\tilde{s}_{p-1,w}^{k_{P-1}}(2e,2f) = \begin{cases} \tilde{s}_{p-1}^{k_{P-1}}(2e,2f) + 1, \text{if } w_r(b) = 1; \\ \tilde{s}_{p-1}^{k_{P-1}}(2e,2f) - 1, \text{if } w_r(b) = 0; \end{cases} for \mid \tilde{s}_{P-1,w}^{k_{P-1}}(2e,2f) \mid \geq \eta, \tag{16.42}$$

where η is a threshold, defined with the relation:

$$\eta = \begin{cases} \alpha s_{P-1}^{k_{P-1}}(0,0) \text{ if } \alpha s_{P-1}^{k_{P-1}}(0,0) > \delta, \\ \delta \quad - \quad \text{in all other cases.} \end{cases} \tag{16.43}$$

Here, α_0 is a coefficient with value $\alpha_0 < 1$ (usually $\alpha_0 = 0.2$); $s_{P-1}^{k_{P-1}}(0,0)$ is the largest coefficient in the corresponding SP layer; and the δ is a positive threshold value (usually $\delta = 0.1$).

The elements $l_{p-1}(2e, 2f)$ of the binary matrix, which defines the retained spectrum coefficients for the layer $P-1$, are defined as follows:

$$l_{P-1}(2e,2f) = \begin{cases} 1 \text{ if } (2e,2f) \in O_{mid}(P-1); \\ 0 \quad - \quad \text{in all other cases,} \end{cases} \tag{16.44}$$

where $O_{mid}(P-1)$ is the area in the transform layer $P - 1$, which corresponds with the middle spatial frequencies. This approach for the spectrum coefficients selection ensures the fragility of the inserted watermark.

For the successful extraction of the fragile watermark, it is necessary to have the original image and to define the spectrum coefficients, which suit the requirements presented with Eqs. (16.44) - (16.46). Each consecutive bit r of the inserted watermark is extracted in accordance with the relation:

$$w_r(b) = \begin{cases} 1 & \text{if } sign[s_{P-1,w_r}^{k_{P-1}}(2e,2f)-s_{P-1}^{k_{P-1}}(2e,2f)]=1; \\ 0 & \text{if } sign[s_{P-1,w_r}^{k_{P-1}}(2e,2f)-s_{P-1}^{k_{P-1}}(2e,2f)]=-1. \end{cases} \qquad (16.45)$$

where $\tilde{s}_{P-1,w_r}^{k_{P-1}}(2e,2f)$ and $\tilde{s}_{P-1}^{k_{P-1}}(2e,2f)$ are correspondingly the coefficients of the watermarked and of the original image, and R is the number of bits of the fragile watermark data sequence $w_r(b)$, for $r = 1, 2, .. , R$.

In case the image does not contain a watermark or the watermark has been destroyed as a result of some kind of editing, then:

$$\tilde{s}_{P-1,w_r}^{k_{P-1}}(2e,2f) - \tilde{s}_{P-1,w_r}^{k_{P-1}}(2e,2f) = 0 \text{ for } r = 1, 2,.., R. \qquad (16.46)$$

The main advantages of the fragile watermarking are:

• The knowledge of the algorithm and the possession of the decoding tools do not permit watermark extraction. This is done using the owner's password;

• Any change, noticed in the watermark, evidences unauthorized access with image contents' editing.

16.3. Data hiding

The described algorithm for multi-layer resistant watermarking could be used for data hiding as well. The hidden data could be another image (compressed or uncompressed) or just binary data. For the successful extraction of the hidden data, it is necessary to have the original image and to perform steps 1- 4 for $p = 0$ and steps 11-14 for $p = 1, 2, ... , P-1$ from the algorithm for multi-layer watermark insertion, described above. This permits definition of all SP coefficients of the processed and of the watermarked image, which answer the requirements for successful phase watermarking. Each consecutive bit r of the hidden data in the layer p of the investigated image is extracted in accordance with the operation:

$$w_r(b_p) = \begin{cases} 1 & \text{if } \tilde{\varphi}_{pw_r}^{k_p}(u,v) - \tilde{\varphi}_p^{k_p}(u,v) > 0 \text{ and } \tilde{\varphi}_{pw_r}^{k_p*}(u,v) + \tilde{\varphi}_p^{k_p}(u,v) < 0; \\ 0 & \text{if } \tilde{\varphi}_{pw_r}^{k_p}(u,v) - \tilde{\varphi}_p^{k_p}(u,v) < 0 \text{ and } \tilde{\varphi}_{pw_r}^{k_p*}(u,v) + \tilde{\varphi}_p^{k_p}(u,v) > 0; \end{cases} \qquad (16.47)$$

$$\text{for } r = 1,2,.., R_p,$$

where $\tilde{\varphi}_{pw_r}^{k_p}(u,v)$ and $\tilde{\varphi}_{pw_r}^{k_p*}(u,v)$ are the phases of coefficients $\tilde{s}_{pw_r}^{k_p}(u,v)$ and $\tilde{s}_{pw_r}^{k_p*}(u,v)$ from the SP of the image, which contains the hidden data; $\tilde{\varphi}_p^{k_p}(u,v)$ and $\tilde{\varphi}_{p_r}^{k_p*}(u,v)$ - the phases of coefficients $\tilde{s}_p^{k_p}(u,v)$ and $\tilde{s}_p^{k_p*}(u,v)$ from the SP of the original image, R_p – the number of bits from the hidden data sequence $w_r(b_p)$

for $r = 1,2,..,R_p$, inserted in the SP layer $p = 1, 2, ..., P-1$. In case the investigated image does not contain hidden data, the following conditions are satisfied:

$$\tilde{\varphi}_{pw_r}^{k_p}(u,v) - \tilde{\varphi}_p^{k_p}(u,v) = \tilde{\varphi}_{pw_r}^{k_p*}(u,v) + \tilde{\varphi}_p^{k_p}(u,v) = 0 \qquad (16.48)$$

$$\text{for } r = 1,2,..,R_p \text{ and } p = 1,2,..,P-1.$$

The resistance of the hidden data is as high as that of the inserted multi-layer watermark.

16.4. Evaluation of the watermarking efficiency

In correspondence with the algorithm, presented above, the data of the multi-layer watermark $w_r(b_p)$ for $r = 1,2,..,R_p$ and $p = 0,1,2,..,P-1$ could be inserted only in the phases of the retained complex-conjugated couples of coefficients, for which the requirements from Eqs. (16.10) and (16.29) are satisfied.

As investigated by Kountchev et al. (2003), the following properties of the CHT-spectrum coefficients were proved:

$$s(2e,2f) = M(2e,2f) \text{ and } \varphi(2e,2f) = 0 \text{ for } e, f = 0, 1, 2, .., \qquad (16.49)$$

$$s(2e+3,2f) = s^*(2e+1,2f), s(2e,2f+3) = s^*(2e,2f+1), s(2e+3,2f+3) = s^*(2e+1,2f+1) \quad (50)$$

i.e. the even coefficients are real, and the odd ones are complex-conjugated couples. In result, the total number of complex-conjugated couples of SP coefficients for the processed image $[B(2^n)]$ is:

$$N(n,P) = 3 \times 4^{n-1} \times P, \qquad (16.51)$$

where P is the number of SP layers, and $n = lg_2 N$ for N – the size of the image matrix.

For the case with an inserted resistant watermark, the elements $l_p(u.v)$ of the matrix-mask $[L_p(2^{n-p})]$ for $p = 0,1, 2,.., P-1$ are set in such a way that to retain the low-frequency complex-conjugated couples only in every transform $[S'^{k_p}_p(2^{n-p})]$. In case half of the coefficients defined with Eq. (16.43) belong to this group, the total number of the retained couples of coefficients is correspondingly:

$$N_g(n,P) = 1.5 \times 4^{n-1} \times P. \qquad (16.52)$$

The total number of bits in the data sequence, representing the multi-layer watermark $w_r(b_p)$, is $R = \sum_{p=0}^{P-1} R_p$. Taking into account Eqs. (16.10) and (16.29), the number of the retained couples of complex-conjugated coefficients $N_\varphi(n, P)$, phases of which are suitable for watermarking, should not be greater than $N_g(n, P)$, defined with Eq. (16.52), i.e.:

$$N_\varphi(n, P) = \sum_{p=0}^{P-1} R_p \le 1.5 \times 4^{n-1} \times P. \tag{16.53}$$

This relation defines the maximum capacity (in bits) of the resistant multi-layer watermark.

The watermark transparency could be evaluated using the Peak Signal-to-Noise Ratio (*PSNR*) for the original and for the watermarked image.

The PSNR of the image, watermarked with a p-layer watermark, is defined with the relation:

$$PSNR_p = 10 \lg_{10}(B_{max}^2 / \overline{\varepsilon_p^2}), \quad [dB]. \tag{16.54}$$

where $\overline{\varepsilon_p^2}$ is the Mean Square Error (MSE) for the layer p:

$$\overline{\varepsilon_p^2} = \frac{1}{4^n} \sum_{i=0}^{2^n-1} \sum_{k=0}^{2^n-1} [B(i, k) - B_{p,w}(i, k)]^2 \quad \text{for } p = 0, 1, 2, ., P-1. \tag{16.55}$$

Here, $B(k, i)$ and $B_{p,w}(k, i)$ are elements of the corresponding matrices of the original and watermarked image in accordance with Eq. (16.33).

The efficiency of the multi-layer watermarking is evaluated using Eqs. (16.53) and (16.54), which define respectively the maximum capacity and the transparency of the inserted watermark.

16.5. Experimental results

The presented algorithm was software-implemented, and the experiments were performed with large number of grayscale and color images. Some examples are presented below. Figure 16.3 shows the original grayscale image "Katia" of size 256×256 pixels. A block size of 16×16 pixels ($n = 4$) was used by the watermarking algorithm for $P = 1$. In accordance with Eq. (16.53), in this case, the maximum watermark capacity for one block is $N_\varphi(4, 1) = R_0 = 1.5 \times 4^3 = 96$ bits, and for the whole image, it is correspondingly $256 \times N_\varphi(4, 1) = 24576$ bits. The real watermark capacity depends on the image contents and is usually in the range (1-8%) of the maximum possible one. The watermarked test image (in which was embedded a digital watermark of 183 bits) is shown in Figure 16.4. In Table 16.1 is shown the amount of the embedded bits for four test images. The results prove that the watermark was embedded in none-homogenous areas of the image only. Despite of the watermark insertion, there are no visible changes. In Figure 16.5, the absolute difference between the original and the watermarked image "Katia" is shown. The real differences are very small and hardly visible. For better visibility of the difference image, a special algorithm for threshold increasing and visualization was used, and the detected differences are shown scaled by 64. As expected, the biggest differences occur around the edges. For the evaluation of the watermark resistance, the watermarked image was compressed with JPEG. The obtained results are shown in Figures 16.6 and 16.7. Figure 16.6 shows the *PSNR* for different values of the parameter Δ_0. The bit-error rate (*BER*) for different values of Δ_0 (the watermark depth) and JPEG quality factor are shown in Figure 16.7.

Fig. 16.3. Original image "Katia"   **Fig. 16.4.** Image watermarked with phase angle $\Delta_0 = 12$

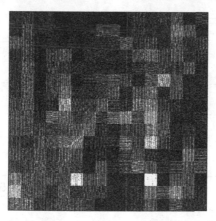

Fig. 16.5. Image, presenting the enhanced absolute differences (scaled up by 64)

Table 16.1. The amount of embedded bits in different test images

Image name (256x256 pixels)	Embedded bits
Katia	183
Baboon	182
Camera	105
Fruits	179

The obtained results were used for the evaluation of the watermark capacity for the famous test grayscale image "Lena" of size 512×512 pixels. In the work of Moulin and Mihcak (2002), an example with the test image "Lena" (of same size) for data hiding in the coefficients of a DCT or wavelet transform in sub-blocks of size 8×8 pixels is presented. The obtained watermark capacity was $C = 0.033$ bpp, and the PSNR of the watermarked image was 38 dB. When the same image was watermarked in the phase domain with Δ=120 and 96 bits for sub-block of size 16×16 pixels the inserted data are $0.08 \times 1024 \times N_\varphi(4,1) = 7864$ bits. In this case the obtained watermark capacity was $C = 0.03$ bpp. The *PSNR* of the watermarked image is 45 *dB*. The comparison shows that for same watermark capacity the quality of the watermarked image is much higher (45 *dB* for the phase watermarking and 38 *dB* for watermarking based on DCT or wavelet transforms). An additional advantage is the lower computational complexity of the new method. The detailed evaluation for 3-layer IDP and wavelet transform with filters of 3 and 5 coefficients for image of size 512×512 pixels, presented in the work of Kountchev et al. (2005), shows that the number of the necessary multiplications in the IDP coder is 10 times lower and the number of additions – more than 2 times lower.

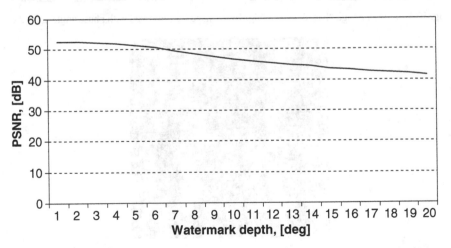

Fig. 16.6. *PSNR [dB]* results for different values of Δ_0

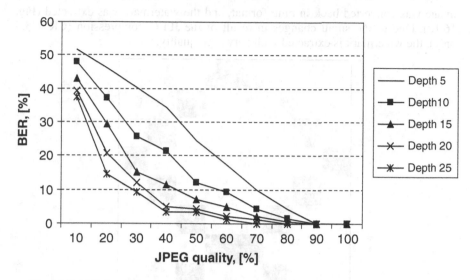

Fig. 16.7. *BER* for different watermark depth

In the figures below, some of the results obtained with fragile watermarking of natural images are presented.

The watermark *"WMD4"*, shown in Fig. 16.8, was inserted in the test image "Fruits" (Fig. 16.9). In this example, the watermark and the processed image are both grayscale, *8* bpp.

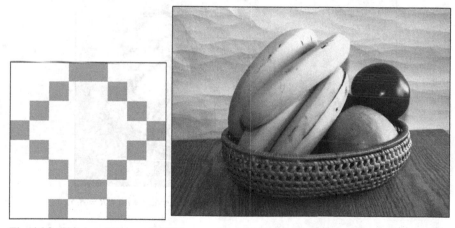

Fig. 16.8. Watermark image *WMD4*   **Fig. 16.9.** The original test image *"Fruits"*
256 x 256 pixels   600 x 450 pixels

The watermark resistance was checked after JPEG compression with compression ratio 2. The conversion to JPEG and the corresponding compression were performed with *Microsoft Photo Editor*. After the compression, the test image was converted back in bmp format, and the watermark was extracted (Fig. 16.10). Due to the small changes in result of the JPEG compression (CR = 3.5 only), the watermark is extracted with very high quality.

Fig. 16.10. Extracted watermark after JPEG compression with *CR = 3.5*

Fig. 16.11. Extracted watermark after JPEG compression with *CR = 8.5.*

For higher compressions, the quality of the extracted watermark is worse; an example is presented in Fig. 16.11. In this case, the watermark was extracted after JPEG compression with *CR = 8.5,* which creates significant changes. This method is suitable for protection of scanned documents, where every change in the extracted watermark would prove unauthorized editing.

Similar results were obtained for the test image *"Decoration"* (Fig. 16.12). The watermarked image is shown in Fig. 16.13. The extracted watermark is shown in Fig. 16.14 and the inserted watermark *"WMD2"* - in Fig. 16.15. The experiment proved that the inserted watermark is transparent, and the visual quality of the processed image is retained.

Fig. 16.12. Test image *"Decoration"* – original; 700 x 570 pixels, 8 bpp.

Fig. 16.13. Watermarked test image with the invisible watermark *WMD2*

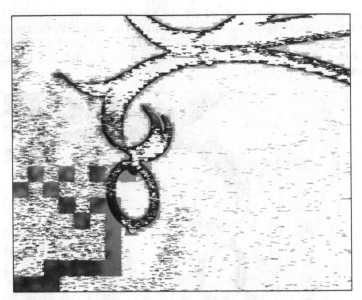

Fig. 16.14. Extracted watermark after JPEG compression (*CR = 18*)

Fig. 16.15. Watermark image *WMD2;* 256×256 pixels, 8bpp

The ability to insert significant amounts of data could be used for hiding important visual information, for example, fingerprints, signatures, etc. For this, a large image size should be used as a hiding media, as this offers enough possibilities to accept the inserted data without noticeable loss of visual quality. For example, a color image of size *1024×1024* pixels can successfully hide a compressed signature or fingerprint image of size 10 - 15 *KB* (the calculations are for block size of *16×16* pixels, 3-layer watermarking). The compressed fingerprints and signature images were obtained with special lossless compression, presented by Kountchev et al. (2007), which ensures very high efficiency. As a result of the ability to hide significant amounts of data containing biometric information, this watermarking is suitable for applications which require distance authentication and secure access control in such applications like bank services, confidential information access and transfer, etc.

Other experiments were performed for contents protection and access control applications. To this end, visible fragile watermarks, which overlap (hide) the whole image or most of its important parts, were used. The watermark removal is performed using a password. The procedure requires the watermarked image to be processed with the watermarking software. After this procedure, the watermark "hides" the whole image or a part of it, as it is shown in Fig. 16.16 below. The example presents a medical ultrasound image. The watermark is shown in Fig. 16.17. In this case, the watermark is smaller than the processed image and hides the region of interest. This approach ensures successful access in image databases and permits watermark removal for authorized users only.

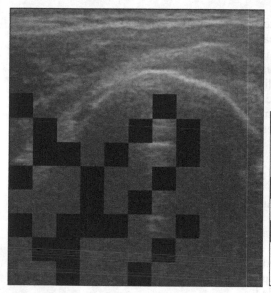

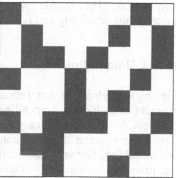

Fig. 16.16. Ultrasound image with hiding watermark   **Fig. 16.17.** Watermark image *WMD1*

16.6. Application areas

16.6.1. Resistant watermarks

The basic application of the resistant watermarks is for IP protection and rights management. There are three important advantages of the watermarking method, which define its main applications: the watermark transparency, the watermark resistance, and the watermark capacity. The watermark transparency is an important quality for retaining the processed image quality. The ability to insert an invisible watermark permits the method to be successfully applied for wide image groups: natural images (color and grayscale), medical information, scanned documents, etc. The high watermark resistance permits its use in any kind of application, where unauthorized editing or use is possible. The high capacity of the presented watermarking method permits the insertion of significant amounts of data.

The presented method for resistant watermarking in the image phase domain is quite suitable for application in up-to-date, high-resolution photo cameras. The relatively low computational complexity of the method permits its real-time applications.

16.6.2. Fragile watermarks

The presented method permits the insertion of two kinds of fragile watermarks: transparent and hiding. The transparent watermarks are suitable for image contents protection and prove any kind of image editing. Their main application areas are: digital libraries, Internet applications using documents or pictures, archiving of important documents, etc. The hiding watermarks are suitable for access control in image databases - for example databases containing medical or biometric information. The fragile watermark is easily destroyed with any kind of compression or editing and is accessible for authorized users only.

16.6.3. Data hiding

The high payload of the presented watermarking method permits its use for efficient data hiding. Depending on the application, the hidden data could be different, for example - binary data or images (compressed or not). In case that the hidden information is binary data or biometrics, it is more suitable to use fragile watermarking. For such applications, the most efficient approach is to compress the image (for example - fingerprint or signature) with some kind of lossless compression, and after that, to hide it.

For applications aimed at proving the authenticity of the original image, the inserted watermark (the hidden information) could be of any kind (another image, sign, data, etc.).

16.7. Conclusion

A new method for image watermarking is developed using the phase spectrum of digital images. The watermarked image is obtained after multi-level IDP decomposition with 2D CHT. The watermark data inserted in the consecutive decomposition layers do not interact, and the watermark could be detected without using the original image. The main advantages of the presented method which result from the high stability of their phase spectrum, obtained with the truncated 2D-CHT are the perceptual transparency of the inserted resistant watermark; its large information capacity; and the high resistance against noises in the communication channel and pirates' attacks for its removal. Specific advantage of the presented method is that the parts of the watermark, inserted in the consecutive decomposition layers, can be treated as different watermarks and can contain independent parts of the inserted information (if necessary). The watermark is highly resistant against cropping, small rotations, or other editing tools, because the watermark data is a part of the image contents and is not lost as a result of such processing. The method ensures high accuracy for the watermark extraction in all pyramid layers, practical watermark invisibility, and resistance against multiple lossy JPEG compression and other manipulations of the watermarked images. The decoding and the corresponding watermark visualization are performed using a secure password and special decoding software.

The method permits the insertion of resistant and fragile watermarks in one image, which ensures higher security for the original image content and provides wider possibilities for multiple applications.

The method is suitable for streaming media as well. In this case, the compressed watermark could be different for every part of the contents. A special version of the method for audio watermarking was presented in the work of Kountchev, Milanova, Todorov and Kountcheva (2007), which proved the method efficiency for such applications.

The future development of the method will be aimed at multi-layer watermarking of multi-spectral images and real-time TV broadcasting.

16.8 Exercises

1. What are the advantages of the presented new method for multi-layer watermarking in the image phase domain, obtained with ordered 2D-CHT and SP?
2. What are the advantages of the ordered complex Hadamard matrix in comparison with the natural one?
3. How are selected the coefficients of the ordered CHT transform, which are suitable for phase watermarking?
4. How is build the pyramid in the image spectrum domain?
5. What technique is used for the extraction of the multi-layer watermark inserted in the image phase domain?
6. How is calculated the capacity of the digital multi-layer watermark?
7. Define please the coefficients $\tilde{s}_0'(u,v)$ of the ordered 2D-CHT if it is applied on input image block of the kind:

$$[B(4)]=\begin{bmatrix} B(0,0) & B(0,1) & B(0,2) & B(0,3) \\ B(1,0) & B(1,1) & B(1,2) & B(1,3) \\ B(2,0) & B(2,1) & B(2,2) & B(2,3) \\ B(3,0) & B(3,1) & B(3,2) & B(3,3) \end{bmatrix}$$

and using the matrix-mask, presented below:

$$[L_0(4)]=\begin{bmatrix} 1 & 1 & 0 & 0 \\ 1 & 1 & 0 & 0 \\ 0 & 0 & 0 & 0 \\ 0 & 0 & 0 & 0 \end{bmatrix}$$

8. Calculate please the capacity of the watermark, inserted in sub-blocks of size 4x4 pixels, for image of size $256x256$ pixels.
9. What are the basic applications of the digital image watermarking?
10. What are the basic methods for image watermarking?

Training example:

The watermarking method will be applied on image block of size 4×4.
The watermark will be inserted in the decomposition layer $p = 0$ of the image block, which elements $B(i, k)$ are as follows:

$$[B(4)]=\begin{bmatrix} B(0,0) & B(0,1) & B(0,2) & B(0,3) \\ B(1,0) & B(1,1) & B(1,2) & B(1,3) \\ B(2,0) & B(2,1) & B(2,2) & B(2,3) \\ B(3,0) & B(3,1) & B(3,2) & B(3,3) \end{bmatrix}=\begin{bmatrix} 0 & 1 & 2 & 3 \\ 1 & 2 & 3 & 4 \\ 2 & 3 & 4 & 5 \\ 3 & 4 & 5 & 6 \end{bmatrix}$$

The transform of the block $[B(4)]$ is calculated first, using the direct ordered 2D-CHT in correspondence with Eq. (16.1):

$$[S_0'(4)]=[CH_0'(4)]\times[B(4)]\times[CH_0'(4)]=\begin{bmatrix} 48 & -4(3+j) & 0 & -4(3-j) \\ -8(1+j) & 0 & 0 & 0 \\ -8(1-j) & 0 & 0 & 0 \\ -8 & 0 & 0 & 0 \end{bmatrix}$$

Then from Eq.(16.4) and using the chosen matrix-mask $[L_0(4)]$ is obtained the transform, which contains the retained complex-conjugated coefficients:

$$[\tilde{S}_0'(4)] = \begin{bmatrix} 48 & -4(3+j) & 0 & -4(3-j) \\ -8(1+j) & 0 & 0 & 0 \\ -8(1-j) & 0 & 0 & 0 \\ 0 & 0 & 0 & 0 \end{bmatrix}$$

The retained complex coefficients are $\tilde{s}_0'(0,1)$, $\tilde{s}_0'(1,0)$ and $\tilde{s}_0'(1,1)$.

The next task is to define the retained coefficients, which satisfy the watermarking condition, presented in Eq. (16.10), when $\alpha_0 = 0.2$ and $\delta_0 = 0.1$. For $\tilde{M}_{0,max} = 48$, the condition $\alpha_0 \tilde{M}_{0,max} > \delta_0$ is satisfied and from this follows $\eta_0 = \alpha_0 \tilde{M}_{0,max} = 9.6$. The modules and phases of the complex-conjugated couples of coefficients are then defined in accordance with the relations:

$$\left| \tilde{M}_0'(0,1) \right| = \left| M_0'^*(0,3) \right| = 12.65 > \eta_0, \ \tilde{\varphi}_0'(0,1) = -\tilde{\varphi}_0'^*(0,3) = 18.43^0,$$

$$\left| \tilde{M}_0'(1,0) \right| = \left| M_0'^*(2,0) \right| = 11.31 > \eta_0, \ \tilde{\varphi}_0'(1,0) = -\tilde{\varphi}_0'^*(2,0) = 45^0,$$

$$\left| \tilde{M}_0'(1,1) \right| = \left| M_0'^*(2,3) \right| = 0 < \eta_0, \ \tilde{\varphi}_0'(1,1) = -\tilde{\varphi}_0'^*(2,3) = 0.$$

From this follows that the phases of coefficients $\tilde{s}_0'(0,1)$ and $\tilde{s}_0'(1,0)$ only are suitable for watermarking in correspondence with Eq. (16.11). Let the chosen phase angle is $\Delta_0 = 10^0$ and the watermark b_0 is with length $R_0 = 2$ and consists of the binary elements $w_1(b_0) = w_2(b_0) = 1$. Then, from Eq. (16.11) and for $r = 1, 2$ is obtained:

$$\tilde{\varphi}_{0w_r}'(0,1) = -\tilde{\varphi}_{0w_r}'^*(0,3) = \begin{cases} \tilde{\varphi}_0'(0,1) + \Delta_0 = 28.43^0 & \text{if} \quad w_r(b_0) = 1; \\ \tilde{\varphi}_0'(0,1) - \Delta_0 = 8.43^0 & \text{if} \quad w_r(b_0) = 0, \end{cases}$$

$$\tilde{\varphi}_{0w_r}'(1,0) = -\tilde{\varphi}_{0w_r}'^*(2,0) = \begin{cases} \tilde{\varphi}_0'(1,0) + \Delta_0 = 55^0 & \text{if} \quad w_r(b_0) = 1; \\ \tilde{\varphi}_0'(1,0) - \Delta_0 = 35^0 & \text{if} \quad w_r(b_0) = 0. \end{cases}$$

The corresponding watermarked coefficients are presented as follows:

$$\tilde{s}_{0w_r}'(u,v) = -\tilde{M}_0'(u,v) \cos \tilde{\varphi}_{w_r}'(u,v) - j \tilde{M}_0'(u,v) \sin \tilde{\varphi}_{w_r}'(u,v),$$

because in this case their modules' signs are presented by the term $sign[\overline{M}_0'(u,v)] = -1$.

From this follows that after rounding is obtained:

$$\tilde{s}'_{0w_r}(0,1) \approx \begin{cases} -11-j6 \ \text{if} \ w_r(b_0)=1; \\ -13-j2 \ \text{if} \ w_r(b_0)=0, \end{cases} \quad \tilde{s}'_{0w_r}(1,0) \approx \begin{cases} -6-j9 \ \text{if} \ w_r(b_0)=1; \\ -9-j6 \ \text{if} \ w_r(b_0)=0. \end{cases}$$

The transform of the zero approximation for block $[B(4)]$, watermarked with the watermark b_0 is:

$$[\tilde{S}'_{0w}(4)] = \begin{bmatrix} 48 & -11-j6 & 0 & -11+j6 \\ -6-9j & 0 & 0 & 0 \\ -6+9j & 0 & 0 & 0 \\ 0 & 0 & 0 & 0 \end{bmatrix} \ \text{if} \ w_1(b_0)=w_2(b_0)=1$$

The watermarked zero approximation is obtained applying inverse ordered 2D DCT in correspondence with Eq. (16.13) on the transform obtained:

$$[\tilde{B}_{0w}(4)] = \frac{1}{16}[CH'_0(4)]^{*t} \times [\tilde{S}'_{0w}(4)] \times [CH'_0(4)]^{*t} = \begin{bmatrix} 0 & 1 & 2 & 4 \\ 0 & 1 & 3 & 3 \\ 2 & 3 & 4 & 4 \\ 3 & 4 & 5 & 5 \end{bmatrix}.$$

The watermarked block $[B_{0w}(4)]$ is calculated in accordance with Eq. (16.17), defining the non-watermarked zero approximation for the layer $p = 0$ from Eq. (16.15) and the inverse ordered 2D-CHT:

$$[\tilde{B}_0(4)] = \frac{1}{16}[CH'_0(4)]^{*t} \times [\tilde{S}'_0(4)] \times [CH'_0(4)]^{*t} = \begin{bmatrix} 0 & 1 & 2 & 3 \\ 0 & 1 & 2 & 3 \\ 2 & 3 & 4 & 5 \\ 2 & 3 & 4 & 5 \end{bmatrix}.$$

Then, in accordance with Eq. (16.16) is calculated the difference matrix for the layer $p = 0$:

$$[E_0(4)] = [B(4)] - [\tilde{B}_0(4)] = \begin{bmatrix} 0 & 0 & 0 & 0 \\ 1 & 1 & 1 & 1 \\ 0 & 0 & 0 & 0 \\ 1 & 1 & 1 & 1 \end{bmatrix}.$$

From Eq. (16.17) is obtained the matrix of the watermarked block:

$$[B_{0w}(4)] = [\tilde{B}_{0w}(4)] + [E_0(4)] = \begin{bmatrix} 0 & 1 & 2 & 4 \\ 1 & 2 & 4 & 4 \\ 2 & 3 & 4 & 4 \\ 4 & 5 & 6 & 6 \end{bmatrix}.$$

The watermarking errors are defined by the matrix:

$$[\varepsilon_0(4)]=[B(4)]-[B_{0w}(4)]=\begin{bmatrix} 0 & 0 & 0 & -1 \\ 0 & 0 & -1 & 0 \\ 0 & 0 & 0 & 1 \\ -1 & -1 & -1 & 0 \end{bmatrix}.$$

The quality of the watermarked block is evaluated by the peak signal-to-noise ratio (PSNR) for the layer $p = 0$ for $B_{max} = 255$, using the error matrix $[E_0(4)]$ and in accordance with Eqs. (16.54) and (16.55).

$$PSNR_0 = 10\lg_{10}(B_{max}^2/\overline{\varepsilon_0^2}) = 10\lg_{10}\left[\frac{255^2\times16}{6}\right] = 52.39, \ [dB].$$

The PSNR value obtained proves that the inserted watermark is practically unnoticeable.

<u>Watermark extraction</u>: for this are first defined the possible transform coefficients suitable for watermarking. Then the watermarked transform for the layer $p = 0$ is calculated.

$$[S'_{0w}(4)]=[CH'_0(4)]\times[B_{0w}(4)]\times[CH'_0(4)]=\begin{bmatrix} 52 & -11-j5 & -2 & -11+j5 \\ -6-10j & -1-j & 2 & -3-j \\ -6+10j & -3+j & 2 & -1+j \\ -12 & -1+j & 2 & -1-j \end{bmatrix}.$$

The modules of the retained coefficients are calculated and then is checked if they satisfy the condition in Eq. (16.10) for $\alpha_0 = 0.2$ and $\delta_0 = 0.1$. It is known, that $M_{0w,max} = 52$ and $\alpha_0 M_{0w,max} > \delta_0$, so then $\eta_0 = \alpha_0 M_{0w,max} = 10.4$.

$$\left|M'_{0w}(0,1)\right|=\left|M'^*_{0w}(0,3)\right|=\sqrt{146} = 12.08 > \eta_0,$$

$$\left|M'_{0w}(1,0)\right|=\left|M'^*_{0w}(2,0)\right|=\sqrt{136} = 11.66 > \eta_0,$$

$$\left|M'_{0w}(1,1)\right|=\left|M'^*_{0w}(2,3)\right|=\sqrt{2} = 1.41 < \eta_0,$$

From this follows that the phases of coefficients $\widetilde{s}'_{0w}(0,1)$ and $\widetilde{s}'_{0w}(1,0)$ only are suitable for watermarking in accordance with Eq. (16.11). The phases are defined by the relations:

$$\tilde{\varphi}'_{0w}(0,1) = -\tilde{\varphi}'^{*}_{0w}(0,3)= 24.4^{0}, \; \tilde{\varphi}'_{0w}(1,0) = -\tilde{\varphi}'^{*}_{0w}(2,0)=59^{0}.$$

The decision for the detection of the searched watermark b_o with elements $w_1(b_o) = w_2(b_o) = 1$ in the layer $p = 0$ is taken using the cross-correlation coefficient $\rho_{m,b}(0)$ for the unknown watermark m_o with length $R_o = 2$. Using the Eqs. (16.35) and (16.39), for $\Delta_0 = 10^0$ and $m_o = b_o$ is obtained:

$$\rho_b(0)=\frac{C_b(0)}{R_0\Delta_0^2} = \begin{cases} \dfrac{1}{2\Delta_0}[\tilde{\varphi}'_{0w}(0,1)+\tilde{\varphi}'_{0w}(1,0)]=4.17 & \text{if } w_1=w_2=1, \\[2ex] \dfrac{1}{2\Delta_0}[\tilde{\varphi}'_{0w}(0,1)-\tilde{\varphi}'_{0w}(1,0)]=-1.73 & \text{if } w_1=1, w_2=0, \\[2ex] \dfrac{1}{2\Delta_0}[-\tilde{\varphi}'_{0w}(0,1)+\tilde{\varphi}'_{0w}(1,0)]=1.73 & \text{if } w_1=0, w_2=1, \\[2ex] \dfrac{1}{2\Delta_0}[-\tilde{\varphi}'_{0w}(0,1)-\tilde{\varphi}'_{0w}(1,0)]=-4.17 & \text{if } w_1=w_2=0. \end{cases}$$

From the values obtained for $\rho_b(0)$ follows that the watermark b_0, detected in the block $[B_{0w}(4)]$, is with elements $w_1(b_o) = w_2(b_o) = 1$, i.e. for the case, where $\rho_b(0)$ has maximum value .

16.9 Acknowledgment

This work was supported by the National Fund for Scientific Research of the Bulgarian Ministry of Education and Science (Contract VU-I -305/07) and the US-Bulgarian project in the Science of Learning, National Academy of Science, USA. Special thanks to the Laboratory for Image and Sound Processing of the Technical University of Sofia – Bulgaria, which provided the test images from their own database.

16.10 References

Arnold M, Schmucker M, Wolthusen ST (2003) Techniques and Applications of Digital Watermarking and Content Protection. Artech House.

Barni M, Bartolini F (2004) Watermarking Systems Engineering: Enabling Digital Assets Security and Other Applications. Marcel Dekker.

Cox I, Miller M, Bloom J (2002) Digital Watermarking. Morgan-Kaufmann, San Francisco.

Furht B (2006) Multimedia Watermarking Techniques and Applications (Internet and Communications Series). Auerbach.

Falkowski B, Lim L (2000) Image watermarking using Hadamard transforms. Electronic Letters Vol 36 No 3 Feb, pp. 211-213.

Katzenbeisser S, Petitcolas F (2000) Information Hiding Techniques for Steganography and Digital Watermarking. Artech House.

Kountchev R, Milanova M, Ford C, Rubin S (2003) Multimedia Watermarking with Complex Hadamard Transform in the Inverse Pyramid Decomposition. Proc. of the 2003 IEEE Intern. Conf. on Information Reuse and Integration, USA pp. 305-310.

Kountchev R, Milanova M, Ford C, Kountcheva R (2005) Multi-layer Image Transmission with Inverse Pyramidal Decomposition. In: Computational Intelligence for Modelling and Predictions, S. Halgamuge, L. Wang (Eds.), Vol. 2, Chapter No 13, Springer-Verlag, pp. 179-196.

Kountchev R, Todorov Vl, Kountcheva R, Milanova M (2006) Lossless Compression of Biometric Images and Digital Watermarking with IDP Decomposition. WSEAS Trans. on Signal Processing Vol. 2 pp. 684-691.

Kountchev R, Milanova M, Todorov Vl, Kountcheva R (2007) Multiple audio Watermarking with Spectrum Pyramid. International Journal of Computer Science and Network Security (IJCSNS) pp. 191-200.

Kountchev R, Todorov Vl, Kountcheva R (2007) Compression and Contents Protection of Images, Texts and Graphics for Distance Learning Applications. Proc. of the 6th WSEAS Intern. Conf. on Signal Processing, Robotics and Automation, Greece pp. 83-90.

Mironov R, Kountchev R, Mirchev V (2007) Ordered Complex Hadamard Transform of Images. XLII Intern. Scientific Conf. on Information, Communication and Energy Systems and Technologies (ICEST'07) Macedonia pp. 369-372.

Moulin P, Mihcak M (Sept. 2002) A framework for evaluating the data-hiding capacity of image sources. IEEE Transactions on Image Processing, Vol. 11, Issue 9, pp. 1029-1042.

O'Ruanaidh J, Dowling W, Boland F (1996) Phase Watermarking of Digital Images. In: Proceedings of Int. Conf. on Image Processing Vol. 3, Sept, pp. 239-242.

Tewfik A (2000) Digital Watermarking. IEEE Signal Processing Magazine Vol. 17, Sept, pp.17-88.

17 Immersive Visualization of Cellular Structures

Sinan Kockara, Nawab Ali, and Serhan Dagtas

Department of Applied Science, University of Arkansas at Little Rock
Little Rock, AR, USA

17.1 Introduction

Bioimaging is an immensely powerful tool in biomedical research that aids the understanding of cellular structures and the molecular events in the cell. Understanding the biological functions within the cell requires an in-depth understanding of all the diverse functions of the microscopic structures and the molecular interactions between macromolecules in their natural environment. Traditionally, cell biologists have used light microscopy techniques to study topographical characterization of cell surfaces. The optical properties of a light microscope give occasion to a blurring phenomenon similar to the one with a conventional microscope with the result that images are characterized by low resolution and magnification. We address the challenging task of enhancing the image produced by a light microscope by reconstructing a stack of monoscopic images from a light microscope to produce a single image with inferential and useful information than that obtained at the best focus level. We believe such an approach will enable a wider base of microscope users to take advantage of light microscope imaging in biological research.

Most of the prior work in this area has focused on reconstruction of the surface model, based on variations of methods such as shape from focus and depth from focus (Nayar and Nakagawa 1990). Shape from focus (SFF) method obtains the surface models of objects from multiple monoscopic images (Nayar and Nakagawa 1990; Nayar 1992; Nayar et al. 1995; Jarvis 1983; Darrell and Wohn 1988; Xiong and Shafer 1993; Yeo et al. 1993; Horn 1968) while depth from focus (DFF) is a model-based method in which the depth map of a scene is computed by solving the inverse problem of blurring process based on camera and edge models (Grossman 1987; Pentland 1987; Subbarao 1988; Lai et al. 1992; Ens and Lawrance 1993). Our work addresses microscopic imaging for the visualization of

Y. Chan et al. (eds.), *Data Engineering*, International Series in Operations
Research & Management Science 132, DOI 10.1007/978-1-4419-0176-7_17,
© Springer Science+Business Media, LLC 2010

the inner structures using translucent images by the reconstruction of the optical sectioning of a specimen from a stack of images.

The inherent imaging properties of a light microscope used in visualization of cellular structures result in images characterized by low resolution and magnification. The images are obtained by using the microscope parameters (typically the focal setting), and are taken from a single point of view. We report a novel mutual information based image clearance algorithm to refine a set of 2D images taken in a light microscope at different focal settings each representing a cross sectional view at the focal plane level and combining the most informative features from each level to produce a single image. The results illustrate that the algorithm produces an image with enhanced visualization of cellular structures than that obtained by the best focus leveled image and thus offers a viable alternative to enhance images produced by a traditional light microscope.

Our goal is to develop a practical, low-cost layer separation method by taking images of cellular structures using multiple focus level of light microscope and visualize the cellular structure in a six-degree of freedom virtual reality environment. We have developed several algorithms that use 2D images obtained at multiple focus levels to construct an image of the object by cleaning other layers' data from focused layer as much as possible. To do that we used statistical distance measures; Kullback-Leibler (KL) divergence and its more intuitive version, the Information Radius (IRad). This has the potential of greatly enhancing the viewing process and expose visual information which is otherwise hidden. The results illustrate that our proposed layer separation from multiple focus levels method is efficient for translucent objects in light microscope.

The rest of the chapter structured as follows. Section 17.2 explains basics of focus. Section 17.3 introduces flat-field correction to eliminate detectors' artifacts. Section 17.4 represents the separation of layers of each focal plane using statistical techniques. Section 17.5 presents 3D Visualization of Cellular Structures. Section 17.6 presents the conclusions of the study.

17.2 Light Microscopic Cellular Images and Focus: Basics

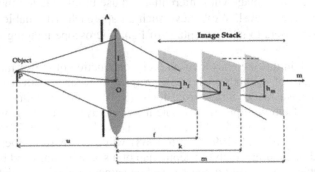

Fig. 17.1. Image formation and volume from focus

Fundamental to the method using the statistical layer separation (SLS) algorithm is the relationship between focused and defocused images. Figure 17.1 is an
illustration of the basic image formation system in a typical light microscope with
different focus level of images (image stack). Light rays from P pass through the
aperture A are refracted by the lens to converge at h_k on the image plane at distance m. The relationship among the object distance u, focal length of the lens f,
and image distances k and m is determined by the lens law (17.1). When an object
is placed at distance u from the lens, the sharply focused image of the object is obtained if the distance between the image plane and the lens is k, where u, k and the
focal length f of the lens satisfy the thin lens formula:

$$\frac{1}{f} = \frac{1}{u} + \frac{1}{k} \tag{17.1}$$

A simple microscope model consists of a lens and an image plane used to derive some fundamental characteristics of focusing based on geometrical optics.
Figure 17.2 shows the depiction of the microscope's optical system and the image
stack with 240 monoscopic images obtained at different focus levels. Here we denote the thickness of the specimen of 240 multiple images as z_0 and the best focused image as k_{150}. Each image in the Figure 17.2 (k_1 ... k_{240}) corresponds to the
image obtained by using focus intervals that gives the information from the specific layer of the specimen. z_0 is the overall thickness of the specimen. z_1 and (z_0-
z_1)are partial thicknesses of the specimen post-best focused image and pre-best focus respectively. Every image layer has its own unique information that is not
present in any other layer. The SLS algorithm first extracts the unique information
from each layer and then combines them to produce an enhanced image. The SLS
does not only produce final image including the most informative data from each
layer but also extracts each layers unique data.

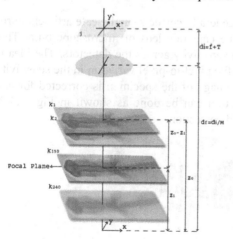

Fig. 17.2. Imaging of volume object, M is magnification of the objective lens, f
is the focal length of the lens and T is the optical tube length

17.3 Flat-Field Correction

A number indicating the quality of the image is the signal-to-noise ratio (SNR). It can be calculated from two independent images I_1 and I_2 of a homogeneous, uniformly illuminated area with the same mean value μ. The variance σ^2 of the difference between the two images depends on photon shot noise, dark current, and readout noise and is calculated as:

$$\sigma^2 = \frac{\text{var}(I_1 - I_2)}{2} \tag{17.2}$$

Then SNR is calculated as:

$$\text{SNR} = 20\log(\frac{\mu}{\sigma})\text{dB} \tag{17.3}$$

Even with a clean specimen preparation and optimal optics, it is possible to get undesired elements in the output image, such as shading or dark current. To eliminate these artifacts, every image taken by a camera (I_o) should be corrected by flat field correction. In addition to the image of the object, an image of the background (I_b) and an image of the camera noise (I_{dark}) are needed (17.4). Dark field image (I_{dark}) is taken by covering the camera's lens with a black cover and the background image (I_b) is taken without a specimen to catch possible undesired noise.

$$I_c = \frac{I_o - I_{dark}}{I_b - I_{dark}} \tag{17.4}$$

The flat-field correction of images generally corrects small-scale artifacts introduced by the detectors e.g. dust on the camera's lens or microscope bulb. This procedure corrects for the variation in sensitivity across the detectors. The idea is that any variation in an image records the pixel-to-pixel variation in the sensitivity of the imaging system. Once the raw image of the specimen is corrected for any dark current (I_{dark}), a flat-field correction can be done as shown in Fig. 17.3, which shows the results of the flat-field correction.

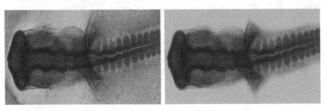

Fig. 17.3. a) Original image k150, b) flat-field corrected image

17.4 Separation of Transparent Layers using Focus

Considerable problem in each layer is that every image contains some of the other layers' data. To clean these data, different classical image subtraction algorithms are not adequate due to minute changes in each layer.

The next step in our approach is to obtain a filtered version of the images captured at each focal plane. Statistical separation algorithms have not been explored widely for layer separation of microscopic translucent image sequences. Schechner et al. (2000) proposes a new method for separation of transparent layers. Several measures have been reported to quantify the difference (sometimes called divergence) between two (or more) probability distributions (Borovkov 1984). Of those measures, the two most commonly used are KL divergence and the Jensen-Shannon divergence (information radius)) measures. KL divergence uses the following formula:

$$D(P \parallel Q) = \sum_i p_i \cdot \log(\frac{p_i}{q_i}) \qquad (17.5)$$

This can be considered as a measure of how different two probability distributions of p and q are. The problem with this method is that it is undefined when $q_i = 0$. In addition, KL divergence is not appropriate as a measure of similarity because it is not symmetric, i.e.,

$$D(P \parallel Q) \neq D(Q \parallel P) \qquad (17.6)$$

If we apply KL divergence to differentiate each specimen-layer's image from others, then the measure can be formulated as

$$D(P \parallel Q) = \sum_{x=1}^{W} \sum_{y=1}^{H} abs(\frac{1}{3} \sum_{z=1}^{3} P(x,y,z) \log \frac{P(x,y,z)}{Q(x,y,z)}) \qquad (17.17)$$

This formula provides a quantitative measure of how much image P differs from image Q. P and Q are images that are taken from different focus levels. W and H are image width and height. Z is RGB color channel.

Φ (x) is regularizing function shown in (17.8). This function is used to keep image's intensity values within the range.

$$\Phi(x) = \begin{cases} x = 0 & \text{,if } x < 0 \\ x = \beta & \text{,if } x > \beta \end{cases} \qquad (17.8)$$

β is a maximum intensity value of the image.
Because the undefined nature of K-L divergence when $Q_i(x,y,z) = 0$ (i is i[th]

image) we used another mutual information approach for layer cleaning which is the Jensen-Shannon divergence (also known as information radius or IRad) (Haykin 1994).

$$\text{IRad}(P_k, Q_i) = D(P_k \| \frac{(P_k + Q_i)}{2}) + D(Q_i \| \frac{(P_k + Q_i)}{2}) \tag{17.9}$$

Information radius is a symmetric function, i.e,

$$\text{IRad}(P_k, Q_i) = \text{IRad}(Q_i, P_k) \tag{17.10}$$

Suppose image $P_k(x,y,z)$ is an RGB image of our specimen at focus level k. $P_k(x,y,z)$ shows probability distribution of image at position x, y, z which can be thought as the source of a certain amount of contribution, which is defined as

$$\log \frac{1}{P_k(x, y, z)} \tag{17.11}$$

and assume $P_k(x,y,z)$ is the probability function associated with the outcome. Then the entropy of this probability distribution is defined as

$$H(P_k(x, y, z)) = -\sum P_k(x, y, z) \log(P_k(x, y, z)) \tag{17.12}$$

Also, joint entropy $H(P_k(x,y,z), Q_i(x,y,z))$ is defined as below (Papoulis 1991),

$$H(P_k(x, y, z), Q_i(x,y,z)) = -\sum_k \sum_i P_k(x, y, z) Q_i(x,y,z) \log(P_i(x,y,z) Q_i(x,y,z)) \tag{17.13}$$

If we normalize (17.9) with joint entropy in (17.13), normalized quantity of difference, which is IRad in our case, with two different images (P and Q) becomes

$$\frac{D(P_k \| \frac{(P_k + Q_i)}{2}) + D(Q_i \| \frac{(P_k + Q_i)}{2})}{H(P_k(x, y, z), Q_i(x,y,z))} \tag{17.14}$$

If we plug normalized IRad (equation (17.14)) into the equation (17.5), then final form becomes

$$\text{Let } \kappa = P_k(x, y, z) \log\left(\frac{P_k(x, y, z)}{\frac{P_k(x, y, z) + Q_i(x, y, z)}{2}}\right) \text{ and } v = Q_i(x, y, z) \log\left(\frac{Q_i(x, y, z)}{\frac{Q_i(x, y, z) + P_k(x, y, z)}{2}}\right) \tag{17.15}$$

where P and Q are two different images. (x,y) values are corresponding to a unique pixel of an image and z value represents 3 channels RGB values of that pixel.

$$\sum_{x=1}^{W}\sum_{y=1}^{H}\Phi(\frac{1}{3}\otimes\frac{1}{k\mu}\sum_{z=1}^{3}\kappa+\nu \tag{17.16}$$

$$\sum_{x=1}^{W}\sum_{y=1}^{H}\Phi(\frac{1}{3}\otimes\frac{1}{k\eta}\sum_{z=1}^{3}\kappa+\nu$$

where η and μ are constants with $\eta < \mu$ and $\eta + \mu = 1$. We assume that the upper layer images affect the current layer image less and the lower layer images affect the current layer image more in a linear way, as the light source is below the specimen. Indices k and i are variables showing layer numbers of the image P and image Q.

As shown in (17.16), correlated information can be used to measure the mutual similarity between two images. This formula measures the mutual dependency or the amount of information one image contains about another. As a result, mutual information can be used to measure mutual difference between two images. Using this basic formulation, we can differentiate one image layer from others. Figure 17.4 demonstrates the significant results of the modified version of IRad algorithm for image separation in (17.16) as applied to the image (k_{150}) in the original image stack. Significance of the results is verified by biologists.

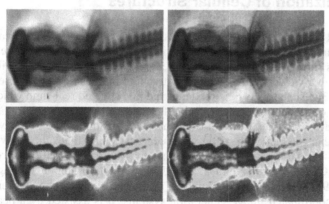

Fig. 17.4. a) Original image k1 (upper left image), b) After IRad applied, c), and d) colored forms

We have summarized below the steps involved in the SLS Algorithm (Algorithm 1). First, we crop every image to eliminate unnecessary data to save on computation time. Second, the flat-field correction of images corrects small-scale artifacts introduced by the detectors. Third, the modified IRad mutual information algorithm is applied to separate each specimen's layer at different focus levels from other (defocused) layers. The separated images are then combined together to establish a new image that contains not only the best focused level of details but also all the informative data from each layer.

```
Image Restoration
INPUTS:
    W, image width
    H, image height
    N, number of images
        I[W, H, N], input matrix-3D image stack (3D Array)
OUTPUTS:
    I_R Restored Image Stack
METHODS:
cropImage(), crops unnecessary data from image
applyFlatField(), applies flat field correction algorithm (Eq. 4)
applyIRAD(), applies information radius algorithm to given image stack (Eq. 23)
VARIABLES:
    I, input matrix
    Index, number of images
for index in 1 to Z
            I[:,:,N] ← cropImage ( I[:,:,N] )
            I[:,:,N] ← applyFlatField( I[:,:,N] )
        I_R ← applyIRAD( I_R )

end for
```

Algorithm 1. Image Restoration (SLS algorithm)

17.5 3D Visualization of Cellular Structures

Virtual Reality (VR) is a virtual environment that provides a user a sense of reality. It's usually a three-dimensional computer generated representation of the real world where user is surrounded by the environment and ideally, can interact with it. This is realized by a viewer centered view by tracking the position of the user. With VR, complex 3D databases can be rendered and investigated real-time which enables exploration of products that are in digital format.

We implemented a user friendly 3D visualization in an immersive VR environment that user can interact with a 3D specimen easily. To that aim, CAVE (CAVE Automatic Virtual Environment) VR system is used. It was first introduced in 1991 by Carolina Cruz-Neira at the University of Illinois at Chicago (Cruz-Neira et al. 1993). The CAVE is composed of three to six projection screens driven by a set of coordinated image-generation systems. It is assisted by a head and hand tracking system that produces stereo perspective.

17.5.1 Volume Rendering

So far, we have primarily focused on image processing algorithms to clean monoscopic images while preserving any informative data from these images for a viable

3D visualization. Our next step is to build 3D volume data using the stack of fil-tered 2D images.

Volume data is most often represented as a mesh (also known as grid). When representing volume data in 2D screen, four basic direct volume rendering methods have been used to depict the data in its entirety (interior as well as the exterior). A comparison of those volume rendering algorithms can be found at Meißner et al. (2000). The rendering times of these methods are very much dependent on the type of the dataset and the transfer functions. Shear-warp and 3D texture-mapping algorithms provide high performance, but at the cost of degraded quality of the output image. However, it is hard to say that one of those algorithms is the winner under all conditions; instead each one of them has certain advantages for the specific conditions.

Texture mapping is a method of adding realism to our images using textures instead of shading it. It was used by Cabral et al. (1994). This process reduces the computing time and makes the algorithm faster. After the volume loaded into the texture memory polygonal slices are rasterized to the view plane. For the interpolation usually a tri-linear function is used but quad-linear interpolation is also available. Also there are texture mappings with shading. We used this approach to exploit the increasing processing power and flexibility of the Graphics Processing Unit. One method to exploit graphics hardware is based on 2D texture mapping (Rezk-Salama et al. 2000). This method stores stacks of slices for each viewing axis in memory as two-dimensional textures. The stack most parallel to the current viewing direction is chosen and then mapped on object-aligned proxy geometry. It is rendered in back-to-front order using alpha blending.

Volume is represented by using texture mapping as the fundamental graphics primitive. The basic principle of three dimensional texture mapping is to apply texture onto the 3D scene. Volumetric data is copied into the two dimensional texture images as a stack of parallel slice planes of specimen and then displayed back-to-front with not sufficiently small intervals. Intervals were not sufficiently small since microscopic images were taken manually adjusted intervals. A number of slices determine the quality of resulting volumetric images. Since the specimen's layer images were taken fairly large intervals; thus, visualized volume data is not appealing.

Each slice plane of the chicken embryo is drawn by sampling the data in the volume by mapping sampled texture coordinates onto the polygon's vertices. Polygons are sliced through the volume perpendicular to the viewing direction. By using ray casting algorithm, the rendering process is done from back-to-front, and each voxel (a pixel representing volume) is blended using alpha blending algorithm with the previously drawn voxel.

The fundamental idea behind the alpha blending is that a third channel or image can be used to drive a blending process which combines the image of the object to be blended and background images. Alpha blending permits two or more images to be composited in such a way that composited image is undetectable whether composited or not. Alpha blending technique presented here combines the two images;

one is the image of the object to be blended called cutout image and the other one is the background image. Alpha blending (Porter and Duff 1984) achieved using the equation below

$$B_{ij}=C_{ij}A_{ij}+(1-A_{ij})B_{ij} \tag{17.17}$$

where i and j are image column and row indexes, respectively, and A_{ij} is a alpha factor that has a value between 0 and 1. B_{ij} is a pixel in the output image and C_{ij} is a pixel in the cutout image. 3D texture mapping allows using tri-linear interpolation supported by the graphics hardware and provides a consistent sampling rate (Meißner et al. 1999). Figure 17.5 represents volumized and cross-sectioned data using 2D texture mapping technique with alpha blending.

Fig. 17.5. Volumized embryo with different rotations and zooming levels

17.5.2 Immersive Visualization: CAVE Environment

Computer graphics and virtual reality technologies have advanced tremendously in recent years. Many application areas have emerged, from telemedicine to military training. A CAVE (Cave Audio Visual Experience Automatic Virtual Environment) is a room-size, immersive VR display environment where the stereoscopic view of the virtual world is generated according to the user's head position and orientation. The CAVE was chosen as a volume visualization environment because it provides an expanded field of view, the larger scale of objects, and suitability for gestural expressions and natural interaction. A participant who is submerged in a VR experience in which all sensory stimuli is cut out except what the computer is sending to the devices worn by the participant. A key advantage that a good VR experience has is real-time responses. The participant has the ability to move in six degrees of freedom within a virtual environment inhabited with virtual 3D objects. With increased flexibility, the users can move and interact in the environment freely and manipulate virtual objects in a virtual environment as the movements are being tracked and monitored as to the position in the x, y and z axis. This function is provided through electromagnetic sensing devices usually warn on the HMD (head mounted stereo displays) and the hands or other body area so that the participant is properly oriented within the environment and to the objects.

VRML (Virtual Reality Modeling Language) is one of the major platform independent development tools for 3D graphics and animation. VRML is rapidly becoming the standard file format for transmitting 3D virtual worlds across the Internet. Static and dynamic descriptions of 3D objects, multimedia content, and a variety of hyperlinks can be represented in the VRML files. Both VRML browsers and authoring tools for the creation of VRML files are widely available for several different platforms. Our VRML conversion method combines accelerated ray casting with VRML for the design of a CAVE based interactive system. The algorithm below summarizes the major steps of our conversion method. The algorithm below (Algorithm 2) produces the final VRMLsurface model of the volume that is produced by our modified IRad algorithm. Also, the configuration file with an extension ".vrd" is produced. VRD files are VRScape server's configuration files which are simple ASCII (text) files and specify the models that comprise a VRScape world. VRScape is a tool used to view VRML files in the CAVE environment (vrco.com 2007). This program also sets preferences on how to rescale and reposition the objects in the immersive world. Figure 17.6 shows VRML output of the example embryo displayed in the CAVE.

```
VRML export
  INPUTS:
          W, image width
          H, image height
          N, number of images
          I[W,H,N], input matrix-3D image stack (3D Array)
          I, input matrix
  OUTPUTS:
          Export.wrl, VRML file
  METHODS:
  importColor, imports colors from 3D array
  importCoordinate, imports coordinates from 3D array
  importPoints, imports points from 3D array
  importColorIndex, imports color indexes from 3D array
  insert, exports 3D array into VRML files
  CreateVRD, creates VRD files for VRSCAPE server to export CAVE environment
  VARIABLES:
          RGB_value, color value of the specific pixel
          Coordinate_Index, coordinate indexes
          Points, vertex points
          Color_Index, color indexes
          I[W,H,N], I is WxHxN matrix
 for index in 1 to W
  for index2 in 1 to H
   for index3 in 1 to N
     RGB_value _ importColor( I[index,index2, index3] )
     Coordinate_Index _ importCoordinate( I[index,index2,index3] )
     Points _ importPoints( I[index,index2, index3] )
     Color_Index _ importColorIndex( I[index,index2,index3] )
     insert( RGB_value, Coordinate_Index, Points, Color_Index, into Export.wrl )
    end for
   end for
  end for
 createVRD(Export.wrl)
```

Algorithm 2. VRML conversion

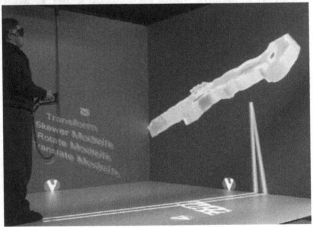

Fig. 17.6. Scientists can view and interact with the example 3D embryonic structure in a CAVE

17.6 Conclusions

We report a novel method to produce refined images of cellular structures from stack of images from a light microscope using the SLS algorithm. Our approach produces an enhanced image of the cellular structures typically obtained only with advanced equipment and is thus a low-cost alternative. The most critical step in light microscopy is focusing. Because our method combines the most informative and unique data from each focal plane, the necessity of finding best focus for light microscopic images may not be necessary. The areas of improvement include; improving the clarity of the output images and using the SLS algorithm to build 3D images by stacking optically sectioned 2D morphologies of living cells and visualize the results in a virtual environment. These images would provide sub-cellular structural details in living cells with image volume projections to create a sense of cell interior depth in living cells taking advantage of real-time operation of SLS algorithm.

17.7 Exercises

1. What does flat-field correction do?
2. Give some examples to possible small scale artifacts introduced by the image detectors.
3. Prove that KL divergence is not symmetric for two different data sets of P and Q with 5 elements by using equation (17.5).
4. Solve the question 3 for information radius by using equation (17.9). See the equality when changing the order of data sets P and Q.
5. When does K-L divergence have undefined nature?
6. When is information radius more useful?
7. What is alpha blending?
8. What are the possible advantages of immersive visualization in a virtual environment?

17.8 References

Borovkov AA (1984) Mathematical Statistics (Mir, Moscow, 1984).

Cabral B, Cam N, Foran J (1994) Accelerated volume rendering and tomographic reconstruction using texture mapping hardware. 1994 Symposium on Volume Visualization, pp. 91-98.

Cruz-Neira C, Sandin D, DeFanti T (1993) Surround-Screen Projection-Based Virtual Reality: The Design and Implementation of the CAVE. Computer Graphics, ACM SIGGRAPH, 135-142.

Darrell T, Wohn K (1988) Pyramid based depth from focus. Proc. CVPR, pp. 504-509.

Ens J, Lawrance P (1993) An Investigation of Methods for Determining Depth from Focus. IEEE Trans. On Pattern Analysis and Machine Intelligence, 15(2):97-108.

Grossman P (1987) Depth from Focus. Pattern Recognition Letters, 5:63-69, 1987.

Haykin S (1994) Communication Systems Chap.10. 3rd ed., John Wiley & Sons, Inc.

Horn BKP (1968) Focusing. MIT Artificial Intelligence Laboratory, Memo No. 160.

Jarvis R (1983) A perspective on range-finding techniques for computer vision. IEEE, Trans. Patt. Anal. Machine. Intell, vol. PAMI-3, pp. 122-139.

Lai SH, Fu CW, Chang S (1992) A Generalized Depth Estimation Algorithm with a Single Image. IEEE Trans. On Pattern Analysis and Machine Intelligence, 14(4):405-411.

Meißner M, Hoffmann U, Straßer W (1999) Enabling classification and shading for 3D texture mapping based volume rendering using OpenGL and extensions. In Proceedings of Visualization 1999, pages 207-214.

Meißner M, Huang J, Bartz D, Mueller K, and Crawfis R (2000) A practical evaluation of popular volume rendering algorithms. In Proceedings of the Symposium on Volume Visualization 2000, pages 81-90.

Nayar SK, Nakagawa Y (1990) Shape form Focus: An Effective Approach for Rough Surfaces. IEEE Intl. Conference on Robotics and Automation, pp. 218-225.

Nayar S.K (1992) Shape from focus system. Proc. CVPR, pp.302-308.

Nayar SK, Walanabe M, Nogouchi M (1995) Real time focus range sensor. Proc. ICCV, pp. 995-1001.

Nayar SK (1992) Shape from Focus System for Rough Surface. In Proc. Image Understanding Workshop, pp. 539-606.

Papoulis A (1991) Probability, Random Variables, and Stochastic Processes Chap.15. 2nd ed., McGrawHill.

Pentland AP (1987) A New Sense of Depth of Field. IEEE Trans. On Pattern Analysis and Machine Intelligence, 9(4):523-531.

Porter T, Duff T (1984) Compositing Digital Images. In Proceedings of the SIGGRAPH.

Rezk-Salama C, Engel K, Bauer M, Greiner G, Ertl T (2000) Interactive volume rendering on standard PC graphics hardware using multi-textures and multi-stage rasterization. In Proceedings of the Workshop on Graphics Hardware 2000, pages 109-118.

Schechner YY, Kiryati N, Basri R (2000) Separation of Transparent Layers using Focus. International Journal of Computer Vision, 39 (1): 25-39, Kluwer Academic Publishers.

Subbarao M (1988) Parallel Depth Recovery by Changing Camera Parameters. In Proc. International Conference on Computer Vision, pp. 149-155.

Xiong Y, Shafer SA (1993) Depth from focusing and defocusing. Proc. CVPR, pp. 68-73.

Yeo TTE, Ong S H, Jayasooriah, Sinniah R (1993) Autofocusing for tissue microscopy. Image and, Vision Comp. vol. 11, pp. 629-639.

18 Visualization and Ontology of Geospatial Intelligence

Yupo Chan

Department of Systems Engineering, University of Arkansas at Little Rock
Little Rock, AR, USA

18.1 Introduction

Recent events have deepened our conviction that many human endeavors are best described in a geospatial context. This is evidenced in the prevalence of location-based services, as afforded by the ubiquitous cell phone usage. It is also manifested by the popularity of such internet engines as Google Earth. As we commute to work, travel on business or pleasure, we make decisions based on the geospatial information provided by such location-based services. When corporations devise their business plans, they also rely heavily on such geospatial data. By definition, local, state and federal governments provide services according to geographic boundaries. One estimate suggests that 85 percent of data contain spatial attributes. This is not even counting the interpretation that internet domain names are the "real estate addresses" of the 21st century. Nor does it include the virtual-reality world, in which one immerses himself or herself in a "fantasy land" without really being there. With geospatial information at one's fingertips, we wish to see how one can use it to ensure public safety and security, which is a most stringent requirement, inasmuch as the relevant information has to be available to make split second decisions.

18.1.1 Premises

As with any database, an objective is to extract cogent information or intelligence for decision making, except that this has to be done in a hurry. In so doing, our basic premise is that humans are much better than machines at detecting patterns in visual scenes, while machines are better at manipulating streams of numbers.

To apply toward an emergency, for example, spatial knowledge discovery alone is not enough. Users, who wish to find temporal patterns, like to visualize

Y. Chan et al. (eds.), *Data Engineering*, International Series in Operations
Research & Management Science 132, DOI 10.1007/978-1-4419-0176-7_18,
© Springer Science+Business Media, LLC 2010

events and data that have a continuous representation over time (such as a series of satellite images). Algorithms of interest include those based on "particle-filtering" methods, as well as adaptive parameter estimation for partially observed non-linear state-space systems. It has to be coupled with good information-delivery mechanisms, which relies upon extracting the information to be presented; and selecting the appropriate presentation method.

The information needs to be presented in a manner appropriate to the needs of the stakeholder. Most important, the research must seek to address algorithmic shortcomings in existing spatial data-mining techniques. Since analysts must quickly view incoming data from various modalities and genres, this chapter seeks to address rapid visual exploration, search, transparent data integration and data integrity. These are all issues that facilitate an effective final product. The end results will allow field personnel react to near real-time changes in geospatial information. This will also support long-term planning and development in such applications as public safety, homeland security and beyond.

18.1.2 Research Agenda

The challenge is that spatial-temporal data violates a key assumption underlying classical statistics and data mining method of independence among learning samples (Brown et al. 2002). For example, the Central Limit Theorem (CLT), a corner stone of classical statistics, breaks down for geospatial information. Also known as the Law of Large Numbers, CLT suggests that a normal distribution becomes a good asymptotic approximation for any distribution when enough data have been collected. This is not at all the case in spatial problems. Consider an $m \times n$ pixel portion of an image. Clearly, either m or n should tend to infinity to include the entire population, but very little can be concluded about the ratio m/n (Ripley 1988). Similarly, when data are used for a cross section of *irregular* spatial units, such as counties, states or provinces, the meaning of *asymptoticity* is not always clear. This is in stark contrast to a regular infinite lattice structure. In essence, the spatial units of observation should typify a larger population, and the number of units should potentially be able to approach infinity in a regular fashion. Clearly, this is not always immediately obvious for the type of data used in applied empirical work in regional science.

The difference between classical and spatial data mining also parallels the difference between classical and spatial statistics. One of the fundamental assumptions that guide statistical analysis is that the data samples are independently generated, as with successive tosses of a coin, or the rolling of a die. When it comes to the analysis of spatial data, the assumption about the independence of samples is generally false. In fact, spatial data tends to be highly self-correlated. For example, people with similar characteristics, occupations, and backgrounds tend to cluster together into the same neighborhoods. The economies of a region tend to be similar. Changes in natural resources, wildlife, and temperature vary gradually over space. In fact, this property of like things to cluster in space is so fundamental that geographers have elevated it to the status of the first law of geography: "Everything is related to everything else, but nearby things are more related than distant things" (Tobler 1979).

We anticipate large volumes of homogeneous data (such as text), and moderate volumes of highly heterogeneous data (such as images). The former allows trends and patterns to be discerned, while the latter suggests precipitous events, which are typical in emergency situations. We are also interested in data with high dimensionality and high degrees of linkages (such as geospatial images combined with ancillary data). The visualization techniques, approaches, and metaphors must be highly flexible. While these visualizations are closely tied to underlying analytic algorithms and techniques, each algorithm and technique should support a number of significantly different databases. For example, it may show all kinds of users how they can interact with and make sense of visual representations of clusters and integrate such representation with analysis tools (Xu 1999). In this regard, we propose an ontology, consisting of several data models, that represents a set of concepts within the geospatial domain and the relationships between those concepts. It is used to reason about the objects within the geospatial domain.

To anticipate the *likelihood* of a particular incident, how can this type of uncertainty be represented in visualizations? How do they implement some sort of visual electronic "sticky notes" that would travel with the data to remind the analyst of unusual events that need further attention (Krizan 1999)? In general, what are the optimal procedures for automatically detecting and identifying temporal changes in geospatial data?

18.2 Semantic Information Representation and Extraction

While researchers can generally analyze text information in a grammatical/semantic structure, images still defy such an approach to date. Mining graphic information remains an art in computer science. Fortunately, it is common knowledge that geospatial representation in GIS takes advantage of the structured vector format. In the vector format of geographic information systems (GIS), for example, data are stored as points, lines, and polygons instead of pixels. This structure might provide an alternative to manipulating graphic information, as noted by Shekhar and Chawla (2002), Chan (2001), Swink and Speier (1999). The readers are referred to these references for the technical details. Aside from a modest storage requirement, vector representation has the semantics and grammar that allow fast analytic processing.

Among today's prevailing philosophies of data sharing between various organizations, federal agencies have begun distributing spatial data using Topological Vector Profile (TVP) as part of the Spatial Data Transfer Standard (SDTS). The most notable of these applications is USGS's conversion of all 1:100 000-scale and 1:2 000 000-scale DLG-3 data to TVP and making it available free of charge on the Internet. SDTS will eventually cover all aspects of spatial-data transfer, including the conceptual modeling of spatial data itself. These encompass the definition of 32 vector and raster spatial *objects*. SDTS would have specifications for data-quality reports, logical specifications for transferring data (what items can be transferred and how they are organized), and the physical field format of the data transfer. Currently, TVP requires several spatial objects to exist in every data-set. Through this approach, TVP provides a common dictionary to unify hitherto diverse spatial-object terminologies.

For example, the following spatial objects are defined:

1. *Planar node*: a zero-dimensional object that is a topological intersection or endpoint of one-dimensional objects,
2. *Complete chain*:   a one-dimensional object that references starting and ending nodes and left and right two-dimensional objects,
3. *GT-polygon*: a two-dimensional object, where the GT stands for `geometry and topology,' and
4. *Universe polygon*:   the special GT-polygon that covers the rest of the universe outside of other GT-polygons; there is always exactly one universe polygon.

An SDTS data-set is referred to as a *transfer*. A transfer consists of a group of files encoded. In the TVP, all files for a particular transfer will be in a single, separate directory for any medium with a directory structure. There is also an ASCII text `README' file associated with it.   Part of the file name refers to a logical grouping of related information. For example, it may facilitate the transfer of one-dimensional spatial objects such as complete chains.

"Such standardization (open geocoding standards) is not only taking place in government agencies but also allowing anyone to contribute to the Google Earth mirror world" (Rouch 2007). Just as Web browsers depend on HTML to figure out how and where to display text and images on a web page, Google Earth depends on a standard called KML, the keyhole markup language, to tell it where geographic data should be placed on the underlying latitude-longitude grid. If one knows how to assemble a KML file, one can make his/her own geographical data appear as a new "layer" on his/her computer's copy of Google Earth; and if s/he publishes that KML file on the Web, other people can download the layer and display it on their own computers. This layering capability transforms Google Earth from a mere digital globe into something more like a 3-D *Wikipedia* of the planet.

18.3 Markov Random Field

In recent years, an increasing amount of raster data are included in GIS. Raster information, the basis of most images, is not as easy a data-set for analytic processing. However, rapid progress has been made recently in processing imagery data, based on contextual information. We will show a couple of motivating examples below.

18.3.1 Spatial or Contextual Pattern Recognition

Images are typically analyzed based on their spectral features, or the "radiance" emanating from the image. Here, we propose a complementary technique utilizing spatial information beside spectral information. Spatial or *contextual* pattern recognition involves the categorization of image pixels based on their spatial relationship with pixels surrounding them. Because of the influence of noise, our target image often includes fluctuations in the gray values (for monochrome images) among adjacent pixels, which cannot be correctly recognized by spectral classification. An important decision in image classification is to strike a balance between spectral and spatial-recognition. By so doing, the weighted combination of contextual (spatial) and non-contextual (spectral) data could provide the best image contours, particularly in the presence of noise. The appropriate weights to be placed on spatial vs. spectral data can best be determined by the analyst as s/he displays the data visually.

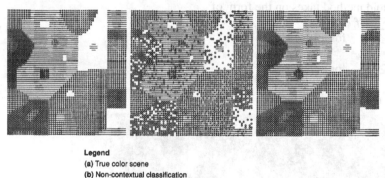

Legend
(a) True color scene
(b) Non-contextual classification
(c) Contextual classification

Fig. 18.1. Contextual vs. Non-contextual Classification [qtd in (Chan 2001)]

Besag (1989) conducted a controlled experiment using synthesized data. The left, middle and right frames—labeled as (a), (b) & (c) —in Fig. 18.1 highlight the difference between contextual and non-contextual classifications. Frame (a) is the "true" image. Frame (b) represents what is normally obtained by any sensor, which is replete with noisy pixels. Using spatial or contextual pattern recognition, the original, true image is "recovered" accurately in Frame (c). Such a procedure, including the Iterative Condition Mode algorithm (McLachlan 1992), is much more effective than non-contextual approaches. This example shows how a raster satellite image, for example, can be processed prior to subsequent analysis.

18.3.2 Image Classification using *k*-medoid Method

Once an image is rid of noise, we wish to discover any underlying pattern in the data. Clustering is the process of grouping a set of physical or abstract objects into classes of similar objects. The purpose of clustering is to divide samples into k groups striving for a high degree of similarity among elements in groups and a high degree of dissimilarity among elements in different groups. We consider the difference in `distance' from the `center' point to a pixel i and to a potential representative pixel j, $|d_i - d_j|$, as the *contextual* part of the formulation. We also define the difference between gray values, $|f_i - f_j|$, as the non-contextual (or 'spectral') part of the formulation. The combination of spectral and contextual data can be accomplished through weights w. The 'cost' of assigning pixel i to representative pixel j is $w|f_i - f_j| + (1 - w)|d_i - d_j|$, where $0 \leq w \leq 1$—which is to be minimized. Such a cost matrix constitutes a typical *symmetric neighborhood matrix*. Based on the experience of the analyst, s/he can adjust the weight w to get the desirable classification result.

Fig. 18.2a shows a GOES satellite (IR2 channel) image downloaded real-time. We use the k-medoid method of Kaufman and Rousseeuw (1989), and its modification as shown above for spatial (contextual) classification (Chan 2005). The k-medoid method takes on the form of

$$\min \sum_i \sum_j f_i\, d_{ij}\, x_{ij} \tag{18.1}$$
$$\sum_j x_{ij} \geq 1 \quad \text{for all } i$$
$$\sum_j x_{jj} = 3$$
$$x_{jj} - x_{ij} \geq 0 \quad \text{for all } i, j;\ i \neq j$$
$$x_{ij} \geq 0 \quad \text{for all } i, j$$
$$x_{ij} \quad \text{binary}$$

Fig. 18.2a. Original Image

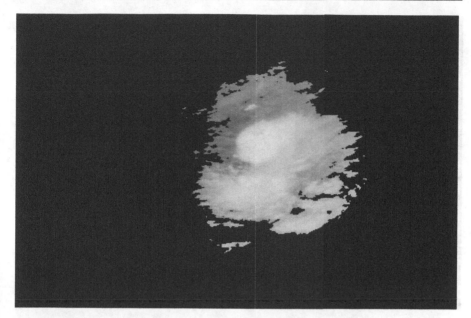

Fig. 18.2b. One Contour, $w = 0.5$

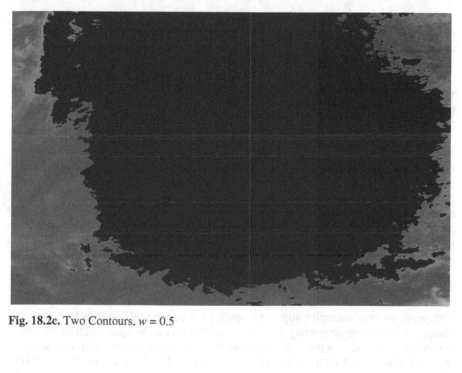

Fig. 18.2c. Two Contours, $w = 0.5$

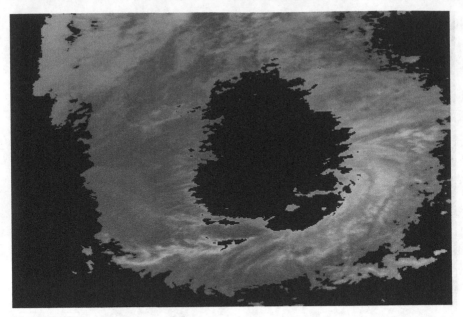

Fig. 18.2d. Three Contours, $w = 0.5$

Notice the objective function contains weights $f_i \, d_{ij}$ values that have been modified above to represent the 'costs' between two pixels. The first constraint in the model assigns each pixel to a 'representative' value defining a grouping. The second constraint establishes the number of groups, in this case $k = 3$. The last 'precedence' constraint simply ties each pixel to a representative ring. The binary variable x_{ij} is zero if a pixel i does not belong to the representative ring j, and is unity otherwise. Similarly, $x_{ij} = 0$ if a pixel i is not chosen as a representative gray value of a ring, and $x_{ij} = 1$ otherwise.

The infrared channel senses the "energy content" of a storm. A hurricane consists of spirals of gusts with different intensity around the "eye" of the storm. The result of a k-medoid classification is a set of infrared contours centered upon a hypothesized *target of interest* (such as the eye of the storm). Figs. 18.2b – d show the construction of one, two, and three contours around the eye. As shown, the k-medoid method is ideally suited for classifying such *non-homogeneous* images. As adapted here, it also highlights the role the analyst plays in pattern recognition, as assisted by visualization.

18.3.3 Random Field and Spatial Time Series

The previous two examples suggest a spatial (or contextual) approach to analyze images. This is complementary to some other familiar techniques such as filtering, sometimes referred as a *particle* based method. An emerging technique in analyzing spatial-temporal data is the *Markov Random Field* paradigm (Chan 2005;

Shekhar and Chawla 2002), of which the previous two techniques in Examples 1 and 2 are special cases. Formally stated, a random field is a set of random variables whose interdependency relationship is represented by a symmetric neighborhood matrix. The Markov property specifies that a variable depends only on its neighbors and is independent of all other variables. While traditional object-relational approaches process GIS information, Markov Random Field can be used to perform image processing. Together, they contribute toward a rich approach to perform geospatial pattern recognition and toward the construction of a Spatial Database Management System.

In the presence of noise, Markov Random Field is characterized by uncertainty. It is particularly suited for distributed disordered systems, which is typical in an act of terror, for example. It provides description, analysis, and prediction. The premise is that under sufficient local averaging, analysts obtain a continuous-parameter Gaussian field. The presence of a Gaussian field facilitates analytical procedures to be employed. We anticipate the Random Field paradigm to be a unifying methodology in this line of research, to the extent that we are concentrating on spatial data or images. The inverse of such a process helps to highlight unusual events. The inverse procedure is a fascinating way to unveil abnormalities or features that we are interested in, including terrorist threats.

The Spatial Temporal Autoregressive and Moving Average (STARMA) procedure is a general way to implement random fields over time (Chan 2005; Pfeifer and Deutch 1980, Pokrajac and Obradovic 2002). While regression mainly entertains the relationship between the dependent and independent variables, autoregressive moving-average (ARMA) models take into explicit account the relationship between the dependent variable and the error (moving average) terms a_t as well (Box et al. 1994). The STARMA model is given by the equation

$$z_t = \sum_{k=1}^{p} \sum_{l=0}^{\lambda_k} \phi_{kl} L^{(l)} z_{t-k} - \sum_{k=1}^{q} \sum_{l=0}^{m_k} \theta_{kl} L^{(l)} a_{t-k} + a_t \qquad (18.2)$$

where z_t is the stationary and homogeneous ARMA time series of lag orders p and q, a_t is the residual series, and ϕ_{kt} and θ_{kt} are calibration constants. In addition to time shifts, L works as the backshift operator on the spatial component. Hence, $L^{(l)} z_t$ is the calculation performed on the lth-order neighbor of z_t. λ_k is the spatial order of the kth auto-regressive term and m_k is the spatial order of the kth moving-average term.

A spatial time-series can sometimes be affected by external events, commonly called *interventions*. Interventions change a stationary and homogeneous *spatial time-series* to a non-stationary and non-homogeneous series. *Intervention analysis* is the classical method of dealing with external events that affect a time series or a process. An intervention is modeled with a transfer function $v(B)$ added to STARMA, where B is a backshift operator in time-series analysis. For example, a bivariate transfer-function model can be represented in general form as

$$Y_t = v(B) X_t + n_t \qquad (18.3)$$

where Y_t is the output spatial time series, $v(B)$ is the transfer function, X_t is input series, n_t is the combined effects of all other factors influencing Y_t (called the noise).

Here we use the transfer function to account for the effects of the intervention on the series. For example, the transfer-function series can be in the form of a simple indicator-variable taking only the values 1 and 0 to indicate (qualitatively) the presence or absence of interference—i.e., a step function. Among other methods, the transfer-function weights identified in the above equation can be classified according to the type of interventions. In these cases, intervention analysis is undertaken to obtain a quantitative measure of the impact of the intervention on the series of interest. Once a STARMA intervention analysis has been performed, we map the STARMA parameters on specific sensor locations—such as their transfer function weights—to vector space. This way, the dimension of the vector can be determined. A subsequent step is to conduct controlled experiments, which allows the corresponding feature-vector classification to be performed. Detailed tasks include identifying different types of interventions at each sensor location. Let us illustrate this via a third example below.

18.3.4 First Persian-Gulf-War Example

The United States Department of Defense (DoD) employs a worldwide-sensor system to detect certain 'events' of interest. A tasking model is designed to allocate the scarce sensor-resources so as to optimize the detection of these events (Greene 1992). Given that an event occurs, where it occurs is controlled by some physical law of detection that is known and/or some exogenous plans or doctrines that are unknown. A historical data-base exists that consists of the relative frequencies of activity occurrences observed by the worldwide sensors from January of 1985 through July of 1991, the time period during which the first Persian Gulf War broke out. Take the example of an intervention such as the outbreak of the Gulf War in 1991, as shown in Fig. 18.3. Such an event affects the time series abruptly. It turns a stationary time series to a non-stationary series. Correspondingly, it cannot be explained by a stationary model such as an autoregressive (AR) model. A STARMA model, complete with intervention analysis, is calibrated based on such a set of data. The data-set is made up of historical monthly relative frequencies for all 22 geographical regions in the world. The accuracy of the model depends critically on the strength of the hypothesized *intervention-model*, which captures the incident or the intervention (or the first Gulf War in this case).

We chose to include this case study here for several reasons. First and foremost, it serves to illustrate "intervention analysis." To account for a known—rather than unanticipated—phenomenon, the data-base was screened by an exogenously-determined filter. The filter represents the telecommunication capabilities as dictated by the laws-of-physics—a fact we can quantify precisely. In this context, the signal range (or maximum distance) in communication imparts a discontinuity on the data—distinguishing regions where the signal is reachable from regions not reachable. Such distinction can be easily filtered out. This approach substantiates our thesis that when the phenomenon being studied is known, it is simpler to take care of it directly. In this case, it is advantageous to account for all the known phenomena (by filtering), rather than relying exclusively on STARMA.

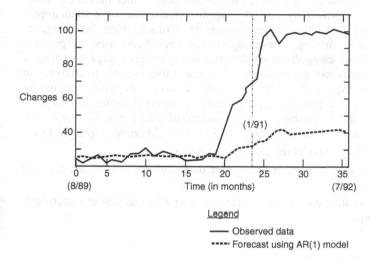

Fig. 18.3. First Persian Gulf War Example (Chan 2005)

Along the same line-of-thought, the unanticipated events exogenous to the systems need to be modeled explicitly. Here, *spatial weights* are used to represent a spatial-interaction, or geospatial activities. These weights, formulated as a *symmetric neighborhood matrix,* are found exogenously. Notice we do not know anything about the underlying process, given the actual information was kept secret by the adversary, hence unknown to DoD. At any rate, the information is unavailable. To the extent that the interaction weights seem to follow a regular pattern among the geographic regions, however, we feel comfortable using these weights, lacking any better information.

A third modeling issue relates to the intervention itself, namely, how do we model the onset of the first Gulf War? Signals picked up by the worldwide sensor system suggest there were activities above and beyond normal geospatial activities. This is depicted as the "ramp" in Fig. 18.3 that is located around January 1991. The existence of this ramp helps to alert the occurrence of an *incident*. And its 'shape' helps us to identify the type of intervention that has occurred.

Most importantly, the case study was a success, in that the STARMA model was able to forecast event-occurrence probabilities better than any prior models assembled by DoD. We feel that such an experience is worth sharing with our readers, to show the potentialities of spatial-temporal modeling. Unlike the other two examples, this has a distinctly different context, falling into the defense-intelligence arena. Its inclusion can only enrich our present discussion in our opinion. For the interested readers, details of the model can be found in (Chan 2005).

18.4 Context-driven Visualization

Among our objectives is the development of an automated as well as interactive algorithm to enhance the spatial knowledge-discovery process. Here, information visualization is an enabler, a facilitator, and an enhancer, rather than a computational engine. This is particularly true when applied in conjunction with an appropriate computational algorithm. Exploration can involve searching, browsing, selecting, filtering, and mining. These algorithms have been used to produce clusters: classifications, categorizations, indexes, sorts, and groupings. Our current task is to adopt various metaphors to visually present these results to analysts, in the hope of helping them with further searching, browsing, exploring, or mining these input data. These algorithms may measure or highlight similarities and differences, linkages, or relationships between individual data items. Following our security example, situations where such visualization could prove helpful include:

- Detect a variety of geospatial threat-warning indicators;
- Alert law-enforcement personnel to evacuate citizens from an affected geographic area; and
- Anticipate bad weather and remaining threats in an area that hinder search-and-rescue operations.

18.4.1 Relevant Methodologies

To alert an analyst of a potential incident, we need to incorporate an understanding about how people perceive visual images (Heuer 1999; Milanova and Elmaghraby 2001). We present a new algorithm for learning an over-complete (redundant) database by viewing it as a probabilistic model (Buxton 2003). This approach is useful for understanding the nature of natural codes in the *cerebral cortex*. This task focuses on two main research themes:

- We follow the flow of visual information in the human (and the primate) visual system, starting with spatial-temporal pre-processing and leading up to the processing of spatial-temporal properties in the visual cortex.
- We segment (or classify the objects in natural images) based of *medial superior temporal* representations.

An interesting problem is how can we go from a distributed neuron-firing response to a binary decision ("seen or not seen")?

Flexible graphical models are useful in cognitive visual-system design with full information integration. The representations reflect dynamic dependencies for interpretation of visual evidence. Flexible models have evolved in the machine-learning community and cover a wide class of parametric models for signal processing, which include

- Principal Component Analysis (PCA)
- Gaussian Mixtures
- Hidden Markov Models, and
- Bayesian Belief Networks (BBN).

We are particularly interested in those that are "generative"— that is, with probability distributions, estimated from input data, over a set of hidden variables. The advantage of such models is that some knowledge of the complexity of the problem, such as number of dimensions of the hidden space, can be built in. The end result is that a large amount of data can be reduced to their essential indicators. These generative models can then adapt to the different types of inputs required by the application, as well as predict and explain the data.

A BBN is a probabilistic graphical model that represents a set of variables and their probabilistic independencies. Formally, BBNs are directed acyclic graphs whose nodes represent variables, and whose arcs encode conditional independencies between the variables. Efficient algorithms exist that perform inference and learning in Bayesian networks. We propose to develop an *intelligent* cognitive visual system: contextual processing with learning capabilities. In our work, BBN is partially structured using *contextual* knowledge. We also take advantage of detailed parameters learned from prior and conditional probabilities between dynamic-scene interpretations. Our modeling approach:

- Accommodates all measurable features useful for prediction,

- Identifies which of the features have the most predictive or explanatory power, and

- Generates probability density estimates over space and time for the occurrence of future events.

18.4.2 Visual Perception and Tracking

As mentioned, our examples focus on automatic incident detection. Let us examine a person's visual perception of, say, a threat. Exploiting statistics of images to predict visual fixation points seems to be a promising research direction, since the eye evolves using these statistics and the visual neurons may be optimized for their inputs.

It has been demonstrated by Reinagel and Zador (1999) that subjects tend to fixate high contrast regions. Also, the intensities of nearby image pixels at the fixation regions are less correlated than in image regions selected at random. In other words, the eye fixates on regions rich in spatial structure. Recent evidence represented by Henderson and Hollongworth (1999) also suggests that perceptual features alone rather than semantic features control initial fixation placements. Based on this interesting finding, we propose to create different attention operators to select image features that are salient based on some low-level criteria (such as edge density or image intensity) and prove that we can select features that are salient at a higher level.

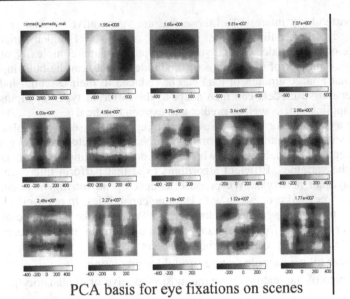

PCA basis for eye fixations on scenes

Fig. 18.4a. PCA basis for eye fixations on a circle (Rajashekar et al. 2002)

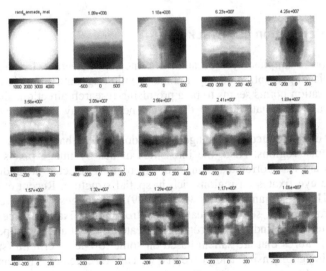

PCA basis for random fixations on scenes

Fig. 18.4b PCA basis for random fixations on a dipole (Rajashekar et al. 2002)

Shown in Figs. 18.4a and 18.4b are the results of a PCA for two different target (circle and dipole). The eigenvalues shown in the panel of Figure 18.5 correspond to the eigenvectors shown in the upper panels (Figs. 18.4a and 18.4b) and were used to select and order the first 15 significant principal components, corresponding to the 15 images generated. The data on the left were generated by the subject searching for the circle, while searching for dipoles generated those on the right. A quick look at the eigenvalues for the circle reveals that the second and third components are about equally attractive to the subject. The eigenvalues for the dipole, however, show a marked preference for horizontal edge information, which means that the subject was actively seeking out potential high-contrast edges in hopes of fortuitously acquiring the target.

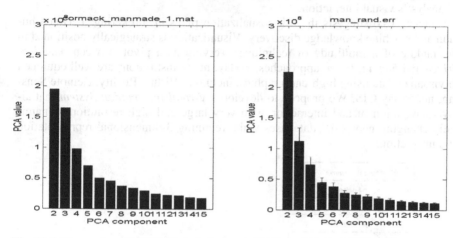

Fig. 18.5. Eigenvalues for PCA (Rajashekar et al. 2002)

While analyzing visual fixation is the first step, the second step is to integrate numerical image features into an intelligent model. Once the trajectories and moving blobs of mobile objects are obtained, the gap between numerical image features and high-level abstract activity description must be bridged. We can use BBN to recognize an "event," such as the subject heading toward a fire, or other threats. A multi-agent event is represented by a number of action threads related by temporal constraints. Multi-agent events are recognized by propagating the constraints and likelihood of event threads in a temporal logic network.

The readers may be familiar with the PCA-based autoregressive method. A key component is the eigen-decomposition of the autocorrelation matrix. The autocorrelation matrix consists of the signal (principal) and noise (non-principal) eigenvectors. In practice, a priori knowledge of the dimensions of the signal and noise subspace should be known.

18.4.3 Visualization

To locate a terrorist activity, for example, analysts conduct a prospective search and impose a reasoning structure. They follow an analytical strategy, modeling the data as well as the analyst (for his visual behavior); they then follow a mutation process to model the threat. The process concludes with a retrospective part that reaches a conclusion regarding the existence of a threat and the type of threat. Together, the procedure might involve these steps (Demirarslan et al. 1998; Tudoreanu and Kraemer 2001):

- Observing the analyst's past activities for his visual behavioral pattern,
- Summarizing the relevant information (including previously retrieved data),
- Examining query-entry techniques in an interactive manner, and
- Fusing different data types into one presentable, easy-to-use format for the analyst's visual interaction.

Figure 18.6 suggests the role visualization plays in 'brokering' between human and machine knowledge discovery. Visualization is strategically positioned in the middle of a multitude of techniques, serving as a pivot between *machine-driven* and *human-driven* approaches. Today, many institutions are well equipped to visualize data using high-end graphics, including Virtual Reality, Remote Sensing, not to say GIS. We propose to develop a *Virtual Information System* that allows navigation of and interaction with very large and high resolution, dynamically changing geospatial databases while retaining 3-dimensional representation and interaction.

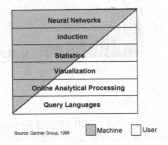

Fig. 18.6. Visualization in Knowledge Discovery

A common knowledge-discovery approach is *correlation* analysis. Such an analysis often assumes *homogeneity* among data. This assumption may often lead toward fallacious inference, however, since data are generally heterogeneous rather than homogeneous. To overcome such fallacious inferences, a combination of *model-driven* and *data-driven* approaches is required (Easa and Chan 2000; Chan 2005). An example is contextual classification techniques, as illustrated in Examples 1, 2, 3 and 4. To the extent that the majority of data contains spatial information, any incident-detection technique should concentrate not only on textual or spectral information but also on contextual information. The premise is:

Context + knowledge base = spatial inference engine.

18.5 Intelligent Information Fusion

In the last dozen or more pages, we introduced a variety of techniques defining an intelligent visualization process, which will assist in the cognition of geospatial information. In terms of implementation, we will define a task associated with each of the activities described above: Spatial databases, Markov Random Field, and Visualization. Here, we name the tasks as *Semantic Information Extraction, Intelligent Contextual Inference*, and *Context-driven Ontology* respectively. On top of these is added another task: *Assessment*, the subject of the next section. This Assessment task provides the verification and validation necessary to ensure that our procedure works in a realistic application. The entire implementation process can be summarized in Fig. 18.7, which will be explained one step at a time.

18.5.1 Semantic Information Extraction

The semantic information extraction subsystem will use semantic analysis and statistical techniques to extract relevant knowledge (content) from maps, images, and other data sources by utilizing a domain-based ontology (Guan et al. 2003). The emergence of distributed computing necessitates newer software models to support and facilitate these applications. This is particularly important for spatial/visual information, since they are often too huge to be transmitted real-time to make critical decisions. In other words, embedded hardware and software elements in these applications will be resource-constrained. This necessitates optimizing implementation strategies such as encoding and data flow. For example, map data-bases can be resident locally, while locational information, expressed in terms of a cursor, can be easily transmitted in real time.

In other words, the activities of these distributed elements are strictly related to the environment in which they reside. Hence the need for information has to be balanced against the constraints that distributed environment entails. By the same token, the system has to operate within, and be acutely aware of dynamically changing group structures and environments; while constantly processing information from multiple sources. In such environments new data (as well as new associates) can arrive, terminate, leave, or suspend at any time, thereby requiring the system to exhibit intelligent, and adaptive behaviors.

Adherence to the above requirements must be accomplished with simple, effective and efficient solutions. Individual software elements need to exhibit simple, yet well-defined underlying patterns, thereby aiding the development of scalable, complex software systems capable of demonstrating domain-specific intelligence (Li 2005). Also, the communicated information has to be simple yet expressive enough to aggregate into intelligent information patterns. We will focus on the supporting infrastructure necessary to physically realize such aggregates and the effects of information multiplicity.

18.5.2 Intelligent Contextual Inference

The integration of spatial data into traditional databases amounts to resolving many nontrivial issues at various levels. They range from deep ontological questions about the modeling of space. For example, should the procedure be field based or object based. The former refers to the Random Field paradigm described above. The latter is more in line with traditional database management.

Once data gathering/extraction is well defined, we need to build scalable, globally consistent views from disparate heterogeneous data sources. Also needed is to assemble relevant data sources and link important image elements and contents intelligently. Querying information in such distributed networks can be difficult for the following reasons, and we offer a solution in each case:

- DATA CONVERSION AND FORMATTING: Similar data can be stored in different formats in a system with heterogeneous networked elements. Often, conversion or normalization of the data into a standard format is necessary before it can be manipulated.
- LOCAL CONTROL: Each local repository will remain under the full control of the site that owns the repository. Initially, we will implement only the ability to query but not modify the data. As a part of our research, we will investigate ways of allowing constrained, distributed updates to the repositories.
- SEMI-STRUCTURED DATA STORAGE AND MANAGEMENT: A unified view of the database will be constructed using semi-structured data-analysis techniques to address the problems of having multiple heterogeneous sources. Semi-structure data format is a "happy median" between the semantics inherent in GIS, and the much less structured format of images.

18.5.3 Context-driven Ontology

The objective in this task is to present large data-sets in a form that is easily visualized and traversed in real time (Shekhar et al. 2002; Shekhar et al. 2002a). Aside from modeling human cognition, issues to be addressed by any of the chosen mechanisms include presentation elegance, and clarity to the user. Our approach will be to provide context-based ontology—i.e., a semantic presentation that displays a particular view of a node based on a specific task. It is particularly suited for geospatial and image data due to its semantics or the unifying random field paradigm—as explained in the previous pages. This approach would also respond to the individual style of an analyst or decision maker, as illustrated in Fig. 18.7.

It should be noted that the proposed visualization procedure is founded on a common methodological framework such as the STARMA model. Likewise, these are common techniques that cut across Markov Random Fields and intelligent cognitive visual system:

- Discriminant Analysis, and
- Cluster Analysis.

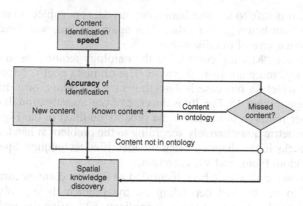

Fig. 18.7. Ontology of Knowledge Discovery (adapted from S. Ramaswamy)

In the knowledge discovery process, a clear distinction is to be made between whether the information content is in the ontology, or that it is not. It is clear that the relationships established in the ontology pertain only to the existing or known information content. Contents outside the ontology must receive special treatment. Perhaps a special pattern classification technique is in order to discover knowledge from such information content.

18.6 Metrics for Knowledge Extraction and Discovery

The "bottom line" is: how do we know that we have extracted the most useful intelligence from the data? For this reason, a set of evaluation metrics is required. Let us walk through Fig. 18.7 together, starting with the "content identification" block at the upper left corner. For real-time applications, the identification speed becomes critical. Unfortunately, identification speed is dependent upon many factors. The previous tasks have identified some of them. To be added is the analysis procedures or the algorithms—a significant component of our discussion. As mentioned, processing visual images is typically data intensive. For that reason, algorithmic efficiency is an area of investigation. The techniques presented in the previous pages have been chosen in part for their reasonable algorithmic performance with respect to execution speed. Obviously, the algorithms can be further improved, depending on the applicational requirements. While addressing an emerging/future threat, new software systems may also need to be assembled from existing components that have been proven to be effective (Yu and Ramaswamy 2006).

The next block in Fig. 18.7—"accuracy of content identification"—is clearly dependent upon the specific application. It is expected that extracting 'shareable' information from new content will be less accurate than from known content due to the ontological learning that has taken place (Frank 2005). Such 'shared' content needs to be appropriately identified and communicated to other interested system components (Ramaswamy et al. 2005). Irrespective, we need to assess how accurate a procedure is. It is safe to say that homogeneous data are subject to more accurate representation than heterogeneous data. But again, dealing with heterogeneous data is the *raison d'etre* of our discussion.

The interrogative block "Missing content" in the ontology requires us to improve extraction accuracy, more so than otherwise. The ultimate goal is "Spatial knowledge discovery," which in our case is detecting an *intervention*, or a threat on a map or spatial image. Figure 18.7 really is the core of our investigation. It can be said that much of our research is to realize the process outlined in the Figure, defining the evaluation metric quantitatively according to the problem at hand, and detailing each of the blocks in the diagram using the identified techniques: Spatial Databases, Markov Random Field, and Visualization.

Two broad evaluation metrics have been identified so far: speed and accuracy. Obviously, they need to be detailed depending on the problem being solved. Evaluation experiments need to be set up for each application to refine the evaluation metrics. Included in these experiments are ways and means to quantify these metrics. For example, the content identification speed is different when a threat is in progress and imminent (rather than latent). More accuracy is also required under this circumstance.

18.7 Conclusions and Recommendations

In this chapter, we seek to identify methods, processes, and guidelines for using visualization in analytic methods (Stredl and Ghosh 2003). We have illustrated with security examples, including an automated procedure to detect and identify threats or an act of terror. The goal of our work is to use an intelligent visualization process, which will complement the regular cognition of geospatial information. This will make advanced information-seeking technology more ubiquitous, useful, reliable, and affordable.

18.7.1 Contributions

We provide these key contributions in this chapter:
- An ontology for vector images and models for raster formats
- Means to visualize meaningful information from the modeled data-sets
- Real world examples to illustrate ontology and visualization concepts
- Identifying implementation tasks for the ontology and visualization of a geospatial data-set
- Metrics to evaluate the effectiveness of our proposed techniques, procedures and standards.

Our work is motivated by the fact that we can exploit the structured semantics and grammar available in GIS; something that is lacking in regular graphic images. Closer examination suggests that data stored in raster format can be similarly analyzed, in addition to data stored in vector format. The ability to concurrently process geospatial data, 3D terrain, and imagery in a timely and reliable manner will provide a definitive advantage to every analyst. To make it useful in an extremely data-rich environment, we must develop an *automated* procedure to detect and identify precipitous events such as threats. Such information must also be displayed in such a way that will immediately catch the attention of the user.

We propose to devise a system that can detect interesting events, anomalies, or alarms in the observed data and computation. An automated system briefly presents them to maintain the user's awareness and ensure that these events are not overlooked. Given the huge amount of geospatial information gathered by satellites and other remote-sensing devices, such a procedure is long overdue. In addition to contributing toward computer science, information science and engineering, we seek an understanding of the complex cognitive processes in human-information processing. In particular, we look for a paradigm shift in the visual-information processing of spatial data. The paradigm includes:

- learning algorithms considering a user's domain knowledge,
- multi-sensory perceptual integration,
- recognition of unusual events in a *dynamic* environment, and
- visual display design, the final product of the research.

18.7.2 Looking Ahead

Google, Microsoft, and Yahoo are racing to transform online maps into full-blown browsers, organizing a diversity of information. Google Earth combines satellite imagery, maps and the power of Google Search to put the world's geographic information at one's fingertips. Since its debut in summer 2005, Google Earth has received attention of an unexpected sort. Officials of several nations have expressed alarm over its detailed display of government buildings, military installations and other sensitive sites within their borders. Beyond Google, Globalsecurity.org has images of nuclear test sites and military bases in much sharper focus than can be found on Google Earth. The company was asked by the National Geospatial-Intelligence Agency, an arm of the U. S. Defense Department, to remove from their site some of the maps of cities in Iraq. The incident was a classic example of the futility of trying to control information.

In this chapter, we have laid out a research agenda for the exciting subject of mining geospatial data. The potential application in safety and security is endless (Rouch 2007). A systems-biology graduate student Andrew Hill and colleagues at the University of Colorado, published a KML file in April 2007, with a grim animated time line showing how the most virulent strains of avian flu jumped from species to species and country to country between 1996 and 2006. What if you could model a Europe where the sea level is 10 feet higher than it is today, or walk around the Alaskan north and see the glaciers and the Bering Strait the way they were 10 years ago? Then perceptions around global warming might change.

While we are laying out a research agenda in this chapter, much of the technology is here already. Digital globes are gaining in fidelity, as cities are filled out with 3-D models and old satellite imagery is gradually replaced by newer high-resolution shots. And today's island virtual worlds will only get better, with more-realistic avatars and settings and stronger connections to outside reality. Map algebra for cartographic modeling was introduced by Tomlin (1990). In parallel, Ritter et al. (1990) introduced image algebra for image processing. It is a fascinatingly visual world for experimentation!

18.8 Exercises

1. Refer to the k-medoid model in this chapter, expressed as Eq. 18.1. A set of water pollution data is collected in a satellite image. The gray value of the 16×16-grid image is shown in Fig. 18.9, where the gray values represent pollution levels. The `proximity' between a pixel with gray-value i and pixel with representative gray-value j is denoted by the 'distance' d_{ij}, where $d_{ij} = |i - j|$. Here, proximity is interpreted as the 'distinction' (or difference) in gray values between these two pixels. By minimizing the 'distances' between pixels of gray-values i and j, we end up grouping pixels of similar gray values together in concentric rings, all centered at the point source. In other words we discern the contours of pollution concentrations from the point source. The number of such contours is determined by the number of "representative values" one wishes to specify.

Suppose the objective function contains weights reflecting the 'intensity' of a gray-value's occurrence. Thus, the most common and most similar gray-values are grouped together. The gray values of pixels in the data-set have the frequency distribution shown in Table 18.1 (Chan 2005).

Table 18.1. Gray-value distribution

Gray value	0	1	2	3	4	5	6	7	8	9
Frequency f_i	109	40	32	28	20	14	6	4	2	1

Please formulate the corresponding k-medoid model and solve it. Show that the pollution contours are as shown in Fig. 18.8. (Chan 2005)

2. Instead of a precise gray-value reading, most images have noise. To handle this, an important decision in image-classification is to strike a balance between spectral vs. spatial pattern-recognition—i.e., classification based on gray-values vs. contiguity respectively. It is proposed that some weighted combination of contextual and non-contextual data could provide, say, the best pollution contours, particularly in the presence of noise.

0	0	0	0	0	1	1	1	1	0	0	0	0	0	0	0
0	0	0	0	0	1	2	2	2	1	1	0	0	0	0	0
0	0	0	1	1	2	3	3	3	2	2	1	0	0	0	0
0	0	0	1	2	3	4	4	3	3	3	2	1	0	0	0
0	1	1	2	3	4	4	5	4	4	3	2	1	1	0	0
0	1	2	3	4	5	5	6	5	4	3	3	2	1	0	0
0	1	2	3	4	5	7	8	6	5	4	3	2	1	0	0
1	2	3	4	5	6	8	9	7	6	5	4	3	2	1	0
0	1	2	3	4	5	6	7	7	5	4	3	2	2	1	0
0	1	2	3	3	4	5	6	5	5	4	3	2	1	0	0
0	0	1	2	3	3	4	5	4	4	3	3	2	1	0	0
0	0	1	1	2	2	3	4	3	3	2	2	1	0	0	0
0	0	0	1	1	2	2	2	2	2	1	1	0	0	0	0
0	0	0	0	0	1	1	1	1	1	0	0	0	0	0	0
0	0	0	0	0	0	0	0	0	0	0	0	0	0	0	0
0	0	0	0	0	0	0	0	0	0	0	0	0	0	0	0

Legend

Number in cells are grey values.

Fig. 18.8. A pollution plume (Chan 2005)

Let us say that pollution contours generally form 'doughnut' shapes about some center point, a source of pollution. These contours, representing the diffusion of certain gray value, can be used as a measure of 'distance.' While the spectral part of the model is quite clear, the contextual part minimizes the variance between the distance pixels are from the source-of-pollution, d_i, and the distance their representative-pixels are from the source, d_j. The combination of spectral and spatial data can be accomplished through a weighted average between the two. The weights range from 0 to 1 for each, and the two weights sum to unity. The weight applied to the contextual part should only be large enough to remove any noise from the data and no larger.

Consider the 6×6 grid shown in Fig. 18.9. The very center of the physical grid—point (3.5, 3.5)—is considered the source-point of pollution, though the center-of-mass of the gray values—(3.5, 3.525)—or the actual point-source of pollution could have been used. Refer to Eq. 18.1, f_i now represents the gray-value of each of the pixels i. The 'cost' of assigning a pixel i to representative pixel j is then $w \,|\, f_i - f_j \,| + (1 - w) \,|\, d_i - d_j \,|$, where $0 \le w \le 1$.

Classify the image with a spectral weight of 1.0 and a spatial weight of 0.0. Do it again for the spatial weight $w \ge 0.5$. Discuss the results. (Chan 2005)

0	0	0	0	0	1
0	2	2	2	1	0
1	1	4	4	2	0
0	2	5	3	2	0
0	2	1	2	1	1
0	0	0	1	0	0

Fig. 18.9. Contextual image classification (Chan 2005)

3. Pfeifer and Bodily (1990), as cited in Chan (2005), applied STARMA to de-mand-related data from eight hotels from a single hotel chain in a large US city. The time-sequence plots of pickup percentages are plotted in Figure 18.10. These hotels are separated by the following symmetrical distances shown in Table 18.2.

Table 18.2. Spatial vs. univariate forecasts

	1	2	3	4	5	6	7	8
1	0.0							
2	3.0	0.0						
3	3.3	3.0	0.0					
4	5.0	3.0	1.0	0.0				
5	25.0	24.5	27.0	27.0	0.0			
6	14.5	10.0	10.0	12.0	13.0	0.0		
7	20.0	14.0	15.0	15.0	28.0	14.0	0.0	
8	30.0	28.0	27.0	26.0	36.0	25.0	10.0	0.0

Suppose spatial weights are simply inversely proportional to distances. Model the time-series data in terms of both univariate analysis and using spatial weights. Compare the results. Use the first 300 data points for model building, and the hold-out sample of 70 points to compare the one-step-ahead forecasting performance of the two approaches.

4. Shekhar and Chawla (2002) propose a paradigm to represent spatial data. They call it an object model vs. a field model. The former refers to the point-line-region vec-tor representation in GIS. The latter, often referred to as raster image, maps the underlying reference frame (typically a grid) into an attribute domain (such as gray values). The vector vs. raster dichotomy can be compared with the 'what' and 'where' in natural language. Discuss.

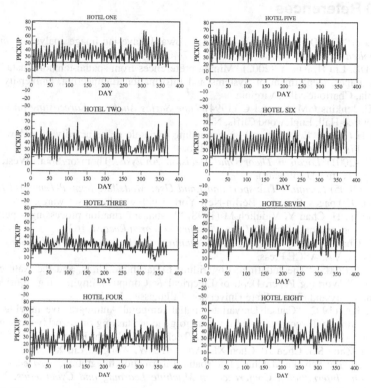

Fig. 18.10. Time sequence plots of pickup percentages (Pfeifer and Bodily 1990)

5. In vector representation, when we draw the boundaries between countries on a map, it shows country A meets country B on a common border. We call *meet* a topological relationship. A state or province is part of a country; it is contained *within* the country. In this example, *within* is also a topological relationship. These relationships are most likely to be queried explicitly by a Data Base Management System (DBMS). Now consider a DBMS organized around raster data representation. Is topology implicit or explicit in raster DBMS (Shekhar and Chawla 2002)?

18.9 Acknowledgements

The authors gratefully acknowledge the contributions of Jim M. Kang, Mariofanna Milanova, Srinivasan Ramaswamy, Shashi Shekhar, and other colleagues toward this research. The authors would also like to express their gratitude toward the referees who offered valuable suggestions for the improvement of this chapter. Obviously, the author alone is responsible for the content of this paper.

18.10 References

Besag, J (1989) "Digital image processing: Toward Bayesian image analysis." *Journal of Applied Statistics*, Vol. 16, No. 3, pp. 397-407.

Brown DE, Liu H, Xue Y (2002) "Mining preferences from spatial-temporal data." Working Paper, Department of Systems and Information Engineering, University of Virginia, Charlottesville, Virginia.

Box GE, Jenkins GM, Reinsel G (1994) *Time Series Analysis: Forecasting and Control.* Prentice-Hall, Englewood Cliffs, N.J.

Buxton H (2003) "Learning and understanding dynamic scene activity: a review." *Image and Vision Computing*, Vol. 21, 125-136.

Chan Y (2001) *Location Theory and Decision Analysis.* Thomson/South-Western, 533 pages (with CD software).

Chan Y (2005) *Location, Transport and Land-Use: Modelling Spatial-Temporal Information.* 930 pages, Springer, Berlin-New York. (with web-based software).

Demirarslan H, Chan Y, Vidulich M (1998) "Visual information processing – perception, decision, response triplet." *Transportation Research Record*, 1631.

Easa S, Chan Y (Eds.) (2000) *Urban Planning and Development Applications of GIS.* Reston, VA: ASCE Press.

Frank MP (2005) "The Indefinite Logarithm, Logarithmic Units, and the Nature of Entropy." Working Paper, Dept. of Electrical & Computer Engineering, Florida A&M University and Florida State University, Tallahassee, Florida.

Greene, KA (1992) "Causal Univariate spatial temporal Autoregressive moving average modeling of Target region information to generate tasking of a worldwide sensor system." MS Thesis, Air Force Institute of Technology, Wright-Patterson AFB, Ohio.

Guan JH, Zhou SG, Chen JP, Chen XL, An Y, Yu W, Wang R, Liu X (2003) "Ontology-Based Gml Schema Matching For Spatial Information Integration." *Proceedings of the Second International Conference on Machine Learning and Cybernetics*, Xian, 2-5 November.

Henderson J, Hollongworth A (1999) "High–level scene perception." *Annual Rev. Psychol.*, Vol. 50, pp. 243–271.

Heuer R (1999) Psychology of Intelligence Analysis. Center for Study of Intelligence, CIA. (http://www.cia.gov/csi/books/19104/).

Kaufman L, Rousseeuw PJ (1989) *Finding Groups in Data.* Wiley-Interscience, New York, New York.

Krizan, L (1999) "Intelligence Essentials for Everyone." Joint Military Intelligence College Occasional Paper No. 6 (June), Government Printing Office, Washington, D.C.

Li, XB (2005) "A scalable decision tree system and its application in pattern recognition and intrusion detection." *Decision Support Systems*, Vol. 41, Issue 1, pp. 112–130.

McLachlan, GJ. (1992) Discriminant Analysis and Statistical Pattern Recognition. Wiley-Interscience, New York.

Milanova M, Elmaghraby A (2001) "A perceptual learning model based on topographical representation." Paper presented at the meeting of the International Joint INNS-IEEE Conference on Neural Networks, Washington, DC.

Pfeifer PE, Deutch SJ (1980) "A three-stage procedure for space-time modeling." *Technometrics*, Vol. 22, pp. 35–47.

Pfeifer PE, Bodily, SE (1990) "A test of space-time ARMA modeling and forecasting of hotel data." Journal of Forecasting, Vol. 9, pp. 255–272.

Pokrajac D, Obradovic Z (2002) "Improved spatial-temporal forecasting through modeling of spatial residuals in recent history." Working Paper, Center for Information Science and Technology, Temple University, Philadelphia, Pennsylvania.

Rajashekar, U, Cormack, LK, Bovik, AC (2002) "Visual Search: Structure from noise." Working Paper, Dept. of Elec. and Comp. Eng. University of Texas at Austin, Austin, TX 78712-1084.

Ramaswamy S, Yamijala G, Neelakantan R, Rajan PK (2005) "Model-driven Design of Stable Software Systems: A Petri Net Based Approach", *International Journal of Intelligent Control and Systems*, Vol. 10, No. 2, pp. 175-187.

Reinagel P, Zador AM (1999) "Natural scene statistics at the centre of gaze." *Network: Comput. Neural Syst.* Vol. 10, pp. 341–350.

Ripley, BD (1988) *Statistical Inference for Spatial Processes*, Cambridge University Press, Cambridge, UK.

Ritter, G; Wilson, J; Davidson, J. (1990) "Image algebra: An overview." *Computer Vision, Graphics and Image Processing*, Vol. 49, pp. 297–3331.

Rouch W (2007) "Second Earth." *Technology Review*, July/August, pp. 39–48.

Shekhar S, Chawla S (2002) *A Tour of Spatial Databases*. Prentice-Hall, Saddle River, N.J.

Shekhar S, Lu CT, Liu R, Zhou C (2002) "CubeView: A System for Traffic Data Visualization." *Proc. 5th IEEE Intl. Conf. on Intelligent Transportation Systems*.

Shekhar S, Lu CT, Zhang P, Liu R (2002a) "Data Mining for Selective Visualization of Large Spatial Datasets." 14th IEEE International Conference on Tools with Artificial Intelligence.

Stredl A, Ghosh J (2003) "Relationship-based clustering and visualization for high-dimensional data mining." *INFORMS Journal on Computing*, Vol. 15, No. 2, pp. 208–230.

Swink M, Speier D (1999) "Presenting geographic information: effects of data aggregation, dispersion, and user's spatial orientation." *Decision Sciences*, Vol. 30, pp. 169–195.

Tobler, W. (1979) "Cellular geography." In *Philosophy in Geography*, Eds., S. Gale and G. Olsson, D. Reidel Publishing Company, Dordrecht, Holland.

Tomlin, C. (1990) Geographic Information Systems And Cartographic Modeling, Prentice-Hall, Upper Saddle River, New Jersey.

Tudoreanu M, Kraemer E (2001) "Automatic presentation of running programs." *Proceedings of the SPIE 2001 Conference on Visual Data Exploration and Analysis VIII*, pp. 143–155.

Xu X (1999) Efficient Clustering for Knowledge Discovery in Spatial Databases. Shaker, Germany: Aachen.

Yu L, Ramaswamy S (2006) "A Configuration Management Model for Software Product Lines", *INFOCOM Journal of Computer Science*, Dec, pp. 1–8.

19 Looking Ahead

Yupo Chan[1], John Talburt[1], and Terry Talley[2]

[1]University of Arkansas at Little Rock
Little Rock, AR 72204-109, USA

[2]Acxiom Corporation
Conway, AR 72202, USA

19.1 Introduction

The enthusiasm of our contributing authors and their convincing messages have demonstrated the great potential of advances in information quality, analytics, and visualization to improve the quality of information-based decision making. We, the editors and the contributing authors, hope that this book will have some impact on the practice of managers and technical personnel immediately upon its publication and in the years to come.

Data Engineering is a field that will continue to evolve. The purpose of this book is simply to lay down some fundamentals such that the readers are better prepared to anticipate future changes. We have organized our discussions using the following taxonomy:

Data Integration and Information Quality
Grid Computing
Data Mining
Visualization

In other words, we start out with how we organize the data and end up with how to view the information extracted out of the data. Following this taxonomy, we will further delineate (and in many cases reinforce) the future directions in data integration, grid computing, data mining and visualization in this final chapter.

Y. Chan et al. (eds.), *Data Engineering*, International Series in Operations
Research & Management Science 132, DOI 10.1007/978-1-4419-0176-7_19,
© Springer Science+Business Media, LLC 2010

19.2 Data Integration and Information Quality

Data integration and information quality are complementary areas that are maturing together. As is common in science, fields of study become increasingly interdisciplinary as they mature. Information quality was essentially born from the 1980's movement to aggregate disparate operational data stored into a single repository (data warehouse), with the goal of extracting non-obvious business intelligence through data mining and other analytical techniques. From these efforts it became clear that independently held and maintained data stores were not easily integrated into a single, logically-consistent knowledgebase. It exposed problems with data accuracy, completeness, consistency, timeliness, and a myriad of other issues. In its earliest form, information quality was focused on methods and techniques to clean "dirty data" to the point that it could be properly integrated.

Information quality as "data cleansing" is a still prominent issue when dealing with databases. In the "Handle the Dirty Data" chapter, a custom name spell-checking algorithm is presented in order to overcome the lack of spelling correction tools for personal names. The results are compared with other known tools to reflect the success of the study. Not only did *Personal Name Recognizing Strategy* (PNRS) provide the most Fixed | Matched corrections, but it also achieved 21 percent more exact corrections than the runner-up algorithm. In future work, a combination of Kullback-Leibler divergence (Pedro et al. 2004) and information-theoretic distortion measures (Cardinal 2002) will be applied to predict how close the obtained results are to the expected ones.

Since its beginnings, information quality has evolved to incorporate a number of new aspects. One of the most significant has been that information systems should be viewed as producing information products analogous to the way in which manufacturing systems produce manufactured products. This has opened the door to many new avenues of research related to the application of quality management principles from the Total Quality Management (TQM) movement to the study of information quality. The result has been a new body of research that delineates and differentiates the characteristics (dimensions) of information quality management vis-à-vis traditional product management. It investigates such questions as: What comprises an information product life-cycle? How can statistical process control be applied in the manufacturing of information products?

The "Information Quality Framework for Verifiable Intelligence Products" is indicative of the information quality research based in the information-product view. It also speaks the need for more research to develop additional information quality frameworks that support other information system models.

The field of information quality management is now advancing even further to include information architecture. Moving beyond the measurement and improvement of information quality in existing systems, it is now incorporating aspects of information architecture in an attempt to thwart quality problems at the earliest stages of information system design.

As noted earlier, almost every information system design will incorporate one or more steps where information from multiple sources must be integrated. More specifically this integration is usually centered on a set of key entities (people, places, and things) that are the critical components of the system model. The integration of entity-based information is the subject of entity resolution, another area of growing research interest.

A key data integration tool is the record-grouping problem, which is called the transitive closure problem. Merging the correct records together constitutes an analysis tool for achieving data quality. The way one groups records affects data accuracy, redundancy, consistency, currency and completeness. In Transitive Closure of Data Records, researchers are currently studying how to further speed-up the proposed parallel and distributed algorithms. Other competing definitions of relatedness and other parameters that might affect the effectiveness of transitive closure computation need to be investigated—e.g., applying different weights to different keys. Last, but not the least, we need to improve the analysis tools, which process the records in a transitive closure, so that the desired data quality can be achieved. One technique might be to use clustering to regroup the over-grouped records in a transitive closure.

In the "Semantic Data Matching" chapter, Latent Semantic Analysis (LSI) is a promising technique for data integration. Nevertheless, the results of this study show that increasing the proportion of shared terms in the data causes degradation in the performance of LSI. For the most part, this degradation is the result of more misclassification with increasing percentages of shared terms. In addition, the best match to a query is highly variable with changing percentages of shared terms. Thus, identification and elimination of shared terms is key to increasing LSI performance. Nevertheless, shared terms often contain information that is useful for classification of records. Therefore, un-important shared terms have to be distinguished from meaningful ones.

Because entities in entity resolution are often people, the access to actual information can be limited by issues of privacy and security. Because of this the IT industry needs synthetic data generation tools for a number of applications, including

- *Regression testing*: Repeatedly generate the same large data set for testing enterprise applications.
- *Secure application development*: Allow developers access to data that looks very much like the real data, but does not contain any sensitive information.
- *Testing of data-mining applications*: Generate data sets with known characteristics to gauge whether data mining tools can discover those characteristics.

Having presented a Parallel Synthetic Data Generator (PSDG), we have identified a number of research areas and potential improvements. .This is also the case for Synthetic Data Description Language (SDDL).

While PSDG does have a functional graphical user interface (GUI), it could use some enhancement, primarily in the area of generating obfuscated versions of existing tables. Currently, the GUI can assist in extracting attribute and domain data from existing tables. It would be nice if it could also perform these additional functions:

- Deduce intra- and inter-column statistical data about existing tables.
- Allow for the specification of a discrete obfuscation level for an attribute when producing obfuscated versions of existing tables. This would relieve the user of the necessity of implementing his/her own obfuscation algorithms.
- Provide streaming, real-time capabilities in the PSDG generation engine. This would allow PSDG to be more useful in a simulation environment.
- Research the idea of composible constraints for SDDL table fields. Currently, only one constraint is allowed per field. Would it make sense to allow multiple constraints? Would they be AND-ed together or OR-ed together?
- Write a translator that could convert an Entity-Relationship Diagram into an SDDL file. This would allow data creators a more comfortable data description mechanism.
- Support logical assertions ("Jazz musicians do not play the harmonica") and fuzzy logic constraints ("Many of the employees are tall") in SDDL table and field descriptions. It is currently possible to describe such constraints, but the SDDL required can be monstrously complicated. It would be nice if the user were allowed to specify such simple assertions.

We would like to explore additional application areas for synthetic data generation. Could SDDL be used to capture some music theory rules, which could be used to generate random (but theoretically sound) music? Could geography and cartography rules be captured in SDDL and used to synthetically generate landscapes? What kind of new functionality would need to be added to SDDL to accommodate these applications?

The chapter "A Declarative Approach to Entity Resolution" is perhaps the most forward looking of the papers related to data integration in that it attempts to move from a process view of entity resolution to a declarative, goal-oriented way to describe the outcome. More work in this area is needed in order to support the design of more robust entity resolution frameworks that impose a logical layer between the information and integration process. Although there are examples of very efficient, high-performance entity resolution systems today, they come at the cost of being very finely tuned to specific data configurations, and are not easily modified to incorporate new sources or integration logic. The ability to create processes from logical formulations of the problem is an important step forward. It is clear that more work in the area is needed.

19.3 Grid Computing

There has been a dramatic increase in the interest and visibility of grid computing during the preparation of this book. Once largely confined to the research community and a few targeted business domains, many of the concepts and techniques of grid computing have emerged as mainstream trends. Adoption of high throughput application paradigms such as Map-Reduce (Dean and Ghemawat

2004) and high performance file systems such as the Google File System (Ghemawat et al. 2003) are becoming increasingly common across a variety of application domains. While some of the initial interest perhaps resulted from the publicity around the phenomenal demonstrated success of Google in exploiting massive processing power on very large amounts of data, the interest has been sustained and increased by the fact that these techniques have proven effectively and efficiently applicable to a wide range of problems. With the advent of processing chips containing many processing cores and with the development and refinement of both virtual machine hardware and software, parallel processing is increasingly considered the standard computing paradigm.

At the same time, deployment of Software-as-a-Service (SaaS) offerings such SalesForce.com have demonstrated the value and convenience of exploiting software on a common shared platform as a consumable resource with usage-based billing. The combination of a flexible grid processing environment, perhaps exploiting the new virtualization technologies, and a set of SaaS offerings billed based upon usage is now described as Cloud Computing (Gruman 2008) and many companies, such as Amazon and Microsoft, are actively deploying cloud computing platforms and selling services within those clouds. As this book is being prepared, most of the services offered within the commercial cloud implementations are relatively simple, often a development machine or a simple web server, but we anticipate rapid expansion of the complexity and range of services offered by cloud providers in the coming months and years. David Patterson has said that "the data center is the computer" (Patterson 2008) and cloud computing environments are one realization of that statement.

Of particular interest from the perspective of this book, it seems likely that future cloud offerings will provide rich environments for data integration, data quality assessment and correction, and data management. We particularly expect this to be the case as advances in network technology and in multi-tenant security makes it more feasible for companies to both quickly transmit their data to cloud environments and also feel comfortable that this sensitive data is protected even within a shared environment. Cloud offerings providing high storage capacity, high computing capacity, and a set of capable software packages can help alleviate some of the current infrastructure challenges associated with high volume data integration and allow the owners of the data to focus on the true value of extracting information from ever larger and more complex sets of raw data.

19.4 Data Mining

A focus of this book is to identify the correct person or object based on the data attributes associated with them. Future research into Entity Resolution could concentrate on integrating data provenance policies, i.e., when to insert, update, and delete based on sources. For law enforcement, for example, it could further refine the path-based prospecting approach, and positive or negative associations between entities. For instance, who bought guns from dealer X and also lived with known suspect Y?

The Intelligence Community (IC) can improve the quality of its intelligence products by incorporating an effective Information Quality framework. We anticipate that intelligence production process will become more visible to the end consumers, and the quality of the products can be examined more easily. Consequently, the finished intelligence products will be more useful because the users can easily assess the confidence level of the products and use the products more appropriately.

Future work will evaluate the proposed solution to identify areas for enhancement, e.g., incorporating entity resolution methods (Talburt et al. 2005; Wang and Madnick 1989) to improve quality of information from multiple sources. Since we have only focused on the traceability aspect so far, future work will develop mechanisms to facilitate the improvement of the validity aspects.

The evaluation results of the techniques mentioned in the "Knowledge Discovery in Textual Databases" chapter show our system could automatically find interesting concepts and their associations from unstructured text data. The experimental results also show that our approach can significantly reduce the number of uninteresting associations. Considering the results from the real-world dataset used, we conclude that the all-confidence measure is quite useful in generating interesting associations. Furthermore, the directed graph that is generated for concept associations not only shows the directed associations represented by association rules but also all transitive associations. The concept association graph can be used to infer new association rules. Therefore, it can lead to the discovery of new knowledge from textual databases.

In the future, we recommend investigating other concept extraction algorithms for knowledge discovery from textual databases. We also recommend developing more efficient algorithms for generating concept association graphs.

In the "Mining E-Documents to Uncover Structures" chapter, a number of algorithms are provided that collectively enable mining an HTML e-document. The goal is to unveil its physical structure—a prelude to discovering its logical structure by the use of explicit terms of the metadata identified through the ontology. The results testify to the effectiveness of the methodology with 91% accuracy. This is particularly valuable to the users who seek finer data granularity in the retrieval of web-based information; conceptual hierarchy within an e-document; semantic web; Internet-based active learning; ontology; e-learning, e-government, e-commerce, and e-military—just to name a few.

The Table Abstract Data Type (ADT) represents a collection of records that can be accessed by the unique keys of the records. The framework design should encompass a wide range of possible implementations of the Table ADT—simple array-based data structures in memory, B-tree file structures on disk, perhaps even structures distributed across a network. By approaching this as a family, the goal is to assemble a Table implementation by selecting the combination of record access structures and storage structures to cater for a specific application.

The chapter "Designing a Flexible Framework for a Table Abstraction" describes how commonality/variability analysis, software design patterns, and formal design contracts are applied advantageously in implementations of the ADT. The framework consists of a group of Java interfaces that collaborate to define the structure and high-level interactions among components of the Table implementations. The key feature of the design is the separation of the Table's key-based record access mechanisms from the physical storage mechanisms. The systematic application of commonality/variability analysis and the Layered Architecture, Interface, Bridge, and Proxy design patterns lead to a design that is sufficiently flexible to support a wide range of client-defined records and keys, indexing structures, and storage media. The use of the Template Method, Strategy, Decorator, and Composite design patterns also enables variant components to be easily plugged into the framework. The Evolving Frameworks patterns give guidance on how to modify the framework as more is learned about the family of applications. The conscious use of these software design patterns increases the understandability and consistency of the framework's design.

19.5 Visualization

The last part of this book examines how useful information can be shown visually to the user, including the authenticity of a document. In the "Image Watermarking" chapter, for example, a new, temper-proof method for image watermarking is developed using the phase spectrum of digital images. The watermarked image is obtained after multi-level "Inverse Difference Pyramid (IDP) decomposition with 2D Complex Hadamard Transform (CHT). The watermark data inserted in the consecutive decomposition layers do not interact, and the watermark could be detected without using the original image. The main advantages of the presented method, which result from the high stability of their phase spectrum, are the following. Perhaps the most important are the perceptual transparency of the inserted resistant watermark; its large information capacity; and the high resistance against noises in the communication channel and pirates' attacks for its removal.

The method permits the insertion of resistant and fragile watermarks in one image, which ensures higher security for the original image content and provides wider possibilities for multiple applications. The method is suitable for streaming media as well. In this case, the compressed watermark could be different for every part of the contents. A special version of the method for audio watermarking was presented in the work of Kountchev et al. (2007), which proved the method's efficiency for such applications. The future development of the method will be aimed at multi-layer watermarking of multi-spectral images and real-time TV broadcasting.

As another visualization application, Google, Microsoft, and Yahoo are racing to transform online maps into full-blown browsers, organizing a diversity of information. Google Earth combines satellite imagery, maps and the power of Google Search to put the world's geographic information at one's fingertips. Since its debut in summer 2005, Google Earth has received attention of an unexpected sort. Officials of several nations have expressed alarm over its detailed display of government buildings, military installations and other sensitive sites within their borders. Beyond Google, Globalsecurity.org has images of nuclear test sites and military bases in much sharper focus than can be found on Google Earth. The company was asked by the National Geospatial-Intelligence Agency, an arm of the U. S. Defense Department, to remove from their site some of the maps of cities in Iraq. The incident was a classic example of the futility of trying to control information.

In the "Visualization and Ontology of Geospatial Intelligence" chapter, we have laid out a research agenda for the exciting subject of mining geospatial data. The potential application in safety and security is endless (Rouch 2007). A systems-biology graduate student Andrew Hill and colleagues at the University of Colorado published a KML file in April 2007, with a grim animated time line showing how the most virulent strains of avian flu jumped from species to species and country to country between 1996 and 2006. What if you could model a Europe where the sea level is 10 feet higher than it is today, or walk around the Alaskan north and see the glaciers and the Bering Strait the way they were 10 years ago? Then perceptions around global warming might change.

While we are laying out a research agenda in this chapter, much of the technology is here already. Digital globes are gaining in fidelity, as cities are filled out with 3-D models and old satellite imagery is gradually replaced by newer high-resolution shots. Moreover, today's island virtual worlds will only get better, with more-realistic avatars and settings and stronger connections to outside reality. Map algebra for cartographic modeling was introduced by Tomlin (1990). In parallel, Ritter et al. (1990) introduced image algebra for image processing. It is a fascinatingly visual world for experimentation, with potential applications to data integration and information quality as discussed early in this chapter!

19.6 References

Cardinal J (2002) Quantization with an information-theoretic distortion measure. Technical Report 491, ULB

Dean J, Ghemawat S (2004) MapReduce: Simplified Data Processing on Large Clusters, OSDI'04: Sixth Symposium on Operating System Design and Implementation, San Francisco, CA.

Ghemawat S, Gobioff H, Leung S (2003) The Google File System, 19th ACM Symposium on Operating Systems Principles, Lake George, NY.

Gruman G (2008) What Cloud Computing Really Means, InfoWorld, http://www.infoworld.com/article/08/04/07/15FE-cloud-computing-reality_1.html, retrieved 2009.

Kountchev R, Milanova M, Todorov Vl, Kountcheva R (Feb. 2007) Multiple audio Watermarking with Spectrum Pyramid. International Journal of Computer Science and Network Security (IJCSNS) pp. 191-200

Patterson D (2008) The Data Center is the Computer, Communications of the ACM, January, 2008, Vol. 51 No. 1.

Pedro JM, Purdy PH, Vasconcelos N (2004) A Kullback-Leibler divergence based kernel for SVM classification in multimedia application. In: Thrun S, Saul L, Scholkopf B (eds) Advances in Neural Information Processing Systems 16, MIT Press, Cambridge, MA

Ritter, G., Wilson, J., Davidson, J. (1990) "Image algebra: An overview." *Computer Vision, Graphics and Image Processing*, Vol. 49, pp. 297–3331.

Rouch W (2007) "Second Earth." *Technology Review*, July/August, pp. 39–48.

Talburt, J., Morgan, C., Talley, T. and Archer, K. (2005) Using Commercial Data Integration Technologies to Improve the Quality of Anonymous Entity Resolution in the Public Sector. *10th International Conference on Information Quality*, Cambridge, MA, 133-142.

Tomlin, C. (1990) Geographic Information Systems And Cartographic Modeling, Prentice-Hall, Upper Saddle River, New Jersey.

Wang, R.Y., Madnick, S.E. (1989) The Inter-database Instance Identification Problem in Integrating Autonomous Systems. In Proceedings of the 5th International Conference on Data Engineering, 46-55.

Index

Y. Chan et al. (eds.), *Data Engineering*, International Series in Operations
Research & Management Science 132, DOI 10.1007/978-1-4419-0176-7,
© Springer Science+Business Media, LLC 2010